WHISKEY OPUS

WHISKEYOPUS

GAVIN D. SMITH & DOMINIC ROSKROW

with contributions by

DAVIN DE KERGOMMEAUX & JÜRGEN DEIBEL

LONDON • NEW YORK
MELBOURNE • MUNICH • DELHI

DK LONDON
Senior Editor Alastair Laing
US Editors Shannon Beatty, Christine Heilman
Project Art Editor Kathryn Wilding
Editorial Assistants David Fentiman, Iska Lupton, Christopher Mooney
Design Assistant Jade Wheaton
Managing Editor Dawn Henderson
Managing Art Editor Christine Keilty
Senior Jackets Creative Nicola Powling
Jackets Assistant Rosie Levine
Senior Production Editor Jennifer Murray
Senior Production Controller Jen Lockwood
Creative Technical Support Sonia Charbonnier
Cartography Martin Darlison at Encompass Graphics Ltd

DK INDIA
Senior Editor Dorothy Kikon
Senior Art Editor Balwant Singh
Art Editor Anjan Dey
Assistant Art Editor Karan Chaudhary
Managing Editor Glenda Fernandes
Managing Art Editor Navidita Thapa
Senior DTP Designer Pushpak Tyagi
DTP Designer Saurabh Chhalaria
CTS Manager Sunil Sharma

First American Edition 2012
Published in the United States by
DK Publishing
375 Hudson Street
New York, NY 10014

12 13 14 15 16   10 9 8 7 6 5 4 3 2 1
001–183116–Sept/2012

Published in Great Britain by Dorling Kindersley Limited

A catalog record for this book is available from the Library of Congress.
ISBN 978-0-7566-9833-1

DK books are available at special discounts when purchased in bulk for sales promotions, premiums, fund-raising, or educational use. For details, contact: DK Publishing Special Markets, 375 Hudson Street, New York, NY 10014 or SpecialSales@dk.com.

Color reproduction by Scanhouse UK, MDP, and Steve Crozier
Printed and bound in China by Hung Hing

Discover more at
www.dk.com

CONTENTS

INTRODUCTION

WHISKEY: THE BIG QUESTIONS

Whiskey is in a very good place at the moment. Global demand is at a record high, and traditional territories, such as Scotland, are working flat out to meet it. And all the indicators suggest the boom days won't end anytime soon. Nor is it just whiskey from traditional territories, either. The whiskey industry is benefiting from a demographic shift toward new emerging middle classes across the planet, combined with a trend in the West of drinking less but better, and seeking heritage and provenance in what is consumed.

Whiskey is both extremely easy to make—it's simply a combination of grain, yeast, and water, brewed into beer and then distilled into grain spirit—and yet extremely difficult to make well. Scotland in particular makes whiskey very well indeed, dominating the category, and drawing on centuries of experience to produce its world-famous single malts and blended whiskeys.

Nevertheless, variations of whiskey have been created successfully in Ireland, the US, Canada, and Japan, all of which are also benefiting from the current boom. But it doesn't stop there. The rise in global demand has been accompanied by an equally dramatic growth in new distilleries appearing in new territories as far afield as Taiwan, India, Australia, and Sweden—many of them producing excellent, world-class tipples. Hundreds of new and small distillers have sprung up, all of them experimenting with wood types, cask finishes, drying techniques, peat, and grains to develop the category into new areas. These are exciting times for whiskey.

An affordable luxury

We live in a rapidly changing world. Countries such as Brazil and others in South America, China, India, nations in Southeast Asia, and emerging states across Africa are growing on a massive scale, and their burgeoning middle classes are seeking to enjoy the rewards of their wealth. When it comes to alcohol, few drinks can match whiskey as an attainable symbol of wealth and luxury. Traditionally, Scotch single malt whiskey has been the greatest beneficiary of this trend for affordable luxury. But in many of the emerging economies, single malt whiskey isn't having it all its own way. Quality blended whiskeys and whiskey from other countries are also benefiting.

A book for the times

Whiskey is a dynamic and organic industry that is constantly evolving. Traditional distilleries are increasing capacity to meet demand and seeking to supply increasingly exotic trading partners. New distilleries are popping up in the most unlikely places to help evolve the category and create new and exciting grain spirits. *Whiskey Opus* provides a detailed and comprehensive account of these changes. Drawing on their extensive experience and contacts in the whiskey world, the authors have not only identified the distilleries and whiskeys that are fueling the current boom, but also sought out and spoken to the people behind them, compiling the most comprehensive and in-depth book about world whiskey ever published.

Whiskey-makers around the world have been asked the "Big Questions," such as "What makes a great whiskey?" and "What were the key historical moments for whiskey?" There are no right or wrong answers to such questions, but they help to reveal how this amazing drink has been reinvented and adapted across the world. From the Orkneys to Auckland and from Bangalore to Baltimore, whiskey-makers have also been asked the little questions that reveal so much, about how they produce and sell their whiskey, and what makes them different from distilleries elsewhere. The result is *Whiskey Opus*: the most detailed and finely researched book ever written on world distilleries and the people who make them tick.

What makes whiskey such a unique drink?

No other spirit attracts the same degree of dedication and loyalty, creates the same frisson of excitement, or prompts so much study and investigation as whiskey. How does whiskey work such magic on its followers? Perhaps it's the heady mix of craftsmanship, history, and mystery wrapped up with the drink. Or because a spirit of such nobility and elegance, which is notoriously difficult to make well, is yet distilled from the roughest, plainest ingredients. Quite how only three basic components—grain, yeast, and water—can be combined to create such a plethora of different flavors has been called "the Great Wonder of Whiskey." Who can resist?

❝ It's the **drink of the people**. It also happens to taste better, have more variety and a greater capacity to **inspire** artists, writers, and musicians, than any other drink.**❞**

STEPHEN MARSHALL, *Senior Global Brand Ambassador, John Dewar & Sons, Scotland*

❝ Whiskey lies at the pinnacle of the long human quest to get alcohol, get more alcohol, and make it taste good. In a world that keeps going faster and faster, it takes **patience and care** both to make whiskey and to enjoy it. A simple beverage built from the simplest and most ordinary ingredients, it manifests in a myriad of wonderful forms, seemingly endless. You would think every possible variation has been tried, yet **whiskey never loses its ability to surprise**. That's a lot to get from a drink.**❞**

CHARLES K. COWDERY, *American whiskey writer and expert, US*

❝ [Whiskey] drieth more and also inflameth lesse than other hot confections doo.**❞**

RICHARD STANHURST, *traveler to Ireland, 1506*

❝ The passion and hands-on **personal touch** of master distillers and master blenders set whiskey apart from other distilled spirits. The process is an art, and as with any great artist, good is never good enough. Renderings of special whiskeys illustrate the **artistry and creativity** of its makers and generate wider interest among consumers, who are thereby inspired to try a greater variety of whiskeys beyond long-time personal favorites.**❞**

JIM RUTLEDGE, *Master Distiller, Four Roses, US*

Water of life A pure and reliable source of water is one of the most basic requirements for distilling whiskey, and many distilleries are located next to springs, streams, and rivers.

Grain to glass The first step in whiskey-making is choosing the grain. Barley is the sole grain in Scotch malt, though corn, wheat, rye, spelt, oats, and even buckwheat can also be used. Corn is the principal grain for making Bourbon and Tennessee whiskey.

❝ While visiting Ireland in 1506, traveler Richard Stanhurst wrote of the Irish, 'They use an ordinarie drinke of Aqua Vitae, being so qualified in the making, that it drieth more and also inflameth lesse than other hot confections doo.' Stanhurst recognized the importance of the "making" process; this remains essential. The manner of distillation enables the **retention of the flavors** of the selected cereals chosen. To this is added the **refinement and mellowing** effect of maturation in select oak casks. Finally, there is the importance of such a **long tradition** offering consistency of flavor and image in a world of volatile change.**❞**

BARRY CROCKETT, *Master Distiller, Midleton, Ireland*

❝ The people, the locations, and the traditions that are **handed down** from one **generation** to another.**❞**

JOHN CAMPBELL, *Distillery Manager, Laphroaig, Scotland*

Unlocking the goodness Malting unlocks sugars in the grains by steeping in water to stimulate germination, then kilning the malt to halt germination. Some distilleries still have their own traditional floor maltings, though most use maltsters.

❝ Whiskey is such a simple concept, and yet highly technical and very complicated at the same time—it is **the perfect blend of science and art**. Perhaps what makes it so special is the infinite number of variables in the process, and the wide range evident in all the whiskeys in the world, which although very different, can trace their core concepts back to the grain, water, and yeast **purity**.**❞**

CAMERON SYME, *Managing Director, The Great Southern Distilling Company, Australia*

❝ The beauty of whiskey rests on the **cask to cask selection**. When new make comes off a still and is filled to the casks, beautiful interplay between the two starts. You taste a balanced whiskey, savoring **multiple layers** of flavors and textures in every mouthful. ❞

JOANIE TSENG, *International Brand Director for Kavalan, Taiwan*

❝ Whiskey **captures the soul**. It is a drink to celebrate special occasions, a product that can leave a special memory of an event. Revisiting a whiskey years down the road can **evoke the memories** of the special occasion when it was first tasted. I haven't found anything else that has such an effect. ❞

CAMERON SYME, *Managing Director, The Great Southern Distilling Company, Australia*

Grist to wash Malt is milled to grist and mixed with hot water in a mash tun to extract the soluble sugars and produce the wort. The wort is then fermented with yeast in brewing vessels called washbacks.

Copper contact The wash produced by fermentation is distilled in either column or pot stills. Stills are made from copper to purify the spirit, with the metal acting as a catalyst to extract sulfur compounds. The size and shape of the still, and how it is operated, will affect the purity and lightness of the spirit.

The basics of whiskey-making

Barley is the most commonly used grain in whiskey-making. It is the sole grain in Scotch malt, and a percentage of malted barley is used in almost all whiskey. Corn, wheat, and rye can also be used.

MALTING Barley goes through a malting process to activate enzymes and maximize its starch content, which is later converted to sugar and then alcohol. If peat is burnt while drying the grains, the whiskey will have a smoky flavor.

MASHING Malt is milled to produce a coarse flour called "grist." The grist is then mixed with hot water in a mash tun to extract soluble sugars. The sugar-laden water, known as "wort," is piped off for use.

FERMENTATION The wort is mixed with yeast and heated in a washback. The yeast feeds off the sugars in the wort, producing alcohol and carbon dioxide. This fermentation results in what is effectively a strong and rather tart beer, called "wash."

DISTILLATION The next stage is for the wash to be distilled in order to extract from it the alcohol spirit. The essential process is simple: the wash is boiled and, as alcohol boils at a lower temperature than water, the alcohol is driven off the wash as vapor; this vapor is then condensed into liquid. Most whiskey is distilled twice.

THE CUT The first and last parts of the "run" during the second distillation are not pure enough for use. Known as the "foreshots" and the "feints," respectively, they will go back for redistillation along with "low wines" from the first distillation. The desired part of the distillation is the middle section, and this is known as the "middle cut," or just "the cut." This usable spirit, which is called "new make," is drinkable and exhibits some of the characteristics that will be found in the final whiskey. The distiller must assess the spirit and identify the cut.

MATURATION The new make will have its strength slightly reduced to about 63 or 64 percent ABV—the optimum strength to begin maturation. The spirit is then piped from a holding tank into oak casks. The process that turns raw, clear, new make into the richly hued, complex-tasting drink we know as whiskey, is maturation. The length of time for maturation varies, depending on climatic conditions, the size and type of casks used, method of storage, and legal requirements.

❝ Scotch whiskey is so special as it incorporates all the **unique flavors and character of Scotland.** It can be smoky, sweet, salty, floral, wild, aggressive, subtle, or warming. Open a bottle of Scotch single malt and no matter where you are in the world, you are immediately transported back to your favorite part of Scotland. ❞

FRANK McHARDY, *Director of Production, J. & A. Mitchell & Company Ltd., Scotland*

❝ Waves of delicious aromas and flavors underlying the surface-level volatiles. ❞

DAVID COX, *Director of Global Experiences, The Macallan, Scotland*

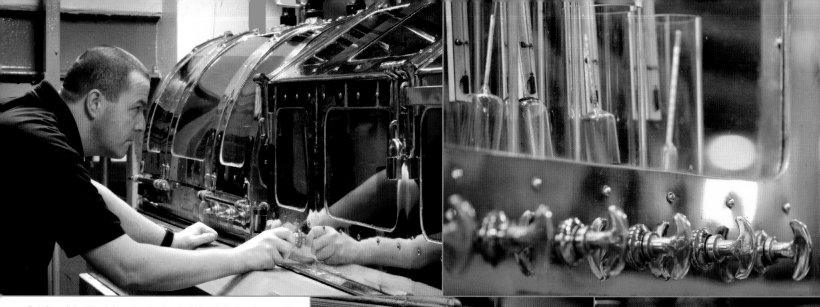

Duty bound A spirit safe is employed at Scotch whiskey distilleries using pot still distillation to enable the distillers to assess the spirit. Dating to the 19th century, the safe is padlocked to prevent the distiller from coming in contact with the spirit, originally so that the new make could not be siphoned off to avoid paying duty on it.

❝ From all existing spirits, whiskey is by a long way the one possessing the **widest variety of characters**, offering a range of flavors that easily compares with those offered by wines. ❞

JEAN DONNAY, *Owner, Glann ar Mor, Brittany, France*

❝ **Whiskey is the glue** that keeps Scotland together. It's a constant: when you're born, graduate, get married, have children; **whenever you celebrate** birthdays, anniversaries, at Christmas and the New Year; whiskey will even be drunk when you've passed away. ❞

GERRY TOSH, *Global Brand Manager, Highland Park, Scotland*

❝ Whiskey is possibly the only drink to give such a diversity of flavors from one distillery to the other. And most of all, **no whiskeys are bad whiskeys**—it's just some are better than others! ❞

ASHOK CHOKALINGAM, *General Manager, Amrut, India*

Maturing spirit Fresh off the still, the new make spirit is crystal clear and fiery, but it can also be fruity and drinkable. New make offers only the barest indication of how the mature whiskey will taste. Some distilleries draw samples intermittently to monitor the progress of the spirit's maturation.

Finishing touches The bottling of the whiskey is often carried out at large, automated plants, but in smaller distilleries and microdistilleries, the bottling, sealing, and labeling can often be done by hand.

What makes a great whiskey?

One of the major fallacies about whiskey is that only Scotland can make great whiskey and that great whiskey can only be single malt. This is just not true. There are great blends from both Scotland and elsewhere, great Irish, Japanese, and Canadian whiskeys, great Bourbons and ryes, and great whiskeys from many other countries. Quality is about fine ingredients and the care and dedication with which those ingredients are used to make the whiskey.

❝ Location, people, production equipment and one of the most important items, **good-quality casks** for maturing the product.❞

FRANK McHARDY, *Director of Production, J. & A. Mitchell & Company Ltd., Scotland*

❝The depth of flavor and character.❞

JOHN CAMPBELL, *Distillery Manager, Laphroaig, Scotland*

❝ **Great people.** The much-overlooked guys and girls who work day in, day out making whiskey—they're the ones we should thank.❞

GERRY TOSH, *Global Brand Manager, Highland Park, Scotland*

❝ Complexity and balance. Also, to me a real whiskey should first start with a short, **nice and gentle little 'bite,'** and should then progressively overflow you with a kind of great tenderness. If it doesn't work like that, then something is missing.❞

JEAN DONNAY, *Owner, Glann ar Mor, Brittany, France*

Whiskey styles

There are several types of whiskey, and the variations depend upon the type and proportion of grains used and the methods employed. Barley, corn, wheat, and rye are the principal grains, while variations in methods that lead to different classifications include the way of distilling (batch or continuous distillation) and the process and period of maturation. American whiskeys are mostly aged in new oak, while Scotch and Irish whiskeys employ reused casks.

SCOTCH SINGLE MALT Made solely from malted barley in copper pot stills, this is the "original" whiskey of the Scottish Highlands. Single malt is the product of an individual distillery. In Scotland it must be matured for at least three years.

PURE POT STILL Made from a mix of malted and unmalted barley, distilled in a pot still, pure pot-still whiskey is unique to Ireland. In the Victorian era it accounted for most of the whiskey made in Ireland, but there are few expressions left.

GRAIN Distilled in a continuous still, grain whiskey is typically made from wheat or corn, along with unmalted and malted barley. Grain whiskey is the mainstay of most blends, though some is bottled as pure grain whiskey.

BOURBON Bourbon is the classic US style of whiskey. To be deemed Bourbon, the whiskey must contain at least 51 percent corn in the mash bill. It must be also be matured in new, charred white oak casks for a minimum of two years.

❝ Cask selection, modern techniques, skilled craftsmanship and also **geographical influences** such as water, air, climate, etc., all contribute to making a great whiskey. **❞**

JOANIE TSENG, *International Brand Director for Kavalan, Taiwan*

❝ Expertise and **patience**. All good whiskey **needs time**—longer fermentations, slower distillation, decent maturation, and marrying. **❞**

STEPHEN MARSHALL, *Senior Global Brand Ambassador, John Dewar & Sons, Scotland*

❝ It is the **love and passion** of the makers of whiskeys that put a wide variety of great whiskeys on the shelves of liquor stores. **❞**

JIM RUTLEDGE, *Master Distiller, Four Roses, US*

❝ Smoothness, taste, uncompromising commitment to quality, individuality, and just having **the X-factor. ❞**

CAMERON SYME, *Managing Director, The Great Southern Distilling Company, Australia*

❝ Flavors, **complexity,** price, and finish. **❞**

ASHOK CHOKALINGAM, *General Manager, Amrut, India*

❝ There are many great whiskey styles. Those that are greatest **capture the essence** of individual whiskey traditions in terms of flavor, taste, and aftertaste. **❞**

BARRY CROCKETT, *Master Distiller, Midleton, Ireland*

❝ A great whiskey is a whiskey that **tells you a story**, teaches you something you didn't know, and also makes you **glad. ❞**

CHARLES K. COWDERY, *American whiskey writer and expert, USA*

AMERICAN RYE By law, rye whiskey has to be made from a mash of not less than 51 percent rye. As with Bourbon, new charred-oak barrels are used for a minimum of 2 years' maturation. Rye has a peppery, slightly bitter character.

CORN Distilled from a mash of not less than 80 percent corn at less than 80 percent ABV, corn whiskey is the one American style with no set minimum period of maturation or cask requirement, and is often sold new and clear.

TENNESSEE Made in a similar way to Bourbon, with at least 51 percent corn in the mash bill, Tennessee whiskey has the distinction of undergoing filtration through a deep bed of sugar-maple charcoal, known as Lincoln County Process.

CANADIAN Most whiskey from Canada is blended. The base spirit often has a light and neutral character. There is no constraint on the mash bill, and a proportion of rye, which adds spice to the mix, tends to give Canadian whiskey its character.

BLENDS A mix of one or more single malts and one or more single grain whiskeys, blends typically have a proportion of 40 percent malt to 60 percent grain. More malt is used in deluxe blends, less in standard blends.

A sociable spirit There is plenty of advice explaining how to drink whiskey. Perhaps the best advice is to drink it any way you want to. Mood, company, memory, time, and place can all affect the appreciation of whiskey.

What is the perfect way to drink whiskey?

Ask any distiller the perfect way to drink whiskey, and they'll say any way you darn well please. Should you add water or pour whiskey over ice? If you want to—it's totally your call. If anyone tells you not to add water to your whiskey, tell them the distillers started it. They add water before the spirit goes in the cask, and they usually dilute it down before it's bottled. Why not add a little more? Water can unlock the aromas and flavors of the whiskey. With ice, too, is the chosen way for many to enjoy drinking Bourbon or blends.

❝For me **whiskey is emotional,** so rather than saying 'in a nosing glass with no ice and a drop of water,' I prefer to think about **times and places**. So it would have to be standing on the cliffs of Yesnaby in Orkney looking out over the Atlantic.❞

GERRY TOSH, *Global Brand Manager, Highland Park, Scotland*

❝It depends on how **good or bad** your wife or husband was on that particular day. If they were good, then 40 percent ABV; if they were hell, **cask strength** please!❞

ASHOK CHOKALINGAM, *General Manager, Amrut, India*

❝The perfect way to drink whiskey is in **whatever manner** pleases you the most.❞

CHARLES K. COWDERY, *American whiskey writer and expert, US*

❝I like my single malt whiskey with **room-temperature water**, to dilute it to around 22–28% ABV. This allows the most flavor to come out. For most mixed grain whiskeys, I prefer to mix with **ginger ale**. That said, I do like a good solid Bourbon **neat on ice**.❞

CAMERON SYME, *Managing Director, The Great Southern Distilling Company, Australia*

Whiskey glasses

To full appreciate the taste of a whiskey you need a glass that will present the aroma to the best advantage. Adapted from a sherry glass, the copita is the industry standard: it has a bowl for swirling the liquid to release the aroma; and the rim narrows, so the aroma is presented to the nose extremely well. The Glencairn offers a more robust version of the copita, while the Glenmorangie has a lid to hold in the aromas.

THE REIDEL "GLAS"

THE GLENCAIRN GLASS

Sensory receptacle Also known as a *catavino*, and adopted and adapted from sherry glasses, the copita glass is the industry standard glass for the organoleptic assessment of whiskey.

❝Master distillers, master blenders, along with aficionados and connoisseurs, prefer tasting, evaluating, and **appreciating their drink neat**—or perhaps with a single ice cube or small splash of water.❞

JIM RUTLEDGE, *Master Distiller, Four Roses, US*

❝With someone who laughs at your jokes.❞

STEPHEN MARSHALL, *Senior Global Brand Ambassador, John Dewar & Sons, Scotland*

❝I can enjoy it in a warm, comfortable, and **cozy place**, or outside in the open air where I can discover new unexpected flavors, related to the time and the place. The same whiskey drunk **by the seaside at sunset** or in a forest at midday will always taste different to me.❞

JEAN DONNAY, *Owner, Glann ar Mor, Brittany, France*

On the rocks Whiskey with ice is a favorite way of drinking Bourbon and blends in particular, when you want to relax over a long drink.

COPITA

SINGLE MALTS OF SCOTLAND GLASS

THE GLENMORANGIE GLASS

TUMBLER

Who invented whiskey?

Asia, the Middle East, Valhalla... There have been lots of claims and counter-claims about the origins of grain distillation. Truth be told, no one really knows, and the chances are that the separating of alcohol from water to make it stronger came about in different parts of the world at roughly the same time. What seems likely is the clergy had something to do with it, and that its origins are tied up with medicine. Alcohol comes from an arabic word, and the theory that traveling priests brought the secrets of distillation back to Ireland and from there to the west coast of Scotland are not without merit.

Ancient origins Many ancient peoples have a claim to being the inventors of whiskey, from the Chinese to the Egyptians. Possibly the most likely candidates are the Mesopotamians, who seem to have used distillation to make perfumes.

❝ Samuel Morewood in his 1838 publication *A History of Inebriating Liquors* offers two thoughts, both of which suggest the importance of Ireland to the invention of whiskey. Firstly, he speculated that if **Egyptians**, or other Asiatics, were acquainted with distillation, it is likely they would have introduced it into Ireland. Secondly, he refers to a statement by the Roman writer Tacitus that 'the ports and landing places of Hibernia [Ireland] were better known than those of Britain.' It is now taken that the skill of distillation was developed in **Mesopotamia**, and that the practice and knowledge was brought to the West. Merchants and other travelers used established **trade routes,** and it is reasonable to suggest the practice came from **North Africa to Ireland**. It is not possible to state who actually invented whiskey, but the practice came to such prominence in Ireland that the name *aqua vitae* became **uisce beatha**, from which the word 'whiskey' derives.**❞**

BARRY CROCKETT, *Master Distiller, Midleton, Ireland*

❝ We trained an **Irish monk** to make whiskey and told him to **keep it secret** or we'd eventually have to pay taxes on it. He just couldn't keep it quiet!**❞**

GERRY TOSH, *Global Brand Manager, Highland Park, Scotland*

Medicinal properties Probably the earliest application of distilling techniques was in the production of perfumes and medicines. Even distilled alcohol was regarded as medicinal and used to treat a variety of diseases.

❝ Whiskey was, as everybody should know, invented in the north, more specifically in **Sweden**. The first person to make whiskey was a **viking called Orm** who had learnt the art of distilling on his travels to the Miklagård (Konstantinopel) over a thousand years ago.**❞**

LARS LINDBERGER, *International Marketing Officer, Mackmyra, Sweden*

Monastic habit Distilling of alcohol was a common activity in medieval monasteries; indeed, it may have been traveling monks who first brought the knowledge back from the Middle East.

❝You must go back centuries to drafty **monasteries** where the monks made a variety of alcoholic drinks, including a spirit which allegedly they consumed to **keep out the cold**. The spirit probably helped fuel their imaginations when illuminating **manuscripts**.❞

FRANK McHARDY, *Director of Production, J. & A. Mitchell & Company Ltd., Scotland*

❝The history, as I understand it, is that the **Irish applied distillation technology** to fermented grain. It was a matter of necessity to help preserve surplus gain. The Scots were the ones who really took it further and applied the concept more broadly. The distillation technology supposedly came out of the Middle East. But **does anyone really know** who invented whiskey? I'm just glad that someone did!❞

CAMERON SYME, *Managing Director, The Great Southern Distilling Company, Australia*

❝I've heard it dates as far back as 8000BC to the **ancient Chinese**. Most cultures have used the same technology and the natural ingredients from the land to flavor the product.❞

JOHN CAMPBELL, *Distillery Manager, Laphroaig, Scotland*

❝I tell people that **the Scots** invented it. I've seen no evidence to the contrary. The feeling in my bones when I visit Finlaggan* certainly makes me think of it as an important place.❞

*A reference to the ruins of Finlaggan Castle on Eilean Mòr in Loch Finlaggan, Islay, where the Council of the Isles once met. The Council was presided over by the Lords of the Isles, ancient rulers of the islands and coastal areas of the west of Scotland, and reputed to be the ancestors of Gaelic invaders from Ireland in the 5th century AD.

STEPHEN MARSHALL, *Senior Global Brand Ambassador, John Dewar & Sons, Scotland*

❝Someone in a beer-making culture made the first whiskey, but it may not have been successful or for some other reason they didn't keep making it, so **history forgot them**. Egyptians made beer and had distillation technology thousands of years ago. It's hard to believe they didn't at least dabble in distilled beer, i.e., whiskey. Someone up there in the North Atlantic apparently made the **first successful whiskey**, so we remember them, and that's what matters.❞

CHARLES K. COWDERY, *American whiskey writer and expert, US*

❝The Irish. But the Scots **matured** it.❞

RONNIE COX, *International Brands Ambassador, The Glenrothes, Scotland*

Spreading the spirit One theory suggests that whiskey was brought to Scotland by the Gaelic Irish Christian missionaries who first landed on Islay and the western coast of Scotland in the 6th century AD.

Orm the whiskey inventor? Could it be that Vikings taught the world to make whiskey, in between launching invasions and discovering America?

What was the defining moment in whiskey history?

The history of whiskey is studded with significant moments both in terms of the drink's discovery and evolution and the economic and political context in which it has developed. The most important moment? The development of the column of Coffey still takes some beating, as does the introduction of oak casks and the charring of oak. Maybe the very greatest defining moment, however, for anyone who enjoys whiskey is the moment when you take a sip and the taste makes total sense. Is there any moment greater than that?

Moonshiners In the 18th and 19th centuries, many Scottish people set up secret stills to avoid taxes, worked at night when the smoke and steam couldn't be spotted.

❝ My personal defining moment was **the day in March 1963** when I decided that my future lay in the whiskey industry and started work at Invergordon distillery.❞

FRANK McHARDY, *Director of Production, J. & A. Mitchell & Company Ltd., Scotland*

❝ It would have to be one of two events: either the first imposition of tax on whiskey, or the first granting of a **license to legally** distill whiskey.❞

CAMERON SYME, *Managing Director, The Great Southern Distilling Company, Australia*

❝ The moment when **Orm the Viking**, returning from his travels, met some French monks who were on their way to establish a monastery in the British Isles. He taught them the **art of distilling** and that's the way Christian monks knew the art of distilling. But they of course only used it for medical purposes.❞

LARS LINDBERGER, *International Marketing Officer, Mackmyra, Sweden*

❝ The **1823** Excise Act.❞

DAVID COX, *Director of Global Experiences, The Macallan, Scotland*

❝ There were two: adoption of routine **aging in oak casks** and the invention and adoption of the continuous still.❞

CHARLES K. COWDERY, *American whiskey writer and expert, US*

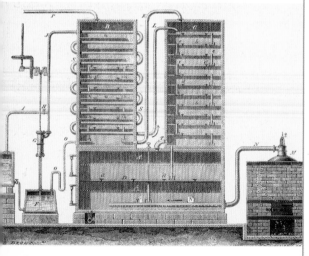

Continuous innovation Known as the Coffey (after its inventor), patent, column, or continuous still, it allowed for continuous rather than batch distillation and led to the production of grain whiskey, a lighter style that could blend with malts for mass appeal.

The evils of excise Government taxes on the production and sale of goods, known as "excise," have frequently been resisted. The 1725 malt tax riot in Glasgow saw the military driven out of the city.

Time Distilled—key events in the history of whiskey

The origins of whiskey are lost in time, but they stretch back hundreds of years, possibly thousands. Moreover, there is great debate as to how the spirit evolved and who was responsible. Here, then, are key signposts.

THE FIRST WHISKEY Nobody knows who first distilled whiskey, but there are suggestions that distillation was first carried out in China or Mesopotamia, for medicine and perfume. Certainly there are big links between health and alcohol: just consider a drinking toast in virtually any language.

BLAME IT ON THE CLERGY The church has a lot to answer for when it comes to alcohol. Pilgrims traveled extensively in the Middle Ages and probably brought distilled spirits back to Europe. Monasteries were the guardians of brewing and distilling, and the dissolution of the monasteries in England probably helped spread these skills.

BY THE LIGHT OF THE MOON Small communities around the world have made grain spirit for hundreds of years, and often it was used as currency to buy other goods. As a result, it attracted tax and was often distilled illicitly. The word "moonshine" refers to a time when illicit whiskey was distilled under cover of darkness.

INTO THE DAYLIGHT In Scotland it took the Excise Act of 1823 to legalize an already thriving trade in whiskey. In Ireland, whiskey went legal in 1608 with the world's first whiskey license. In North America, it took a rebellion and a resettlement into new frontiers in the South to establish whiskey-making on the banks of the Ohio River.

> There are quite a few to pick from but I'd have to say the invention of the Coffey still, which basically takes Scotch from being a **small cottage industry** into the huge spirit it is today.

GERRY TOSH, *Global Brand Manager, Highland Park, Scotland*

> One of the defining periods in the history of Irish whiskey dates to between 1780 and 1826. The earlier of these two dates refers to the establishment of the **John Jameson distillery** in Dublin, followed in 1791 by the establishment of the John Power distillery, also in Dublin. The later date refers to the establishment of the **Midleton distillery**. A second defining moment dates to 1975 with the building of a modern distillery at Midleton, which replaced the old one. It also enabled the restart of the renaissance of the **Irish whiskey industry**.

BARRY CROCKETT, *Master Distiller, Midleton, Ireland*

> When you look at the history of whiskey you can see there have been, and continue to be, lots of interesting times, from the passing of laws, to the invention of continuous distillation, and even an epidemic of **phylloxera beetles**.

JOHN CAMPBELL, *Distillery Manager, Laphroaig, Scotland*

A useful pest An unlikely "hero" of whiskey, the phylloxera beetle devastated Europe's grape crop, allowing whiskey to overtake brandy as the drink of the elite.

Japan's whiskey master Masataka Taketsuru learned the secrets of single malt production in Scotland and used this knowledge to help create the Japanese whiskey industry, known today for producing possibly the best single malts in the world.

Global spirit Whiskey production in the 20th century expanded across the globe and continues to grow in the 21st century—from Japan to South Africa, Switzerland to Taiwan, India to Australia.

> After the second world war, continental distillers of brandies and small breweries began to produce whiskeys, and have now spread even further: from **Sweden, France,** and **Germany** to **Japan, India,** and **Taiwan**. With the development of production techniques, distillers from the rest of the world are able to make quality whiskey for discerning consumers.

JOANIE TSENG, *International Brand Director for Kavalan, Taiwan*

> If one moment had to be singled out, that could well be when Scottish producers **first started to blend** grain whiskey with malt whiskey.

JEAN DONNAY, *Owner, Glann ar Mor, Brittany, France*

A chance cask Whiskey cannot legally be called "whiskey" until it has matured for a period in oak casks, but it wasn't always this way. The discovery that the flavors of malt spirits improve if stored for a time in wooden casks was most likely made by chance: a barrel of spirit forgotten about for years, then tasted.

ROLL OUT THE BARREL Nobody can pinpoint exactly when oak casks became part off the whiskey story, but it was almost certainly a happy accident. As the need to export grew, containers were required. In Scotland, it's likely whiskey was stored in casks that had previously carried all manner of things—including fish.

BLAZING A TRAIL There are many legends surrounding the "invention" of Bourbon whiskey in America. In fact, the technique of charring casks crossed over from the Old World to the New, and the corn in the mash bill was simply the most abundant local grain.

STAMP OF APPROVAL Even the Bourbon name is a happy accident: whiskey-makers didn't realize drinkers were enjoying a spirit that had matured in casks stamped with the word "Bourbon." Whiskey was never actually made in Bourbon County, but the name stuck.

FROM POT TO COFFEY Scotch's world story began with the invention of the Coffey still in 1826, perfected by Irishman Aeneas Coffey and then rejected by the Irish. The new still was adopted by Scotland to make grain whiskey, which, when added to single malts, made the smooth, easy-to-drink whiskey that we know today as blended whiskey.

BEETLE MANIA Meanwhile, the dominance of brandy on the high tables of the well-to-do came to an end when a devastating "plague" caused by the phylloxera beetle wiped out grape production across Europe toward the end of the 19th century—leaving whiskey without competition.

Why oak casks and from when?

It's true that whiskey is made of just three ingredients, but there are two other major contributors to flavor: the peat that is sometimes used in drying the green malt, and the oak used in maturation. Malt spirit comes off the still as a clear liquid and is placed in oak casks to start its journey to whiskey. How long it stays there depends on a myriad of different factors, including what country you are making it in, what style of whiskey it is, and how light or robust the spirit is to stand up to the strong flavors from the oak. Up to three-quarters of the flavor of a single malt whiskey will come from the cask, and considerably higher than that for Bourbon. It's from the oak that the magic and mystery of whiskey stems.

The mighty oak European oak *(Quercus robur)* and American white oak *(Quercus alba)* are the most common types of oak used to make whiskey casks.

❝ Small oak casks were **less likely to break** than jars when whiskey used to travel on the backs of donkeys. The use of oak in order to improve the spirit came only after, when results were observed.❞

JEAN DONNAY, *Owner, Glann ar Mor, Brittany, France*

❝ If you've ever tasted whiskey from **cherry wood** you'll know why. I've always assumed that it made sense with the herring industry, as oak casks were used to **store the fish.**❞

STEPHEN MARSHALL, *Senior Global Brand Ambassador, John Dewar & Sons, Scotland*

❝ One of the reasons is that oak has a unique physical and **chemical nature**. It is also a pure wood without passing strong flavors to the whiskey. In addition, it **adds to the aromas** of the spirits and removes the undesirable elements from new-make spirit. Back in the 18th century, around one-third of the goods for exports were contained in casks. At the same time someone started using oak casks for whiskey and it was realized that storing in oak **improved the flavor** of the spirit.❞

JOANIE TSENG, *International Brand Director for Kavalan, Taiwan*

A taste of Jerez Usually made from European oak, sherry casks will have previously been used to store the fortified wine called sherry. The type of sherry held in the barrel will affect the flavor of the whiskey.

About time The length of maturation is the single most influential factor in the flavor of the mature whiskey. There is no optimum time—this depends on the history of the cask. Each is unique, and whiskeys of the same vintage and distillery are nevertheless still discernibly distinct from one cask to the next.

Barrel recycling Most casks used by the whiskey industries of Scotland, Japan, and Ireland began life as American barrels. Having been used to mature American whiskey, the barrels are taken apart and transported in bundles to be "remade" by coopers as hogsheads.

Purifying flame Burning the inside of the cask causes chemical changes to the wood, without which the spirit will not mature. European casks tend to be lightly toasted, while American barrels are charred.

> ❝ Medieval and pre-medieval Europe was heavily **covered in oak forests**. Oak was a most suitable wood for the construction of holding vessels. Much later it was recognized that **oak compounds** and the interchange between the flavors of distilled spirits generated a further range of special characteristics particular to whiskey. ❞

BARRY CROCKETT, *Master Distiller, Midleton, Ireland*

> ❝ Not many woods are **watertight**. These properties were well known to naval Britain more than 500 years ago. Some oaks are native to Europe. The **French taught the Romans** to put wine into wooden casks. Amphorae are tough to roll. ❞

RONNIE COX, *International Brands Ambassador, The Glenrothes, Scotland*

Casking explained

Much of the final taste of a whiskey can come from both the type of oak used to make the cask and what that cask contained before whiskey spirit was put into it, though the finest whiskeys have their flavors enhanced by the cask and not dominated by it. Advanced age is not necessarily a good thing: long maturation in an over-active cask can cause the spirit to be dominated by wood-derived flavors.

INTERACTION OF SPIRIT AND WOOD Whiskey spirit enters the cask as a clear liquid, but once in wood, four reactions take place. First, as the spirit gently expands and retracts and moves in the cask with the passing of the seasons, spirit is forced into the oak, taking from it flavor and color. But a second effect takes place: the wood also removes impurities and negative compounds in the spirit. Thirdly, the wood and spirit react with each other to produce a myriad of flavors; this is the unexplained magic of whiskey. The final part of the maturation is created by oxidization, because oak allows air to pass into the cask.

CASK SIZE Although whiskey is nearly always matured in oak, the size of the cask varies, affecting the speed of maturation because the smaller the cask, the more the spirit comes into contact with the wood and the greater the effect on maturation. Sherry butts and puncheons hold 132 gallons (500 liters), hogsheads hold 66 gallons (250 liters), and American barrels hold 53 gallons (200 liters).

AGE OF CASK Whether the cask is new or used will also affect maturation. Bourbon must be matured in a new cask that has had its inside toasted or charred, for instance. Scotch single malt spirit will be spoiled by virgin oak, so it is matured in a cask that has already been used for producing something else, normally for Bourbon or sherry. Different types of casks are increasingly being used, however, particularly casks first seasoned with port wine.

ATMOSPHERIC FACTORS Maturation will also be affected by average temperature, extremes of temperature, humidity and atmospheric pressure, and the size and type of warehouse. The traditional Scottish dunnage warehouse is cool, damp, earth-floored, and with casks racked three high, which causes spirit to reduce its strength but retain high volume. In the US, by contrast, racked warehouses stack casks up to 80 high and the atmosphere can be warm—even hot—close to the roof, and dry. In these conditions, the volume reduces but the strength remains high.

New filled The ABV of new make spirit is reduced slightly to the optimum strength to begin maturation, before being piped from a holding tank into the cask.

❝ Legend has it that originally spirit was collected in **stone jars** and consumed fairly quickly. At some point a distiller stored his spirit in a **wooden receptacle** and forgot where he hid it. When the spirit was eventually found, it was noticed that there was an **improvement in the flavor**, and maturation was born. ❞

FRANK McHARDY, *Director of Production, J. & A. Mitchell & Company Ltd., Scotland*

❝ Try maturing spirit in **rubber barrels** and see what the whiskey ends up tasting like. That's if you're **brave enough.** ❞

ASHOK CHOKALINGAM, *General Manager, Amrut, India*

This way up The location of a warehouse and the position of the barrels can affect maturation. Casks at the bottom of a row will mature at a different rate from those at the top, and a warehouse by the sea may contribute salty characteristics.

❝ As the oak for a Viking was a holy tree, Orm [the Swedish 'inventor' of whiskey] thought that the oak must be the best wood for making casks for the **divine beverage** he had made. But there is also another story of why the use of oak casks became popular in Scotland. This happened when Orm's great-grandson was plundering in Scotland. By this time, the monk who had learnt the art of distilling had passed the knowledge to some local villagers. The people had heard the **Vikings were on the way** and had placed thistles around the village to prevent them from sneaking in. When the Vikings tried to enter, they stepped on the thistles and started to scream and make a noise. This gave the villagers time to defend themselves and beat back the Vikings. And that's why the **thistle is Scotland's national flower**.

What has this to do with the oak? As we all know, Scottish people can be stingy, and it was no different a thousand years ago. One of the men who had just distilled some alcohol heard the screams. And as he didn't want either the Vikings or his fellow villagers to steal his alcohol, he took the first vessel he could find to put it in, and that was an oak cask. Then he **buried the cask**. The greedy man was killed in the battle and it took ten years before the man's son dug up the cask. But then he realized that the oak worked wonders on the alcohol. ❞

LARS LINDBERGER, *International Marketing Officer, Mackmyra, Sweden*

❝ For Laphroaig it was to ensure a consistent product that Ian Hunter **searched the world** for the correct casks. He decided upon reaching Kentucky in the 1920s that he had found his cask. Prohibition was a problem at the time, however, and it wasn't until after prohibition came to an end that Laphroaig obtained its **final ingredient** and our recipe was complete. And we still stay true to the recipe.❞

JOHN CAMPBELL, *Distillery Manager, Laphroaig, Scotland*

❝ I can't respond to this relative to Scotch, but only a **brand new barrel** may be used for each filling in the Bourbon process. The **natural sugars** present in the white oak barrels dramatically impact the distinct **sweet flavors** associated with Bourbon.❞

JIM RUTLEDGE, *Master Distiller, Four Roses, US*

Test of spirit At some distilleries, the master distiller will monitor the progress of the spirit's maturation by drawing samples using a simple tubular instrument called a valinch.

❝ When our distillery was first brought to life it would have used **whatever was available** to store the whiskey. The earliest record I have seen is an account from 1890 where it talks about the sole use of the **best sherry cask**—and it's never changed.❞

GERRY TOSH, *Global Brand Manager, Highland Park, Scotland*

❝ Find the most readily available, continuous supply of casks and be amazed at what changes they effect on the spirit over a few years maturation! **Spain** obligingly provided the first wave via the British sherry bottlers, and then the **United States** followed after the second world war.❞

DAVID COX, *Director of Global Experiences, The Macallan, Scotland*

Straight from the barrel At the US microdistillery Copper Fox, makers of Wasmund's Single Malt, visitors are encouraged to learn about the maturing process and can even take part by buying a barrel kit to mature Wasmund's spirit in their own way.

What does the future hold and what are the challenges?

Whiskey finds itself in a very good place. As traditional producers seek to take advantage of growing global demand, they realize that whiskey's attraction is centered on heritage, provenance, and integrity, and when making fine spirits you cannot cut corners. Meanwhile, we're seeing a new generation of producers turning to innovation. Much of it cannot be called whiskey, but all bets are off as to whether new, closely-related drinks categories will be invented in the future.

Grain store Global grain prices have been following a general upward trend, placing pressure on raw material costs for whiskey producers.

❝Stock supply and **raw material costs**. Everything is getting more expensive and there are more people in the world drinking whiskey, so finding a balance is key.❞

GERRY TOSH, *Global Brand Manager, Highland Park, Scotland*

❝The future is bright. Demand is increasing and there is great innovation within the market, but there are some clouds on the horizon. We need to make sure that we **maintain quality** while increasing production to satisfy growing world demand. We also need to make sure the industry can survive the inherent **boom–bust cycles** that we see repeated throughout history.❞

CAMERON SYME, *Managing Director, The Great Southern Distilling Company, Australia*

❝One of the biggest challenges could be the **shortage of old whiskeys**. Consumers, particularly from the key emerging markets, are still chasing rare and old whiskeys. With limited quantities, the supply will be unable to meet rising demand.❞

JOANIE TSENG, *International Brand Director for Kavalan, Taiwan*

❝That we produce great whiskey **faster** than we can **convert** the unconverted.❞

RONNIE COX, *International Brands Ambassador, The Glenrothes, Scotland*

Industrial Goliaths versus small-scale Davids
As established producers expand capacity with huge, mechanized distilling operations, they risk losing out to smaller, more traditional operations and new microdistilleries better able to boast of their heritage, provenance, and personal touch.

❝The biggest challenge facing the world of whiskey is success, because success tempts people to cut corners and **make hay** while the **sun shines**, and it's hard to make a case that whiskey is threatened when it's selling as fast as you can make it. Whiskey-makers need to tell the truth about whiskey and not just tell people what they want to hear. We should all make lots of **money** but also **keep the love.**❞

CHARLES K. COWDERY, *American whiskey writer and expert, US*

❝As always, one of the biggest challenges facing the world of whiskey at present is to compete against the **white spirit market**. At the present time, rising costs in utilities, casks, raw materials, and labor bring pressure to bear on the unit costs.❞

FRANK McHARDY, *Director of Production, J. & A. Mitchell & Company Ltd., Scotland*

❝Whiskey has to be very careful not to lose the strong and well-asserted identity it enjoys. With whiskey now being made in all corners of the planet **under different regulations**, there is a genuine risk of consumers drinking some spirits **labeled as whiskey**, which will not offer the true depth and complexity of character a whiskey should offer.❞

JEAN DONNAY, *Owner, Glann ar Mor, Brittany, France*

" I see a **great future** for lots of new whiskey brands. If people are **open-minded** and will accept new distilleries and **new countries** making whiskey, they will discover lots of new ideas and new flavors. "

ASHOK CHOKALINGAM, *General Manager, Amrut, India*

" There are lots of opportunities for whiskey **across the world** as more people find out about it. They want to know more and understand that whiskey can come from **lots of places** and not just the traditional countries. "

JOANIE TSENG, *International Brand Director for Kavalan, Taiwan*

" I would like to see some **real innovation** in **blended whiskey** to bring new flavors to new drinkers and show them that Scotch whiskey can be an exciting category. "

GERRY TOSH, *Global Brand Manager, Highland Park, Scotland*

" The world economy is a major concern; it is so easy for governments, in no matter what part of the world, to **tax distilled spirits** with the perception that the income generated does not harm the general public. "

JIM RUTLEDGE, *Master Distiller, Four Roses, US*

" Trade barriers and **counterfeiting** are two of the problems the industry currently has. "

JOHN CAMPBELL, *Distillery Manager, Laphroaig, Scotland*

" The biggest challenge in today's world is to maintain the highest quality standard in a world where much is **treated as a commodity**. Maintaining a high premium through sourcing the best cereals, superior quality casks, and optimizing distillation techniques will help **guarantee ongoing success**. "

BARRY CROCKETT, *Master Distiller, Midleton, Ireland*

Euro stills Global expansion is not restricted to the developing economies: Europe is cashing in on the whiskey boom too, in places like Sweden and Germany.

Liquid gold In some quarters, whiskey is considered a safer investment than gold. A super-premium category has emerged to cater to the millionaire market, which seeks ever rarer, more mature malts in ever more elaborate packaging—a trend online retailer Master of Malt parodied with its April 1 "release" of a bogus 105-year-old single malt.

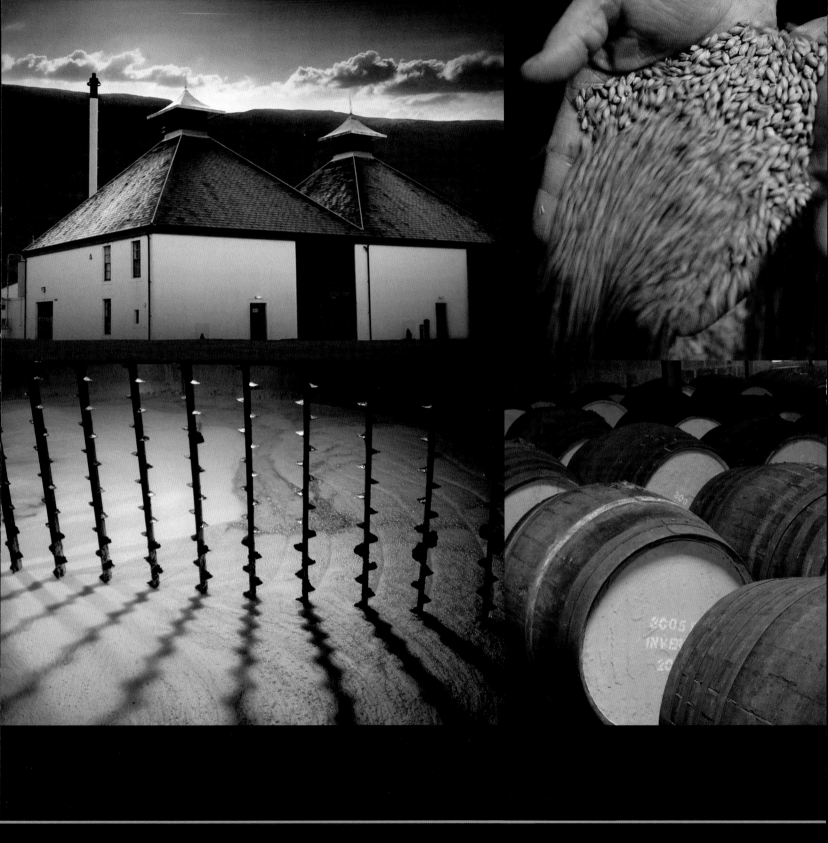

SCOTLAND

SCOTLAND

Whiskey may now be a truly global drink, enjoyed in many countries around the world and produced in a number of them, but to most people its roots lie in the Scottish Highlands (though the Irish would certainly dispute that Scotland was the birthplace of whiskey). The popular image of whitewashed distilleries silhouetted against the grandeur of a heather-clad moor with a burn of pure water flowing by is derived partly from the work of generations of advertisers and marketers, who wish to equate their product with the beautiful, the natural, and the archetypally "Scottish." Most consumers don't want to imagine high-speed bottling lines in 1980s concrete structures located in industrial parks when they pour a dram and raise it to their lips.

Scotch Whiskey Events

Scotch whiskey has long been at the heart of many of the country's principal celebrations. A dram to welcome in the New Year at midnight on Hogmanay is practically mandatory, while Burns' Night Suppers, held to commemorate the birth of Scotland's national bard on January 25, 1759, always feature the national drink. In 2012 an Aberdeen University student by the name of Blair Bowman came up with the concept of World Whisky Day (www.worldwhiskyday.com), initially staged on March 27 and hopefully the foundation for ongoing initiatives. Meanwhile, www.scotlandwhisky.com is a partnership between public and private sectors intended to promote Scotch whiskey, offering invaluable information to novices and aficionados, locals and visitors alike.

While it's easy to be cynical about marketing ploys, the fact remains that Scotland does boast an extraordinarily diverse range of distilleries scattered across some of the most scenic parts of the country, and the survival of almost 100 malt distilleries is in itself remarkable in an unsentimental, commercial world where policies of consolidation and rationalization have long been preeminent.

Many of those distilleries still surviving were founded during the remarkable Victorian period of popularity when blended Scotch ruled the waves. And Scotch is once again in the ascendancy, with producers discovering ever more emerging markets, particularly in Asia, eager to sample the delights of a dram, though the US and France remain the two most valuable overseas markets. Record export sales have led to the expansion of existing distilleries and the creation of entirely

The landscape of the Highlands and Islands *is synonymous with Scotch whiskey worldwide.*

Speyside's Glenfarclas distillery *has been owned by J. & G. Grant since 1865 and is still a family-run concern.*

new ones in recent years, and most distillers are cautiously optimistic about ongoing growth.

While a remarkable number of malt distilleries have survived, ownership is concentrated into relatively few hands, with the two major players, Diageo and Pernod Ricard subsidiary Chivas Brothers, operating between them 40 of the 97 commercial malt-producing facilities.

SCOTCH WHISKEY REGIONS

The regions of Scotch malt whiskey production have evolved for both practical and administrative reasons and also as a result of perceived stylistic similarities between whiskeys distilled within proximity of each other. The division between "Highland" and "Lowland" came about as a result of the 1784 Wash Act, which imposed varying levels of duty in the two areas, while the whiskeys produced on Islay, for example, were noted for their heavily peated profile.

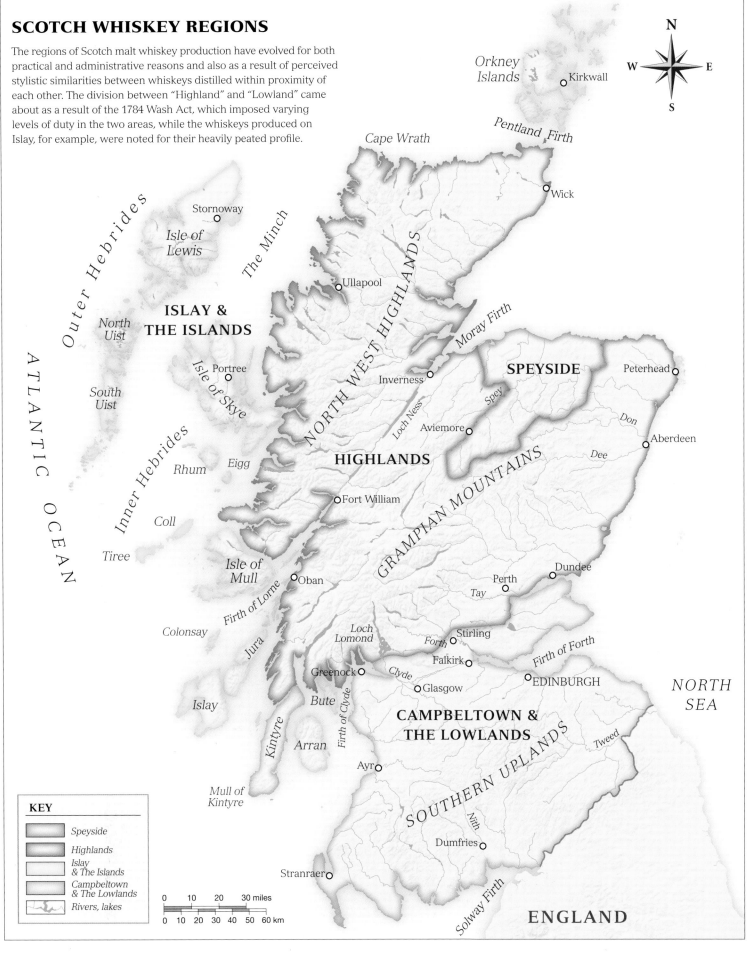

N
W · E
S

Orkney Islands
Kirkwall
Pentland Firth
Cape Wrath
Wick

Stornoway
Isle of Lewis
The Minch
Outer Hebrides
North Uist
South Uist
ATLANTIC OCEAN

ISLAY & THE ISLANDS

NORTH WEST HIGHLANDS
Ullapool
Moray Firth
Inverness
SPEYSIDE
Peterhead
Spey
Loch Ness
Aviemore
Don
Aberdeen
Dee

Portree
Isle of Skye
Inner Hebrides
Rhum
Eigg
HIGHLANDS
Coll
Tiree
Fort William

GRAMPIAN MOUNTAINS

Isle of Mull
Oban
Firth of Lorne
Colonsay
Jura

Dundee
Perth
Tay

Loch Lomond
Stirling
Forth
Falkirk
Firth of Forth
Clyde
Greenock
Glasgow
EDINBURGH

NORTH SEA

Islay
Bute
Firth of Clyde
Arran
Kintyre
Mull of Kintyre

CAMPBELTOWN & THE LOWLANDS

SOUTHERN UPLANDS
Tweed

Ayr
Nith
Dumfries

Stranraer

Solway Firth

ENGLAND

KEY
- Speyside
- Highlands
- Islay & The Islands
- Campbeltown & The Lowlands
- Rivers, lakes

0 10 20 30 miles
0 10 20 30 40 50 60 km

SPEYSIDE

Known as the "Golden Triangle," Speyside is the very heartland of malt whiskey production. The adjective "golden" is apt in two ways: not only does it imply something precious, but Speyside is also a center for the cultivation of malting barley, and the summer months see acre after golden acre of the raw material of Scotch whiskey swaying in the breeze.

Regional Styles

Traditionally, Speysides have been known as elegant, complex whiskeys, but there are dramatic differences between the light, grassy, floral profile of a single malt such as Glen Grant and the full, rich, sherried character of The Macallan nearby.

Author's Choice

BALVENIE A classic Victorian distillery in family ownership and one of only a handful still operating floor maltings. Its single malt is widely available yet never commonplace and its owners are not afraid to innovate.

TORMORE Not a "big hitter" but still a must-see for its visionary architecture.

Regional Events

Eight distilleries, including Historic Scotland's silent Dallas Dhu site, plus the fascinating Speyside Cooperage, are part of the official Malt Whisky Trail (www.maltwhiskytrail.com), while a number of other distilleries also provide facilities for visitors. For details, visit www.scotlandwhisky.com. Two annual whiskey festivals are staged, with the Spirit of Speyside Whisky Festival (www.spiritofspeyside.com) taking place over five days in May and the Autumn Speyside Whisky Festival occupying four days during September or October (www.dufftown.co.uk).

Located in northeastern Scotland, the Speyside single malt region is also a place of remote highland glens where winter lingers long and where, in days gone by, illicit distillers were able to ply their trade in relative safety.

At the center of the region is the great Spey River, Scotland's fastest-flowing and second-longest river, which has a fine reputation among anglers for its world-class salmon fishing. The river rises in the highlands of Badenoch and flows past Grantown, Aberlour, and Rothes until it reaches the sea between Elgin and Buckie. From a whiskey-making perspective, however, Speyside embraces an area extending from the Findhorn River in the west to the Deveron in the east, and as far south as the city of Aberdeen.

Speyside's historical popularity as a location for distilleries is due to the fact that the area provided the key ingredients needed for making whiskey: plentiful pure water, high-quality barley, and peat, all within relatively close proximity. It is now home to about half of all Scotland's malt whiskey distilleries.

The arrival of the railroads in the second half of the 19th century meant that the Speyside distilleries could transport their spirit to the great blending centers farther south, and when the increasing popularity of blended whiskey caused a distilling bonanza, it was on Speyside that development was at its most dramatic. Today, the Scotch whiskey industry is experiencing another such bonanza and Speyside remains firmly at the center of activities, with major distillers such as Diageo and Chivas Brothers investing heavily in its future. For the whiskey-lover, visiting Speyside offers wonderful opportunities for exploration and discovery.

The pagoda-capped kilns *of Strathisla distillery.*

N W E S

NORTH SEA

Speyside is centered on the whiskey-making settlements of Elgin, Keith, Rothes, and Dufftown. Principal roads into the region are the A96 from Aberdeen via Huntly and Keith to Elgin, the A96 from Inverness, and the A9/A95 from Perth by way of Aviemore and Aberlour to Keith. Public transportation is principally limited to local buses, though a train service operates between Inverness and Aberdeen, with stations at Elgin, Keith, and Huntly.

Scotland
Speyside

North Sea

Speyside

SCOTLAND

Glasgow ○ EDINBURGH

ENGLAND

Burghead

Burghead Bay

Lossiemouth

Spey Bay

Cullen

Glenglassaugh

Portsoy

Macduff

Roseisle

Buckie

Inchgower

Tugnet

Elgin

Glen Moray Linkwood

Benromach

Forres

Glenburgie

Miltonduff

BenRiach
Longmorn

Mannochmore

Glenlossie

Glen Elgin

Fochabers

Macduff

Knockdhu

Aberchirder

Aultmore
Strathisla

Auchroisk

Glen Grant
The Glenrothes

Speyburn

Rothes

Keith

Strathmill

Glen Spey

Glentauchers

Craigellachie

The Macallan

The Balvenie

GlenDronach

Cardhu

Aberlour

Kininvie
Glenfiddich
Glendullan

Dailuaine

Knockando

Dufftown

Glenallachie

Mortlach
Dufftown

Huntly

Glenfarclas

Benrinnes

Cragganmore
Tormore

Ben Rinnes △
2759ft
(841m)

Allt-a-Bhainne

Ardmore

Lochindorb

Cromdale

CROMDALE HILLS

The Glenlivet

Tamnavulin

Balmenach

Tomintoul

Livet

Oldmeldrum

GLENLIVET

Avon

Braeval

Tomintoul

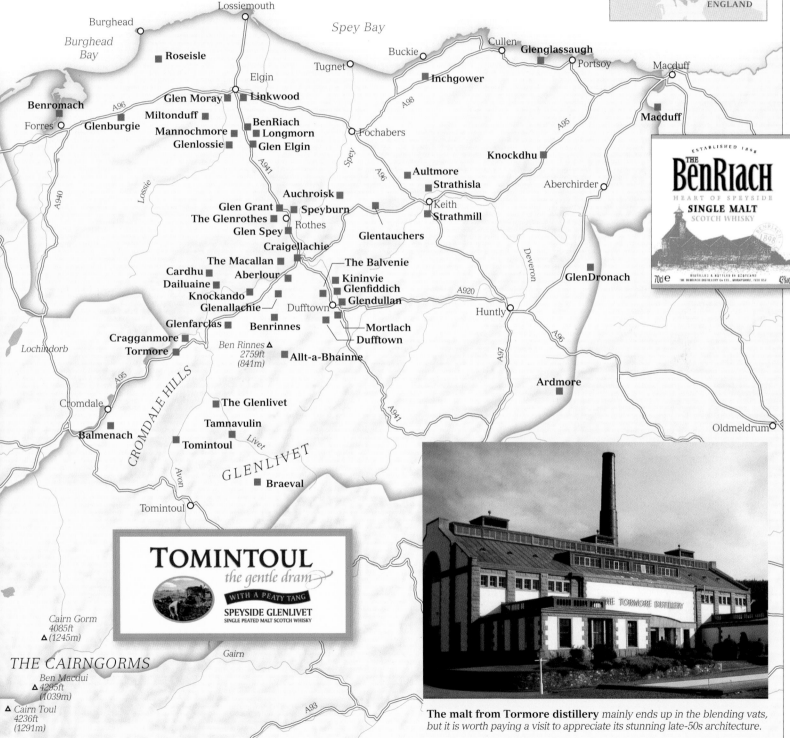

The malt from Tormore distillery *mainly ends up in the blending vats, but it is worth paying a visit to appreciate its stunning late-50s architecture.*

THE CAIRNGORMS

Cairn Gorm
4085ft
△ (1245m)

Ben Macdui
△ 4295ft
(1039m)

△ Cairn Toul
4236ft
(1291m)

Gairn

THE BenRiach
HEART OF SPEYSIDE
SINGLE MALT
SCOTCH WHISKY

ESTABLISHED 1898

TOMINTOUL
the gentle dram
WITH A PEATY TANG
SPEYSIDE GLENLIVET
SINGLE PEATED MALT SCOTCH WHISKY

ABERLOUR

OWNER Chivas Brothers Ltd. (Pernod Ricard)
FOUNDED 1826 CAPACITY 977,000 gal (3.7m liters)
ADDRESS Aberlour, Banffshire AB38 9PJ
WEBSITE www.aberlour.co.uk

The late-Victorian distillery *was designed by Charles Doig after a fire destroyed the original building in 1898.*

Close to the busy A95 road on the south-western outskirts of Aberlour, the distillery stands at the opposite end of the village from a factory that produces one of Scotland's other great iconic products, namely shortbread.

Walkers Shortbread Ltd. is an independent family firm, which makes one of the best-known brands, and while Aberlour single malt is not such a household name in the UK, mention single malt Scotch whiskey in France, and Aberlour is likely to be the name on almost everyone's lips.

According to Neil Macdonald, Chivas Brothers Brand Director, Malts, "Aberlour was one of the first single malt distilleries to be acquired by a non-British company when France's Pernod started its acquisition in 1974. One consequence was that Pernod focused on building the reputation of Aberlour in France and played a key role in building the single malt category there. To this day, Aberlour is brand leader in this key market.

"Whiskey in France is generally drunk straight, which allows the long, soft, and warming finish of Aberlour to shine through. Aberlour is rated one of the top two single malts in France, which is the world's biggest Scotch market, and is currently the seventh most popular malt whiskey in the world. More than half of Aberlour's sales are taken from France."

Sherried heritage

Aberlour Distillery was founded by Peter Weir and James Gordon in 1826, though the present plant actually dates from 1879, when the banker James Fleming built it close to the site of the original, which had been seriously damaged by fire. Aberlour remained in a variety of independent hands until 1974–75, when Pernod purchased its then owner, Campbell Distilleries. In 2001, Pernod Ricard, as the company had become, acquired Chivas Brothers, and Aberlour joined the Chivas group of distilleries.

Aberlour is one of a number of single malts that have clung to the tradition of using significant amounts of ex-sherry wood for maturation purposes, highlighted by the cask strength, Oloroso sherry cask-aged Aberlour "a'bunadh" (Gaelic for "of the origin") expression, launched in 2000. Neil Macdonald notes that "Aberlour's relationship with the finest sherry cask maturation has defined it as one of the best

sherry-matured whiskeys in the world, with Aberlour "a'bunadh" attaining cult status among whiskey connoisseurs.

"Throughout the rest of the range we are proud to showcase a definite sherry influence, although we often prefer that this is part of our double-cask maturation style, which mixes whiskey matured in sherry casks with whiskey from Bourbon casks, giving great depth and versatility to the range. From its medium-sized pot stills Aberlour produces a balanced spirit that takes well to maturation in ex-sherry casks, but has the elegance to shine through in ex-Bourbon cask maturation as well."

The principal bottlings of Aberlour include a 10-year-old, 12- and 16-year-olds, both of which are double-cask matured, an 18-year-old, and "a'bunadh."

TASTING NOTES

ABERLOUR "A'BUNADH"
single malt, 59.6% ABV, cask strength, matured in ex-Oloroso sherry casks, non-chill-filtered
Rich on the nose, with sherry, furniture polish, nutty malt, apples, and smoke. The full palate is intensely sherried and fruity, with more apples, nuts, and smoke, plus ginger. The finish is long, with honey, spices, and dark chocolate.

ABERLOUR 10-YEAR-OLD
single malt, 40% ABV, matured in a mix of ex-Bourbon and ex-sherry casks
A sweet sherry and honey nose, balanced by spiciness and a touch of Jaffa oranges. Caramel and quite dry sherry on the palate, with barley sugar in the medium-long sweet finish.

ABERLOUR 18-YEAR-OLD
single malt, 43% ABV
The nose offers sweet sherry, honey, and orange creams. Spices and figs emerge. The palate is rich, with spicy sherry, apricots, and peaches. The finish is long, with cream, more spices and figs, and gentle oak.

ABERLOUR 10-YEAR-OLD

While Aberlour was a late starter when it came to offering public access to the distillery, since getting in on the visitor center act in 2002, it has become synonymous with in-depth connoisseur tours, opting for quality over quantity. The Aberlour Distillery Experience embraces comprehensive access to the production plant and a tutored nosing and tasting session in No. 1 Warehouse, together with the option of filling a bottle to purchase from a dedicated single cask. The Founder's Tour allows participants the rare chance to sample spirits with a variety of "cut points," and even enjoy a whiskey and chocolate pairing session.

ABERLOUR 18-YEAR-OLD

ABERLOUR "A'BUNADH"

THE BALVENIE

OWNER William Grant & Sons Ltd.
FOUNDED 1892 **CAPACITY** 1.48m gallons (5.6m liters)
ADDRESS Dufftown, Banffshire AB55 4BB
WEBSITE www.thebalvenie.com

O ne of the great pleasures of Scotch whiskey is the almost infinite number of variables that shape the essential style of each single malt and make it different from all others. The Balvenie is distilled on a site adjacent to its big brother Glenfiddich, yet produces a spirit with an entirely different profile.

As David Stewart, The Balvenie Malt Master, explains, "There is a honeyed sweetness right through The Balvenie from the new make spirit. It's sweet, biscuity, and malty. It's more fruity, floral, and aromatic than Glenfiddich, with deeper malt notes."

William Grant & Sons Ltd. is known as a company in which members of staff serve for long periods of time, with several generations of the same family often being employed. David Stewart began his career with Grant's in 1962. He became Master Blender a dozen years later, remarkably being only the fifth person to occupy that role in the history of the firm. In 2009, Stewart handed over the blending reins to his long-standing "apprentice" Brian Kinsman, while Stewart continued in his parallel role as The Balvenie Malt Master.

The Balvenie is also an important component of William Grant's major blended brand Family Reserve, and David Stewart explains, "When it comes to blending, Glenfiddich adds fruity, floral, estery, aromatic character, while The Balvenie gives malty, nutty depth and sweetness to a blend."

A sister to Glenfiddich

The Balvenie dates from 1892–93, when it was constructed as a sister distillery to Glenfiddich. While Glenfiddich had been built on a shoestring, by the time The Balvenie was established, the Grant family's financial fortunes had improved to the extent that it was possible to spend much more money on the new distillery—more than two and a half times the outlay for Glenfiddich.

Nonetheless, secondhand stills from Lagavulin on Islay and Glen Albyn in Inverness were acquired, the reason being not so much a desire to save money but rather a wish to have "seasoned" stills, which had already proved themselves capable of producing good whiskey.

The single malt produced by the distillery was first officially bottled in its own right during 1973, and today, Balvenie boasts five wash stills and six spirit stills. The brand is now in the top ten single

THE BALVENIE 12-YEAR-OLD "DOUBLEWOOD"

THE BALVENIE 17-YEAR-OLD "NEW OAK"

Turning the barley *as it germinates is a skilled job. At The Balvenie distillery, it is turned up to four times a day.*

malts in the US, and enjoys strong sales in the UK, Taiwan, France, Canada, and travel retail outlets.

Approximately 80 percent of new make spirit is filled into ex-Bourbon casks and another 20 percent goes into former sherry casks, with maturation taking place in some of the 40-plus warehouses, which also hold the make of Glenfiddich and Kininvie distilleries.

In addition to its own maltings, The Balvenie boasts a cooperage and coppersmith facilities. The cooperage and maltings are popular elements of the distillery tour, which is aimed at the more knowledgeable whiskey aficionado, lasting for about three hours and limited to a maximum of eight people.

An esoteric whiskey

David Stewart says, "With The Balvenie we have created an esoteric image—it's easier to do smaller bottlings here than it is at Glenfiddich, due to the scale of the operations. The Balvenie brand tends to be where we experiment a little and offer limited editions. We used to bottle The Balvenie 'Classic,' and it was finished in a sherry cask. In fact it was probably the first-ever cask finish, although that wasn't mentioned on the label. That led directly to 'DoubleWood' and 'PortWood.'"

The Balvenie 12-year-old "DoubleWood" and 21-year-old "PortWood" expressions are both part of the current core range, along with 12-year-old "Signature," 15-year-old "Single Barrel" (matured in former Bourbon casks), and 30- and 40-year-old variants. "DoubleWood" is initially filled into ex-Bourbon casks, then transferred to sherry casks for the final two years of maturation. "PortWood" is first matured in ex-Bourbon casks before spending a secondary period of maturation in 20-year-old port pipes. "Signature" is made up of whiskey matured in first-fill ex-Bourbon barrels, refill Bourbon barrels, and Oloroso sherry butts. It was released in 2008 and replaced the existing 10-year-old "Founder's Reserve."

Rare expressions

As well as being smaller in scale than Glenfiddich, The Balvenie is able to trade on its traditional "craft" image, giving scope for the sort of bottlings already noted, and other more obscure expressions. These have embraced releases such as The Balvenie 14-year-old "Roasted Malt" and 17-year-old "Peated Cask." The former was the first single malt Scotch whiskey to be made using a batch of dark, roasted malted barley, more commonly used to make stout, while the latter comprises a mixture of 17-year-old matured in new wood and 17-year-old finished in casks that previously contained a heavily peated batch, distilled in 2001 and not so far released. According to David Stewart, "There is peatiness in the expression, but you still get the honey and other essential Balvenie characteristics."

Another Balvenie rarity is the 2006 release, The Balvenie 17-year-old "NewWood." "It's about taking the idea of how much oak you can add to a whiskey," explains Stewart. "We started with fully matured whiskey and put it into the most active casks you could find—namely virgin oak. We found we got intense, sweet vanilla and spices." "NewWood"—initially matured in ex-Bourbon casks—was succeeded by "New Oak," which differed from its predecessor in having an original maturation period in a mixture of ex-Bourbon and ex-sherry casks.

TASTING NOTES

THE BALVENIE 12-YEAR-OLD "DOUBLEWOOD"
single malt, 40% ABV, matured in ex-Bourbon casks, finished sherry casks
Nuts and spicy malt on the nose, with banana, vanilla, and sherry. Full-bodied, with soft fruit, vanilla, sherry, cinnamon, and a hint of peat on the palate. Dry and spicy in a luxurious finish.

THE BALVENIE 17-YEAR-OLD "NEW OAK"
single malt, 43% ABV, matured in ex-sherry and ex-Bourbon casks, finished in new oak casks
Vanilla, honey, spice, and lively oak on the nose. More oak, spice, and vanilla on the palate, along with figs and dates. The finish is quite lengthy, with honey and soft, warm oak.

THE BALVENIE 40-YEAR-OLD
single malt, 48.5% ABV, matured in 4 refill hogsheads and 3 sherry butts, non-chill-filtered
Rich and mellow on the nose, with oak, raisins, peaches, honey, vanilla, and worn leather. The palate features ginger, stewed fruits, and developing bitter chocolate. Elegantly drying in the finish, with aniseed and licorice.

THE BALVENIE 40-YEAR-OLD

NEW USE FOR THE NEW HOUSE

Most distilleries, whatever their vintage, were created from scratch for the role of distilling whiskey. The Balvenie is unusual in that, while the majority of its structures were newly built, the derelict mansion of Balvenie New House was incorporated into the design, serving as extremely unconventional maltings and warehousing. This situation continued until 1929, when the upper floors of Balvenie New House were demolished and the stone was used to build more conventional malt barns. Today, The Balvenie is one of only a handful of Scotch whiskey distilleries to continue malting a percentage of the barley it uses on its own floor maltings.

BENROMACH

OWNER	Gordon & MacPhail
FOUNDED 1898	CAPACITY 132,000 gal (500,000 liters)
ADDRESS	Invererne Road, Forres, Morayshire IV36 3EB
WEBSITE	www.benromach.com

In common with many other Speyside distilleries, Benromach dates from the last decade of the 19th century, when the Scotch whiskey industry expanded dramatically to service the increased demand for blends. The distillery was founded in 1898 by the Benromach Distillery Company, opening two years later, but closing almost immediately, with a crisis of overproduction decimating the distilling landscape. The plant was revived between 1907 and 1910, and again after World War I, but was silent for much of the economically troubled 1930s.

Benromach changed hands several times during its first half-century of existence, before finding itself part of the Distillers Company Ltd. portfolio in 1953. Thirty years later, however, Benromach was to cease production once again, when the same problem of overproduction that eventually ended the Victorian whiskey boom caused major rationalization during the 1980s, with the Distillers Company alone closing 23 of its distilleries.

Happily, Benromach was one of those shuttered distilleries that were subsequently revived, thanks in this instance to the foresight of renowned Elgin-based bottlers and retailers Gordon & MacPhail, who took over Benromach in 1993, a decade after its closure. Production resumed five years later, coinciding with the distillery's centennial.

A new and smoky style

Gordon & MacPhail's Associate Director and Whiskey Supply Manager, Ewen Mackintosh, explains, "When we purchased Benromach distillery we undertook a great deal of work and research to identify the type of whiskey we wished to create. When sampling Speyside whiskeys from the 1960s and before this time, we identified that each retained a smoky characteristic. We attributed this smokiness to the use of traditional floor maltings at the time. At Benromach we wished to create a whiskey that embraced the smoky style that is prevalent in whiskeys pre-1960s."

Accordingly, malt for general production is peated to a level of 10–12 parts per million, or ppm, and given that many Speyside malts are only very lightly peated, this is a significant element in the ultimate character of the whiskey. "Benromach is a medium-to-heavy style of spirit, helped by the use of malt peated to this level," says Distillery Manager Keith Cruickshank.

In May 2004, the new style of Benromach was showcased with the release of "Traditional,"

BENROMACH "ORGANIC"

BENROMACH "TRADITIONAL"

an expression with no age statement and the first release of spirits to have been distilled under Gordon & MacPhail's ownership of the distillery.

An innovative range

Innovation has continued ever since, with variants such as the heavily peated "Peat Smoke" and "Organic," the first single malt whiskey certified by the UK's Soil Association, which guarantees that the whole production process, from raw materials to bottling, meets organic standards. Maturation is in virgin oak casks, made with wood sourced from sustainable forests in Missouri.

The "Origins" range is intended to demonstrate how apparently minor differences in whiskey-making can exert a significant influence on the finished product, with batches being distilled from Golden Promise and Optic barley varieties, as well as a quantity entirely matured in ex-port pipes.

As Keith Cruickshank notes, "At Benromach we believe that making single malt whiskey is a little like creating a jigsaw. Like each part of a jigsaw, each element of the whiskey-making process plays a tiny but important role in the overall picture."

Consistency of distillation

While an increasing amount of the spirits bottled as Benromach has now been distilled under the Gordon & MacPhail regimen, older expressions such as the "Vintage 1969" were produced when the distillery was owned by the Distillers Company.

The new Benromach *distillery, the smallest in Speyside, was officially opened in 1999 by the Prince of Wales.*

Consumers could be forgiven for expecting little similarity between the "old" and "new" Benromachs, but Ewen Mackintosh says, "We feel there is a common thread that connects vintages distilled by the previous owners and spirits distilled by Gordon & MacPhail. When Gordon & MacPhail purchased Benromach we were fortunate to obtain a sample of the new-make spirit from the previous owners. When we analyzed this sample against our distillations, we noticed this common thread. This is despite the fact that we reequipped Benromach with all-new equipment. The only constant that remains the same is the water source!"

TASTING NOTES

BENROMACH "TRADITIONAL"
single malt, 40% ABV, 80% first-fill ex-Bourbon, 20% ex-sherry casks
A nose of citrus fruit, pine needles, malt, and discreet aromas of peat. Floral and smoky on the palate, with barley, vanilla, cloves, spice, and pepper. Sweet and smoky in the finish.

BENROMACH "VINTAGE 1969"
single malt, 42.6% ABV, refill sherry hogsheads
Spicy sherry on the nose, with floral notes and a hint of peat. Sweet sherry and stewed fruits on the palate, along with subtle bonfire smoke. Toffee and dark chocolate in the long finish.

BENROMACH "ORGANIC"
single malt, 45% ABV, virgin American oak casks, non-chill-filtered
Sweet on the nose, with bananas, toasted malted bread, and fresh oak aromas. Sweet in the mouth, with vanilla, brittle toffee, and a hint of resin. The finish features fruity, lively oak.

AN EARLY-MATURING SPIRIT

Benromach is the smallest distillery on Speyside, operated by just two members of staff, one of whom is the manager. Benromach's current production facilities differ quite significantly from those originally in place, having been redeveloped during the 1990s on a much more modest scale. The new stills installed there were considerably smaller than those they replaced, and were designed with relatively broad necks to capture the heavier flavors created during the first distillation. The aim is to produce a spirit that matures early, but also has enough substance to last in cask for two or three decades prior to bottling.

BENROMACH "VINTAGE 1969"

CARDHU 12-YEAR-OLD

CARDHU

OWNER Diageo PLC	
FOUNDED 1824	**CAPACITY** 845,000 gal (3.2m liters)
ADDRESS Knockando, Aberlour, Banffshire AB38 7RY	
WEBSITE www.discovering-distilleries.com	

The first licensee of what was originally known as Cardow Distillery was John Cumming, who possessed three convictions for illicit distilling. He took over the lease of Upper Cardow farm in 1813, settling there with his wife, Helen.

Elizabeth's regime

Cumming was persuaded to operate on the right side of the law as a result of the groundbreaking Excise Act of 1823 and was granted a license to make whiskey the following year. After his death in 1846, his son, Lewis, and daughter-in-law, Elizabeth, ran the distillery, and upon Lewis's death in 1872, Elizabeth adopted the role of principal distiller. She was one of the first women in Scotland to hold such a position.

Under Elizabeth Cumming's regime, the distillery was extended in 1887, with the old equipment, including a somewhat worn pair of stills, being sold to a Johnny-come-lately former shoemaker by the name of William Grant, who was establishing his own Glenfiddich distillery just across the valley.

Six years later Cardow was acquired by John Walker & Sons of Kilmarnock and the Cumming family continued to run the operation for a time under the new name of Cardhu. This was the era when blended Scotch whiskey was taking the world by storm, and as a leading proponent of blending, the Walker company required a sizable distillery to supply it with malt.

Walker heart malt

Today, an expanded and upgraded Cardhu is part of the Diageo portfolio and serves as the "brand home" for Johnnie Walker, remaining a key component of the world's best-selling blended Scotch whiskey.

The Johnnie Walker blend has its origins in the Ayrshire town of Kilmarnock, where a youthful John Walker established a licensed grocery business during 1820. Little is known of his life, although he did retail whiskey and probably assembled his own vattings for customers. When John Walker died in 1857, his son Alexander took over the business, and a decade later copyrighted the now famous slanted Old Highland Whisky label with its distinctive gold writing.

However, it was under the stewardship of his son, also Alexander, who joined the company in 1888, that John Walker & Sons really began to emerge as a significant force in the world of whiskey, with the popular cartoon illustrator Tom Browne drawing the first "Striding Man"—the symbolic figurehead for the brand—in 1908.

Today, the blend sells in excess of 130 million bottles a year, and the old, familiar Red Label and Black Label variants have been augmented by the likes of Green Label (a blended malt), Gold Label (carrying an 18-year-old age statement), and Blue Label (the super-premium offering of the family).

Cardhu's Spanish market

Cardhu itself has the status of Diageo's leading single malt in terms of sales, with Spain as its principal market, and the early years of the 21st century saw growth of the brand outstrip available supplies of the liquid itself.

According to Diageo's Dr Nick Morgan, "We drastically reduced the number of markets we supplied in order to focus stocks on strategic markets. Having seen the issue of increasing demand coming we had also made some long term decisions about production, which included putting in a new mash tun a number of years ago. This has allowed us to get supplies and demand back in balance."

Apart from the 12-year-old expression, bottlings of Cardhu are rare, with a 1997 variant appearing in 2009 as part of Diageo's comprehensive "Managers' Choice" lineup of single cask, cask-strength malts. Independent bottlings of Cardhu are also elusive, though the Aberdeenshire-based bottler Duncan Taylor & Company Ltd. released 222 bottles of a 26-year-old 1984 version in 2011.

TASTING NOTES

CARDHU 12-YEAR-OLD
single malt, 40% ABV
The nose is relatively light and floral, quite sweet, with pears, nuts, and a whiff of distant smoke. Medium-bodied, malty, and sweet in the mouth. Medium-length in the finish, with sweet smoke, malt, and a hint of peat.

CARDHU "MANAGERS' CHOICE" 1997
single malt, 57.3% ABV, single cask, cask strength, matured in a first-fill ex-Bourbon American oak hogshead (252 bottles)
Attractive, floral nose of light malt, pixie sticks, and delicate spices. Sweet and rich palate, with vanilla, toffee, and Bourbon. The finish is medium in length, with persistent spice, slowly drying to dark chocolate.

CARDHU 26-YEAR-OLD "DUNCAN TAYLOR RARE AULD COLLECTION"
single malt, 54.4% ABV
Sweet and malty on the nose, with vanilla, cinnamon, orange-flavored chews, and figs. Very sweet and fruity on the palate, with rum and raisin ice cream and hazelnuts. The finish is long and malty, with rich chocolate notes.

CARDHU "SPECIAL CASK RESERVE"

CRAGGANMORE

OWNER Diageo PLC
FOUNDED 1869 **CAPACITY** 528,000 gal (2m liters)
ADDRESS Ballindalloch, Banffshire AB37 9AB
WEBSITE www.discovering-distilleries.com

Spend time on Speyside today and it is as though the great railroad revolution passed by this corner of northeast Scotland. Sharp-eyed observers will, however, spot stretches of track bed and inexplicable arched bridges, while walkers on the popular Speyside Way are actually traveling on much of the route once occupied by trains. Far from omitting Speyside, the 19th-century rail revolution embraced the region broadly, and the sites chosen for many distilleries took into account the proximity of railroad lines.

It's fair to say that from the late 1860s onward, the presence of the rail network was second in importance only to the availability of a good water supply for the many promoters of Speyside distillery projects. Trains brought in supplies of barley for malting and coal for firing the stills, and in return removed casks of spirits destined for the blending halls and bottlers further south.

Cragganmore, in the parish of Ballindalloch, was the first distillery on Speyside to be deliberately sited close to a rail line, with the Strathspey Railway having opened a branch from Boat of Garten near Aviemore to Craigellachie and Dufftown in 1863. The distillery's founder, John Smith, had a private siding constructed to facilitate use of the neighboring line. Indeed, Smith was a great fan of this rapidly developing form of transportation, even though his huge bulk meant that he had to travel in the caboose because he could not fit through the passenger car doors.

In 1887—one year after John Smith's death—the first "whiskey special" train left Ballindalloch Station with a load of 19,000 gallons (73,000 liters) of whiskey, and many more "whiskey specials" followed in the years to come.

The origins of Cragganmore

By the time Smith set out to establish Cragganmore in 1869, he could already boast a strong track record as a distiller, having managed Wishaw in Lanarkshire and the distilleries of Macallan and Glenlivet in Speyside before leasing Glenfarclas. Persistent rumors marked him out as the illegitimate son of Glenlivet founder George Smith.

When it came to designing his own distillery, close to the Spey River, Smith called upon the in-demand services of Elgin's Charles Doig, who was later engaged again to modernize the distillery in 1901. The Smith family's control of the distillery lasted until 1923; four years later 50 percent of Cragganmore passed to Distillers Company Ltd., while the remaining half belonged to Sir George Macpherson-Grant of Ballindalloch Estate. DCL didn't acquire the Macpherson-Grant share of the distillery until 1965, a year after the capacity of Cragganmore had been doubled by the addition of two new stills.

In 1988 DCL's successor firm, United Distillers, selected Cragganmore 12-year-old as the regional

The site for Cragganmore distillery *was chosen to be close to the Strathspey railroad line, which closed in 1968.*

CRAGGANMORE 12-YEAR-OLD

representative in its Classic Malts portfolio. Cragganmore had long enjoyed the reputation of being a first-class blending malt, as well as a fine dram in its own right, but many observers were nonetheless surprised that it fought off the likes of Glen Elgin and Mortlach for the accolade.

Making the malt

The essential character of Cragganmore single malt is partly due to comparatively lengthy fermentations of around 60 hours. Diageo's Andy Cant says, "Fermentation times, while not excessive, are long enough to produce some of the floral, light fruit notes that make Cragganmore such an interesting single malt."

However, it is the distillation regimen that has the greatest influence on the style of Cragganmore. Cant explains that "the wash still lyne arms slope downward toward the worm tubs, thereby limiting the opportunity for the vapor to interact with copper, while the T-shaped tops of the spirit stills encourage a degree of reflux." The wash stills thereby produce a comparatively sulfury character, while the spirit stills give a lighter spirit, but "sulfury" and "meaty" are desirable components of Cragganmore, so in order to combat the lighter style of spirits produced in the spirit stills, they are not given time to rest, which would allow the copper to rejuvenate. The stills are recharged as soon as they are empty, making the copper less active than would otherwise be the case. Andy Cant considers that the fermentation and distillation regimens "together contribute to the complexity associated with Cragganmore."

TASTING NOTES

CRAGGANMORE 12-YEAR-OLD
single malt, 40% ABV
A complex nose of sherry, brittle toffee, nuts, heather, mild wood smoke, and mixed peel. Malty on the palate, with almonds, herbal, and fruit notes. Medium in length, with a slightly peppery, smoky finish.

CRAGGANMORE 21-YEAR-OLD (SPECIAL RELEASES 2010)
single malt, 56% ABV, cask strength, matured in refill American oak casks (5,856 bottles)
Orange fondant cream on the nose, with marzipan and malt, deepening to molasses. Fresh citrus fruits on the palate; lively and spicy, becoming drier and more oaky, with ginger and licorice in the lengthy finish.

CRAGGANMORE "DISTILLERS EDITION" (BOTTLED 1997)
single malt, 40% ABV, matured for a secondary period in ex-port pipes
The nose is waxy and floral, with fresh fruit, vanilla, and a wisp of smoke. The palate is oily, with smoke, malt, oranges, and spice. The lengthy finish features ripe bananas and oak, drying steadily.

CRAGGANMORE CLUBROOM

Traditional in appearance, with white-washed stone walls and contrasting slate roofs, Cragganmore is set in a peaceful location, despite the fact that the busy A95 road is not far away. In addition to the Cragganmore Distillery Tour, visitors may also participate in an Expressions Tour, which includes the opportunity to sample three different variants of the single malt in the Cragganmore Clubroom, a venue not usually open to the public, featuring a fascinating array of historical Cragganmore-related memorabilia. While its Diageo sister distillery of Cardhu is open to visitors year-round, Cragganmore operates only between April and November.

CRAGGANMORE 21-YEAR-OLD

CRAGGANMORE "DISTILLERS EDITION"

GLENDRONACH

OWNER	The BenRiach Distillery Company Ltd.
FOUNDED 1826	**CAPACITY** 370,000 gal (1.4m liters)
ADDRESS	Forgue, Huntly, Aberdeenshire AB5 6DB
WEBSITE	www.glendronachdistillery.com

The story of GlenDronach is an object lesson in how a niche operator can acquire a once-cherished whiskey from a global company with an overlarge portfolio of brands and restore it to its rightful eminence. Established in 1826 by James Allardice, who headed a consortium of local farmers and businessmen, GlenDronach was taken over in 1852 by Walter Scott, formerly manager of Teaninich distillery, who proceeded to expand the operation. On his death in 1887, the distillery was acquired by a Leith partnership.

Famous names acquire GlenDronach
A significant part of GlenDronach's subsequent heritage was intertwined with two famous Scotch whiskey families, the Grants and Teachers. Captain Charles Grant, fifth son of William Grant, founder of Glenfiddich, bought GlenDronach in 1920 and it remained with the family until 1960, when it was acquired by the Teachers. Passing to Allied Breweries Ltd. in 1976, GlenDronach fell silent from 1996 to 2002. Until the 1996 closure, floor maltings were in operation—much later than at most Scotch whiskey distilleries. GlenDronach is also notable for being the last distillery in Scotland to operate coal-fired stills, though health and safety issues precipitated conversion to steam in 2005, when Allied (now Allied Domecq) was taken over by Chivas Brothers.

GlenDronach did not fit comfortably into the Chivas Brothers portfolio, which was overburdened with riches after the acquisition of Allied, and it was not surprising when, in August 2008, it was announced that The BenRiach Distillery Company had purchased GlenDronach. This distillery had already done a fine job of giving the low-profile BenRiach single malt a whole new identity and impetus. Buying GlenDronach gave the consortium of owners, headed by Billy Walker, a heavily sherried single malt to complement BenRiach.

Reinventing GlenDronach
"GlenDronach was a single malt of substance in terms of market presence, and it was always on our radar," says Walker, who proceeded to copy the BenRiach capitalization quirk, changing to upper case the "D" in what had previously been known as Glendronach. "The whiskey is now back to where it should be," notes Walker, explaining, "We only had one product when we took over and we have totally reinvented GlenDronach.

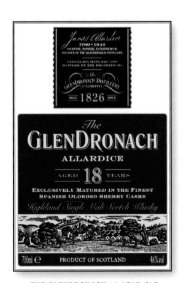

THE GLENDRONACH 18-YEAR-OLD
"ALLARDICE"

THE GLENDRONACH 12-YEAR-OLD "ORIGINAL"

We've brought in new wood management, extended the range, and made the whiskey more muscular."

While some new-make spirit is filled into ex-sherry butts, a significant proportion is put into ex-Bourbon casks before being transferred into sherry wood for a final maturation. Around 9,000 casks of whiskey were acquired with the distillery, and a program of re-racking up to 50 percent of the spirit into fresh Oloroso casks has been undertaken. As a result, GlenDronach now competes strongly against the likes of Glenfarclas, The Macallan, and The Dalmore.

The GlenDronach lineup

The year following the takeover saw the release of 12-, 15-, and 18-year-old expressions, along with a limited edition 33-year-old and five single-cask bottlings. While the 12-year-old is matured in a mixture of Pedro Ximénez and Oloroso sherry casks, the 15- and 18-year-olds are matured exclusively in ex-Oloroso casks. In 2010, the GlenDronach lineup was further enhanced by a 31-year-old, intended to replace the 33-year-old, and a 1996 single-cask bottled to celebrate the opening of the distillery's new visitor center, together with no fewer than 11 vintages and four wood-finished expressions.

These were the first GlenDronach finishes ever to be offered, and included Sauternes, Moscatel, tawny port, and a virgin oak finish, all initially matured in European oak. Subsequently, 11 more vintages were released, while a 21-year-old variant was added to the core range. The 21-year-old is named "Parliament" after the parliament of rooks that has been a feature at GlenDronach for centuries. The rooks were said to have provided advance notice of the approach of excise officers by their crowing, in the days when the GlenDronach area was a hotbed of illicit distilling.

STREET MARKETING

Soon after establishing GlenDronach distillery, James Allardice ventured to Edinburgh in search of markets for his whiskey, taking with him copious amounts of the spirit. However, he failed to interest the many tavern landlords he approached with his new single malt. According to legend, while heading wearily back to his hotel he was accosted on the Canongate by two prostitutes whom he invited to his room for a drink. When they left, he gave them the remainder of his whiskey, only to find word of GlenDronach spreading on the streets, and being requested by name in the city's hostelries. The orders soon followed.

TASTING NOTES

THE GLENDRONACH 12-YEAR-OLD "ORIGINAL"

single malt, 43% ABV, Pedro Ximénez and Oloroso sherry casks, non-chill-filtered
A sweet nose of fruitcake. Smooth on the palate, with sherry, soft oak, fruit, almonds, and spices. Dry, nutty finish, ending with bitter chocolate.

THE GLENDRONACH 14-YEAR-OLD "VIRGIN OAK FINISH"

single malt, 46% ABV, non-chill-filtered
Slightly smoky nose with lively oak, sweetening with banoffee pie and cocoa. Spicy in the mouth, with vanilla, cereal, hazelnuts, and sawn wood. Gingery dry finish.

THE GLENDRONACH 31-YEAR-OLD "GRANDEUR"

single malt, 45.8% ABV, cask strength, Oloroso sherry casks, non-chill-filtered
Malt, sherry, ginger, and coffee nose. Sherry and stewed fruits on the palate, with molasses and almonds. Long finish with hints of coal tar, honey, licorice, and chocolate.

THE GLENDRONACH 14-YEAR-OLD "VIRGIN OAK FINISH"

THE GLENDRONACH 31-YEAR-OLD "GRANDEUR"

GLENFARCLAS

OWNER J. & G. Grant

FOUNDED 1836 **CAPACITY** 793,000 gal (3m liters)

ADDRESS Ballindalloch, Banffshire AB37 9BD

WEBSITE www.glenfarclas.co.uk

When it comes to the Scotch whiskey equivalent of the French *grand cru* designation for top-quality wines, Speyside is home to a comparatively high number of the leading contenders. Among these are two single malts whose expressions are principally defined by their heavily sherried style, namely The Macallan and Glenfarclas.

While The Macallan is probably the most collectible whiskey in the world, with the rarest expressions commanding record-breaking prices of up to £125,000 (about $185,000), connoisseurs of Glenfarclas tend to buy it simply in order to consume the product rather than look at the bottle or hope that it will appreciate in value. This is partly due to the prevailing philosophy of Glenfarclas supremo John Grant, who represents the fifth generation of his family to own the distillery. Son George continues the family tradition by serving as Brand Ambassador.

Whiskey for drinking

John Grant believes that whiskey is for drinking, and prices Glenfarclas accordingly. He eschews the contemporary trend for overly elaborate packaging, noting of the Glenfarclas 40-year-old expression, launched in 2010, "It's affordable because it's not overpackaged—it just comes in a plain carton—and we have lots of it. We make a reasonable margin, and I'd rather people drank it than collected it.

"I think we should ban all secondary packaging—cartons, tubes, and so on—from a carbon footprint point of view. If you buy a bottle of Château Latour or something similar, no matter how expensive and prestigious the wine, all you get is a bottle with a label. So why has the Scotch whiskey industry gone down the route of using so much extravagant packaging?"

Although Glenfarclas distillery was first established in 1836 by Robert Hay, in the shadow of Ben Rinnes in the parish of Ballindalloch, it was not acquired by the Grant family until 1865. It was then a further five years before it actually came to be operated by J. & G. Grant Ltd., as father John and son George initially leased the plant to John Smith, until he left to establish nearby Cragganmore distillery. Since then various members of the Grant family have presided over the distillery to the present day, through both good times and bad.

GLENFARCLAS "175TH ANNIVERSARY"

GLENFARCLAS 10-YEAR-OLD

An independent spirit

"The great advantage of being independent is that we can take a long-term view and plan long-term strategies," says John Grant of the current generation. "We aren't answerable to those terrible men in boardrooms who are only interested in higher share prices and bigger dividends and don't care how it is achieved. We don't have that burden."

Having the ability to take a long-term view of the business is one of the reasons why the distillery's inventory boasts the sort of quantities of old whiskey stocks most distillers would kill for. Long-term strategic thinking also explains the well-established use of Oloroso sherry casks, rather than ex-Bourbon barrels. If the need to restrain costs in order to maintain or increase shareholder dividends were the overriding consideration, it would be ex-Bourbon barrels all the way, since a good European oak ex-sherry butt can cost up to 10 times as much as its American oak cousin.

Much of the distillery that we see today, standing in the bulky, broad shadow of the mountain of Ben Rinnes and within sight of the A95 road connecting Aberlour to Grantown on Spey, was constructed in the postwar era, with the original pair of stills being augmented by two more in 1960, while a major rebuilding program during the mid-1970s added yet another pair.

Given the distillery's well-deserved reputation for producing a consistently high-quality sherried Speyside whiskey, it is not surprising that larger rivals have often cast covetous eyes over the fiercely independent Glenfarclas operation. "I regularly get offers for the distillery," says John Grant. "But I just say 'no, thank you.' We are in charge of our destiny, because we do everything, including our own bottling, at Broxburn, near Edinburgh. The distillery will only be sold over my dead body, and I hope it will carry on after me."

The Glenfarclas lineup

Glenfarclas can now offer a wide range of aged single malt expressions, from 10 to 50 years old. This is thanks to a concerted effort to market Glenfarclas as a single malt, first begun in the mid-1970s when John Grant joined the firm, then headed by his father George.

"By 1979–80 we had enough stock to offer a 15-year-old," says Grant, "and by the mid-1980s we could offer a 21-year-old. In the late 80s we added 25- and 30-year-olds. Now we are able to have a 40-year-old as part of the current permanent range."

GLENFARCLAS 40-YEAR-OLD

Direct-fired copper pot stills, *the largest in Speyside, help to produce a characterful malt.*

DIRECT-FIRED STILLS

Glenfarclas boasts six of the largest stills on Speyside, and unusually, they are direct-fired by gas, rather than heated by steam. According to company Chairman John Grant, "We once put a steam coil borrowed from Miltonduff into one of our spirit stills for a few weeks, and what came out nosed bland. All the character and body and guts had gone. You definitely do get a different spirit. You get really individual character from direct-fired stills. A lot of character has gone from many whiskeys and the change from direct-firing to indirect was enormous. It's much more efficient, but different alcohols come off at different rates."

In 2007 came the release of the innovative and highly collectible Family Casks range, which comprises single-cask bottlings of Glenfarclas from every year between 1952 and 1994. As John Grant notes, "We do it because we have the stock, whereas many of our competitors don't—it's as simple as that."

Glenfarclas celebrated the 175th anniversary of the founding of the distillery in 2011, and a special commemorative bottling was launched to mark the occasion. The bottling includes whiskey from 1952, the oldest of the stocks now held, along with casks of spirits distilled during each of the successive five decades. A limited edition "Chairman's Reserve," drawn from four casks from the 1960s, was also released as part of the celebrations.

TASTING NOTES

GLENFARCLAS 10-YEAR-OLD
single malt, 40% ABV, ex-sherry casks
Aromas of sherry, raisins, nuts, and spices on the nose, with just a lingering hint of smoke. The palate offers quite dry sherry, with a developing and gradually sweetening full body. The finish is long, nutty, and comparatively dry.

GLENFARCLAS 40-YEAR-OLD
single malt, 46% ABV, ex-sherry casks
Full and lush on the nose, with aromas of sweet sherry, orange marmalade, new leather, and spicy fruit. Big-bodied and rich on the fruity palate, with developing flavors of black coffee and some licorice notes. The spicy finish is very long.

GLENFARCLAS "175TH ANNIVERSARY"
single malt, 43% ABV, ex-sherry casks
Vanilla, barley sugar, and toffee aromas on the nose, with flavors of honey, sherry, cinnamon, black pepper, old leather, and oranges on the palate. The finish offers just a hint of cocoa.

GLENFARCLAS "105 CASK STRENGTH"

GLENFARCLAS 12-YEAR-OLD

GLENFARCLAS 17-YEAR-OLD

49

GLENFIDDICH

OWNER William Grant & Sons Ltd.

FOUNDED 1886 **CAPACITY** 3.17m gal (12m liters)

ADDRESS Dufftown, Banffshire AB55 4DH

WEBSITE www.glenfiddich.com

There is a tendency among those who consider themselves whiskey aficionados to dismiss Glenfiddich because of its popularity, much as they might dismiss Toyota cars because so many people drive them. But just as Toyotas are well-made and reliable vehicles, so Glenfiddich is actually a very good whiskey. Selling nearly a million bottles per year, the brand has been the world's top single malt for longer than anyone cares to remember.

As Glenfiddich's Master Blender, Brian Kinsman declares, "You get some people coming into whiskey who say Glenfiddich is old hat. But the more they learn, the more they appreciate what we've done. We've paved the way for lots of other single malts. The more they learn, the more polite they become!" Kinsman does concede, however, that the whiskey itself has evolved. "We've been very protective of the distillery character but it's now 12 years old, where previously it didn't carry an age statement, and it's deeper, richer, and more complex than it was back in the 1970s."

A giant among distilleries

Glenfiddich currently operates no fewer than 28 stills, spread across two still houses. The scale of production has risen enormously since its establishment by William Grant, at which point it was only the second distillery in Dufftown after Mortlach. What has not changed, however, is the ownership. The current chairman of the firm is Peter Gordon, great-great-grandson of William Grant and a member of the fifth generation of the family to run the organization.

As the largest family-owned distilling company in Scotland, William Grant & Sons Ltd. embraces Glenfiddich and the neighboring Balvenie distillery, along with Kininvie, established in 1990 and adjacent to Balvenie. Kininvie was built to provide additional malt whiskey for the firm's "Grant's Family Reserve" blend, the world's fourth-biggest blended Scotch whiskey. Since 1963 Grant's has also operated Girvan grain distillery and its blending and warehousing facilities on the Ayrshire coast, while a new and highly flexible malt distillery was developed within the Girvan complex during 2007–08. Named Ailsa Bay, it has an annual capacity of 1.6 million gallons (6.25 million liters).

Glenfiddich was the first Scottish distillery to open its doors to the public on a regular basis, back in 1969, and since then more than 3 million visitors have sampled its delights.

GLENFIDDICH 15-YEAR-OLD
Whiskey matured in new oak casks gives this expression sweetness and flavors of honey and spice on the palate.

The extent of the range

Brian Kinsman explains, "With Glenfiddich we have 12-, 15-, 18-, 21-, and 30-year-olds as core bottlings, plus a 40- and a 50-year-old, of which just 50 bottles are released each year. The 12-, 18-, and 30-year-olds give a straight line, as it were, through the ongoing effects of maturation. Beyond those, we have moved off that straight line with expressions like the 15-year-old, which contains some whiskey matured in new oak casks, making it more honeyed, sweet, and spicy."

The component whiskeys in Glenfiddich 15-year-old are also married in a Solera system, more commonly associated with sherry. The wooden Solera vat is regularly topped off with whiskey to ensure continuity and quality.

Kinsman adds, "Glenfiddich 21-year-old is not, as you might expect, a more intense version of the 18-year-old. It's the sweetest whiskey in the range, which is achieved by the use of American oak casks and some Spanish oak casks, plus a rum finish for a few months. A third 'spike' on the straight line comes with Glenfiddich 'Rich Oak,' which features American and Spanish oak finishes, though it's still recognizably Glenfiddich."

Phoenix from the snow

In 2010 there came the introduction of an innovative limited release by the name of "Snow Phoenix." The severe winter of 2009–10 caused damage to several of the Glenfiddich warehouses, and Brian Kinsman selected a number of casks from each of these warehouses and blended them together to create "Snow Phoenix." Comprising whiskeys from 13 to 30 years, Kinsman describes it as "a great Glenfiddich single malt born of chance and adversity."

TASTING NOTES

GLENFIDDICH 12-YEAR-OLD
"SPECIAL RESERVE"
single malt, 40% ABV
A delicate, floral, slightly fruity nose; well-mannered in the mouth, malty, elegant, and soft. Rich fruit flavors dominate the palate, with a developing nuttiness and an elusive whiff of peat smoke in the fragrant finish.

GLENFIDDICH 30-YEAR-OLD
single malt, 43% ABV, vatting of ex-Oloroso sherry and ex-Bourbon casks
Coconut, fruit salad, oak, and sherry on the nose. Complex palate, with cinnamon, ginger, oak, and dark chocolate. Long and honeyed with sweet oak in the finish.

GLENFIDDICH "SNOW PHOENIX"
single malt, 47.6% ABV, matured ex-Oloroso sherry and ex-Bourbon casks, non-chill-filtered
A sweet nose of clotted cream, orchard fruits, and sherry. The oily palate embraces ripe apples, honey, brown sugar, instant coffee, and a suggestion of smoke. The finish is very long, with dry sherry gradually sweetening.

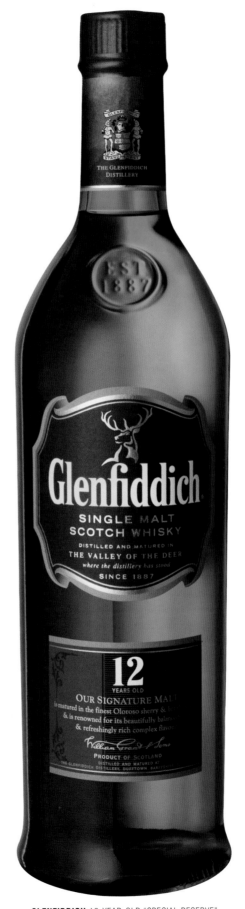

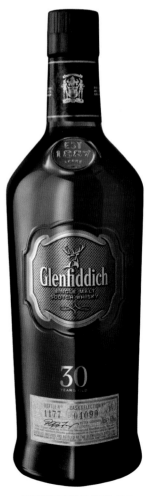

A FAMILY BUSINESS

The story of the establishment of Glenfiddich during 1886–87 is a remarkable one by any standards. Former shoemaker, lime works clerk, and Mortlach distillery manager William Grant enlisted the help of five of his sons, and together the family virtually built their own distillery on the outskirts of Dufftown from start to finish. That they were able to accomplish this was due in no small measure to the availability of bargain-priced second-hand distilling equipment from Cardow (now Cardhu) distillery. The final bill for constructing Glenfiddich, including all equipment and labor, came to the extraordinarily modest sum of just over £700 (about $3,400).

GLENFIDDICH "SNOW PHOENIX"

GLENFIDDICH 12-YEAR-OLD "SPECIAL RESERVE"

GLENFIDDICH 30-YEAR-OLD

GLEN GRANT SINGLE MALT

GLEN GRANT

OWNER Gruppo Campari	
FOUNDED 1840	**CAPACITY** 1.6m gal (5.9m liters)
ADDRESS Elgin Road, Rothes, Morayshire AB38 7BS	
WEBSITE www.glengrant.com	

Glen Grant has the distinction of being the only Scottish distillery directly named after a person or persons, in this case the brothers John and James Grant, who established the first distillery in the town of Rothes during 1840. In 1872, the distillery was inherited by James Grant's son, also James, frequently referred to simply as "the Major"—an astute businessman who carried on the work of his father and uncle in developing Glen Grant into one of the largest distilleries of its day.

While the Major was a traditional figure in many ways, the woodland garden he made at Glen Grant was planted with new and exotic species not usually found in northern Scotland. One feature of it always remembered by visitors was the "dram safe" set in the rocky bank of the burn that flows through the picturesque glen in the distillery grounds. Installed by the Major, this provided the *pièce de résistance* of a walk through the gardens in his company; visitors were suitably astonished when the Major unlocked the safe, pulled out a bottle of Glen Grant, and poured drams for them, accompanied, if required, by crystal-clear water from the burn itself.

Glen Grant expands

At the height of the Victorian whiskey boom, in 1897, the Major constructed an entirely new Glen Grant No. 2 distillery on the opposite side of the main road through Rothes in order to increase capacity. Later rechristened Caperdonich, this facility was demolished in 2010.

In 1953, J. & J. Grant, Glen Grant Ltd. merged with George & J. G. Smith of Glenlivet to form Glenlivet & Glen Grant Distillers Ltd., and in 1972 the company became part of The Glenlivet Distillers Ltd., acquired five years later by The Seagram Company Ltd. The complement of stills was increased from four to six in 1973, and from six to ten in 1977. During 2001 Glen Grant was one of the Seagram distilleries acquired by Chivas Brothers, and in 2006 the distillery and brand name were sold to the Italian drinks company Campari.

Italian style

One of the first and most astute decisions made by Campari was to headhunt Dennis Malcolm to manage their new acquisition. Nobody knows Glen Grant better than Malcolm, who was born in a distillery house on the site where his father was a stillman and his grandfather had also served as a

GLEN GRANT 25-YEAR-OLD

GLEN GRANT 1955 (GORDON & MACPHAIL)

GLEN GRANT "THE MAJOR'S RESERVE"

mashman and stillman. Malcolm started working at Glen Grant in 1961 as an apprentice cooper, and has had a connection with the distillery in one capacity or another for most of his working life.

"Campari bought Glen Grant because they wanted a really good spirits brand. Glen Grant has a huge following in Italy. In terms of volume, it's the leading single malt Scotch in the country," explains Malcolm. Of the spirits, he says, "The wash still had what you might term a 'German helmet' to it, which helps to prevent a buildup of solids from the fermented wash. The stills are fitted with purifiers, which work all the time, and they create a huge amount of reflux, which gives the spirit a comparatively light and delicate character. Using wooden washbacks also adds to the character."

He adds, "The entire volume of spirit we are producing now is for Glen Grant expressions, and the percentage of sherry wood that I lay down is around 10 percent. It mostly goes into the 10-year-old and 16-year-old expressions."

The drams

The Campari regime has seen the release of a number of limited editions and single-cask bottlings, with a "Distillery Edition" non-chill-filtered, cask-strength expression becoming available in 2012. Core variants include "The Major's Reserve" (no age statement), a five-year-old exclusive to Italy, and 16- and 25-year-olds. Remarkably, the Elgin-based bottler Gordon & MacPhail offers expressions of Glen Grant dating back to 1948.

Although Glen Grant has the image of a pale and youthful whiskey, Dennis Malcolm says, "Just because our whiskey is usually light and young doesn't mean it can't grow old very gracefully. It matures beautifully. It's very dense and complex when it's matured in a sherry cask."

TASTING NOTES

GLEN GRANT "THE MAJOR'S RESERVE"
single malt, 40% ABV
Delicate on the nose, with gentle vanilla, malt, lemon, and the aroma of damp leaves. Malt and vanilla take center stage on the palate, too, along with citrus fruit and hazelnuts. The finish is brisk.

GLEN GRANT 1955 (GORDON & MACPHAIL)
single malt, 40% ABV, matured in ex-sherry butts
A rich, sherried nose, with ginger, honey, citrus fruit, spices, and oak char. The palate is peppery, slightly smoky, with very dry sherry and a note of oranges. Long and spicy, with aniseed in the finish.

GLEN GRANT 25-YEAR-OLD
single malt, 40% ABV, matured in first-fill and refill sherry casks
Peaches, toffee, worn leather, and tea leaves on the nose. Full on the palate, with strawberries, developing plums, and spicy oak. The finish is short, with ginger and oak.

BYE-WAY OF ROTHES

James "the Major" Grant was in many ways an archetypal Victorian Highland laird and, in later life, a passionate sportsman, devoted to shooting, fishing, and big game hunting. During a safari in Matabeleland (now part of Zimbabwe) in 1898, the Major and his party came across an abandoned child and took him home to Rothes. The boy was christened Biawa Makalaga, having been discovered in Makalaga state, and was known locally as "Bye-way." He was educated in Rothes and subsequently became butler to the Major. After the Major's death, Biawa lived on in Glen Grant House until he died in 1972.

THE GLENLIVET

OWNER Chivas Bros. Ltd. (Pernod Ricard)
FOUNDED 1824 **CAPACITY** 2.8m gal (10.5m liters)
ADDRESS Ballindalloch, Banffshire AB37 9DB
WEBSITE www.theglenlivet.com

The Glenlivet is arguably the most famous distillery name in the world, and its single malt is the global number two after Glenfiddich. However, The Glenlivet has ambitions to take the top spot, and to do so, a long-term, large-scale supply of maturing whiskey must be guaranteed. You cannot fight a war without ammunition.

Accordingly, the beautifully situated Speyside distillery was the subject of a $15 million expansion program during 2008–09, when a new production area was developed, housing an ultra-efficient mash tun, eight washbacks, and six new stills, virtually doubling the distillery's potential capacity; it now ranks just below Diageo's Roseisle and the aforementioned Glenfiddich in terms of potential output. The Glenlivet is another of those historic distilleries where the impetus to expand swiftly at various periods in its history has led to the construction of some less-than-attractive structures, but its most recent growth spurt has gone a long way toward righting past aesthetic wrongs.

Preserving the old, creating the new

The Glenlivet's Master Distiller is Alan Winchester, a Speyside man born and bred, who began his distilling career at Glenfarclas distillery in 1975. "The Glenlivet had lost a lot of its original features during the 1960s when expansion took place," explains Winchester, "and so when a new production area was planned, it was decided to construct a feature building, and part of the brief was that the stills should be visible through a window from the outside.

"We set out to create something that is in keeping with the older parts of the distillery, clad in local stone. We knew how to reproduce the style of whiskey we were already making at The Glenlivet, and we installed wooden washbacks, like in the old side of the distillery, and copied the still design, which dates back to the 19th century."

Smith's Glenlivet

The Glenlivet was the first distillery to be granted a license in the wake of the highly influential 1823 Excise Act, and its owner and licensee was George Smith, whose family had been distilling whiskey on his farm at Upper Drumin, about a mile (1.6 km) from the present Glenlivet distillery, since 1774.

In 1840 George Smith leased the Cairngorm distillery at Delnabo, near Tomintoul, and his son, William, took charge of the distillery at Upper Drumin. However, demand for Smith's whiskey outstripped supply, and in 1858 a new, significantly larger distillery named Glenlivet was established on the present Minmore site, with Upper Drumin and Cairngorm closing the following year.

Family ownership continued for almost a century, with George & J. G. Smith Ltd. merging with J. & J. Grant Glen Grant Ltd. to form Glenlivet & Glen Grant Distillers Ltd. in 1953. In 1972 the company joined Hill Thompson & Company Ltd. and Longmorn-

THE GLENLIVET 12-YEAR-OLD

The magnificent scenery *that surrounds The Glenlivet distillery is an added attraction for visitors.*

Glenlivet Distilleries Ltd. to create The Glenlivet Distillers Ltd.; Seagram of Canada then acquired that company in 1977, and in 2001 The Glenlivet was one of the former Seagram assets purchased by Pernod Ricard subsidiary Chivas Brothers, for whom it is now the jewel in their Scotch whiskey portfolio.

The definite article

The powers that be at Chivas Brothers are eager to stress that the distillery should always be referred to as The Glenlivet. The definite article usage stems from an 1880 legal action, fought by John Gordon Smith, who felt that the name was being devalued by its widespread employment by distilleries often many miles from the glen itself.

Indeed, so many distilleries attempted to capitalize on the fame and reputation of The Glenlivet that during the second half of the 19th century the place was jokingly referred to as "the longest glen in Scotland." The court decided that only Smith's Glenlivet distillery could use the definite article in front of its name, while all other distillers had to use "Glenlivet" as a hyphenated prefix or suffix.

The Glenlivet today

The core or "Classic" range comprises single malts from 12 to 25 years of age, including 15-year-old "French Oak," 18-year-old, 21-year-old "Archive," and "XXV," introduced in 2007, which is the oldest expression in the permanent range.

The core lineup is supported by an array of rare bottlings under The Glenlivet Cellar Collection label, while "Nàdurra" is a non-chill-filtered, cask-strength variant of The Glenlivet. Bearing no age statement, it is bottled in batches to accommodate natural strength variations. *Nàdurra* is the Gaelic word for "natural."

TASTING NOTES

THE GLENLIVET 12-YEAR-OLD
single malt, 40% ABV
A honeyed, floral, fragrant nose. Medium-bodied, smooth, and malty on the palate, with vanilla sweetness; not as sweet, however, as the nose might suggest. The finish is pleasantly lengthy and sophisticated.

THE GLENLIVET 16-YEAR-OLD "NÀDURRA"
single malt, 55.1% ABV, matured first-fill American oak casks, cask strength, non-chillfiltered
Floral, fruity, creamy notes on the nose, with vanilla and gentle spice. The fruity, floral notes continue on the palate, before a long drying oaky and nutty finish kicks in.

THE GLENLIVET "XXV"
single malt, 43% ABV, finished first-fill sherry butts for around two years
Sherry, cherry cake, raisins, and English Breakfast tea on the nose. A quite intensely fruity palate, with nuts, spices, and raisins. The finish embraces steadily drying oak.

THE GLENLIVET "XXV"

THE GLENLIVET 16-YEAR-OLD "NÀDURRA"

GLEN MORAY

OWNER	La Martiniquaise
FOUNDED 1897	CAPACITY 608,000 gal (2.3m liters)
ADDRESS	Bruceland Road, Elgin, Morayshire IV30 1YE
WEBSITE	www.glenmoray.com

Glen Moray represents a good example of a single malt that does not have too many competing high-profile brands and is flourishing under the ownership of a company that is prepared to focus on its merits.

Back to capacity

While in the Glenmorangie PLC portfolio, this whiskey from the Speyside capital of Elgin was always going to play second fiddle to Glenmorangie itself, and could sometimes be found in supermarkets at a price that was more or less comparable with some of the higher-quality blends.

Fortunately for Glen Moray, that's no longer the case, despite initial fears that when French beverage company La Martiniquaise took control the distillery's output might all disappear into the Glen Turner and Label 5 blending vats. In fact, as distillery manager Graham Coull says, "At a brand level there has actually been an increased focus on Glen Moray as a single malt.

"Glen Moray is running at full capacity, and we are currently looking at expansion options for the distillery. Over 50 percent of our total production is now being retained for single malt use, while 25 percent is retained for our own company's blends and 25 percent is swapped in reciprocal deals to bring in other single malts to use in our blends."

La Martiniquaise has the option of creating new production capacity by building a substantial malt whiskey distillery alongside the Starlaw grain plant on its site near Bathgate, where the company has blended and bottled its whiskeys since 2004, rather than export spirits from Scotland in bulk to be processed in France.

Peaty possibilities

In common with several other Scottish distilleries whose make has long been at the opposite end of the stylistic spectrum from peaty malts, Glen Moray now distills from heavily peated malt for a short period each year. "Just less than 9 percent of the annual production is peated spirit," says Graham Coull, "with 2012 being the third year in which we produced peated spirit, and the volume has remained pretty much constant year on year. The vast majority will be used in our own blends, but we will mature some spirit for longer to see how it develops."

GLEN MORAY 10-YEAR-OLD "CHARDONNAY"

GLEN MORAY "CLASSIC"

Brewery background

There is a close relationship between brewing beer and distilling whiskey, with both breweries and distilleries requiring a guaranteed supply of grain for malting and pure process water, and whiskey is, in essence, simply distilled beer. Several breweries have been converted into distilleries over the years, including Glenmorangie, the late, lamented Lochside in Montrose, and Glen Moray itself.

The distillery was established in 1897, when the Speyside region was at the heart of a vast expansion in whiskey production, and was developed within the former West Brewery of Henry Arnot & Company, trading as the Glen Moray Glenlivet Distillery Company Ltd.

After the whiskey bubble burst amid a crisis of overproduction around the turn of the 20th century, expansion was swiftly followed by contraction and Glen Moray closed in 1910. With the exception of a brief revival two years later, the Elgin distillery was silent until 1923, when it reopened in the hands of new owners Macdonald & Muir Ltd. The Leith-based company already owned Glenmorangie, and it was left up to the manager of that distillery to choose between Aberlour and Glen Moray to add to the portfolio. He chose the latter.

During 1958 a degree of reconstruction took place at Glen Moray, with the existing floor maltings being replaced by Saladin boxes, though on-site malting ended entirely in 1978. A year after malting ceased, the complement of stills was doubled to four.

French connections

Macdonald & Muir changed its name to Glenmorangie plc in 1996, and in 2004 the company was acquired by French luxury goods group Louis Vuitton Möet Hennessy (LVMH). It would be unfair to suggest that LVMH had little interest in Glen Moray, since they invested in a new visitors' center at the distillery and proceeded to release various limited editions and vintage expressions.

"The Fifth Chapter," a 1992 cask-strength bottling, appeared during 2005, while two well-regarded cask-strength limited editions of Glen Moray "Mountain Oak" were released in 2003 and 2007. The whiskey for "Mountain Oak" had been matured since filling during 1991 in what Glen Moray described as "a unique selection of toasted and charred mountain oak casks from North America." A number of vintage bottlings are always available, with the oldest to date being distilled in 1962 and marketed under the "Manager's Choice" banner.

Despite such innovations at Glen Moray, however, in 2008 LVMH divested itself of its blending operations, blended Scotch whiskey brands, and the Glen Moray operation in order to concentrate on its Ardbeg and Glenmorangie single malts. Ownership of the Glen Moray distillery and single malt brand remained in French hands, however, with a buyer found in the form of the French beverage firm La Martiniquaise.

La Martiniquaise opts for a much lower profile than the owner of the Louis Vuitton designer fashion house and the Moët Champagne and Hennessy Cognac brands. Indeed, if you read most whiskey books, you won't find any mention of the fact that the company now operates a large grain distillery near Bathgate in West Lothian. The Starlaw Distillery has a capacity of 6.6 million gallons (25 million liters) per year, and provides grain spirits for La Martiniquaise's Glen Turner malt whiskeys, the best-selling malt brand in France, and the Label 7 blend, both of which also enjoy strong sales in overseas markets.

Glen Moray today

Under the La Martiniquaise regime, the principal Glen Moray lineup of expressions embraces "Classic" and 12- and 16-year-old variants, with "Classic" replacing the previous eight-year-old and containing three-, five-, and seven-year-old whiskey. In 2011 there came the release of port and Madeira cask-finished expressions and a 10-year-old fully matured in ex-Chardonnay casks, while a 2003 Glen Moray, fully matured in a Chenin Blanc cask and bottled at cask strength, appeared in 2012.

GLEN MORAY 8-YEAR-OLD

GLEN MORAY "PORT WOOD"

TASTING NOTES

GLEN MORAY "CLASSIC"
single malt, 40% ABV
Notably fresh on the nose, with aromas of barley, wet grass, and gentle fruit notes. The palate is balanced and mild with a taste of nuts, citrus fruit, and oak. Citrus notes continue in the finish with a little extra spice.

GLEN MORAY 16-YEAR-OLD
single malt, 40% ABV
Dried fruits, cloves, and a hint of leather on the nose. The palate is oily, sweet, and rounded, with brittle toffee and oak tannins. The finish is medium in length, with nuts and gentle spice.

GLEN MORAY 10-YEAR-OLD "CHARDONNAY"
single malt, 40% ABV, fully matured in ex-Chardonnay casks
The nose presents baked apples and pears, with a sprinkling of cinnamon. Soft in the mouth, with vanilla, more cinnamon, and floral notes. The finish is medium in length, fruity, and spicy.

GLEN MORAY 16-YEAR-OLD

THE MACALLAN

OWNER The Edrington Group

FOUNDED 1824 **CAPACITY** 2.3m gal (8.75m liters)

ADDRESS Easter Elchies, Craigellachie, Aberlour, Banffshire AB38 9RX **WEBSITE** www.themacallan.com

In single malt global sales, The Macallan occupies third place behind Glenfiddich and The Glenlivet, but when it comes to sheer whiskey cachet, it surely ranks highest of them all. The brand boasts an unparalleled reputation for both the quality of its liquid and the high prices that rare and collectible bottlings command at auction. In November 2010, a bottle of 64-year-old Macallan—the oldest whiskey ever bottled by the distillery—became the most expensive whiskey in the world when it sold at a charity auction in New York for $145,000.

Collaborations

Part of The Macallan's attraction for collectors is the fact that they are guaranteed a regular supply of limited edition releases, which are very likely to appreciate in value over the years. The "Fine & Rare" range comprises vintage expressions dating from 1926 to 1989, while the ongoing "Masters of Photography" series combines exclusive bottlings with unique photographic items from leading photographers, such as Rankin and Albert Watson.

Another innovative collaboration involved The Macallan working with furniture-maker Viscount Linley to create a custom whiskey cabinet from English bur oak, complete with six bottles of vintage Macallan malt whiskey dating from 1937, 1940, 1948, 1955, 1966, and 1970. The ensemble sells at Harrods in London for £55,000 ($88,000).

Ken Grier is Director of Malts for The Macallan and he explains the rationale behind their brand positioning as a notably high-end and collectible whiskey. "Firstly, you've got to have heritage, provenance, and reputation," he says. "These factors give a reassurance of the value of the whiskey. Secondly, you must have very high-quality liquid, and not just elaborate packaging.

"Also, you must have a creative point of difference, something that ensures it is worth the money. For example, when we did the Rankin collaboration, we took the cost of a bottle of "Fine Oak" 30-year-old and a Rankin Polaroid photograph at retail price and sold the item for the sum of the two costs. You can't rip people off."

The Macallan heritage

Today's iconic Macallan single malt first saw the light of day in 1824 when the distillery was licensed to Alexander Reid, though for much of its subsequent existence it was in the hands of the Kemp family, with the Japanese distilling giant Suntory acquiring 25 percent of the stocks in what had become Macallan-Glenlivet PLC in 1986. A decade later, Highland Distilleries Ltd. bought the rest of the stocks, and in 1999 a partnership of The Edrington Group and William Grant & Sons Ltd. purchased Highland Distilleries, going on to form the 1887 Company.

The Macallan distillery has been progressively expanded over the years and now operates two separate production areas with a total of 21 stills. Long renowned for its adherence to ex-sherry casks for maturation, The Macallan has actually exhibited a dual personality since 2004, when the "Fine Oak" range was introduced alongside "Sherry Oak." This was a bold move that risked diluting the potency of the brand, but the result of producing a lighter Macallan by a judicious blending of ex-sherry and ex-Bourbon casks has been to give the single malt a whole new fan base. The "Sherry Oak" range extends from a 10- to a 30-year-old, while "Fine Oak" runs from a 10- to a 25-year-old; travel retail outlets boast a variety of expressions in The Macallan 1824 Collection.

TASTING NOTES

THE MACALLAN 12-YEAR-OLD "SHERRY OAK"
single malt, 40% ABV, matured in ex-sherry casks
Buttery sherry and fruitcake on the nose, rich and full on the palate, with ripe oranges and sweet oak. Long and malty in the finish, with gently smoked, spicy oak.

THE MACALLAN 12-YEAR-OLD "FINE OAK"
single malt, 40% ABV, matured in a combination of ex-sherry and ex-Bourbon casks
The nose is complex and fragrant, with malt, marzipan, and hard toffee. Orange marmalade, milk chocolate, and gentle oak figure on the palate, along with lively spice. The finish is fruity and spicy.

THE MACALLAN 25-YEAR-OLD "FINE OAK"
single malt, 43% ABV, triple matured in sherry-seasoned Spanish and American oak casks, and Bourbon-seasoned American oak casks
Peaches and wood spice on the rich nose. Vanilla, lemon, and coconut on the palate, balanced by deeper raisin, fig, and peat notes. The long finish features Jaffa oranges, spice, and a suggestion of sherry.

THE MACALLAN 30-YEAR-OLD "SHERRY OAK"
single malt, 43%ABV, matured in ex-Oloroso sherry casks
Big sherry notes on the full, mature nose, with spice and tangerines. Luxurious rounded palate with sherry, honey, raisins, and allspice. Long, fruity finish with coffee and dark chocolate.

THE MACALLAN 30-YEAR-OLD "RANKIN"
single malt, 43% ABV, triple matured in sherry-seasoned Spanish and American oak casks, and Bourbon-seasoned American oak casks
An aromatic nose, with soft sherry, malt, honey, and Jaffa oranges. The palate is smooth and malty, with vanilla, peaches, oak, honey, and caramel. Toffee and oak in the medium-length finish.

THE MACALLAN 30-YEAR-OLD "SHERRY OAK"

FROM BARLEY TO CASKS

A number of factors influence the character of The Macallan single malt, starting with the barley. The use of a proportion of the Minstrel variety helps to produce a rich, oily new-make spirit character. The spirit stills are notably small and are run slowly, with a narrow cut of around 16 percent being filled into casks, again helping to ensure an oily, rich new-make spirit that is ideally suited to lengthy maturation in ex-sherry casks. The Macallan also has its own Spanish oak casks custom-made and seasoned with sherry in Spain, while American oak cask staves are also imported to Spain for sherry seasoning.

THE MACALLAN 12-YEAR-OLD "FINE OAK"

THE MACALLAN 25-YEAR-OLD "FINE OAK"

THE MACALLAN 30-YEAR-OLD "RANKIN"

STRATHISLA

OWNER Chivas Brothers Ltd. (Pernod Ricard)
FOUNDED 1786 **CAPACITY** 634,000 gal (2.4m liters)
ADDRESS Seafield Avenue, Keith, Banffshire AB55 5BS
WEBSITE www.maltwhiskydistilleries.com

Like Dalwhinnie, Strathisla is one of those Scotch whiskey distilleries that appear to have been built with modern-day tourists in mind. Arguably the oldest working distillery in the Scottish Highlands, Strathisla is marvelously photogenic, featuring an exaggerated pair of pagoda-capped kilns and even a waterwheel. It stands on the outskirts of the town of Keith, which also has a second operational distillery in the shape of the low-profile Diageo-owned Strathmill.

Miltonic beginnings

The history of Strathisla begins in 1786, when it was established by Alexander Milne and George Taylor under the name of Milltown. The distillery officially became known as Milton when it was acquired by McDonald Ingram & Company. in 1825; just five years later, William Longmore purchased the plant. The name Strathisla was adopted for the first time during the 1870s, though in 1890 the name reverted to Milton. Isla is the river that cuts through the town of Keith, and "strath" means a river valley.

In 1940, London financier Jay Pomeroy purchased the distillery from what had become William Longmore & Company. Pomeroy was subsequently found guilty of tax evasion in 1949, and the business was declared bankrupt.

Seagram on the scene

At this point, the most significant development in the history of the distillery took place. Acting on behalf of the Seagram Company of Canada, James Barclay bought Milton at auction for the Canadian distilling giant's recently acquired Chivas Brothers subsidiary. A program of refurbishment and upgrading was instigated, and the name became Strathisla again in 1951.

With sales of Chivas Regal growing in North America during the postwar period, Chivas Brothers built an entirely new distillery named Glen Keith (currently inactive), adjacent to Strathisla, in order to boost the volume of malt whiskey production, and in 1965 the number of stills at Strathisla was doubled to four. The company proceeded to develop a significant power base in Keith, constructing vast tracts of warehousing outside the town where about 100 million casks of malt whiskey are now maturing, and bonds where Chivas Regal is blended, prior to bottling near Glasgow.

Seagram expands

In 1978, The Glenlivet Distillers Ltd. was acquired by Seagram, adding a number of prestigious distilleries such as The Glenlivet itself to the company's portfolio, along with a pair of Speyside distilleries created purely to supply malt whiskey for blending.

Braes of Glenlivet (later rechristened Braeval) had been built in 1973 and Allt-a-Bhainne two years later. Both now provide a significant amount of spirits for use in the Chivas Regal family of blends.

Strathisla Distillery, along with Seagram's other spirits assets, was purchased by Pernod Ricard in 2001 and subsequently became the "Home of Chivas Regal," reflected in the emphasis on the popular visitors' center and the presentation to visitors of a dram of 12-year-old Chivas Regal while they watch a DVD presentation, followed by a measure of 18-year-old Chivas Regal or Strathisla 12-year-old single malt after the distillery tour and warehouse visit.

Chivas Regal

Chivas Brothers' Master Blender Colin Scott says, "With its long-established reputation as a distinguished dram, Strathisla 12-year-old single malt is prized by the industry as the 'connoisseur's best-kept secret.' Strathisla has been sold as a single malt Scotch whiskey for more than two centuries, and the 12-year-old offers full, fruity, and haylike flavors with a mellow nutty sweetness, which adds to the heart of the Chivas Regal blend.

"Chivas Brothers maintains an extensive aged whiskey inventory of more than 6 million casks, with an emphasis on aged Scotch whiskey for luxury products. Strathisla production contributes to these."

Regarding the style of Chivas Regal, Scott declares, "Its distinctive character encapsulates the classic Speyside fruity profile. Strathisla has this fruity Speyside aspect in abundance and also has a very good weight for bringing body to the blend. Over and above this there must be careful cask selection for the Strathisla new distillate, so that when the spirit is mature it gives just the right character we are looking for when blending."

Super-premium sales

Key markets for Strathisla are Scotland and Sweden, while Chivas Regal sells in more than 150 countries across Europe, Asia Pacific, and the Americas. Annual sales amount to more than 50 million bottles, with the brand being the leading

STRATHISLA 12-YEAR-OLD

STRATHISLA 16-YEAR-OLD "CASK STRENGTH"

REGAL BLENDING

The single malt from Strathisla is at the heart of Chivas Regal, one of the best-known premium blends of Scotch whiskey in the world. The brand traces its roots back to Aberdeen in 1801, when William Edward opened a grocery emporium, later to be joined by James Chivas in 1836. The firm of Chivas Brothers was then established in 1857 by James Chivas with his brother John and, after laying down stocks of whiskey, it began blending in its own right. The firm had gained a reputation as purveyors of fine goods to royalty and the Scottish nobility, and began blending in order to satisfy the demands of their wealthy customers for a smoother-drinking whiskey. Chivas Regal was their third and most aged proprietary blend. Launched in 1909 to capitalize on the booming US economy, it was soon enjoying strong sales in a number of global markets.

The Strathisla distillery cuts a handsome figure, embellished with a high gabled roof and two pagodas.

super-premium Scotch whiskey in Europe. Available expressions include 12-, 18-, and 25-year-olds. As for Strathisla, the principal house bottling is the 12-year-old expression, but Gordon & MacPhail has enjoyed a long association with the single malt brand and offers a wide range of variants, with the oldest having been distilled back in 1949.

TASTING NOTES

STRATHISLA 12-YEAR-OLD
single malt, 43% ABV
Sherry, stewed fruits, spices, and malt on the nose. Almost syrupy on the palate, with toffee, honey, nuts, a whiff of peat, and oak. The finish is slightly smoky, with more oak and a final flash of ginger.

STRATHISLA 16-YEAR-OLD
"CASK STRENGTH EDITION"
(DISTILLED 1994, BOTTLED 2011)
single malt, 55.3% ABV, cask-strength, non-chill-filtered
A rich and beguiling nose of honey, bananas, vanilla, and nutmeg. The same characteristics carry through onto the palate, along with a little planed lumber and white pepper. The fruity finish is notably long, with spices.

STRATHISLA 25-YEAR-OLD
(GORDON & MACPHAIL)
single malt, 43% ABV, matured in first-fill and refill sherry casks
A soft, fragrant, buttery nose, with a whiff of warm leather. Full-bodied in the mouth, with sherry, malt, plums, and oak, plus gentle background smoke. The finish is long, with drying, gingery oak.

STRATHISLA 25-YEAR-OLD (GORDON & MACPHAIL)

CHIVAS REGAL 18-YEAR-OLD
The classic Speyside profile of Strathisla malt lies at the core of the Chivas Regal family of blends, contributing fruitiness and body.

ARDMORE

OWNER Beam Global Spirits & Wine
FOUNDED 1898 **CAPACITY** 1.37m gal (5.2m liters)
ADDRESS Kennethmont, Huntly, Aberdeenshire AB54 4NH
WEBSITE www.ardmorewhisky.com

In 1898–99, Ardmore Distillery was constructed by the Glasgow-based firm of Teacher & Sons to provide malt whiskey for their increasingly popular Highland Cream blend, created by William Teacher in 1863. Today, the distillery, on the eastern fringes of Speyside, continues to fulfill that role, providing malt for what is now the top premium blended whiskey in India and Brazil.

The distillery and the Teacher's brand are now in the ownership of Beam Global Spirits & Wine, and Ardmore produces the bulk of its spirit from malt peated to 12–14ppm. This was once the norm among Speyside distillers, but while most competitors have appreciably reduced their peating levels, the smoky style of Ardmore gives the Teacher's blend its distinctive full and rich character. This is emphasized by a notably high malt content of 45 percent, and more than 30 different component malts go into the blend, though Ardmore remains its heart malt.

Ardmore's capacity was gradually increased from the original pair of stills to the present eight, and it was one of the few distilleries that continued to direct-fire its stills using coal until 2002, when a switch was made to steam heating.

The Scottish golden eagle *can often be seen flying above Ardmore and has become the distillery's symbol.*

New releases

Until 2007 Ardmore was generally only available in independent bottlings, but in that year the innovative Ardmore "Traditional Cask" was launched. This has been matured initially in ex-Bourbon barrels and hogsheads for 6–13 years before receiving a second year-long period of maturation in handmade quarter casks. It carries no age statement, but the small quarter casks are a proven way of adding maturity to spirits because of the higher level of contact with the wood. Subsequently, 25- and 30-year-old expressions of Ardmore were released in limited quantities for duty-free outlets in the UK and North American markets during 2008.

TASTING NOTES

ARDMORE "TRADITIONAL CASK"
single malt, 46% ABV
Sweet and initially creamy on the palate, with spices, peat smoke, tobacco, and vanilla emerging and blending together. Water releases ripe fruits and accentuates the peat. Long and mellow in the finish.

ARDMORE 21-YEAR-OLD "SIGNATORY"
single malt, 59.2% ABV, cask strength, single cask, wine-treated cask # 30118, non-chill-filtered
Lots of peat smoke on the full, oily nose, with allspice and a grassy note. The palate features a big hit of peat, with citrus fruits and black pepper. The peaty citrus fruits continue through the lengthy finish.

ARDMORE 25-YEAR-OLD
single malt, 51.4%ABV, cask strength, non-chill-filtered
Soft peat, marzipan, and cream crackers on the nose, becoming fruitier with cherries. Slightly savory on the palate, with peat, vanilla, and freshly peeled oranges. The finish is earthy, with salt and subtle oak.

ARDMORE 21-YEAR-OLD "SIGNATORY"

ARDMORE "TRADITIONAL CASK"

BENRIACH

OWNER The BenRiach Distillery Company Ltd.
FOUNDED 1898 **CAPACITY** 739,700 gal (2.8m liters)
ADDRESS Longmorn, Elgin, Morayshire IV30 3SJ
WEBSITE www.benriachdistillery.co.uk

For much of its existence, BenRiach lived in the shadow of its larger neighbor, Longmorn. Fortunes change in the whiskey business, however, and while Longmorn today produces whiskey mainly for blending, BenRiach enjoys a high profile among single malt aficionados, due to a wide core range of expressions and an energetic release program.

Benriach, as it was originally spelled, was founded in 1898, but shut down from 1900 until 1965, though its floor maltings continued to be used by Longmorn. Revived in the mid-1960s, Benriach was again closed in 2002 by then owners Pernod Ricard.

Small-scale individuality

However, two years later the BenRiach Distillery Company Ltd. was formed by a consortium of businessmen, led by industry veteran Billy Walker, and production recommenced later that year. Under the new regime, the middle "r" in the brand name was capitalized, and like the Islay distillery Bruichladdich, a virtue was made of the small-scale operation's flexibility and individualistic inventory.

"Heart of Speyside," 12-, 16-, and 20-year-olds, and 10-year-old "Curiositas Peated" remain at the core of the range, along with heavily peated 21-year-old "Authenticus Peated," a quartet of "Fumosus" heavily peated wood finishes, and six "standard" wood finishes. The occasional true curiosity is also released, such as 12-year-old triple-distilled "Solstice", which appeared in 2010.

TASTING NOTES

THE BENRIACH "HEART OF SPEYSIDE"
single malt, 40% ABV, ex-Bourbon casks
Fresh nose, nutty, honeyed, and spicy. Honey and spice on the palate, with a touch of black pepper and cooked oranges. Medium finish with pepper and lively oak.

THE BENRIACH 10-YEAR-OLD "CURIOSITAS PEATED"
single malt, 40% ABV
Initially medicinal notes, with peat and tar, followed by citrus fruit, honey, and soft oak. The palate is smoky and sweet, with iodine and fruity, spicy oak. Sweet and mildly phenolic finish.

THE BENRIACH 30-YEAR-OLD
single malt, 50% ABV, vatting of Bourbon-matured whiskey finished in Oloroso sherry butts and whiskey fully matured in Gomez fino sherry butts, non-chill-filtered
The nose reveals raisins, dark chocolate, sherry, cinnamon, and dried fruits. Rich, sweet and full-bodied in the mouth, with sherry, honey, smoky oak, and ginger. The finish is malty and gently oaky.

THE BENRIACH "HEART OF SPEYSIDE"

THE BENRIACH 10-YEAR-OLD "CURIOSITAS PEATED"

THE BENRIACH 30-YEAR-OLD

GLEN ELGIN

OWNER Diageo plc
FOUNDED 1898 **CAPACITY** 449,000 gal (1.7m liters)
ADDRESS Longmorn, Elgin, Morayshire IV30 3SL
WEBSITE www.malts.com

Given that it operates 28 malt distilleries in Scotland, Diageo does not give single malt prominence to the whiskey produced in all of them, but focuses on a core range representing a variety of regions and styles. Yet, away from the Taliskers and Cardhus, Lagavulins and Dalwhinnies, there are some seriously fine single malts waiting to be discovered. One such is Glen Elgin, long favored by blenders and an important component of the historic White Horse blend, but since 2005 also embraced by Diageo's Classic Malts portfolio.

Low-profile classic

Glen Elgin is one of Speyside's more elusive distilleries, in keeping with its profile. With three pairs of relatively small stills and traditional wooden worm tubs to condense the spirits, it offers a good example of how a distillery can be set up to produce a style of spirit that is essentially at odds with the expectations of its equipment. In theory, that spirit should be relatively full-bodied and rich, but lengthy fermentation and slow distillation actually result in a comparatively fruity and light character.

Established in 1898, production began in May 1900, just as the industry suffered a dramatic downturn from which it took more than 50 years to recover. Glen Elgin made whiskey for just five months before closing. In 1930 the distillery was acquired from Glasgow blender J. J. Blanche & Company by the Distillers Company Ltd. subsidiary Scottish Malt Distillers (SMD), becoming part of Diageo.

GLEN ELGIN 12-YEAR-OLD

GLEN ELGIN 32-YEAR-OLD "GREEN ELGIN"

TASTING NOTES

GLEN ELGIN "MANAGERS' CHOICE"
single malt, 61.1% ABV, single cask, cask strength, matured in rejuvenated European oak butt (534 bottles)
Furniture polish and brittle toffee on the nose, with raisins, prunes, and spice. Smooth-bodied, with a palate of oranges and peaches, then ginger root and black pepper. The finish dries to licorice.

GLEN ELGIN 12-YEAR-OLD
single malt, 43% ABV
A nose of rich, fruity sherry, figs, and fragrant spice, plus honey and cut flowers. Full-bodied, soft, malty, and honeyed in the mouth, with ginger and orange. Lengthy and slightly perfumed, with spicy oak in the finish.

GLEN ELGIN 32-YEAR-OLD "GREEN ELGIN"
single malt, 42.3% ABV, cask strength
Fragrant and honeyed, with black cherries, walnuts, and mild smoke on the nose. The palate is sensuous and rich, with honey, ripe oranges, and a little more wood smoke. The finish is nutty and slowly drying.

GLENGLASSAUGH

OWNER Glenglassaugh Distillery Company Ltd.
FOUNDED 1873 **CAPACITY** 290,600 gal (1.1m liters)
ADDRESS Portsoy, Banffshire AB45 2SQ
WEBSITE www.glenglassaugh.com

There are few sadder sights for the whiskey-lover than a silent distillery, its copper pots cold and tarnished, with no smell of mash on the air or bustle of human activity. Fortunately, some stories have happy endings, and Glenglassaugh is one such.

The distillery stands close to the southern shores of the Moray Firth, most of the structures visible today dating from 1957–59, with the exception of the warehouses and former malt barns. The original distillery was built in 1873–75 and for over a century, from the 1890s onward, it was in the ownership of Highland Distilleries Ltd., latterly part of The Edrington Group. Continuity of ownership did not equate with continuity of operation, though, and even after investing in the construction of their new distillery, Glenglassaugh was mothballed in 1986.

A new spirit

The distillery found its savior in Scaent Group, which has global energy interests and was eager to expand into Scotch whiskey. Scaent bought the distillery in early 2008, forming the Glenglassaugh Distillery Company Ltd. Around $1.6 million was spent refurbishing the distillery, and on December 4, spirits ran from the stills once more.

The core range now includes a 26-year-old, along with "Aged over 30 Years" and "Aged over 40 Years" expressions. An innovative single-mash variant of new-make spirit came out in 2009, while 2011 also saw the release of a three-year-old single malt distilled under the Scaent regime.

TASTING NOTES

GLENGLASSAUGH "CLEARAC" SPIRIT DRINK
new-make spirit, 50% ABV
A cereal-like nose of cream and summer meadows. Initially peppery on the palate, with pleasing brittle toffee notes emerging with time along with fruity and spicy overtones. The medium-length finish is sweet and spicy.

GLENGLASSAUGH 26-YEAR-OLD
single malt, 46% ABV, non-chill-filtered
The nose offers vanilla, cinnamon, wild berries, and hazelnuts. Notably fruity on the palate, with raisins, figs, and spice. The fruits turn to ripe oranges in the slightly peppery finish.

GLENGLASSAUGH "AGED OVER 40 YEARS"
single malt, 44.6% ABV, single cask, cask strength, refill sherry casks, non-chill-filtered
Floral and herbal on the complex nose, with dried fruits and worn leather. The palate is full and rich, with the dried fruits merging with old oak, cinnamon, and roasted coffee beans. The finish is fruity and pleasingly oaky.

THE GLENROTHES

OWNER The Edrington Group/Berry Brothers & Rudd
FOUNDED 1878 **CAPACITY** 1.48m gal (5.6m liters)
ADDRESS Burnside Street, Rothes, Morayshire AB38 7AA
WEBSITE www.theglenrothes.com

As a malt whiskey, The Glenrothes has long enjoyed a high reputation among blenders, one of only a few Speyside whiskeys accorded the blender's grading of "Top Class." The Glenrothes has a long-standing relationship with the Cutty Sark and The Famous Grouse blends, but its profile as a single malt has grown significantly since the distillery's owners, The Edrington Group, decided to offer vintage releases of its single malt rather than age-specific expressions.

An unusual arrangement

Established by James Stuart of the Macallan distillery, Elgin solicitor John Cruikshank, and bankers Robert Dick and William Grant, the distillery, hidden away next to the town cemetery in Keith, first made whiskey in December 1879. Financial difficulties forced Stuart out, and the other partners formed William Grant & Company.

In 1887, the company amalgamated with the Islay Distillery Company, and the new concern took the name Highland Distilleries, which today, as Highland Distillers, is part of The Edrington Group. However, the present ownership situation is highly unusual in that while Edrington owns the actual distillery, the Glenrothes brand has belonged to Berry Brothers & Rudd since 2010, with the London wine and spirits merchants having handed over the historic Cutty Sark blend to Edrington in return.

TASTING NOTES

THE GLENROTHES "SELECT RESERVE"
*single malt, 43% ABV, matured ex-sherry
and ex-Bourbon casks*
Ripe fruits, spice, and toffee on the nose, with a whiff of cane syrup. Faint wood polish in the mouth, vanilla, spicy and slightly citric. Creamy and complex. Slightly nutty, with some orange, in the drying finish.

THE GLENROTHES "VINTAGE 1998"
*single malt, 43% ABV, approx. one-third matured
ex-Oloroso sherry casks, remainder ex-Bourbon casks*
A nose of cereal, honey, and sweet, tropical fruits and raspberries. The palate is gentle and quite sweet, with vanilla custard, coconut, and cinnamon notes. Nutmeg and cinnamon in the medium-length finish.

THE GLENROTHES "ALBA RESERVE"
single malt, 40% ABV, matured refill ex-Bourbon casks
An attractive, if youthful, nose of pears, cloves, coconut, and white chocolate. The palate is soft and approachable, with ripe berries and coconut, while the finish is relatively sweet and consistently elegant.

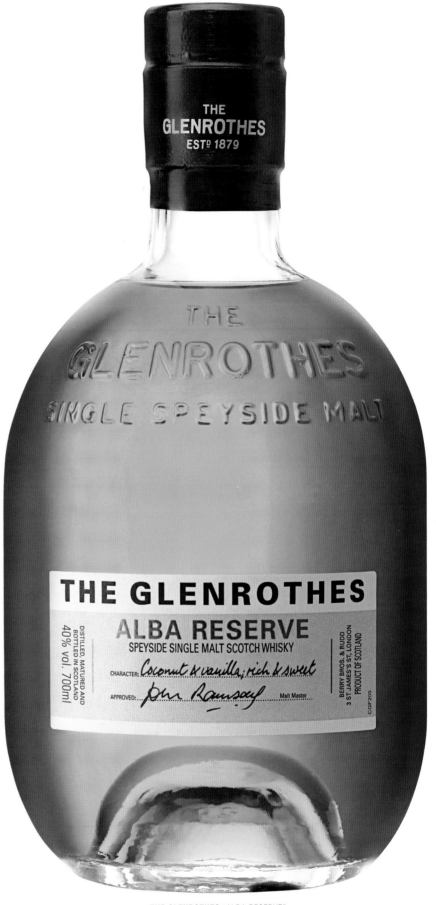

THE GLENROTHES "ALBA RESERVE"

KNOCKANDO

OWNER Diageo plc
FOUNDED 1898 **CAPACITY** 343,000 gal (1.3m liters)
ADDRESS Knockando, Morayshire AB38 7RT
WEBSITE www.malts.com

KNOCKANDO 25-YEAR-OLD

Knockando has long been the heart malt in the J&B blended Scotch whiskey brand, globally the third-best seller behind Johnnie Walker and Ballantine's, and particularly popular in France, Spain, Portugal, South Africa, and the United States. The J&B "Rare" blend was established by the fashionable London wine and spirits merchants Justerini & Brooks especially for the US market during the era of Prohibition (1920–33); its pale color and light style suited the mood of the era, making it serious competition for Cutty Sark.

Born in the whiskey boom
However, the history of Knockando began in 1898–99, when it was established just before the end of the great Victorian whiskey boom. Knockando was only active for about 10 months before being forced to close, with Gilbey's purchasing it at a bargain price in 1904.

The connection between Knockando and J&B dates back to a 1962 merger between W. & A. Gilbey Ltd. and United Wine Traders (then owners of J&B), which led to the creation of International Distillers & Vintners and the doubling of Knockando's capacity in 1969 by the installation of a second pair of stills. Subsequent mergers and acquisitions eventually led Knockando and the J&B brand into the Diageo portfolio. From the 1970s onward, Knockando has mainly been bottled according to vintage rather than carrying a specific age statement, though a 12-year-old expression is now available.

TASTING NOTES

KNOCKANDO 12-YEAR-OLD
single malt, 43% ABV
Delicate and fragrant on the nose, with hints of malt, worn leather, and hay. Quite full in the mouth, smooth and honeyed, with gingery malt. Medium length in the finish, with cereal and more ginger.

KNOCKANDO 21-YEAR-OLD "MASTER RESERVE"
single malt, 43% ABV
A hint of yeast on the nose, followed by honey, malt, and stewed fruits. Smooth and malty on the palate, with discreet fruit notes. Slightly savory toward the long finish, which features pepper and spice.

KNOCKANDO 25-YEAR-OLD
single malt, 43% ABV, first-fill ex-sherry casks
Aromas of wood polish, new leather, and brittle toffee, plus overripe bananas. Coal fires with time. Rich on the palate, with molasses and dried fruits. The finish is long, with cocoa powder and developing tannins.

KNOCKANDO 21-YEAR-OLD "MASTER RESERVE"

J&B "RARE"

66

LONGMORN

OWNER Chivas Brothers Ltd. (Pernod Ricard)
FOUNDED 1894 **CAPACITY** 924,600 gal (3.5m liters)
ADDRESS Elgin, Morayshire IV30 3SJ
WEBSITE www.maltwhiskydistilleries.com

While The Glenlivet is Chivas Brothers' pinup single malt and Strathisla is notable for its popularity with visitors and its role as the brand home of "Chivas Regal," Longmorn principally provides malt whiskey for blending. This may mean that its popularity as a single malt is confined to a relatively small but growing group of aficionados, but it fulfills its role as the provider of malt for the "Chivas Regal," "Queen Anne," and "Something Special" blends with aplomb.

Longmorn has an enviable reputation among blenders as one of the top-flight Speysides, and back in 1897, when the distillery had been in production for less than three years, *The National Guardian* declared that "Longmorn jumped into favor with buyers from the earliest day on which it was offered."

The distillery was constructed by John Duff and his associates, but Duff took sole control in 1897. This was clearly not a judicious move, since he filed for bankruptcy the following year, with Longmorn being bought by one James Grant. Private ownership continued until 1970, when The Glenlivet Distillers Ltd. was formed, and in 1978 Seagram of Canada acquired it. Longmorn was one of the former Seagram assets subsequently acquired by Pernod Ricard subsidiary Chivas Brothers Ltd. in 2001.

Longmorn operates eight stills, and until 1994 the wash stills were direct-fired, using coal, while the spirit stills, located in a separate still house, were heated by steam.

TASTING NOTES

LONGMORN 16-YEAR-OLD
single malt, 48% ABV, non-chill-filtered
The nose offers cream, spice, toffee apples, and honey. Medium-bodied in the mouth, this Longmorn displays fudge, butter, and lots of spice. The finish is quite long, with oak and late lingering dry spices.

LONGMORN 17-YEAR-OLD "CASK STRENGTH EDITION"
single malt, cask strength, 58.2% ABV, non-chill-filtered
Peach, orange, and vanilla notes on the malty, spicy nose. The palate is rich and fruity, with pears, brittle toffee, spice, and clover. The finish is lengthy and slowly drying.

LONGMORN 30-YEAR-OLD (GORDON & MACPHAIL)
single malt, 43% ABV, ex-sherry casks
Old sherry and fruitcake mix on the rich nose. More sherry on the creamy palate, with rum and raisins. Drying steadily with sherry, oak, licorice, and dark chocolate.

LONGMORN 30-YEAR-OLD (GORDON & MACPHAIL)

LONGMORN 16-YEAR-OLD

LONGMORN "CASK STRENGTH EDITION"

MORTLACH

OWNER Diageo PLC

FOUNDED 1823 **CAPACITY** 1m gal (3.8m liters)

ADDRESS Dufftown, Banffshire AB55 4AQ

WEBSITE www.malts.com

Of all Scottish distilleries, Mortlach deserves a prize for having the most complex whiskey-making regimen, with the spirit distilled 2.8 times. Key to the process is the role of No. 1 spirit still, nicknamed the "Wee Witchie." In total there are six stills, all of different shapes and sizes, and the "Wee Witchie" is charged three times during each run. Condensation of spirits takes place in six worm tubs, five made of wood and one of stainless steel. The spirit that results from this unique distillation process is notably rich and robust, suited to lengthy maturation in ex-sherry casks.

The development of Mortlach

Mortlach was the first distillery to be built in Dufftown and William Grant worked there for 20 years, latterly as manager, before leaving to establish his own Glenfiddich operation in 1886. From 1853, members of the Cowie family were at the helm of Mortlach until the distillery's sale to John Walker & Sons in 1923. Mortlach became part of the Distillers Company Ltd. two years later, when Walker's was absorbed into its empire.

The Johnnie Walker connection continues as Mortlach is an important component of Black Label, and when demand grew in recent years, Mortlach became even more elusive as a "house" bottling. However, an increase in production at the distillery means that the 16-year-old "Flora & Fauna" bottling is now more readily available. For lovers of full-bodied, sherry wood-matured, complex single malts, Mortlach is a connoisseurs' classic.

TASTING NOTES

MORTLACH "MANAGERS' CHOICE"
single malt, 57.3% ABV, single cask, cask strength, matured first-fill, ex-Bourbon American oak barrel
Light and gently fruity on the nose, with peaches and an undertone of butcher shops. The palate is notably sweet and fruity, with lots of vanilla, while the medium-length finish is steadily drying, with cocoa powder.

MORTLACH 16-YEAR-OLD
single malt, 43% ABV
A rich, spicy, sherried nose, with sweet treacle, pepper, and peat smoke. Complex, elegant, yet masterful. Palate of sherry, fruitcake, gunpowder, and black pepper. A long, quite dry, and slightly smoky, gingery finish.

MORTLACH 32-YEAR-OLD 1971
single malt, 50.1% ABV, cask strength
A nose of barley, new-mown hay, honey, and oak. Palate is buttery and spicy, with pepper, honey, and a hint of char. Long and spicy with licorice in the fruity finish.

MORTLACH "MANAGERS' CHOICE"

MORTLACH 16-YEAR-OLD

SPEYBURN

OWNER Inver House Distillers Ltd. (Thai Beverages PLC)
FOUNDED 1897 **CAPACITY** 528,300 gal (2m liters)
ADDRESS Rothes, Aberlour, Morayshire AB38 7AG
WEBSITE www.speyburn.com

On the outskirts of the distilling town of Rothes, Speyburn is one of five Scottish distilleries operated by Inver House Distillers Ltd., part of the mighty Thai Beverages PLC since 2001. As a single malt, Speyburn is best known in the US, but the majority of the distillery's "make" finds its way into Inver House blends such as Catto's, Hankey Bannister, and Pinwhinnie.

Established in 1897, when Speyside was at the center of a distillery boom, Speyburn was designed by Elgin architect Charles Doig, and the structures remain little changed. Doig is the doyen of distillery architects, and his most enduring creation, the Chinese-style kiln pagoda head, is regarded as a symbol of Scotch whiskey distilling.

Diamonds and gold

Speyburn was commissioned by John Hopkin & Company, already owners of Tobermory distillery, and operated under the auspices of the Speyburn-Glenlivet Distillery Company Ltd. The founders were anxious to distill some spirits during Queen Victoria's Diamond Jubilee year (1897) for a commemorative release, but this could only be accomplished by working the stills in a snowstorm in December, before the doors or windows had been installed in the newly constructed stillhouse.

The Distillers Company Ltd. purchased Speyburn in 1916 and the distillery served as a production facility for the supply of blending malt until 1991, when Inver House Distillers Ltd. took control. The following year they released a 10-year-old expression of the single malt, and in 2009 a new expression "Bradan Orach" was released without an age statement. "Bradan Orach" is Gaelic for "golden salmon," in tribute to the Spey River, one of Scotland's finest salmon rivers.

TASTING NOTES

SPEYBURN 10-YEAR-OLD
single malt, 40% ABV
The nose is spicy and nutty, with pencil shavings and sweet malt. In the mouth, sweet and easy-drinking, with herbal notes and a hint of smoke. Medium length in the finish, with barley and oak.

SPEYBURN "BRADAN ORACH"
single malt, 40% ABV
The nose is fruity and floral, with oranges, honey, and malt; the palate is nicely balanced, with fresh fruit, vanilla, spice, and subtle oak. Spicy oak features in the relatively lengthy finish.

SPEYBURN "BRADAN ORACH"

SPEYBURN 10-YEAR-OLD

THE SPEYSIDE

OWNER Speyside Distillers Company Ltd.

FOUNDED 1990 **CAPACITY** 158,500 gal (600,000 liters)

ADDRESS Tromie Mills, Kingussie, Inverness-shire PH21 1NS

WEBSITE www.speysidedistillery.co.uk

Although the first spirits flowed from The Speyside's stills in December 1990, the founding year could easily be stated as 1956 or 1962. The former date was when Glasgow whiskey broker George Christie bought the site on the banks of the Tromie River, not far from Kingussie, and the latter was the year in which dry-stone wall-builder Alex Fairlie began constructing the distillery.

Building proceeded on a leisurely basis, taking almost three decades. Once completed, Christie's project was christened Speyside, which may seem slightly generic but was actually the revival of an old, local distillery name. The original Speyside distillery had been established in Kingussie during 1895, though it operated for only a decade before falling into disuse.

The "new" Speyside may have taken a long time to build, but it did not take long for its whiskey to find its way into bottles, with the "Drumguish" single malt first released in 1993, when it could only just have been legal as Scotch whiskey. A decade after the stills were fired up, ownership passed to a group of private investors, including the founder's son, Ricky Christie, and since 2006 a small amount of peated spirit has been distilled each year. "Speyside Single Malt" was first released as an eight-year-old in 1999. The current core range comprises 12- and 15-year-old variants, "Drumguish," and the idiosyncratic "Cú Dhub." This near-black single malt is designed to replicate the late and largely unlamented Loch Dhu brand, created by United Distillers in the 1990s using Mannochmore single malt matured in double-charred casks.

TASTING NOTES

THE SPEYSIDE "CÚ DHUB"
single malt, 40% ABV
Damp ashtrays and a hint of sherry on the nose. Smoke and malt, dark caramel notes, and dried fruits on the palate. The finish is smoky-sweet and medium in length.

THE SPEYSIDE 12-YEAR-OLD
single malt, 40% ABV
Barley and herbs on the toasted, well-balanced nose. Medium-bodied, with vanilla, hazelnuts, oak, and a hint of peat on the palate. Toffee and orange in the relatively lengthy finish.

THE SPEYSIDE 15-YEAR-OLD
single malt, 40% ABV
Oranges, malt, and honey on the nose. Lots of malt on the palate, with more honey and hints of orchard fruits. The finish focuses on caramel and slightly spicy oak.

THE SPEYSIDE "CÚ DHUB"

THE SPEYSIDE 12-YEAR-OLD

TOMINTOUL

OWNER Angus Dundee Distillers PLC
FOUNDED 1964 **CAPACITY** 872,000 gal (3.3m liters)
ADDRESS Ballindalloch, Banffshire AB37 9AQ
WEBSITE www.tomintouldistillery.co.uk

Tomintoul is one of those distilleries best described as "functional," and its workaday appearance is emphasized all the more by contrast with the grandeur of the surrounding Highland scenery. The distillery, located in the parish of Glenlivet, is equipped with six stills, and takes its name from the nearby settlement of Tomintoul, the highest village in the Highlands. The Tomintoul distillery is located in the Glenlivet Estate at Ballantruan, on the east side of the Avon River and in the valley between the Glenlivet Forest and the hills of Cromdale.

It took more than a year to find the pure water source of the Ballantruan Spring in the Cromdale hills. Once discovered, the distillery was subsequently built close to the spring. Given the high, remote site chosen for the distillery, the story goes that when the plant was being constructed during 1964–65, the contractors made sure they always had several weeks' worth of materials on hand, in case they were cut off by bad weather.

Tomintoul was created for the Tomintoul-Glenlivet Distillery Ltd., a company set up by whiskey blenders and brokers Hay & Macleod & Company Ltd. and W. & S. Strong & Company Ltd. Then in 1973, Scottish & Universal Investment Trust went on a shopping spree, acquiring Whyte & Mackay Distillers Ltd. and also the Tomintoul operation.

The Tomintoul range
Tomintoul was first marketed as a single malt during the 1970s, and examples dating from that time and presented in distinctive "perfume bottles" are now sought after by collectors. However, the brand became best known after Angus Dundee Distillers PLC bought the distillery from Whyte & Mackay in 2000, going on to add a blend center on the site three years later. Today there is also maturation capacity for 116,000 casks, and stocks of whiskey up to 40 years old are held there.

The single malt range, starting with a 10-year-old, was progressively augmented, and now comprises nine principal expressions, namely 10-, 14-, 16-, 21-, and 33-year-olds, along with Oloroso cask-finished and port wood cask-finished 12-year-olds, plus a 1976 vintage and "Peaty Tang."

For more than a decade Tomintoul has produced annual batches of heavily peated

Stunning landscapes *surround the distillery near Tomintoul, the highest village in the Highlands.*

spirits in addition to its standard make. Principally, this is intended to give Angus Dundee peated malt for blending purposes, but the youthful peated Tomintoul was also bottled in its own right, being issued in 2005 as "Old Ballantruan." This was followed three years later by "Peaty Tang," which comprises four- and five-year-old peated Tomintoul, along with a percentage of unpeated eight-year-old whiskey.

TASTING NOTES

TOMINTOUL 10-YEAR-OLD
single malt, 40% ABV
A light, floral, and pleasantly malty nose. Light-bodied and delicate, with vanilla fudge, apples, and lemon on the palate. The finish is medium in length, with honey and lingering malt.

TOMINTOUL 21-YEAR-OLD
single malt, 40% ABV
Melons, pears, warm spices, and barley sugar on the nose. A rich, spicy palate presence, plus toffee and malt notes. Quite lengthy in the finish; mildly mouth-drying, with cocoa powder, and spicy to the end.

TOMINTOUL "PEATY TANG"
single malt, 40% ABV
A lively nose of peat-reek, with floral background notes, malt, and something close to carbolic soap. Soft on the palate, malty, and sweet, overlaid with a nutty, smoky coating. The finish is dry and smoky.

TOMINTOUL 33-YEAR-OLD

TOMINTOUL 10-YEAR-OLD

ALLT-A-BHAINNE

WEBSITE www.aberko.com

Located between Dufftown and Glenlivet, Allt-a-Bhainne Distillery dates from 1975, when it was built by Chivas Brothers for the express purpose of providing bulk malt whiskey for blending. The architectural style is bold and modern, and the distillery was designed to be operated by one person per shift. There are no official Allt-a-Bhainne bottlings, but a 12-year-old expression appears under the Deerstalker label.

Deerstalker 12-year-old (single malt, 46% ABV, non-chill-filtered) *Flint and toffee on the nose, with pixie sticks. Delicate fruit notes on the palate and a soft, warming finish.*

AUCHROISK

WEBSITE www.diageo.com

Like Allt-a-Bhainne Distillery, Auchroisk was built during the 1970s, in this case by Justerini & Brooks Ltd. In the hands of Diageo, this modern distillery provides malt whiskey for a range of blends, and the site is also used to mature malt spirits made in other Diageo distilleries in the area. Additionally, malts are vatted together at Auchroisk and transported by tanker to bottling plants, where the grain element of blended Scotch whiskeys is introduced.

Auchroisk 10-year-old (single malt, 43% ABV) *Spice and citrus fruits, nuts and malt on the nose. Fresh fruit and malt on the palate, with more malt plus milk chocolate in the finish.*

Auchroisk "Managers' Choice" (single malt, 60.6% ABV) *The nose offers orange and vanilla, with a slightly dirty malt backdrop. On the palate gingery oak and caramel blend with tropical fruit notes. Drying in the relatively short finish, with some nutty oak.*

AULTMORE

WEBSITE www.dewars.com

Established in 1896, Aultmore has had a long association with the Dewar's blend of Scotch whiskey. The distillery that stands today close to the town of Keith largely dates from a rebuilding project carried out at the beginning of the 1970s, and there is little trace of its Victorian roots.

Aultmore 12-year-old (single malt, 40% ABV) *A floral and fudge note on the nose with elements of spice. Fresh citrus fruits on the palate, with vanilla, more spice, and lemon zest. The finish is nutty and quite drying.*

AUCHROISK 10-YEAR-OLD

CRAIGELLACHIE 14-YEAR-OLD

BALMENACH

WEBSITE www.inverhouse.com; www.aberko.com

Situated in a remote, rural location off the main road from Grantown-on-Spey to Aberlour, Balmenach dates back to 1824 and is now owned by Inver House Distillers. The distillery has also made gin since 2009.

Balmenach 12-year-old (single malt, 43% ABV) *A big nose of sherry and honey leads into a smooth, full-bodied palate, featuring dry sherry, honey, and ginger. Rounded and relatively lengthy finish.*

Deerstalker 18-year-old (single malt, 40% ABV) *Pine, grapefruit, eucalyptus, and sherry on the nose. Full-bodied on the palate, with sherry, malt, and subtle peat. Long in the finish, with a final citrus note.*

BENRINNES

WEBSITE www.diageo.com

The distillery stands below the eponymous mountain that is a distinct Speyside landmark, and although established in 1826, the present plant dates from a mid-1950s reconstruction program. The relatively meaty spirit produced is used in a variety of Diageo blends.

Benrinnes 15-year-old (single malt, 43% ABV) *Caramel, old leather, black pepper, and sherry on the nose. Full-bodied, with sherry, figs, and savory notes on the palate. Spice and delicate smoke in the complex finish.*

BRAEVAL

WEBSITE www.aberko.com

Originally christened Braes of Glenlivet, Braeval dates from the 1970s and is mainly available in single malt format (10- and 15-year-old expressions) with the Deerstalker label.

Deerstalker 10-year-old (single malt, 40% ABV) *Lemon grass, sherbet, and light vanilla on the nose. The palate is clean and uncomplicated, with citrus fruit; refreshing finish is short to medium in length.*

CRAIGELLACHIE

WEBSITE www.dewars.com

Dating from 1891, Craigellachie enjoyed a lengthy association with the White Horse blend. Today, most of its output goes to Dewar's.

Craigellachie 14-year-old (single malt, 40% ABV) *Cereal and citrus fruits on the nose, with honey and new-mown hay. Quite full-bodied, spicy, and nutty on the palate, with a soft, mildly oaky finish.*

DAILUAINE

WEBSITE www.diageo.com

The main purpose of Dailuaine malt spirits is blending, and in recent years Diageo has distilled three different styles there. As a single malt, Dailuaine usually enjoys greater sherry wood maturation than most Diageo whiskeys.

Dailuaine 16-year-old (single malt, 43% ABV) *Sherry, nuts, and toffee on the full nose. The palate is rich and malty, with ripe oranges, spices, and some smoke. Fruity and slightly smoky in the finish.*

Dailuaine "Managers' Choice" (single malt, 58.6% ABV) *A nose of toffee apples and sherry, progressively sweeter, ending at powdered sugar. Mouth-coating, with sherry, toffee, ripe bananas, and ginger. Lengthy and gently drying spicy finish.*

DUFFTOWN

WEBSITE www.diageo.com

After Roseisle and Caol Ila, Dufftown has the third-largest capacity of any of Diageo's 28 malt distilleries. After a long association with the Bell's blend, since 2006 the single malt has enjoyed a higher profile under the Singleton banner.

Singleton of Dufftown (single malt, 40% ABV) *Sweet and floral nose, with peaches, apricots, and malt. Spicy cereal and Jaffa oranges on the palate. Warm spices and sherry in the relatively long finish.*

Dufftown "Managers' Choice" (single malt, 59.5% ABV) *Fragrant, sweet, and gently spicy on the nose. Rich, substantial, and warming palate, with mixed spice and fudge. Ginger in the finish.*

GLENALLACHIE

WEBSITE www.maltwhiskydistilleries.com

Not far from Aberlour, Glenallachie dates from 1968 and is now owned by Pernod Ricard. It has an ultra-low profile as a single malt, with most of the make finding its way into the Clan Campbell blend.

Glenallachie 16-year-old "Cask Strength Edition" (single malt, 58% ABV) *Scented on the nose, with polished oak, honey, and sherry. The palate majors in sweet sherry, stewed fruit, and spice. Long in the finish, with treacle toffee and dark chocolate.*

Glenallachie 1992 (Gordon & MacPhail) (single malt, 43% ABV) *A fresh, fragrant nose, with grass and barley, fudge, and a herbal edge. The palate offers black pepper and oak, with emerging spicy malt and honey. Becomes more tannic in the medium-length finish.*

GLENBURGIE

WEBSITE www.maltwhiskydistilleries.com

Glenburgie is a workhorse distillery for Pernod Ricard, producing one of the "heart" malts of the best-selling Ballantine's blend. Founded in 1810, the present distillery dates from 2004.

Glenburgie 15-year-old "Cask Strength Edition" (Distilled 1992, Bottled 2007) (single malt, 58.8% ABV) *A delicate floral and fruit nose, featuring grapefruit, pears, and eating apples. The palate is fruity and sweet, with vanilla and honey, plus a fizz of pixie sticks in the medium-length finish.*

Glenburgie 10-year-old (Gordon & MacPhail) (single malt, 40% ABV) *Citrus fruits and floral notes on the nose, with cream and malt. Notably fruity on the palate, with peppery oak and developing toffee and sherry. The finish dries subtly.*

GLENDULLAN

WEBSITE www.diageo.com

Along with Mortlach, Glendullan is one of two Diageo distilleries in the malt whiskey capital of Dufftown. Founded in 1896, the present buildings date from a 1970s redevelopment. It is best known through its Singleton expression.

Singleton of Glendullan (single malt, 40% ABV) *Spicy and herbal on the nose, with melon, vanilla, and brittle toffee. Citrus fruits, malt, vanilla, and oak on the palate. A sprinkling of pepper in the finish.*

Glendullan "Managers' Choice" (single malt, 58.7% ABV) *A nose of spicy malt, toasted cereal, and vanilla. Full-bodied, with fresh fruit, cooked oranges, cloves, and oak on the palate. The finish features aniseed and a final hint of ginger.*

GLENLOSSIE

WEBSITE www.diageo.com

Located in rolling countryside to the south of Elgin, Glenlossie shares its site with Mannochmore. While Glenlossie dates from 1876, its younger sister was established in 1971. It is also now home to a bio-energy plant, fueled by draff.

Glenlossie 10-year-old (single malt, 43% ABV) *A light, gristy nose, with vanilla and freshly planed wood. The full palate gives ginger, barley sugar, and spice. The finish is lengthy and mouth-coating, with developing oak.*

Glenlossie "Managers' Choice" (single malt, 59.1% ABV) *Zesty on the nose, with lemonade, vanilla, and wood glue. Very sweet on the palate, with effervescent spice and lemon. Lengthy and fruity in the finish, with vibrant, youthful oak.*

GLENLOSSIE 10-YEAR-OLD

GLENALLACHIE 16-YEAR-OLD

GLEN SPEY

WEBSITE www.diageo.com

One of four distilleries operating in Rothes and the lowest-profile of them all, Glen Spey has contributed malt whiskey to the J&B blend for well over a century. In 1887 it became the first Scottish distillery to be bought by an English company.

Glen Spey 12-year-old (single malt, 43% ABV) *The nose is floral and delicate, with notes of tropical fruit. Citrus fruit, vanilla, honey, and hazelnuts on the palate. The finish features soft oak and cinnamon.*

Glen Spey "Managers' Choice" (single malt, 52% ABV) *Delicate and fragrant on the nose, with notes of vanilla, spring flowers, and some resin. Fresh fruit flavors in the mouth, with developing malty notes. The finish features notes of butter and fudge.*

GLENTAUCHERS

WEBSITE www.chivasbrothers.com

From the onset of production in 1898, the distillery's make was destined for the blending vats, as one of the founders was James Buchanan of Black & White fame. Over the years Glentauchers has also been associated with Teacher's, and today contributes significantly to the Ballantine's blend.

Glentauchers 1991 (Gordon & MacPhail) (single malt, 43% ABV) *Fresh and initially estery on the fruity nose, with sweet sherry, honey, and toffee influences. Sweet and malty with new-mown hay and allspice on the palate. The finish features spicy banana.*

INCHGOWER

WEBSITE www.diageo.com

Located close to the northeast fishing port of Buckie, Inchgower has enjoyed a long association with the Bell's blend. It is now part of the Diageo portfolio, and spirit from the four stills remains a staple of Bell's.

Inchgower 14-year-old (single malt, 43% ABV) *Light and zesty on the nose, with cooking apples and wet grass. Subtle on the palate, with orange, ginger, and mild licorice. Medium length in the spicy, clean finish.*

Inchgower "Managers' Choice" (single malt, 61.9% ABV) *Sweet and fruity, with caramel and sherry on the nose. Tarmac, treacle, and cough syrup on the full palate. Complex finish, with bitter oak notes vying with sea salt and even molasses.*

GLENTAUCHERS 1991 (GORDON & MACPHAIL)

ANCNOC "VINTAGE" 1996

KININVIE

WEBSITE www.williamgrant.com

Kininvie shares a site with The Balvenie Distillery on the outskirts of Dufftown and is effectively just a stillhouse, boasting nine stills, with the rest of the distilling apparatus being located within The Balvenie's production buildings. Kininvie came on line in 1990 and contributes spirit to the Grant's family of blends and also the blended malt Monkey Shoulder. Rare single malt releases carry the Hazelwood name.

Hazelwood Reserve 17-year-old (single malt, 52.5% ABV) *The nose features leather, nougat, and ultimately a note of treacle. The palate is full, sherried, and spicy, with chocolate orange. Long and supple in the finish.*

KNOCKDHU

WEBSITE www.ancnoc.com

One of those rare beasts, a Scottish distillery which chooses to market its single malt under another name, Knockdhu Distillery is near Huntly. AnCnoc was introduced in 1993 to avoid potential confusion with Knockando. The late-Victorian distillery is owned by Inver House Distillers.

AnCnoc 12-year-old (single malt, 40% ABV) *Delicate and floral on the nose, with oranges and white pepper. Palate of gentle peat, hard candy, and spice. More orange in the spicy, drying finish.*

AnCnoc 16-year-old (single malt, 46% ABV) *The nose features fresh citrus fruit and vanilla toffee. Quite full-bodied, with spices and chewy toffee on the palate. The medium finish boasts vanilla, gentle oak, and a hint of mint.*

AnCnoc "Vintage" 1996 (single malt, 46% ABV) *Initial resin on the nose, then sherry and leather, salted nuts, and barbecue fumes. Mouth-coating, with dry sherry and nougat on the palate, but also strong tea and a savory note. Spicy peanuts and finally cocoa powder in the long finish.*

LINKWOOD

WEBSITE www.diageo.com

This distillery in the suburbs of Elgin dates back to 1821, though the current stillhouse with two pairs of stills dates from a 1971 expansion. For a time both the original "A" side and the modern "B" side were operational.

Linkwood 12-year-old (single malt, 43% ABV) *The nose is sweet, with soft fruit and almonds. Vanilla, spice, and marzipan on the rounded palate. Dry and citric in the finish, with a hint of aniseed.*

MACDUFF

WEBSITE www.dewars.com

Located near the port of Banff, Macduff Distillery dates from the early 1960s. Most of the Macduff spirit finds its way into owner Bacardi's William Lawson blend. As a single malt, house bottlings carry the Glen Deveron name.

Glen Deveron 10-year-old (single malt, 40% ABV) *Nose of planed lumber, resin, and malt. Peanuts, spicy malt, and tangerines on the palate. Short-to-medium finish, with grist and wood.*

Glen Deveron 15-year-old (single malt, 40% ABV) *The nose features vanilla, honey, and a hint of wood smoke. The palate is smooth and soft, with malt and butterscotch. Hazelnuts and brittle toffee in the medium finish.*

MANNOCHMORE

WEBSITE www.diageo.com

Built in 1971, Mannochmore shares a site with Glenlossie, near Elgin. Its six stills provide malt for Diageo blends, but the distillery is best known for producing the almost black "Loch Dhu" single malt, matured in double-charred casks.

Mannochmore 12-year-old (single malt, 43% ABV) *A floral, perfumed nose, with marshmallows and a hint of lemon. Sweet, malty palate, with ginger and vanilla. Almonds in the short-to-medium finish.*

Mannochmore "Managers' Choice" (single malt, 59.1% ABV) *Sweet on the nose, with apricots, ginger, cream soda, and unrefined sugar. Rich on the palate, with milk chocolate, orange marmalade, and raisins. Dark chocolate orange in the lengthy, luscious finish.*

MILTONDUFF

WEBSITE www.maltwhiskydistilleries.com

Along with Glenburgie, Miltonduff provides one of the key malts in the Ballantine's blend. The distillery, near Elgin, dates from 1824, though most of the plant was built in the mid-1970s.

Miltonduff 10-year-old (Gordon & MacPhail) (single malt, 40% ABV) *Initially estery, with eating apples and fudge notes developing. Spicy cereal, malt, and vanilla on the palate, with emerging treacle. Slowly drying in the medium-length finish.*

Miltonduff 19-year-old "Cask Strength Edition" (distilled 1991, bottled 2009) (single malt, 51.3% ABV) *Pears and oranges on the soft nose, with developing marmalade and cinnamon notes. Soft fruits carry over onto the palate, along with vanilla pods. Long and sweet in the finish.*

STRATHMILL "MANAGERS' CHOICE"

TORMORE 12-YEAR-OLD

ROSEISLE

WEBSITE www.diageo.com

Environmentally sustainable technology is at the heart of this new distillery built by Diageo not far from Elgin during 2007–09. Situated beside the company's Roseisle Maltings, it has a capacity of 3.3 million gallons (12.5 million liters) per year, making it potentially the most productive malt distillery in Scotland. Equipped with 14 stills, it is capable of producing light and heavy Speyside styles of blending spirit.

STRATHMILL

WEBSITE www.diageo.com

The status of Strathmill could hardly offer a greater contrast to that of its Keith neighbor Strathisla. While the latter is a high-profile element of the "Malt Whisky Trail," Strathmill goes largely unnoticed by visitors. The vast bulk of its output is for the J&B blend.

Strathmill "Managers' Choice" (single malt, 60.1% ABV) *Fragrant nose, with quite intense floral aromas, notably violets. Comparatively big-bodied, syrupy, and sweet on the palate, with sherbet and spice. The medium finish dries steadily, with ginger.*

TAMNAVULIN

WEBSITE www.whyteandmackay.co.uk

Established not far from Glenlivet during the mid-1960s, Tamnavulin was recommissioned in 2007 after a lengthy period of closure. It is elusive as a single malt, principally because of owner Whyte & Mackay's blending requirements.

Tamnavulin 12-year-old (single malt, 40% ABV) *Gentle malt and hay on the delicate nose. Malty and spicy on the palate, with lots of fruit. Spice, caramel, and a wisp of smoke in the finish.*

TORMORE

WEBSITE www.chivasbrothers.com

From an architectural viewpoint, Tormore, established in 1958–60, makes a lavish statement. However, its principal role has always been to provide malt for blending, being created in the first place to contribute to Long John.

Tormore 12-year-old (single malt, 40% ABV) *Fresh on the comparatively light nose, with newly mown grass and spring flowers. The smooth palate features fudge, hay, barley sugar, mixed spices, and almonds. The finish is soft and gently oaky.*

HIGHLANDS

As the Highlands is geographically the largest of all the single malt regions the landscape in which distilleries are located can vary dramatically, embracing farmland, moorland, mountains, lochs, and lengthy stretches of coastline. Much of the Highlands is sparsely populated and distilleries often inhabit remote locations, chosen for the availability of pure, reliable water sources and sometimes occupying sites that were formerly home to illicit whisky-making operations. Distances between distilleries can be quite long, but one of the benefits of travelling from one to another is the opportunity to experience the natural beauty of the Highlands in every season, to appreciate its wildlife, and to meet the people who inhabit this distinctive and beautiful part of the world.

The Highlands region encompasses all of mainland Scotland, with the exception of Speyside, north of a theoretical 'Highland Line' that follows the old county boundaries between Greenock on the Firth of Clyde in the west and Dundee on the Firth of Tay in the east. The first official geographical definition of a Highland region of malt whisky production occurred in 1784, when the Wash Act specified the division behind Highland and Lowland for the purposes of variable levels of excise duty.

The sheer scale of the region and diversity of its physical features, make it difficult to specify a generic Highland style of single malt whisky than it is with other categories. What we ultimately pour from the bottle owes more to methods of production and maturation regimes than any geographical proximity between distilleries.

The Perthshire distillery of Aberfeldy *is home to the innovative Dewar's World of Whisky visitor centre.*

Balblair distillery *was relocated in 1895 to make use of the new railway line.*

Glenmorangie and Dalmore stand little more than 19 kilometres (12 miles) apart on the same coastline, but the two malts produced vary enormously in character.

The Highland region is home to some 20 operational malt whisky distilleries, and while the area has not seen the same large-scale investment in major distillery expansions and new-builds like Roseisle on Speyside in recent times, most of the distilleries produce malts that are of great importance for blending, while many also enjoy high profiles in their own right.

GETTING AROUND

Perth and Inverness are the principal population centers in the Highlands, with the A9 road from Glasgow connecting the two and then heading on into Sutherland and Caithness, leading to Wick and Thurso. In the west, Fort William and Oban are the main towns, best reached from Glasgow via the A82. In the east, the A90 runs between Dundee and Aberdeen. Train services connect Glasgow to Oban and link Perth, Dundee, Aberdeen, Inverness, and Wick with Edinburgh and England.

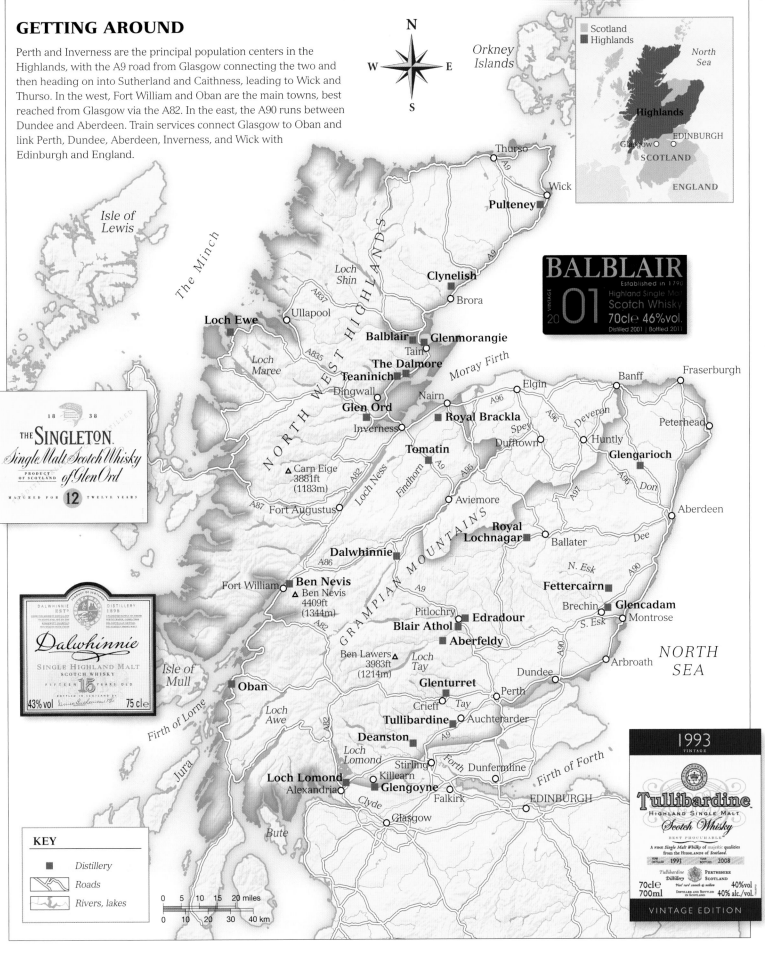

Scotland
Highlands
Orkney Islands
North Sea
Highlands
EDINBURGH
Glasgow
SCOTLAND
ENGLAND

Isle of Lewis

The Minch

Thurso
Wick
Pulteney

Loch Shin
Clynelish
Brora

Ullapool
Loch Ewe
Balblair **Glenmorangie**
Tain
The Dalmore
Teaninich
Loch Maree
Dingwall
Nairn
Elgin
Banff
Fraserburgh
Glen Ord
Inverness
Moray Firth
Spey
Peterhead
Royal Brackla
Dufftown
Huntly
Glengarioch
Tomatin
Carn Eige 3881ft (1183m)
Loch Ness
Findhorn
Don
Aberdeen
Fort Augustus
Aviemore
Dee
Dalwhinnie
Royal Lochnagar
Ballater
N. Esk
Fort William
Ben Nevis 4409ft (1344m)
Fettercairn
Brechin
Glencadam
Montrose
Pitlochry
Edradour
Blair Athol
S. Esk
Aberfeldy
Ben Lawers 3983ft (1214m)
Loch Tay
Arbroath
NORTH SEA
Glenturret
Dundee
Oban
Crieff
Perth
Loch Awe
Tullibardine
Auchterarder
Isle of Mull
Deanston
Loch Lomond
Stirling
Dunfermline
Firth of Lorne
Loch Lomond
Killearn
Falkirk
Firth of Forth
Jura
Alexandria
Glengoyne
EDINBURGH
Clyde
Glasgow
Bute

NORTH WEST HIGHLANDS
GRAMPIAN MOUNTAINS

BALBLAIR
Established in 1790
VINTAGE
01
20
Highland Single Malt
Scotch Whisky
70cle 46%vol.
Distilled 2001 | Bottled 2011

THE SINGLETON.
Single Malt Scotch Whisky
PRODUCT OF SCOTLAND
of Glen Ord
12
MATURED FOR TWELVE YEARS

Dalwhinnie
DISTILLERY
SINGLE HIGHLAND MALT
SCOTCH WHISKY
FIFTEEN YEARS OLD
15
43% vol
75 cle

1993
VINTAGE
Tullibardine
HIGHLAND SINGLE MALT
Scotch Whisky
BEST PROCURABLE
A FINE Single Malt Whisky of majestic qualities from the HIGHLANDS of Scotland.
YEAR DISTILLED 1993 YEAR BOTTLED 2008
Tullibardine Distillery PERTHSHIRE SCOTLAND
70cle 40%vol
700ml 40% alc./vol.
DISTILLED AND BOTTLED IN SCOTLAND
VINTAGE EDITION

KEY

- ■ Distillery
- Roads
- Rivers, lakes

0 5 10 15 20 miles
0 10 20 30 40 km

ABERFELDY

OWNER	John Dewar & Sons Ltd.
FOUNDED 1896	**CAPACITY** 766,000 gal (2.9m liters)
ADDRESS	Aberfeldy, Perthshire PH15 2EB
WEBSITE	www.dewars.com

Aberfeldy is one of those curious distilleries that has a physical profile higher than that of the single malts it produces. This is largely because Aberfeldy is home to Dewar's World of Whiskey, an interactive visitor experience that set the bar high when it opened in 2000. Dewar's is one of the most iconic names in Scotch whiskey, even if "Aberfeldy" has less international cachet.

Although the small market town of Aberfeldy is located about 10 miles (16 km) west of the busy A9 road from the Central Belt of Scotland into the Highlands, it stands in the heart of an area that is notably popular with visitors to Perthshire. This ensures a steady stream of around 40,000 visitors a year from all over the world wishing to experience the various touch-screen displays, handheld audio guides, and the Brand Family Room, where they can pit their skills against a large-scale blender's nosing wheel.

Given all the interactive, crowd-pleasing aspects of the visitor center, it would be easy for the distillery itself to become overshadowed, but such is the timeless allure of a row of hot, hissing stills that Aberfeldy never becomes a visitor center with a distillery attached.

The distillery in question was built by the burgeoning Perth-based family business of John Dewar & Sons during 1896–98. By this time, blended Scotch whiskey was taking the world by storm, and the new distillery, like so many constructed at the time, was intended solely to provide malt whiskey for the company's increasingly popular blends.

An advantageous location

A number of factors have informed the locations of Scotland's distilleries, and Aberfeldy was no exception to the usual criteria. All have been constructed with access to a guaranteed supply of pure water, so vital to whiskey-making, and in past times they were often situated comparatively close to the barley-growing areas, which provide the main raw material of malt whiskey, and near the deposits of peat required to fire the furnace and dry the malting barley.

Many, however, were built in close proximity to the intricate network of railroads that covered Scotland during the second half of the 19th century and the first half of the 20th. Aberfeldy was one such distillery, being developed alongside the Aberfeldy-to-Perth railroad line, which provided a direct link into the sidings of John Dewar & Sons' vast bonding and blending facilities in Perth, from where blended Scotch whiskey was subsequently transported to the thirsty markets of England and abroad.

New developments in a new century

Aberfeldy passed to the mighty Distillers Company Ltd. in 1925 when the latter merged with Dewar's, but in 1998 it was one of four distilleries acquired by Bacardi Ltd., which subsequently increased the product range and gave the brand much more of a family ethos once again. "I guess people in other companies probably forget that," says Stephen Marshall, Senior Global Brand Ambassador, "but it's reassuring to know that the family is at the helm. There are great internal communication systems too, so everyone always knows what's going on."

A 25-year-old single malt expression of Aberfeldy was released in 2000, but was replaced by the currently available 21-year-old in 2005. A number of highly regarded single-cask bottlings have also been marketed during the past few years, showcasing the single malt at its best and most distinctive. A 14-year-old, bottled in 2011, was notable for the fact that, after hogshead maturation, the whiskey ultimately underwent a period of finishing in an ex-sherry cask prior to bottling.

With Dewar's occupying the number one blended Scotch whiskey position in the US, still globally the leading market for Scotch whiskey sales, it is inevitable that most of the output of Aberfeldy finds its way into the blending vats. Stephen Marshall points out that the five distilleries under the control of John Dewar & Sons, namely Aberfeldy, Aultmore, Craigellachie, Macduff, and Royal Brackla, produce around 2.6 million gallons (10 million liters) of spirits per year. "We sell around 50,000 cases of single malt, so the majority of our production is certainly used for blending," he confirms.

However, sales of Aberfeldy single malt have grown by about 400 percent over seven years to reach 25,000 cases per year, though Marshall says that "Aberfeldy single malt hasn't been a particular focus up to this point—we've been concentrating on Dewar's. Since Bacardi took over, the range of whiskeys has expanded considerably and will continue with some exciting new whiskeys. The main market for Aberfeldy 12-year-old is the USA."

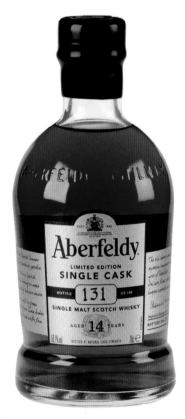

ABERFELDY 14-YEAR-OLD "SINGLE CASK"

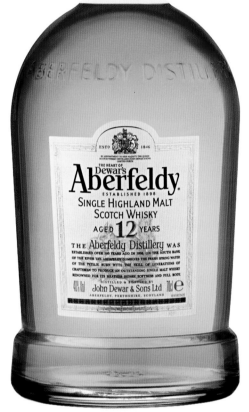

ABERFELDY 12-YEAR-OLD

A FLAMBOYANT FIGURE

Aberfeldy distillery was established by brothers John and Tommy Dewar, the latter renowned as one of the most flamboyant figures in Scotch whiskey. An entrepreneur of the late-Victorian blended Scotch boom, "Whiskey Tom" sailed yachts, bred racehorses, and worked tirelessly as the charismatic ambassador for the family business. He once declared, "A teetotaller is one who suffers from thirst instead of enjoying it."

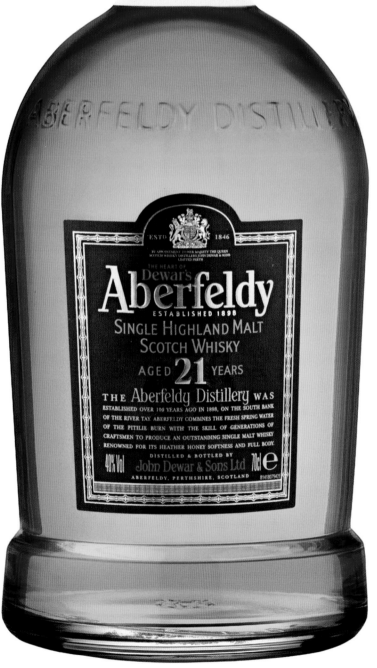

ABERFELDY 21-YEAR-OLD

TASTING NOTES

ABERFELDY 12-YEAR-OLD
single malt, 40% ABV
Sweet, with honeycombs, breakfast cereal, and stewed fruits on the nose. Quite full-bodied and sweet on the elegant palate, with malty notes. The finish is long and complex, becoming spicier and drying.

ABERFELDY 14-YEAR-OLD "SINGLE CASK"
single malt, 58.1% ABV, single cask, matured ex-Bourbon cask, finished sherry butt, non-chill-filtered
The nose offers raisins and hot chocolate, developing vanilla and overripe bananas with burnt sugar and caramel. Syrupy on the palate, with apricots, dried fruits, honey, and sherry. Gently spicy, with licorice in the long finish.

ABERFELDY 21-YEAR-OLD
single malt, 43% ABV
A nose of honey, soft fruits, vanilla, and lightly charred wood notes; full-flavored and sweet on the palate, with a suggestion of chocolate oranges. Long, spicy, and addictive in the finish.

BEN NEVIS

OWNER Ben Nevis Distillery (Fort William) Ltd
FOUNDED 1825 **CAPACITY** 476,000 gal (1.8m liters)
ADDRESS Lochy Bridge, Fort William, Inverness-shire PH33 6TJ
WEBSITE www.bennevisdistillery.com

A long with Oban, Ben Nevis is one of only two surviving commercial distilleries in the Western Highlands classification. However, unlike the more easterly and northerly areas of the Highlands, the west was never home to many distilleries. Despite this, Fort William once boasted three distilleries, namely Glenlochy (1898–83), Nevis (1878–10), and the currently operational Ben Nevis.

Colin Ross is the longstanding manager of Ben Nevis, and he recalls that "as a northeast lad myself growing up on Speyside, I was used to there being many distilleries around us. As the son of a haulage contractor, I had been in and out of distilleries since I was seven or eight years old, collecting draff for delivery to the Aberdeen-shire farms and assisting with deliveries of empty casks."

Western scarcity

Speculating on the relative lack of distilleries in the West Highlands, Ross suggests that "the drove roads in the Central Highlands would have proved easier to access from the Eastern Highlands than perhaps from the west. Another factor that may have been of benefit in the Eastern Highlands was a ready source of fuel in the peat mosses of Dallas, Knockando, and at New Pitsligo in Aberdeenshire.

"But I think the strongest reason why there were few distilleries compared to Speyside and the rest of the Highlands would have to be to do with the availability of good-quality barley for malting. After all, in Alfred Barnard's *The Distilleries of the United Kingdom and Ireland* it is mentioned that Donald Peter McDonald, the son of 'Long John' McDonald, had his own small ships sailing through the Caledonian Canal to the lands of the Moray Firth to load barley for the production of his whiskey in Fort William."

Ben Nevis distillery was established two miles northeast of Fort William in 1825 by a farmer, the aforementioned "Long John" McDonald, who stood six feet four inches tall, hence his nickname. McDonald's whiskey was marketed as Long John's Dew of Ben Nevis, though the name "Long John" subsequently came to be applied to a blended Scotch whiskey, now owned by Chivas Brothers. The distillery remained in the hands of the McDonalds until 1941, and between 1878 and 1908 the family operated a second distillery, named Nevis, which was then absorbed into the main Ben Nevis plant.

The dubious Hobbs

The most colorful owner of Ben Nevis distillery was Joseph Hobbs, who bought the distillery from the McDonald family. He was born in Hampshire, England, during 1891, and migrated with his parents to Canada in 1900. There he made a fortune, which he subsequently lost during the Great Depression. Hobbs returned to the UK and proceeded to develop significant whiskey-related interests in Scotland, where, among other distilleries, he owned Ben Nevis from 1941 until his death 20 years later.

One of Hobbs' rather dubious innovations was the installation of concrete washbacks, and he also installed a Coffey still, in order to produce both grain and malt spirits and blend them on the premises. When he acquired the former Deuchar's brewery in the east coast port of Montrose during 1957 and converted it to a whiskey distillery, Hobbs replicated the Ben Nevis distillation regimen by installing four pot stills and a Coffey still to produce malt and grain whiskey, which was then blended on the premises.

A Japanese connection

Ben Nevis has had a number of owners during its lengthy existence, and has endured several periods of closure, but its future was assured when the facility was purchased from the brewing giant Whitbread & Co. Ltd. by the Japanese Nikka Whisky Distilling Company Ltd. in 1989.

At present Ben Nevis distills two types of spirits; one, which undergoes a relatively lengthy period of fermentation, is exported to Japan as "new make," where it is ultimately used in Nikka blended whiskeys. The second style, with a fermentation time of around 48 hours, is destined for single malt bottlings and as a component of the range of Dew of Ben Nevis blended Scotch whiskeys.

Colin Ross describes the character of Ben Nevis single malt as a "cross between a Speyside and an Islay malt. Perhaps this is down to location, in that we are midway between these two famous whiskey regions, with the lighter Speyside types contrasting with the heavier, more robust malts of Islay. Another malt that I feel is similar to Ben Nevis is Dalwhinnie, and perhaps that backs up this theory. The large capacity of our stills may also have a bearing on this fuller flavor, with hints of chocolate, nuts, and dried fruits. One group distilleries manager I worked for at one time described the new make spirit as reminiscent of 'heather and honey.'"

Of the maturation regimen, Ross says "We fill a high percentage of refill casks of all sizes—butts, hogsheads, and barrels, but introducing new sherry, new Bourbon, and port casks every year. We are also experimenting with differing types of

"McDONALD'S TRADITIONAL BEN NEVIS"

BEN NEVIS 25-YEAR-OLD

wine casks. In order to maintain uniformity in our 10-year-old single malt we use refill casks, fresh Bourbon barrels, and fresh sherry casks. The percentage of each can vary in an attempt to ensure consistency in this, our flagship whiskey."

Current whiskeys

As Ross notes, the "flagship" bottling is a 10-year-old single malt expression, but he has also presided over the release of a number of limited, cask-strength variants, notably 19-, 25-, and 26-year-olds, not to mention a 40-year-old Dew of Ben Nevis "Blended at Birth" blended whiskey expression. The latter was distilled during 1962 in the distillery's pot stills and in the Coffey still installed by owner Joseph Hobbs, who then filled a blend of the new-make grain and malt spirits directly into casks for maturation.

In 2011, "McDonald's Traditional Ben Nevis" single malt appeared, and Colin Ross notes that "the idea behind McDonald's Traditional Ben Nevis was to see if we could produce a whiskey of the quality that had once been so popular when Donald Peter McDonald was responsible for the production of whiskey at his two distilleries. I had read somewhere that at that time Long John's Dew of Ben Nevis far outsold many of the larger and more famous malts of today, and I felt that by introducing a peated malt we may be able to replicate the whiskey of that era. This whiskey differs from the 'standard' bottlings of Ben Nevis single malt in that it has been produced from peated malt and is being sold at a younger vintage, having been matured in fresh sherry casks."

TASTING NOTES

BEN NEVIS 10-YEAR-OLD
single malt, 46% ABV, matured in a mixture of refill casks, fresh Bourbon barrels, and fresh sherry casks
The initially quite green nose develops nutty, orange notes. Full-bodied, with coffee, brittle toffee, and peat, along with chewy oak, which persists to the finish, together with more coffee and a hint of dark chocolate.

BEN NEVIS 25-YEAR-OLD
single malt, 56% ABV, single cask, cask strength, distilled December 1984, filled into freshly dumped ex-Bourbon barrels, vatted into ex-sherry butts in October 1998; 628 bottles from cask 98/35/1 released January 2010
The nose offers smoky sherry, cocoa, and maraschino cherries. Full-bodied on the palate, with plums, prunes, and a hint of smoke. Lingering in the finish, with dry sherry, fruity oak, and a tang of licorice.

"McDONALD'S TRADITIONAL BEN NEVIS"
single malt, 46% ABV
Initial starch on the nose, then buttery smoked haddock, a hint of chili, sherry, and wood smoke. Full-bodied, spicy on the palate, with hazelnuts and peat. Stewed fruit and lingering spicy cigarette ash in the finish.

BEN NEVIS 10-YEAR-OLD

BLAIR ATHOL

OWNNER Diageo PLC
FOUNDED 1798 **CAPACITY** 476,000 gal (1.8m liters)
ADDRESS Perth Road, Pitlochry, Perthshire PH16 5LY
WEBSITE www.discovering-distilleries.com

Like its Perthshire neighbors Aberfeldy and Glenturret, Blair Athol is better known as a distillery than it is as a single malt. Diageo's third-busiest distillery visitors' center, after Talisker and Oban, stands on the outskirts of the bustling tourist center of Pitlochry, now bypassed by the A9 road between Perth and Inverness. The name is slightly confusing, as the village of Blair Atholl, with an extra "l," is located some 7 miles (11 km) northwest of Pitlochry.

Blair Athol is one of Diageo's oldest distilleries, dating from the late 18th century, when it was established by John Stewart and Robert Robertson under the name of Aldour. The Allt Dour burn runs through the distillery grounds, and translates from the Gaelic as "Burn of the Otter," which explains the presence of an otter on the label of the 12-year-old "Flora & Fauna" expression of Blair Athol single malt. The Blair Athol name was adopted in 1825, when Robert Robertson expanded the distillery.

Just as Aberfeldy is the spiritual home of the Bacardi-owned Dewar's blend, and Glenturret performs the same function in relation to The Famous Grouse for The Edrington Group, so Blair Athol serves as the "brand home" of Bell's blended Scotch whiskey.

BLAIR ATHOL 12-YEAR-OLD

Bell's blends

The distillery was purchased by Perth-based Arthur Bell & Sons Ltd. in 1933, but due to the prevailing economic climate remained silent until 1949, when it was substantially rebuilt and reequipped prior to the recommencement of production. The rise of Bell's blend mirrored that of Dewar's and The Famous Grouse during the later decades of the 19th century, with all three subsequently best-selling brands being created by Perth wine and spirits merchants.

Today, Diageo uses Blair Athol distillery to relate the story of the blend, though compared to Dewar's World of Whisky and Glenturret Distillery's Famous Grouse Experience, the Blair Athol visitor experience is altogether more traditional in its approach.

Although only eighth in the global top ten of blended Scotch whiskeys, and playing a supporting role to Diageo's Johnnie Walker and J&B in most territories, Bell's enjoys notably strong sales in the UK. Indeed, it vies with The Famous Grouse for supremacy in the domestic market.

The Bell's blend gained a greater following when an 8-year-old age statement was applied to it in 1993, at a time when distillers had surplus stocks of older whiskeys. Those days are long gone, however, and Diageo subsequently removed the age statement, declaring in 2008 that the

Blair Athol distillery takes its name *from Blair Atholl village, home to Blair Castle, the seat of the Dukes of Atholl.*

revamped recipe for "Bell's Original" was closer to that first formulated by Arthur Bell.

As a company, Bell's retained its independence until taken over by the brewer Guinness in 1985, subsequently being absorbed into what was to become Diageo plc. In 1998 the Bell's brand lost its last connection with its home city of Perth when the Cherrybank sales, marketing, and distribution function was relocated to Harlow in Essex.

In 2010 six new stainless steel washbacks replaced the existing four wooden and four stainless steel vessels at Blair Athol. Diageo's Dr Nick Morgan explains that "We wanted a consistent production regime at Blair Athol and it made more sense to go down the stainless steel route, particularly as we had already been using them there for many decades."

Two pairs of stills are in place, the second being added in 1973, and the distillery operates on a seven days per week basis.

Single Malt

As most of the Blair Athol "make" is earmarked for blending, the single malt is a relatively rare beast, with a 12-year-old "Flora & Fauna" bottling now being augmented by a distillery-exclusive expression which has been matured in first fill ex-sherry casks, and by a release in Diageo's "Managers' Choice" range.

According to Diageo Master Blender Jim Beveridge, "Blair Athol spirit character lends itself particularly well to sherry cask maturation, and the percentage of sherry cask-matured spirit in Blair Athol 12-year-old is appreciably higher than in many Diageo single malts."

TASTING NOTES

BLAIR ATHOL 12-YEAR-OLD
single malt, 43% ABV
The nose is moist, mellow, and sherried, with brittle toffee, sweet and fragrant. Relatively rich on the smooth palate, with malt, raisins, and sherry. The finish is lengthy, elegant, balanced, and slowly drying.

BLAIR ATHOL "DISTILLERY-EXCLUSIVE BOTTLING"
single malt, 55.8% ABV
The nose is initially slightly prickly, with sweet notes emerging—canned peaches in syrup and developing marshmallow. Mouth-coating, with a palate of toffee, dried fruits, spice, and a hint of aniseed. Lengthy and steadily drying in the finish.

BLAIR ATHOL 1995 "MANAGERS' CHOICE"
single malt, 54.7% ABV, cask strength, single cask, matured in a bodega sherry European oak cask (570 bottles)
A rich, fruity nose with figs and faintly herbal notes. Malt and spice on the palate, with dark chocolate whiskey liqueurs. The finish is medium in length and drying, spicier when diluted, with lingering orange marmalade.

THE BELLS OF BLAIR ATHOL

Arthur Bell joined TH Sandeman's Perth wine and spirits business in 1840, setting up on his own 11 years later from the same Kirkside premises. Using the expertise he had gained in blending tea, Bell began to blend grain and malt whiskeys, using Blair Athol malt and the make of several other distilleries. By the time Arthur Bell died in 1900 and his son Arthur Kinmont "A.K." Bell took over the firm, the blend was on sale across the British Empire, with strong markets in Europe too. The story of the blend's slogan "Afore ye go" is rather mysterious. Some claim it derives from World War I when the men of the distillery were given a free bottle of Bell's whiskey as they left for the front. Yet it was only adopted for the centennial in 1925, and the firm itself cites its origins in a "Gaelic war cry."

BLAIR ATHOL 18-YEAR-OLD "BICENTENNIAL LIMITED EDITION"

CLYNELISH

OWNER	Diageo PLC
FOUNDED 1819	**CAPACITY** 1.1m gal (4.2m liters)
ADDRESS	Clynelish Road, Brora, Sutherland KW9 6LR
WEBSITE	www.discovering-distilleries.com

Clynelish stands close to the East Sutherland village of Brora, some 50 miles (80 km) northeast of Inverness, and is the northernmost distillery in Diageo's portfolio. Only Pulteney in Wick has a more northerly location on the Scottish mainland. There are actually two distilleries on the Clynelish site, with the original stone structures built for the Marquess of Stafford, latterly the Duke of Sutherland, standing alongside their 1960s replacements. The Duke's distillery benefited from a supply of locally grown barley as well as abundant peat for fueling the malt kilns, while fuel was provided by the local Brora coal mine, which had been in use since the 16th century.

The changing fortunes of Clynelish
Clynelish had a number of owners before John Walker & Sons Ltd. bought into it during 1916 and Walker's duly became part of the Distillers Company Ltd. in 1925. Within five years, DCL owned the entire share capital of Clynelish, subsequently moving the distillery into the care of its Scottish Malt Distillers subsidiary. However, Clynelish was silent for most of the economically troubled 1930s, only resuming production just before the outbreak of World War II.

During the 1960s, DCL expanded and rebuilt many of its existing distilleries to cope with the increasing demand for blended Scotch whiskey, and in the case of Clynelish, an entirely new modernistic plant was built during 1967–68 alongside the old production buildings. The original distillery closed down in May 1968, but was revived the following year, renamed Brora.

During 1969–73, Brora distilled relatively heavily peated spirits, with more batches being produced periodically in subsequent years, as DCL required additional stocks of Islay-style spirits for blending purposes. Today, bottlings of peaty Brora have achieved a cult status among connoisseurs, second only to those from the now-defunct Islay distillery of Port Ellen. Bottlings of Brora ranging from 25 to 32 years of age have been issued in Diageo's annual Special Releases program, to great acclaim.

Brora finally closed permanently in 1983, but the distillery remains largely intact, and its quirky, tarnished pair of stills remains in place. Meanwhile, the new Clynelish plant, with its six stills, serves as a workhorse for DCL, turning out large amounts of spirits for blending, and it was only in 2002 that a 14-year-old house bottling of Clynelish was released.

JOHNNIE WALKER "GOLD LABEL"
Clynelish spirit is a key component in Diageo's Johnnie Walker range of blended whiskeys, contributing a unique "waxy" profile.

CLYNELISH 14-YEAR-OLD

CLYNELISH "DISTILLERS' EDITION"

The original Clynelish distillery was established by the second Marquess of Stafford in 1819 to provide an outlet for the barley crops grown by tenants on his estate. The Marquess married Elizabeth, 19th Countess of Sutherland, and in 1833 was created Duke of Sutherland. At the time the Clynelish distillery was constructed, the Sutherlands were the largest private estate owners in Europe, and the family is closely associated with the Highland Clearances, in which thousands of tenants were evicted from their homes. An imposing stone statue of the first Duke of Sutherland dominates the landscape from the summit of Ben Bhraggie, near Golspie.

Dunrobin Castle *is a fine example of the Scottish Baronial style and remains the seat of the Dukes of Sutherland.*

Waxing technical

Douglas Murray, Diageo's Process Development Manager, says, "I led the team that worked to identify the key building blocks that allowed us to understand what was important to the uniqueness of spirit produced by each of our distilleries. It's not about changing their character, it's about being able to improve the consistency by knowing how we get the characteristics we do. Clynelish is unique in being the only Diageo distillery to offer spirit with a 'waxy' profile, and it's an important factor in a lot of our older blends, especially the Johnnie Walker range—most notably Johnnie Walker "Gold Label." There are undertones of grassy and fruity in Clynelish, but these are swamped by waxy. Waxy is all about mouthfeel in a blend."

Murray explains, "In most distilleries there is one combined vessel for low wines and feints and foreshots, but Clynelish has a separate low wines receiver and a foreshots and feints tank. The low wines from the wash still are pumped into the low wines receiver, and from there into the spirit still via the spirit still charger. The foreshots and feints from the spirit still are collected in a receiver and then briefly added to the low wines in the spirit still charger.

"Because of the comparatively long time the liquid sits in the low wines and foreshots and feints tanks prior to being mixed to create the spirit still charge, you get a buildup of waxiness.

The wash distillation is similar in technique to that required to make fruity character, but the use of the intermediate tanks ensures the low wines are converted to waxy as a result of the spirit still distillation."

The whiskeys

In 2006 the 14-year-old was joined by a bottling in the "Distillers' Edition" series, which had enjoyed a period of secondary maturation in ex-sherry casks. Next, 2008 saw a cask-strength edition exclusive to distillery visitors, and 2009, a cask-strength, single cask bottling in the "Managers' Choice" portfolio.

TASTING NOTES

CLYNELISH "DISTILLERS' EDITION"
single malt, 46% ABV, matured ex-Bourbon cask, finished Oloroso Seco sherry casks
Sweet sherry and honey on the nose, with cloves. The palate initially offers sherry, with cloves, angelica, and spices developing. The finish is medium in length, with a mild note of ginger.

CLYNELISH "MANAGERS' CHOICE"
single malt, 58.8% ABV, single cask, cask-strength, first-fill ex-Bourbon cask, 232 bottles, non-chill-filtered
The nose offers vanilla, gingery spice, and a faintly maritime background note. Full and rich on the palate; malty, with fresh fruit and a lively, spicy edge. The finish is lengthy, with oak and aniseed.

CLYNELISH 14-YEAR-OLD
single malt, 46% ABV
The nose is fragrant and spicy, with candle wax, malt, and discreet smoke. Slightly waxy in the mouth, with honey, citric orange, spice, and peat. Brine and spicy tropical fruit in the finish.

THE DALMORE

OWNER	Whyte & Mackay Ltd. (United Spirits Ltd.)
FOUNDED 1839	CAPACITY 977,000 gal (3.7m liters)
ADDRESS	Alness, Ross & Cromarty IV17 0T
WEBSITE	www.thedalmore.com

The Dalmore's transformation from a well-regarded single malt to one of the two most collectible and highly prized whiskeys in Scotland has been a remarkable one. Along with The Macallan, The Dalmore is able to release extremely limited editions of very old whiskey and sell them for the sort of sums many rival distillers can only dream of.

According to David Robertson, Director of Whiskey for The Dalmore, "It's partly about building up the reputation of a distillery and the quality of the whiskey it produces over a number of years. The quality of the liquid itself and the efforts of the brand custodians have made possible what has been achieved, I think. Master Distiller Richard Paterson has nurtured and retained old casks of The Dalmore so that selling it at 40, 50, and even more than 60 years of age is a viable proposition."

Record-breaking luxury

The Dalmore's dramatic move upmarket from respected Highland single malt to multiple record-breaker has really come about since the brand's owner, Whyte & Mackay Ltd., was acquired by the India-based company United Spirits Ltd. in 2007.

"By then it had become apparent that The Dalmore was massively undervalued, both by ourselves and also in the marketplace," says David Robertson. "It was terrific liquid with great credibility, and we were doing the guys who make it a disservice by the way the brand was being handled. Similarly Master Distiller Richard Paterson, who had so brilliantly nurtured the spirit."

The result was a major packaging makeover, a broadening of the range, and the start of an ongoing program of ultra-limited releases, which have included 40-, 45-, 58-, and 59-year-old whiskeys, with just a dozen decanters of the 58-year-old from two sherry casks being released in 2010 under the "Selene" banner, followed by 20 decanters from the same cask in 2011, named "Eos." Also in 2011 came "Astrum," distilled in 1966 and finished for 18 months in Gonzalez Byass casks.

Rarest of all, however, was "Trinitas," a 64-year-old expression of The Dalmore, in which some of the component whiskeys have been maturing for more than 140 years. Just three bottles were

The Dalmore distillery lies beside *the calm waters of the Cromarty Firth, a sea loch to the north of Inverness.*

filled, each with an asking price of £100,000 (about $150,000). Two were immediately acquired by collectors, while the third bottle subsequently sold at Harrods in London for £120,000 ($180,000).

The Dalmore began setting records for the price of its whiskey in 2002, when a bottle of 62-year-old Dalmore changed hands for £25,877.50 (about $38,800), then the world's most expensive whiskey ever sold at auction. Just 12 bottles of the expression were produced, and more headlines were garnered in April 2005 when one of them was bought at the Pennyhill Park Hotel in Surrey, England, by an anonymous businessman who proceeded to share it with five of his friends during the course of the evening. Then, in September 2011, another record fell when the last bottle of "The Dalmore 62" was sold at Changi Airport in Singapore for $200,000.

Starting out

Such luxury is a very long way from The Dalmore's origins, with the distillery having been established beside the Cromarty Firth, close to Alness, in 1839 by Alexander Matheson, who had made a fortune in the opium trade. Matheson turned over the running of his distillery to various estate tenants, and in 1867 Andrew Mackenzie and his family took the reins.

The Mackenzies eventually bought The Dalmore distillery from the Matheson family in 1891 for £14,500 ($65,000), by which time the number of stills had been doubled to four.

THE DALMORE 12-YEAR-OLD

THE DALMORE 40-YEAR-OLD

The distillery remained in the Mackenzie family until 1960, when Mackenzie Brothers (Dalmore) Ltd. merged with the Glasgow blending firm of Whyte & Mackay Ltd., who were long-standing customers for The Dalmore single malt. In 1966, with the Scotch whiskey industry booming, another four stills were installed to double capacity.

That is the status quo today, but the stillhouse is one of the most quirky in Scotland, featuring four flat-topped wash stills of diverse shapes and sizes and four spirit stills with "boil balls" and distinctive cooling copper water jackets, while a section of "number two spirit still" dates back to 1874.

Sherried spirit

The Dalmore is characterized by its richly sherried house style and its ability to flourish during extended periods of aging. The principal casks used for maturation are first-fill ex-Bourbon barrels and former sherry butts, with The Dalmore being the only Scotch whiskey distillery with access to Matusalem Oloroso sherry butts from the historic house of Gonzalez Byass.

Core bottlings of The Dalmore include 12-, 15-, and 18-year-old expressions, along with "Cigar Malt Reserve"—aged in 30-year-old Oloroso sherry butts, American White Oak, and *premier cru* Cabernet Sauvignon wine barriques—and "King Alexander III." This expression takes its name from the fact that in 1263 an ancestor of the Clan Mackenzie saved Alexander III, King of the Scots, from being gored by a stag. The stag's head duly became the emblem of Clan Mackenzie, and adorns all expressions of The Dalmore.

THE DALMORE "GRAN RESERVA"

THE DALMORE "KING ALEXANDER III"

TASTING NOTES

THE DALMORE 12-YEAR-OLD
single malt, 40% ABV, matured 50% ex-Oloroso sherry wood and 50% ex-Bourbon American white oak
Malt, orange marmalade, sherry, and a hint of leather on the nose. Full-bodied and sherried on the palate, with spice and balancing citrus notes. The finish is long, with spices, ginger, and lingering oranges.

THE DALMORE 40-YEAR-OLD
single malt, 40% ABV, matured American white oak, finished Gonzalez Byass Oloroso sherry butts
Orange marmalade combines with fruitcake and mild oak on the nose. Brittle toffee and bitter chocolate on the palate with spicy orange and almonds. The finish is lengthy, with malt and dark chocolate.

THE DALMORE "KING ALEXANDER III"
single malt, 40% ABV, matured vintage Oloroso and Madeira butts, vintage Bourbon barrels, and Cabernet Sauvignon barriques
The nose presents almonds, fencerow berries, plums, brittle toffee, and treacle. Sherry and fresh berries merge with plum notes on the palate, plus vanilla and toffee. Oak, red wine, and black pepper in the finish.

DALWHINNIE

OWNER Diageo PLC
FOUNDED 1897 **CAPACITY** 581,000 gal (2.2m liters)
ADDRESS Dalwhinnie, Inverness-shire PH19 1AB
WEBSITE www.discovering-distilleries.com

Dating from 1897–98, Dalwhinnie was created just before the great Victorian whiskey bubble burst. It was developed for £10,000 ($48,000) under the auspices of the Strathspey Distillery Company Ltd. by local businessmen John Grant, Alexander Mackenzie, and George Sellar, originally bearing the name Strathspey.

However, just a few months after production started in February 1898, the distillery's founders were forced to sell their new plant to AP Blyth & Son and John Somerville & Company, who changed the distillery name to Dalwhinnie.

Takeover bids

Dalwhinnie had the distinction of becoming the first Scottish distillery to fall into US hands, with Cook & Bernheimer of New York and Baltimore purchasing it at auction for a mere £1,250 ($6,000) in 1905. Dalwhinnie's decline in value reflected the collapse of confidence and activity in the Scotch whiskey industry. Cook & Bernheimer operated Dalwhinnie as part of its James Munro & Son Ltd. subsidiary, and this name was retained when ownership changed again in 1920, with Sir James Calder buying the distillery.

The Distillers Company Ltd. (DCL) acquired Dalwhinnie six years later, and in February 1934 a major fire led to the closure of the distillery for

DALWHINNIE 15-YEAR-OLD

four years while reconstruction took place. In the hands of DCL, Dalwhinnie was licensed to James Buchanan & Company Ltd., and to this day Dalwhinnie malt whiskey is an important part of the Buchanan family of blends, which enjoy notably strong sales in South America.

Black & White whiskey

The Black & White blend was established in 1884 by James Buchanan, a Canadian-born, Northern Ireland–educated individual of Scottish parentage. He took up employment as an office boy in Glasgow at the age of 15, before going on to work for 10 years in his brother's grain business.

However, 1879 saw Buchanan take his first steps into the Scotch whiskey industry, when he moved to London as an agent for the Leith blenders Charles Mackinlay & Company. Five years later he was in business for himself, developing his personal blended whiskey, which was designed to appeal to the discerning palates of English drinkers. After being known as House of Commons whiskey and Buchanan's Special, the brand was finally christened Black & White, due to the eye-catching white label on a dark bottle.

The worms return

In 1987, the Dalwhinnie 15-year-old was chosen as part of Diageo predecessor United Distillers' Classic Malts range, and a visitors' center opened four years later. The period 1992 to 1995 saw

Located on the edge *of the Monadhliath and Cairngorm mountains, Dalwhinnie is one of the highest distilleries.*

a $5 million refurbishment program, though just a single pair of stills remained at the end of the work. Dalwhinnie is one of comparatively few Scottish distilleries still equipped with "worm tubs" for condensing purposes, and in 1986 the existing two tubs were removed in favour of "shell and tube" condensers, but these altered the character of the Dalwhinnie "make" in a way considered undesirable, and a new pair of worm tubs was installed.

Cool character

Diageo's Process Development Manager Douglas Murray explains that "Using worms rather than shell and tube condensers tends to create a complex spirit character. At Dalwhinnie this is accentuated by icy cold water (often snow melt) used in our worm tubs. It allows us to cool the spirit vapor very quickly, reducing the copper conversation to a minimum. This helps us to create a particular new make spirit character that goes on to develop into the wonderfully complex 15-year-old Dalwhinnie single malt."

At Dalwhinnie around 1,500 casks are maturing on site, with the resultant whiskey being earmarked for bottling as single malt. Ewan Mackintosh of Diageo says that "Weather conditions are severe and can create plenty of challenges for living and working here. However, we don't believe maturing whiskey at this altitude affects the final taste of the 15-year-old Dalwhinnie, though we may lose slightly less spirit to the "angels."

The Dalwhinnie line-up consists of a 15-year-old and a "Distillers Edition" variant, introduced in 1998, though in the past there have been limited edition 20-, 29-, and 36-year-olds, and in 2010 a "Managers' Choice" expression was also released.

TASTING NOTES

DALWHINNIE 15-YEAR-OLD
single malt, 43% ABV
An aromatic nose, with pine needles, heather, and vanilla, plus delicate peat notes. Sweet on the smooth, fruity palate, with honey, malt, and a subtle note of peat. The medium-length finish dries elegantly.

DALWHINNIE "DISTILLERS EDITION" (1995)
single malt, 43% ABV, matured for a secondary period in ex-Oloroso sherry casks
The nose offers medium-sweet sherry, raisins, and sweet smoke. Big, yet elegant on the palate, with malt, cloves, sherry, and fruit notes, plus muted honey and peat. The finish is long, smooth, and gently drying.

DALWHINNIE "MANAGERS' CHOICE"
single malt, 51% ABV, single cask, cask strength, matured in a refill American oak cask (270 bottles)
Quite a reticent nose: mildly herbal and sherried. Medium-sweet and spicy in the mouth, with graham crackers, honey, oranges, and lemons. Medium-to-long finish, with lingering spices, notably cinnamon.

ON A WHISKEY HIGH

At 1,073 feet (327 m) above sea level, Dalwhinnie is the second-highest operational distillery in Scotland after Pernod Ricard's Braeval, located south of Glenlivet. Its lofty situation makes it one of the coldest places in Britain, and the Met Office, the UK's national weather service, uses it as an official weather station. One of the duties of the distillery manager is to take readings from the on-site meteorological station. Still within sight of the main A9 Perth to Inverness road through the Highlands, before the village of Dalwhinnie was bypassed in the 1970s it was located right next to the road. Dalwhinnie also used to be served by the adjacent Perth to Inverness railroad line courtesy of its own siding, but now all transportation is by road.

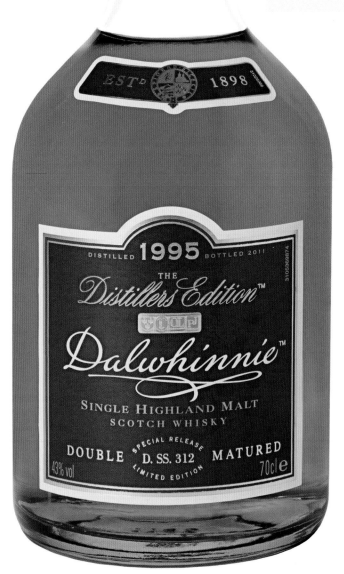

DALWHINNIE "DISTILLERS EDITION" (1995)

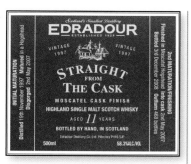

EDRADOUR 11-YEAR-OLD

EDRADOUR

OWNER Signatory Vintage Scotch Whisky Co. Ltd.
FOUNDED 1837 **CAPACITY** 29,000 gal (110,000 liters)
ADDRESS Balnauld, Pitlochry, Perthshire PH16 5JP
WEBSITE www.edradour.com

Given that its annual output is roughly equal to a week's production at one of the larger Speyside distilleries, it seems baffling that the "make" of Edradour was ever given over to blending rather than being treasured as a unique, boutique single malt. However, that was indeed the fate of most Edradour spirits until the distillery was acquired by its present owner, Andrew Symington of independent bottler Signatory Vintage Scotch Whisky Co. Ltd., in 2002.

The Edradour heritage
Edradour boasts a fascinating heritage pre-Symington, having received its first official mention in 1837. Along with Glenturret, it can be seen as one of the two surviving examples of the once-numerous Perthshire "farm distilleries" operating as a farmers' cooperative before being formalized as John MacGlashan & Co. in 1841.

In 1922, William Whiteley & Co. Ltd., a subsidiary of American distiller J. G. Turney & Sons, purchased Edradour to provide malt for its blends, including King's Ransom and House of Lords. Whiteley renamed the distillery Glenforres-Glenlivet, despite its remoteness from the famous glen.

At this point the history of Edradour becomes as colorful as its famous red paintwork, with Whiteley's blends being distributed in the US during the Prohibition era by Frank Costello, of Mafia fame, upon whom the *Godfather* movies were supposedly based. Indeed, there is strong evidence to suggest that Costello indirectly owned Edradour for a time from the late 1930s through his associate Irving Haim, via J. G. Turney & Sons.

In 1982 Edradour was acquired by the Pernod Ricard subsidiary Campbell Distilleries, which introduced Edradour as a 10-year-old single malt bottling four years later. But in 2002, Pernod Ricard declared Edradour surplus to requirements, following its acquisition of Seagram's extensive Scotch whiskey operations. Andrew Symington had been in the market for a distillery for some time and saw the potential in Edradour, as only 20 percent of the modest output was ever bottled as single malt under the Pernod Ricard regime.

Signatory and Symington
Des McCagherty is Symington's principal lieutenant at Edradour, where the whole Signatory operation is now housed. "The inventory we got with the distillery was really quite young," says

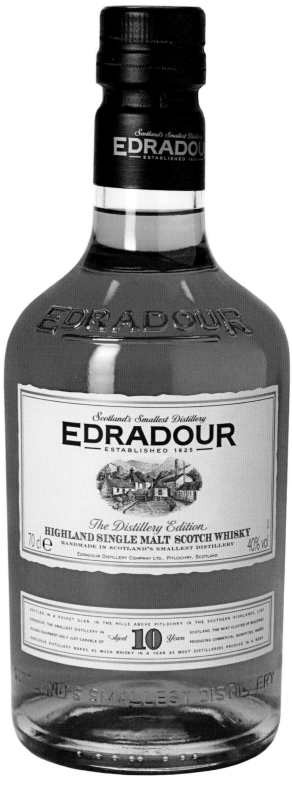

EDRADOUR 10-YEAR-OLD

EDRADOUR 12-YEAR-OLD "CALEDONIA"

McCagherty. "Previously, the House of Lords 12-year-old and five-year-old blends had taken up most of the output. We therefore had to service our growth ambitions for the core 10-year-old initially by branching out into wood finishes."

McCagherty adds, "Edradour was traditionally presented as a single malt with a sherry wood profile, but lots of the stock we acquired with the distillery was in ex-Bourbon casks because it had been destined for blending, so we have recasked much of it into sherry casks. The new-fill is mainly going into first-fill or second-fill sherry casks, with some into first-fill Bourbon and wine casks."

Peated Edradour

One significant innovation of the Signatory regime has been the introduction of a heavily peated spirit (over 50 ppm), named "Ballechin" after a long-lost nearby farm distillery. Des McCagherty explains the rationale thus: "The Islay sector is the fastest growing, and Iain Henderson, formerly of Laphroaig and later manager here, was of the view that the Edradour stills would produce good peated spirits. We did the first batch in 2003 and were very happy with it. Now 25 percent of our output is "Ballechin" and we are laying down stocks for a 15-, 18-, and 21-year-old lineup."

Edradour retains the sense of being a true distilling community, with Des McCagherty and Andrew Symington both occupying houses on site. Despite his official role as Managing

Picturesque Loch Tummel lies just west of Edradour, and is seen at its best from the "Queen's View" point.

Director and Chief Executive, Symington is usually found dressed in his trademark coveralls. "I like to get my hands dirty and enjoy chatting with visitors around the place," he says. "You can find me supervising the bottling line, being involved in the actual production, driving a forklift truck to move casks, or unblocking a drain. I can be found anywhere on the site except in the office. I never go in there!"

As well as a number of cask finishes, single cask and vintage expressions of Edradour have also been bottled. The permanent portfolio comprises the 10-year-old and 12-year-old "Caledonia," while new editions of "Ballechin" are regularly released.

TASTING NOTES

EDRADOUR 10-YEAR-OLD
single malt, 40% ABV, ex-sherry casks
Cider apples, malt, almonds, vanilla, and honey on the nose, along with a hint of smoke and sherry. The palate is rich, creamy, and malty, with leathery sherry and persistent nuttiness. Spices and sherry dominate the finish.

EDRADOUR 12-YEAR-OLD "CALEDONIA"
single malt, 46% ABV, finished 4 years in ex-Oloroso sherry casks
A plump, fruity nose, featuring figs, raisins, and a hint of cloves. Rich and full-bodied in the mouth, nutty and orangey, with plenty of attractive spice and a slowly drying, well-balanced finish.

EDRADOUR "BALLECHIN #6 BOURBON CASK"
single malt, 46% ABV
Sweet peat, maple, emerging subdued vanilla, and dried fruit on the nose. The palate offers more peat, earth, lemon, and berries. Hazelnuts, plain chocolate, and a sprinkling of salt in the bonfire-like finish.

EDRADOUR "BALLECHIN #6 BOURBON CASK"

FETTERCAIRN

OWNER Whyte & Mackay Ltd.

FOUNDED 1824 **CAPACITY** 608,000 gal (2.3m liters)

ADDRESS Distillery Road, Fettercairn, Laurencekirk,
Kincardineshire AB30 1YE **WEBSITE** www.whyteandmackay.com

FETTERCAIRN 13-YEAR-OLD 1991
"OLD MALT CASK" (DOUGLAS LAING)

For many years Fettercairn was a low-profile single malt with no shortage of detractors. The distillery itself is one of the most attractive and beautifully situated in the Highlands, with a dedicated and talented staff, yet it produced a whiskey that sometimes received less than flattering reviews—due in part to the use of stainless steel rather than copper condensers until 1995.

Then, in 2009, Whyte & Mackay addressed the problem of Fettercairn's image with sweeping changes to the range, introducing 24-, 30-, and 40-year-old vintages, followed in 2010 by Fettercairn "Fior" (meaning "pure" or "true" in Gaelic), a replacement for the existing 12-year-old. "Fior" comprises a significant amount of 14- and 15-year-old spirit along with 15 percent heavily peated five-year-old whiskey from first-fill Bourbon barrels, and it represented a sea change in the brand's profile in terms of perceived quality.

Fettercairn reformed

David Robertson, Whyte & Mackay's Director of Rare Whiskies, says of the revamp, "Fettercairn has always been a bit of a hidden gem for us and in 2009 we decided that the time was right to really make some more noise about this great whiskey. I think it's fair to say that some people had certain preconceptions about the whiskey from

Fettercairn, but Master Blender Richard Paterson and Distillery Manager Dave Doig have always been confident in the whiskey they produce there, which is why they introduced the new range. Since we brought out these new products we have seen an increase in positive chatter about the brand, as well as increased sales. The new range won over the majority of the press skeptics, and whiskey writers have been extremely positive about it."

Richard Paterson has been with Whyte & Mackay since 1970, and this third-generation blender is one of the highest-profile characters in the Scotch whiskey industry. "The real value of Fettercairn from a blending perspective is its uniqueness," says Paterson. "I can use it to give body, muscle, and structure to a blend when it is combined with Speyside single malts.

"Fettercairn is a truly Highland style of single malt of body and character. It's physically isolated from most other distilleries and it produces an individualistic whiskey. With "Fior" we tried to create something totally different by introducing the 15 percent peated component which had never been marketed before—we found that was just perfect for what we wanted. "Fior" has certainly done a lot to gain new converts for the brand."

The heavily peated component of "Fior" has been made on an annual basis for several years in line with Whyte & Mackay Ltd.'s policy of quietly distilling batches of peated malt at its operational distilleries, including those in Dalmore and Jura.

Nestled at the foot *of the Cairngorms, Fettercairn has received royal visitors including Queen Victoria.*

PORTRAIT OF A MARRIAGE

Fettercairn Distillery has been under the ownership of Glasgow-based blenders Whyte & Mackay Ltd. since 1973, so it is not surprising that it provides a significant proportion of the malt content for the company's popular family of blended Scotch whiskeys. Whyte & Mackay traces its origins back to 1844, and prides itself on a "double marriage" process in which the component single malts are married together and held in sherry butts for several months. This blended malt is mixed with up to six different grain whiskeys and returned to another set of sherry butts for further maturation prior to bottling.

Back in time

Fettercairn Distillery is unique in being equipped with two spirit stills that are cooled by the release of water externally onto the still necks, from where it flows down the bodies of the stills before being collected and recycled. This has the effect of increasing "reflux," leading to a cleaner and lighter spirit.

The distillery is located in the foothills of the Cairngorm Mountains, in an area once noted for illicit distilling, and dates back to 1824, when it was converted from a former corn mill by local landowner Sir Alexander Ramsay. It was first licensed to James Stewart & Co. the following year. In 1830, Ramsay sold his Fasque Estate, including the distillery, to Sir John Gladstone, father of the future four-times British prime minister William Ewart Gladstone.

The distillery effectively remained in the hands of the Gladstone family until its closure in 1926, after which, in 1939, it was purchased by Ben Nevis owner Joseph Hobbs of Associated Scottish Distillers Ltd.

The whiskey boom of the 1960s saw the number of stills at Fettercairn doubled to four in 1966, and five years later the distillery was acquired by the Tomintoul-Glenlivet Distillery Company Ltd. This company had been formed by the whiskey-broking firms of Hay & MacLeod & Company Ltd. and W. & S. Strong Ltd. to build Tomintoul Distillery during 1964–65. In 1973 Tomintoul-Glenlivet was purchased by Whyte & Mackay Ltd., which became part of Indian entrepreneur Vijay Mallya's United Breweries Group in 2007.

TASTING NOTES

FETTERCAIRN 13-YEAR-OLD SINGLE CASK DISTILLERY EXCLUSIVE
single malt, 58.2% ABV, distilled December 10, 1997, cask #7753, second-fill Oloroso sherry hogshead
A nose of toffee, orange marmalade, caramelized fruits, and licorice. Caramel, honey, pineapple, marzipan, and sherry on the smooth and substantial palate. Long and richly sherried in the finish.

FETTERCAIRN "FIOR"
single malt, 42% ABV, principally 14- and 15-year-old spirits, with 15% heavily peated five-year-old whiskey from first-fill Bourbon barrels
Sherry and smoke on the nose, with ginger, orange peel, toffee, and vanilla. Smoke on the palate, with orange, treacle toffee, dark chocolate, and a sherried nuttiness. Smoky toffee, licorice, and mildly spicy oak in finish.

FETTERCAIRN 30-YEAR-OLD
single malt, 43.3% ABV
Marmalade, plum jam, and toffee notes on the nose, plus hints of sherry. Pineapple, marzipan, and soft fudge on the rich, complex palate. Treacle toffee, licorice, and peat smoke in the long finish.

FETTERCAIRN "FIOR"

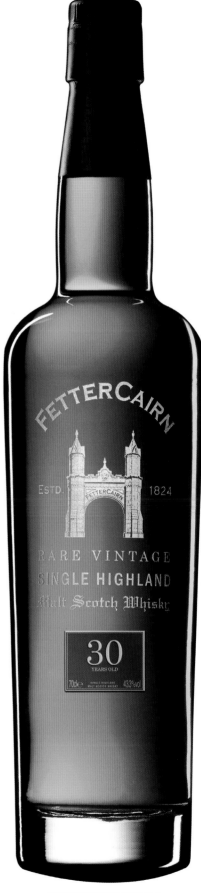

FETTERCAIRN 30-YEAR-OLD

GLENGARIOCH

OWNER Morrison Bowmore Distillers Ltd. (Suntory Ltd.)
FOUNDED 1797 **CAPACITY** 263,000 gal (1m liters)
ADDRESS Distillery Road, Oldmeldrum, Inverurie,
Aberdeenshire AB51 0ES **WEBSITE** www.glengarioch.com

GLEN GARIOCH 12-YEAR-OLD

GLEN GARIOCH "1797 FOUNDER'S RESERVE"

Glengarioch (pronounced "Glen-geery") is one of those lesser-known distilleries, being located some distance from a concentration of other whiskey-making operations and even from a major distilling region. For the purposes of classification, it produces an Eastern Highlands single malt, like Fettercairn, and in common with that distillery, Glengarioch is not on a major tourist trail either. It is, however, situated about 17 miles (27 km) from Aberdeen on the outskirts of the historic town of Oldmeldrum, which is popular with commuters working in Scotland's oil capital and is in the Valley of the Garioch, sometimes known as the "granary of Aberdeenshire" and renowned as the finest barley-growing area in Scotland.

Somewhat confusingly, while the distillery is known as "Glengarioch," the single malt it produces is always described as "Glen Garioch."

Early days

Glengarioch is one of the oldest distilleries in Scotland, the site originally incorporating a brewery and tannery also. As in so many cases, there's a degree of doubt about the actual date when distilling began on the present site, but the owners of Glengarioch have nailed their colors to the mast and declared 1797 to be its date of establishment, producing a "1797 Founder's Reserve" expression—though it has been claimed that whiskey-making could have been taking place at the distillery a dozen years earlier.

It's widely accepted that in 1798 the distillery was in the hands of one Thomas Simpson. Though the distillery owners declare that brothers John and Alexander Manson founded the plant, other sources have it that John Manson & Co. of the Strathmeldrum Distillery bought Glengarioch in 1837. What can be said with certainty is that in 1884, Glengarioch was acquired by the Leith blending firm J. G. Thomson & Co., with fellow Leith blender William Sanderson taking an interest in the distillery and its whiskey. Sanderson had launched his Vat 69 blend in 1882 and Glen Garioch went on to become the heart malt of this brand.

Sanderson gained ownership of Glengarioch in 1908 through the Glengarioch Distillery Company Ltd., which was bought by Booth's

Glengarioch has been the most easterly *distillery in Scotland since the closure of Glenugie in Peterhead in 1983.*

Distilleries Ltd. in 1933. Glengarioch then became part of the Distillers Company Ltd. when DCL acquired Booth's Distilleries Ltd. in 1937.

Silent spring

DCL closed Glengarioch in 1968, claiming there was insufficient water available for distillation, but two years later Bowmore Distillery's owner, Stanley P. Morrison Ltd., purchased the Oldmeldrum distillery and recommenced production.

The water issue was solved in 1972 when a spring was discovered on neighboring Coutens Farm, nicknamed "The Silent Spring of Coutens Farm" as it could not be seen or heard. What it did do, however, was to allow distillery output to be increased tenfold. Under the Morrison regime a third still was added in 1972, followed by a fourth in 1973, the same year in which the first official bottling of Glen Garioch took place.

The distillery's floor maltings were operational until the comparatively late date of 1993. A year later, what was now Morrison Bowmore Distillers Ltd. came under the total control of Japanese distillers Suntory Ltd., which had owned a 35 percent stake in the company since 1989.

Glen Garioch reborn

The distillery was silent from October 1995 to August 1997, but then in 2004 a 1958 expression of Glen Garioch appeared—the oldest bottling of the whiskey ever undertaken. The following year a visitors' center opened in the former cooperage, and around that time Glen Garioch sales peaked in the region of 250,000 bottles per year. In 2009 a radical revamp of the Glen Garioch range took place, with the distinctive

"tartan and stag" packaging dropped in favor of a more modern and restrained appearance. The existing lineup of 8-, 12-, 15-, and 21-year-old expressions was replaced by "1797 Founder's Reserve," without an age statement, a 12-year-old, and an ongoing program of annual vintage releases, beginning with 1978 and 1990, and followed by 1991, 1986, and 1994.

The older vintages display a significant difference in character from younger bottlings, due to the influence of the more heavily peated malt made on the distillery's floor maltings until 1993. The maltings remain intact and the distillery's owners have not ruled out the possibility of reinstating them at some future date.

Rare and fine

Morrison Bowmore's CEO Mike Keiller says, "With only small batches of hand-selected stock available worldwide, Glen Garioch leads the way in this new era of rarity within the whiskey arena. Suited to the enthusiast, the collector, and those with a genuine appreciation of craft and quality, Glen Garioch now complements the already successful single malt portfolio of Morrison Bowmore Distillers."

John Mullen, Glen Garioch Brand Manager, adds, "Quality and provenance are key to the positioning. For us, this has to start with the spirit itself. For example, with '1797 Founder's Reserve' our Senior Blender, Iain McCallum, was determined to craft an expression that could serve as a tribute to our visionary original distillery owners while doing something particularly special with a non-age-statement malt. With its fruity, sweet vanilla and spice flavor, we're convinced that we have remained true to our heritage."

TASTING NOTES

GLEN GARIOCH 12-YEAR-OLD
single malt, 48% ABV, non-chill-filtered
Sweet on the nose, focusing on fresh fruit—peaches and pineapple—plus vanilla, malt, and a hint of sherry. Full-bodied, with more fresh fruit on the palate, along with spice, brittle toffee, and finally quite dry oaky notes.

GLEN GARIOCH "1986 VINTAGE"
single malt, 54.6% ABV, cask strength, non-chill-filtered
Peaches and ginger on the nose, with fudge and a wisp of smoke. Full-bodied, rich, and sweet in the mouth, with fresh fruit and violet creams. Finally a slightly earthy, peaty note. The finish is long and gently smoky.

GLEN GARIOCH "1797 FOUNDER'S RESERVE"
single malt, 48% ABV, non-chill-filtered
A nose of soft fruits (pears, peaches, and apricots), together with butterscotch and vanilla. Quite full-bodied, with vanilla, malt, melon, and light smoke on the palate. The finish is clean and medium in length.

LEADER IN THE FIELDS

The dramatic rises in fuel costs in the 1970s led several distillers to develop energy-saving projects that prefigured more recent innovations in this field. At Glengarioch, a waste heat recovery system heated the malt kiln and preheated the wash prior to distillation, extending in 1977 to embrace 1 acre (4,000 sq m) of greenhouses and a similar area of hoop houses in which tomatoes, cucumbers, peppers, and eggplants were cultivated, along with flowers such as geraniums and tulips. In 1982, Glengarioch also became the first Scottish distillery to use North Sea gas for heating purposes.

GLEN GARIOCH "1986 VINTAGE"

GLENGOYNE

OWNER Ian Macleod Distillers Ltd.

FOUNDED 1833 **CAPACITY** 291,000 gal (1.1m liters)

ADDRESS Dumgoyne, near Killearn, Glasgow G63 9LB

WEBSITE www.glengoyne.com

Glengoyne could have reason to doubt its identity. Classified as being in the Highlands region for malt whiskey making, its production buildings do lie just that side of the theoretical "Highland Line." Once distilled, however, the spirits are transported across the A81 road to be matured in warehouses on the other side of the Line, in the Lowlands. Until the 1970s Glengoyne was categorized as a Lowland single malt, and the presence of three stills (one wash and two spirit) in the still house points toward the potential for a Lowland-like triple-distillation tendency. Furthermore, the distillery boasts a longstanding use of unpeated malt, and is sometimes compared with Auchentoshan in style.

Prolonged distillation

What really matters, of course, is the quality of the whiskey being distilled, and with single malt sales having grown dramatically in recent years, the Glengoyne team prides itself on both its use of unpeated malt and the slow rate of distillation.

Stuart Hendry, Brand Heritage and Commercial Manager, says, "Glengoyne has always distilled slowly. There are different ways to impart flavor to your new-make spirit. You can add most of the flavor at the start through the addition of peat at the drying stage in the malting process, or you can dry your barley with warm air, then use your stills to create flavor nuances in the unsmoked version. Most peaty distillers go at it hammer and tongs to get the spirit out of the stills as quickly as possible.

"Our way is to prolong copper contact for as long as possible, which strips out much of the sulfur. Copper also acts as a catalyst which brings together the sugars and amino acids created during fermentation to give a new range of molecularly light, intense, sweet, estery flavors. These we call 'early boilers' and they come across as soon as we start collecting. It's our desire to capture these flavor congeners that leads us to collect our middle cut so early."

Illicit origins?

Glengoyne sits just 12 miles (19 km) from Glasgow, but despite its comparative proximity to the city, the location in a wooded glen at the foot of Dumgoyne Hill could hardly be bettered. It was first licensed in 1833, but it's believed that distilling on the site predated official sanction; certainly the area was once a hotbed of smuggling.

GLENGOYNE "THE TEAPOT DRAM"

GLENGOYNE 12-YEAR-OLD "CASK STRENGTH"

The distillery was built by George Connell, who leased the land, and the license was held by members of the MacLellan family for many years. Originally christened Glenguin, the distillery was known as Burnfoot at the time it was bought by Lang Brothers Ltd. in 1876. They changed the name back to Glenguin, or Glen Guin, and the present spelling was adopted around 1905.

Bottlers take charge

A modernization program followed the acquisition of Lang by the Robertson & Baxter Group in 1965, and a third still was added during reconstruction work in 1966–67. Robertson & Baxter is now part of the Edrington Group, and under its ownership a great deal of Glengoyne found its way into Lang's Supreme and other blends. Then, in April 2003, the distillery, the Glengoyne and Lang's brand names, and a significant amount of maturing stock were acquired by Ian Macleod Distillers Ltd., old established blenders and bottlers but never previously owners of a distillery.

The new proprietors doubled output and began to market Glengoyne energetically as a single malt. As Stuart Hendry says, "Essentially, we don't cut corners, we buy the best barley that we can, we don't smoke it, we distill at a snail's pace and source sherry casks from our long-term partners in Jerez."

Principal bottlings available include 10-, 12-, 17-, and 21-year-old expressions, with the 12-year-old also available at cask strength along with a 13-year-old "Port Cask Finish." A variant by the name of "Burnfoot" without an age statement is offered in travel retail outlets. "The Teapot Dram," named after the copper teapot formerly used to dispense drams to the distillery workforce, is exclusively available to distillery visitors.

TASTING NOTES

GLENGOYNE 12-YEAR-OLD
single malt, 43% ABV
Malt and light honey on the nose, with nuts and citrus fruit; palate of spices, toffee, and chocolate orange. Consistent, medium finish with mellow oak and a hint of ginger.

GLENGOYNE 21-YEAR-OLD
single malt, 43% ABV, matured in first-fill European oak sherry casks
The nose offers immediate and accessible sherry, spices, and black treacle. Mouth-coating, bold, and sherried on the palate, with aromatic spice and nutty notes. Licorice and chocolate caramels dominate the finish.

GLENGOYNE "THE TEAPOT DRAM"
single malt, 58.8% ABV, cask strength, matured in five first-fill sherry casks 9–11 years old
The nose is spicy, with brown sugar, rosewater, dark chocolate, sherry, and a hint of pepper. Stewed fruits, almonds, and cinnamon on the big, oily palate. Long in the finish, with oak and licorice.

GLENGOYNE 21-YEAR-OLD

TOP TOURS

Just outside Glasgow and within relatively easy reach of Edinburgh, Glengoyne attracts around 40,000 visitors each year and offers one of the most comprehensive tour menus of any Scottish distillery. Five different options are available, ranging from the standard Glengoyne Tour up to the ultimate Glengoyne Masterclass, claimed to be the most in-depth and comprehensive distillery experience in Scotland. It includes presentations on new-make spirits, the maturation process, and grain whiskeys, and culminates in a hands-on whiskey blending session in the Sample Room. At the end of the visit, guests are presented with a small bottle of the blend they have created, along with a personalized bottle of Glengoyne 10-year-old and a certificate.

GLENMORANGIE

OWNER The Glenmorangie Company Ltd.	
FOUNDED 1843	**CAPACITY** 1.6m gal (6m liters)
ADDRESS Tain, Ross-shire IV19 1PZ	
WEBSITE www.glenmorangie.com	

Innovation is essential in a competitive commercial environment, although to an extent Scotch whiskey distillers are limited by the very specific terms of the legal definition of Scotch whiskey. However, that does not mean that within the industry clever minds are not coming up with innovative ideas and putting them into practice. A prime example of this is Glenmorangie's Bill Lumsden, Head of Distilling and Whisky Creation. Lumsden has a PhD in biochemistry, so he brings a solid science background to the business of creating whiskeys that stand out from the crowd yet have total integrity.

The whys and wherefores of wood

One of Bill Lumsden's particular areas of interest is wood management, and he declares, "My philosophy on wood is that it doesn't matter how good your new spirit is if you don't fill it into good-quality wood which is also sympathetic to the style of your whiskey. No other company has gone into such detail with their wood policy as Glenmorangie." Indeed, the distillery has gone so far as to buy an area of woodland in Missouri's Ozark Mountains, from where the wood for "designer casks" is sourced. These are used to mature some of the spirit that finds its way into various bottlings in the Glenmorangie portfolio.

Thanks in part to Lumsden's pioneering work with wood, Glenmorangie was the first single malt to offer its own bottlings of finished whiskey, initially from ex-port casks, and the brand has remained at the forefront of the process, working with a wide range of finishes, including Burgundy, Sauternes, Madeira, and sherry.

Early years

For the first 150 years of its existence, however, Glenmorangie offered one style of whiskey, in common with every other distillery in Scotland, though it used—and continues to use—hard water for processing, while most distilleries use soft.

Glenmorangie was developed between 1843 and 1849, when the first spirits flowed. Its founder was William Mathieson, who utilized existing elements of the defunct Morangie Brewery, and in 1887 the Glenmorangie Distillery Company Ltd. was formed. The plant was entirely rebuilt at that time, and Glenmorangie became the first distillery in Scotland to use steam to heat its stills rather than coal.

GLENMORANGIE 18-YEAR-OLD
The malt in this expression is first matured for 15 years in American white oak, with a portion transferred to ex-Oloroso casks for the remaining time.

THE TALLEST STILLS

Whiskey stills come in all shapes and sizes, and their many variations play a significant part in shaping the character of the spirits they produce. Perhaps no distillery has placed more emphasis on the individuality of its stills than Glenmorangie. One print advertising campaign carries an illustration of the vessels in question and declares, "There are a lot of perfectly good single malts made in shorter stills. We have the tallest stills in Scotland." They are based on the design of the original ex-gin stills from London, installed when the distillery was founded, and contribute significantly to the light, fruity, floral character of Glenmorangie.

GLENMORANGIE 10-YEAR-OLD "THE ORIGINAL"

Macdonald & Muir Ltd., owners of the Highland Queen blended brand, took a majority share in Glenmorangie in 1918, and the distillery went on to survive a period of closure in the mid-1930s.

Rising capacity

The more recent history of Glenmorangie has been notably positive, with the complement of stills being doubled from two to four during a reconstruction program in 1979, and doubled again just a decade later.

In 2004 Glenmorangie PLC, as it had now become, was bought by Louis Vuitton Moët Hennessy (LVMH) for £300 million ($540 million), placing Ardbeg, Glen Moray, and Glenmorangie distilleries in the hands of the French corporation. Today Glenmorangie is the second-best-selling single malt in the UK after Glenfiddich, and globally it occupies the number five position.

Innovation continues

As well as three wood finishes, "Lasanta" (sherry), "The Nectar d'Òr" (Sauternes), and "Quinta Ruban" (port), notable among the current core lineup is "Signet," one of Lumsden's proudest innovations. Twenty percent of its component whiskey is made from "chocolate" malt, matured 10 years in a combination of ex-Bourbon and new oak casks, then blended with other Glenmorangie whiskeys, some up to 35 years old, from a variety of cask types, including sherry and wine. Lumsden is also responsible for the "Private Collection" bottlings, including "Sonnalta PX" (finished in ex–Pedro Ximénez sherry casks), "Finealta" (containing some whiskey from lightly peated malt and whiskey of varying ages, matured in a mix of ex-sherry casks and plain, new American oak), and "Pride 1981."

GLENMORANGIE "THE NECTAR D'ÒR"

TASTING NOTES

GLENMORANGIE 10-YEAR-OLD "THE ORIGINAL"
single malt, 40% ABV
Fresh fruit, butterscotch, and toffee on the nose. Smooth palate of nuts, spice, vanilla honey, Jaffa oranges, and hard toffee. Fruity in the finish, with a hint of ginger.

GLENMORANGIE "SIGNET"
single malt, 46% ABV
A nose of rich fruit, honey, marmalade, maple, sherry, sweet oak, and spice. Lots of fruit and spice on the palate, with dark chocolate, vanilla, and leather. The finish is spicy and medium in length.

GLENMORANGIE "PRIDE 1981"
single malt, 56.7% ABV, cask strength, matured 18 years in ex-Bourbon casks, 10 years in Sauternes barriques
An intense, pungent, earthy nose, with polished furniture, spices, oak tannins, and licorice. Waxy palate with sherbet, honey, baked apples, orange marmalade, raisins, and a hint of smoke in the lengthy finish.

GLENMORANGIE "SIGNET"

GLENMORANGIE "PRIDE 1981"

GLENTURRET

OWNER The Edrington Group	
FOUNDED 1775 **CAPACITY** 79,000 gal (300,000 liters)	
ADDRESS The Hosh, Crieff, Perthshire PH7 4HA	
WEBSITE www.thefamousgrouse.com	

If the visitor to Glenturret is in any doubt as to the primary focus of this distillery, a vast sculpture of a grouse at the entrance to the parking lot provides a clue, while a sign above the main door declares "The Famous Grouse Experience at Glenturret Distillery."

Glenturret has been one of Scotland's most popular whiskey-related destinations since becoming the brand home of The Famous Grouse blend in 2002, though it already boasted a well-used visitors' center prior to what might be termed its rebranding. The distillery's new role included the installation of *The Flight of the Grouse*, a state-of-the-art, award-winning interactive show, which was significantly upgraded in 2008, when $500,000 was spent on even more advanced interactive technology. The brand's marketing focus is now based around the trio of "Snow Grouse," "Naked Grouse," and "Black Grouse" in addition to the standard blend, and the Taste Experience area has been introducing visitors to the "Famous Family" since 2010.

Home of the Grouse
The Edrington Group, which owns The Famous Grouse and is principal owner of Glenturret Distillery, wanted a location in Perthshire for the brand home of their best-selling blend. "Glenturret had a genuine connection to The Famous Grouse as it was a working Perthshire distillery whose single malt was a contributor to the blend," says Ken Grier, Director of Malts. He also admits that The Edrington Group would probably no longer retain the distillery in its portfolio if The Famous Grouse Experience did not exist, with the Group having sold off distilleries such as Bunnahabhain, Glengoyne, and Tamdhu over the years.

Glenturret receives little promotion as a single malt. Grier explains, "It's a small distillery with limited output, and we have two major single malt brands in Highland Park and The Macallan which we focus on." In 2003 a 10-year-old expression of Glenturret single malt replaced the existing 12-year-old as the principal version, and a number of single cask bottlings have since been released.

Distilling details
For the connoisseur of historic distilleries, however, Glenturret has much to commend it, being equipped with a unique open mash tun in which there are no rakes or stirring equipment. A wooden pole is used to turn the contents by hand. The pair of manually controlled stills is run very slowly, processing

THE GLENTURRET 10-YEAR-OLD

THE GLENTURRET 29-YEAR-OLD

Glenturret lies just east of the Trossachs, *a gentle
landscape of wooded hills and peaceful lochs.*

around 2 gallons (9 liters) per minute, whereas some
distilleries would double that rate of throughput.
The wash still is equipped with a large boil ball,
giving a significant amount of reflux and copper
interaction. Combined with the slow rate of
distillation, following lengthy fermentation in
wooden washbacks, this makes for fruity, floral
notes in the spirit being produced.

Around half of the 40,000–52,000 gallons
(150,000–200,000 liters) currently being distilled
each year is made from malt peated to 80–120 ppm,
and this is destined to feature in the peaty "Black
Grouse" variant. "From the point of view of
integrity we want some Glenturret in The Famous
Grouse blend, although the quantity is necessarily
small," says Ken Grier. "A lot of effort is going
into promoting "Black Grouse", and the peated
Glenturret malt means we will be less reliant
on buying in peated malt."

Famous heritage

The sign above the main door describes Glenturret
as "Scotland's oldest distillery," established in 1775.
Certainly illicit distilling took place there at that
time, and it was first licensed to John Drummond,
under the name Hosh, in 1818, with the Glenturret
name being adopted in 1875. The distillery closed
in 1921 and eight years later the equipment was
dismantled, with the buildings subsequently being
used for agricultural storage. Glenturret remained
silent until businessman James Fairlie acquired the

premises in 1957 and reequipped it for distilling,
with production starting two years later. Ownership
passed to Remy-Cointreau in 1981, with Highland
Distillers taking over nine years later. In 1999 The
Edrington Group and William Grant & Sons Ltd.
purchased Highland Distillers, operating as
The 1887 Company, with Edrington owning
70 percent of the shares.

The grouse sculpture is a relatively recent
addition to the distillery, but another animal has
been immortalized for much longer. A bronze
bust commemorates the achievements of Towser,
the former distillery cat, who earned a place in
The Guinness Book of Records by accounting for
28,899 mice during her 24 years at the distillery.

TASTING NOTES

THE GLENTURRET 10-YEAR-OLD
single malt, 40% ABV
Nutty and slightly oily on the nose, with barley and citrus
fruits. Sweet and honeyed on the full, fruity palate, with a
balancing note of oak. Medium length in the sweet finish.

THE GLENTURRET 16-YEAR-OLD
single malt, 58.4% ABV, single cask, cask-strength
Spice, vanilla fudge, and honey on the sweet, malty nose.
The palate continues the honey and malt themes,
along with barley and a hint of cocoa. Spicy oak
and milk chocolate in the lengthy finish.

THE GLENTURRET 29-YEAR-OLD
single malt, 55.6% ABV, single cask, cask-strength
A delicate nose, fragrant, with lemonade and vanilla.
Floral on the palate, with hay, honey, spicy oak,
and wood tannins. The finish is medium in length,
with toffee and developing oak.

THE FAMOUS GROUSE

OBAN

OWNER Diageo PLC	
FOUNDED 1794	**CAPACITY** 177,000 gal (670,000 liters)
ADDRESS Stafford Street, Oban, Argyll PA34 5NH	
WEBSITE www.discovering-distilleries.com	

John and Hugh Stevenson were local entrepreneurs in the Oban area, establishing a boat-building business, a tannery, and a brewery, with the brewery being converted into a distillery by 1794. This places Oban among a historically elite group of working Scottish distilleries that have their roots in the 18th century.

The Stevensons' business ventures, which included slate quarries, made a significant contribution to paving the way for the development of Oban that was to take place over the next century, as Victorian steamers began to use Oban as a regular port of call and the railroad arrived in the town during 1880.

Hugh Stevenson's son, Thomas, left Oban to farm in Buenos Aires, but returned after the death of his father in order to purchase the distillery and the slate-quarrying enterprise. He was also responsible for constructing Oban's grandiose Caledonian Hotel, but financial difficulties caused by supporting his brother's printing business led to a situation where creditors were paid in whiskey and slates.

A change of hands

Oban distillery remained in the Stevenson family until 1866, when it was bought by Peter Cumstie, who sold it to James Walter Higgen in 1882.

Higgen rebuilt the distillery between 1890 and 1894, but managed to continue producing spirits while doing so, due to its great demand. While many of today's most prestigious single malts spent much of their history as "blending fodder," Oban enjoyed strong sales as a single malt from the 1880s onward.

Ownership of Oban passed to Oban & Aultmore Glenlivet Distilleries Ltd. in 1898, with the Oban Distillery Company Ltd., held by Buchanan-Dewar, gaining ownership in 1923. Buchanan-Dewar went on to become part of the Distillers' Company Ltd. two years later.

DCL days and onward

Oban was one of numerous Scottish distilleries to endure a period of silence during the economically depressed interwar years, closing from 1931 until 1937. Between 1968 and 1972, however, the distillery underwent a major refurbishment program, with its floor maltings ceasing to operate at that time.

Although the distillery had been refurbished, there was physically very little room to expand operations due to the constricted nature of the site, and even if DCL had wanted to add more stills, this was not a feasible option.

Accordingly, today's distillery still has just one pair of lantern-shaped stills, among the smallest in Scotland, and Oban's output is the second-lowest in the Diageo portfolio after Royal Lochnagar.

Known as "Gateway to the Isles," *the town of Oban is the main ferry terminal for many Hebridean islands.*

OBAN "MANAGERS' CHOICE"

The stills are actually large enough to produce more spirits per annum than is currently being achieved, but are unable to do so due to the fact that the character of Oban single malt is dependent upon long fermentation times of up to 110 hours, which limits production to six mashes per week. Diageo's Mike Tough explains that "the lengthy fermentation time ensures we obtain the light character required in our spirit."

All of the precious Oban spirit is currently earmarked for single malt bottling, and a 14-year-old Oban expression was one of the "founding fathers" of United Distillers' Classic Malts range in 1988, with a dedicated visitors' center opening the following year.

In 1998 an Oban "Distillers Edition" was introduced, employing Montilla Fino sherry wood for a secondary period of maturation. Montilla Fino sherries are light in color and dry and salty in character, which makes them an ideal match for Oban with its salty, slightly peaty characteristics.

A limited edition of the oldest Oban to be bottled to date by its proprietors appeared in 2002, in the form of a 32-year-old expression, followed two years later by a 20-year-old. Subsequently, a "Managers' Choice" bottling of 2000 whiskey, matured in a European oak bodega butt, was added to the lineup, while 2010 saw the arrival of a distillery-exclusive variant, which carries no age statement. Like the "Distillers Edition," it is finished in ex-fino sherry casks.

If seeking out a bottle of this distillery-exclusive, the distillery itself is impossible to miss. Fronting Oban Bay, it is set into the base of a steep cliff, above which rises the unfinished folly of McCaig's Tower, the philanthropic venture of a local banker, constructed in 1897 to provide local employment.

TASTING NOTES

OBAN 14-YEAR-OLD
single malt, 43% ABV
The nose offers soft smoke, heather honey, toffee, and a whiff of seashore. Spicy, cooked fruits on the palate, with malt, oak, and a little smoke. The finish is rounded and aromatic, with spices and oak.

OBAN "DISTILLERS EDITION" (1995)
single malt, 43% ABV, finished in ex-fino sherry casks
Rich, spicy, confident, with caramel, milk chocolate, orange, and smoke on the nose. Spicy chocolate, malt, rich fruit, and brine on the palate. The fruit and salt linger though a long finish.

OBAN "DISTILLERY EXCLUSIVE"
single malt, 55.2% ABV, cask strength, finished in ex-fino sherry casks
Honey, fudge, sherry, cloves, and a hint of smoke on the nose. Gently spicy on the palate, with Jaffa oranges and an edge of subtle salt and smoke. Oak, ginger, and cloves in the lengthy finish.

GATEWAY TO THE ISLES

Oban distillery stands proudly in the center of the town from which it takes its name, and this is no accident, for the town actually grew up around the distillery. *An t-Òban* or "The Little Bay" in Gaelic, Oban was originally a small fishing village before the founding of the distillery and arrival of the railroad turned it into a busy port, handling wool and slate shipments, as well as whiskey. Today Oban is the largest population center in the West Highlands, a magnet for visitors and also a busy ferry port in its role as "Gateway to the Isles." Oban is the principal ferry terminal for Mull, Coll, Tiree, Colonsay, Barra, and South Uist. Not surprisingly, Oban distillery is notably popular among visitors, receiving in excess of 30,000 per year.

OBAN "DISTILLERS EDITION" (1995)

OBAN 14-YEAR-OLD

PULTENEY

OWNER	Inver House Distillers Ltd. (Thai Beverage PLC)
FOUNDED 1826	**CAPACITY** 449,000 gal (1.7m liters)
ADDRESS	Huddart Street, Wick, Caithness KW1 5BA
WEBSITE	www.oldpulteney.com

In the hands of current owners Inver House Distillers Ltd., Old Pulteney single malt has been a notable success story, rising from relative obscurity to become a global performer in little more than a decade. In 2011 the brand enjoyed a sales growth in excess of 60 percent in the UK, combined with significant sales increases in key international arenas.

Maritime malt

Marketed as "The Genuine Maritime Malt," the Old Pulteney brand makes good use of its home town's fascinating fishing-related heritage, given added relevance by the subtle briny characteristic present in most expressions of the whiskey. The packaging of Old Pulteney is designed to reflect its home town's fishing history, bearing a prominent image of a herring drifter on both bottle and carton. While Scotland's northernmost distillery is always known as Pulteney, its single malt has long had the prefix "Old" attached to it.

The distillery has an urban location in the Pulteneytown district of Wick, an area named after Sir William Pulteney, a governor of the British Fisheries Society, which created the settlement of Pulteneytown and a capacious harbor alongside the existing burgh of Wick during the early years of the 19th century.

Drunk as a herring

The herring industry may have made Wick its fortune, but it also contributed to a significant degree of drunkenness among the population. Indeed, it was estimated that during the 1840s, a staggering 590 gallons (2,230 liters) of whiskey was being consumed in the port each day during the height of the herring fishing season.

Certainly some of that whiskey was being supplied by Pulteney distillery, which had been established in 1826 by James Henderson, who had previously distilled at Stemster, near Halkirk. After almost a century of operation, Pulteney was acquired by the Dundee blending firm of James Watson & Company Ltd. in 1920.

Five years later, Watson's was absorbed into the mighty Distillers Company Ltd., and in 1930 production ceased at Pulteney. Not only was the world in the grip of the Great Depression, but Pulteney had the added problem of being a whiskey distillery located in the middle of an ostensibly "dry" town.

WHISKEY TALES...

THE DRY TOWN

Prohibition will forever be closely associated with the United States and its 1930s period of bootleggers, speakeasies, and "the real McCoy." Yet Scotland had its very own era of prohibition—or, to be precise, the burgh of Wick did, being declared dry between 1925 and 1947. This ban resulted from opposition to the hard-drinking reputation of the town during the 19th and early 20th centuries, when Wick was at the center of the herring fishing industry, whose hard workers also tended to be hard drinkers. Wick may have officially been dry, but at least one illicit still supplied the town with whiskey, while a café on Bridge Street served it to diners in an ornate silver teapot.

OLD PULTENEY 12-YEAR-OLD

Pulteney revived

Pulteney was silent until 1951, when it was owned, along with Balblair, by Banff-based lawyer Robert "Bertie" Cumming. However, the lure of Canadian gold was too much for Cumming, who sold out to Hiram Walker, which was eager to expand its Scotch whiskey interests in the postwar period. A comprehensive rebuilding program was undertaken during 1958–59, resulting in the external appearance of the distillery as it is today. Allied Breweries Ltd. bought Pulteney in 1961, and operated it until what was then Allied Domecq sold the distillery and single malt brand to Inver House Distillers Ltd. in 1995.

Two years later, a 12-year-old official bottling was released, and that remains the core bottling, along with 17- and 21-year-olds, introduced in 2004 and 2005 respectively, while a 30-year-old appeared in 2009, followed in 2012 by a 40-year-old, the most ancient expression released by the distillery. Visitors to the Pulteney distillery have the opportunity to personally fill, seal, and purchase a bottle of whiskey from one of several unique single casks usually available.

In 2010, Pulteney introduced into the travel retail arena an expression with no age statement called "WK499 Isabella Fortuna," which takes its name from the one of the last surviving herring drifters, built in 1890 and now preserved by the Wick Society. This was followed in 2012 by "WK209," matured in European sherry casks and named after another herring drifter, WK209 *Good Hope*, built in Wick during 1948. These bottlings further reinforce Pulteney's role as the "Genuine Maritime Malt" and with the same marketing position in mind, the brand teamed up with adventurer Jock Wishart on his "Row to the Pole" expedition to the magnetic North Pole in 2011.

Each May, Pulteney hosts a Prohibition Ball, instituted in 2007 and intended to celebrate the repeal of "prohibition" in Wick during May 1947, with proceeds being donated to a local charity. The Prohibition Ball has been a great success, but around the time of its inauguration there were high hopes that an ambitious biomass, wood-burning power source at Pulteney distillery would provide cheap fuel to local homes, businesses, and even Caithness General Hospital; this plan rather obscurely ended in failure.

Gunn on Pulteney

Twentieth-century Scottish novelist, nationalist, and one-time excise officer Neil M. Gunn was a native of Caithness, and writing in his 1935 book *Whisky and Scotland*, Gunn declared, "I must say something of Pulteney—the whisky of my native county—Old Pulteney as it was always called,

OLD PULTENEY 17-YEAR-OLD

OLD PULTENEY 21-YEAR-OLD

though I have childhood memories of seeing it perfectly white and certainly new. In those days it was potent stuff, consumed, I should say, on the quays of Wick more for its effect than its flavor! When I got of an age to understand Old Pulteney, I could admire its quality when well matured, recognizing in it some of the strong characteristics of the northern temperament." Old Pulteney is sometimes referred to as the "Manzanilla of the North" because its clean, salty style evokes the type of sherry also produced in proximity to the sea.

Sawn-off still

Pulteney distillery is equipped with a single pair of highly individual stills, with condensing taking place in a pair of stainless steel worm tubs. Both stills boast large "boil balls," which encourage reflux, while the dramatically truncated, flat-topped appearance of the wash still is said to have resulted from an incident many years ago when a new still was fabricated for the distillery but turned out to be too tall to fit. The solution was to have a coppersmith remove the top and seal it. There seems to be no proof of this tale, but no alternative explanation for the still's appearance either, and the roof of the stillhouse has since been raised in height.

The overall effect of the prevailing distilling regimen is to produce a relatively oily new-make spirit, some 95 percent of which is filled into ex-Bourbon casks if being retained by the distillers, while approximately 40 percent is sold on for blending purposes and is removed from the site by tanker. Around 24,000 casks can be retained in five on-site warehouses.

TASTING NOTES

OLD PULTENEY 12-YEAR-OLD
single malt, 40% ABV
The nose presents fresh malt and floral notes, with a touch of pine. The palate offers a sweet whiskey, with more malt, spices, fresh fruit, and a suggestion of salt. The finish is lightly drying and nutty.

OLD PULTENEY 21-YEAR-OLD
single malt, 46% ABV, matured in a mix of ex-fino sherry casks and former Bourbon barrels, non-chill-filtered
Vanilla, furniture polish, and old leather on the nose. Full-bodied, balanced, and smooth, with fresh fruits, more vanilla, honey, and dry sherry on the spicy palate. The finish is silky and long.

OLD PULTENEY 30-YEAR-OLD
single malt, 44% ABV, matured in American oak barrels, non-chill-filtered
The nose is sweet and malty, with delicate vanilla, tropical fruits, and ripe peaches. The palate is voluptuous, with more fruit, honey, and a hint of wood. The finish is long, with spicy oak.

ROYAL LOCHNAGAR

OWNER Diageo PLC
FOUNDED 1823 **CAPACITY** 92,000 gal (349,000 liters)
ADDRESS Crathie, Aberdeenshire AB35 5TB
WEBSITE www.discovering-distilleries.com

Lochnagar distillery was established south of the Dee River in 1845 by John Begg. It was built on the opposite side of the river from a distillery that had been created by James Robertson of Crathie in 1826 and was destroyed by fire in 1841, though that whiskey-making operation was rebuilt the following year and remained in production until 1860.

Royal seal of approval

Begg christened his distillery "New Lochnagar," and his fledgling enterprise was blessed with a great stroke of luck when Queen Victoria purchased the Balmoral Estate close by in 1848. With sights set high, John Begg soon invited Prince Albert to visit Lochnagar, keenly aware of the Prince's fondness for technology.

The day after this invitation was dispatched, Queen Victoria, Prince Albert, and their three eldest children duly visited Begg's establishment, with Prince Albert declaring, "We have come to see through your work, Mr. Begg."

As part of her fascination with all things Highland, Queen Victoria was not averse to taking a dram herself, was once observed by Prime Minister William Gladstone mixing whiskey with her claret, and at times also had whiskey served from a teapot. Accordingly, John Begg received a Royal Warrant of Appointment as a supplier to the Queen, enabling him to style his distillery Royal Lochnagar.

Changing times

The plant was substantially rebuilt in 1906, and a decade later passed out of the Begg family, being acquired by John Dewar & Sons Ltd. When Dewar's became part of Distillers Company Ltd. in 1925, Lochnagar entered the DCL fold.

Another major program of refurbishment and reconstruction took place in 1963, when the tun room was enlarged, the still house altered, and a mechanical stoking system for the pair of stills was installed. Remarkably, until that time a steam engine and waterwheels had powered the distillery plant, but these were replaced by electrical equipment.

In 1987 the old farmstead was converted into a visitors' center, while 11 years later a shop was developed in the center, providing a showcase for the Diageo Malts portfolio, which includes a number of rare whiskeys. At the same time, Lochnagar became home to the Malt Advocates Course, which provides company employees and selected guests with the opportunity to gain detailed knowledge of all stages of whiskey production and marketing.

Royal Lochnagar is the smallest of Diageo's 28 malt distilleries, and operates a cast-iron mash tun, complete with rakes, a pair of wooden

Royal Lochnagar has pride of place *as the distillery closest to Balmoral, the Royal Family's summer home.*

ROYAL LOCHNAGAR "SELECTED RESERVE"

ROYAL LOCHNAGAR "DISTILLERS EDITION"

washbacks, and cast iron worm tubs to condense the spirits. Unusually for Diageo, casks are filled on site, rather than spirits being tankered away to a centralized filling facility, and up to 1,000 casks are stored in the single distillery warehouse.

Why Lochnagar?

Because of the modest size of the enterprise, making spirits at Lochnagar is significantly more expensive than at larger distilleries, where economies of scale come into play, but the survival of relatively small distilleries is highly significant in rural areas, which often have quite fragile economic environments

Nonetheless, one may question why Diageo persists in retaining distilleries like Lochnagar, apart from the prestigious, if understated, royal connections. The answer, according to Diageo's Knowledge & Heritage Director, Dr. Nick Morgan, is that "we have 28 distilleries, and a number of them might be considered to be 'expensive,' either because of size, location, or the additional costs associated with the way we choose to make whiskey, like using traditional worm tubs at nine of our sites. But we make whiskey this way to ensure that we deliver the variety of characters that our blenders need to make great whiskeys like Johnnie Walker. Regardless of size, or royal connections, Lochnagar has an important place in the blender's tool kit, which is why we still make whiskey there."

Much of the make of Lochnagar is destined for the more exclusive Johnnie Walker bottlings, while the principal single malt is a 12-year-old, along with "Selected Reserve," which contains a vatting of whiskies around 20 years of age, and a "Distillers Edition" variant, introduced in 2008.

TASTING NOTES

ROYAL LOCHNAGAR 12-YEAR-OLD
single malt, 43% ABV
Sherry, malt, vanilla, coffee, and oak on the aromatic nose, along with a wisp of smoke. Lots of spicy malt, grapes, molasses, and later oak on the palate. Drying oak and peat feature in the finish.

ROYAL LOCHNAGAR "SELECTED RESERVE"
single malt, 43% ABV
Malt, sherry, green apples, and peat on the rich nose. The richness carries over onto the palate, which features flavors of fruit cake, ginger, malt, and fudge. The elegant finish showcases toffee and smoke.

ROYAL LOCHNAGAR "DISTILLERS EDITION" (VINTAGE 1998)
single malt, 40% ABV, matured for a secondary period in Muscat casks
Fruit malt loaf, almonds, and a hint of leather on the nose. Sweet and rounded on the palate, with raisins dipped in honey. Graham crackers and dates in the medium-length finish.

ROYAL LOCHNAGAR 12-YEAR-OLD

OLD MAN OF LOCHNAGAR

Royal Lochnagar distillery is located in magnificent countryside on what has become known as "Royal Deeside." The buildings stand close to the bulk of the mountain of Lochnagar, which features in the illustrated children's book *The Old Man of Lochnagar*, written by none other than Prince Charles, heir to the British throne. The Prince has spent a great deal of time in close proximity to the distillery, as the Royal Family's home of Balmoral is less than a mile (1.5 km) away, and His Royal Highness makes no secret of the fact that he feels more at home on the Balmoral Estate than almost anywhere else in the world. Given his fondness for fine single malt, he has been known to make occasional low-key visits to Lochnagar distillery.

TULLIBARDINE

OWNER Tullibardine Distillery Ltd.
FOUNDED 1949 **CAPACITY** 713,000 gal (2.7m liters)
ADDRESS Stirling Street, Auchterarder, Perthshire PH4 1QG
WEBSITE www.tullibardine.com

Consistently topping the list of Scotland's most-visited distilleries, Tullibardine saw no fewer than 120,000 people pass through its doors in 2010. Part of the distillery's popularity is due to its location alongside the busy A9 road that connects the city of Glasgow with Perth, and in addition to the distillery itself and associated café and visitor center, the site on the outskirts of the village of Blackford also houses a number of prominent retail outlets.

Although the present distillery, built on the site of an ancient brewery, only dates from 1949, whiskey-making had previously been conducted under the Tullibardine name in this area of Perthshire during the late 18th and early 19th centuries. Today's Tullibardine distillery was designed by William Delmé-Evans—who went on to create the Isle of Jura and Glenallachie distilleries—and it was operated by Brodie Hepburn Ltd. from 1953 until 1971, when that Glasgow whiskey-broking firm was taken over by Invergordon Distillers Ltd.

Tullibardine's capacity was subsequently increased by the installation of a second pair of stills in 1973, and when Invergordon was acquired by Whyte & Mackay Distillers Ltd. in 1993, the Perthshire plant was considered surplus to requirements, closing the following year.

A new presence in the marketplace
Happily for Tullibardine, however, a business consortium bought the site from Whyte & Mackay Ltd. for $1.8 million in 2003. A retail development was created alongside the distillery and this was subsequently sold to a property development company, leaving Tullibardine Distillery Ltd. to get on with the business of resuming whiskey-making and establishing a credible presence in the marketplace.

Accordingly, Tullibardine became well known for releasing an apparently ever-widening range of cask-finished whiskeys. As International Sales Manager James Robertson explains, "The reason for releasing cask finishes in the first place was because we had a gap in our inventory for the years between 1995 and 2003 when there was no production."

"The finishes gave the distillery the chance to sell a range of malts, and we went down the route of releasing vintages, starting with 1993, to avoid confusion with the old 10-year-old

bottling, which had been sold during the Whyte & Mackay era. We wanted to start afresh."

Aware that the quality of early finishes tended to be somewhat variable, and the portfolio potentially confusing, a decision was made around 2007 to concentrate on five core finishes, which now embrace sherry, port, rum, Sauternes, and Banyuls.

"Where possible we are stating the name of the specific vineyard which supplied the casks in question," says Robertson, "and in addition to the core finishes we will always offer a new one each year that is interesting and unusual."

While the finished single malts formerly contained 1992- or 1993-distilled whiskey, a switch has now been made to using five-year-old spirits, allowing a reduction in price, which places the finished single malts between the entry level "Aged Oak" and the vintage expressions in terms of cost.

A French Scotch whiskey
After operating in the hands of a consortium of businessmen since 2003, Tullibardine distillery was purchased in 2011 by the third-generation family-owned French company Maison Michel Picard, based in Chassagne Montrachet, Burgundy. Maison Michel Picard was an existing customer for the distillery's new-make spirits, which it used for its own-brand whiskey business, and virtually all of Tullibardine's output not intended for single malt bottlings is now destined for Picard's popular Highland Queen and Muirhead brands, which it acquired from the Glenmorangie Company Ltd. in 2008. In addition to owning vineyards, Maison Michel Picard also operates four distilleries in France.

TASTING NOTES

TULLIBARDINE "AGED OAK EDITION"
single malt, 40% ABV, ex-Bourbon casks
The nose exhibits barley, light citrus fruits, Juicy Fruit gum, marzipan, and cocoa. Oily in the mouth, slightly earthy, with Brazil nuts and developing vanilla and lemon on the palate. The finish is drying, with lingering spices.

TULLIBARDINE "VINTAGE 1988"
single malt, 46% ABV, non-chill-filtered
Fresh and citric on the nose, with some honey. Full-bodied, smooth, and fruity in the mouth, with a syrupy finish in which the sweetness of white chocolate persists along with spice.

TULLIBARDINE "BANYULS FINISH"
single malt, 46% ABV, matured ex-Bourbon cask, finished ex-Coume del Mas Banyuls red wine casks
Sweet and fragrant on the nose, with rose hips, cream toffee, and a hint of damp earth. Mouth-coating and spicy, with wild berries. Fruity in the finish, with raspberries, black currants, and milk chocolate. Ultimately drying oak.

TULLIBARDINE "VINTAGE 1988"

TULLIBARDINE 15-YEAR-OLD

TULLIBARDINE "AGED OAK EDITION"

TULLIBARDINE "BANYULS FINISH"

BALBLAIR

OWNER Inver House Distillers Ltd. (Thai Beverages PLC)
FOUNDED 1790 **CAPACITY** 370,000 gal (1.4m liters)
ADDRESS Edderton, Tain, Ross-shire IV19 1LB
WEBSITE www.balblair.com

Attractively located overlooking the Dornoch Firth, Balblair is one of the most northerly of the mainland distilleries in Scotland. It also has a claim to being one of the oldest surviving whiskey-making plants in Scotland, with the year of its founding given as 1790. In reality, however, the present distillery actually dates from the 1890s, with the 18th-century original being located ½ mile (800 m) away.

Farm origins

That original was the work of John Ross of Balblair Farm, and the distillery remained in the Ross family until 1894, with major rebuilding taking place in 1872. Despite that program of reconstruction, when Inverness wine merchant Alexander Cowan took on the lease of Balblair distillery from its owners, the Balnagowan Estate, the plant was relocated to its present site during 1894–95, taking advantage of the adjacent railroad line to facilitate the import of raw materials and the export of casks of whiskey. Despite relocating, Balblair has continued to draw upon the same soft water source since its 18th-century foundation, in the form of the Allt Dearg stream (pronounced "jerak" and meaning "red burn"), which flows down from the hills behind the distillery.

A dram back on track

Balblair was silent from 1915 until 1947, when Banff solicitor Robert "Bertie" Cumming purchased it, restarting distilling two years later after investing significantly in upgrading the distillery and increasing output. When Cumming retired in 1970, he sold Balblair to the Canadian distiller Hiram Walker & Sons Ltd. Hiram Walker merged with Allied Vintners to become Allied Distillers in 1988, and Allied sold Balblair to Inver House eight years later.

In 2007 the Balblair range was given a radical shake-up by Inver House, which removed the existing Balblair Elements (with no age statement) and 10- and 16-year-old expressions and instigated a program of vintage releases in their place, complete with dramatically restyled packaging. New vintages are released as stocks of existing ones become depleted, and the current lineup comprises 2001, 1989, and 1978 vintages.

BALBLAIR "VINTAGE 2001"

TASTING NOTES

BALBLAIR "VINTAGE 2001"
single malt, 46% ABV, ex-Bourbon barrels, non-chill-filtered
The nose offers lemonade, vanilla, allspice, and developing caramel notes. Sweet and spicy, with tangerines, apples, toffee, and milk chocolate on the palate. Cocoa powder in the spicy, relatively lengthy finish.

BALBLAIR 12-YEAR-OLD "SINGLE PEATY CASK"
single malt, 61% ABV, cask strength, ex-Bourbon cask previously filled with an Islay malt
Freshly cut peat, new oak, straw, developing toffee, and coffee beans on the nose. More peat on the slightly peppery palate, plus stewed tea and a hint of rum. The finish is medium in length, peppery, and oaky.

BALBLAIR "VINTAGE 1978"
single malt, 46% ABV, ex-Bourbon barrels, non-chill-filtered
Vanilla, honey, banoffee pie, and cloves on the aromatic nose. Honey, soft toffee, milk chocolate, almonds, and spice on the palate, while the lengthy finish offers cinnamon and gentle oak notes.

BALBLAIR 12-YEAR-OLD "SINGLE PEATY CASK"

DEANSTON

OWNER	Burn Stewart Distillers Ltd. (CL World Brands)
FOUNDED 1965	**CAPACITY** 793,000 gal (3m liters)
ADDRESS	Deanston, by Doune, Perthshire FK16 6AR
WEBSITE	www.deanstonmalt.com

Deanston is one of those rare Scotch distilleries to have been developed within an existing structure, the former Adelphi cotton mill, an 18th-century listed building by the Teith River.

Conversion work was carried out during the mid-1960s whiskey boom by the Deanston Distillery Company Ltd., formed by James Finlay & Company and Tullibardine owner Brodie Hepburn Ltd. Deanston was purchased by Invergordon Distillers Ltd. in 1972, being bottled as a single malt two years later. The distillery then closed in 1982 as the Scotch whiskey industry reined in production, but was reopened in 1991, having been acquired by Burn Stewart Distillers.

Green traditions

Despite its relatively modern origins, Deanston is a notably traditional distillery, featuring a rare surviving open cast-iron mash tun, and no computerization of processes. It boasts the quirkiest maturation warehouse in Scotland, namely a vaulted ex-weaving shed constructed in 1836, and was operating in an eco-friendly manner long before "green" became such a hot topic, courtesy of a pair of water-driven turbines.

Deanston distills from 100 percent Scottish barley and was one of the first distilleries to make organic whiskey, with regular batches being produced since 2000. In 2012 a 10-year-old bottling of organic Deanston was released.

Under the Burn Stewart regime, Distilleries Manager Ian Macmillan has improved the quality and enhanced the reputation of Deanston single malt, first by opting for longer fermentation periods and a slower rate of distillation, and more recently by increasing the strength and eschewing chill-filtration. Deanston single malt is also a major component of Burn Stewart's popular "Scottish Leader" blend.

TASTING NOTES

DEANSTON "VIRGIN OAK"
single malt, 46.3% ABV,
finished in virgin oak casks, non-chill-filtered
Sweet and grassy, with vanilla and fresh oak notes on the nose. Light-bodied, youthful spice, and zest on the fruity palate. The finish is spicy and drying.

DEANSTON 12-YEAR-OLD
single malt, 46.3% ABV, non-chill-filtered
A fresh, fruity nose with malt and honey. The palate displays cloves, ginger, honey, and malt, while the finish is long, quite dry, and pleasantly herbal.

DEANSTON 30-YEAR-OLD
single malt, 46.7% ABV, matured ex-Bourbon and sherry casks, finished in Oloroso sherry casks for two years, non-chill-filtered (US exclusive)
Milk chocolate, nuts, and fruit malt loaf on the nose. Oranges, almonds, and drying oak on the palate. Drying and nutty in the finish.

Housed in an old mill warehouse *dating back to the 18th century, Deanston was actually founded in the 1960s.*

DEANSTON "VIRGIN OAK"

DEANSTON 12-YEAR-OLD

GLENCADAM

OWNER Angus Dundee Distillers PLC
FOUNDED 1825 **CAPACITY** 343,000 gal (1.3m liters)
ADDRESS Park Road, Brechin, Angus DD9 7PA
WEBSITE www.glencadamdistillery.co.uk

The historic Angus town of Brechin lies between the cities of Dundee and Aberdeen in the Eastern Highland region of malt whiskey production. Until 1983 the former royal burgh was home to two distilleries, Glencadam and North Port, with the latter falling victim to the Distillers Company Ltd.'s sweeping round of plant closures during that troubled decade for Scotch whiskey distilling. In 2000 it looked as though Brechin was losing its surviving distillery, when Glencadam's then owner Allied Domecq Ltd. closed it down. Happily, however, export blend specialist Angus Dundee Distillers PLC came to the rescue in 2003, adding the Eastern Highland plant to its existing Tomintoul facility on Speyside. In addition to the actual distillery, Angus Dundee also operates a blending and bottling facility at Glencadam, which is capable of blending nearly a million gallons (4 million liters) of Scotch whiskey per year. The site's six warehouses, two of which date back to 1825, have a capacity of around 20,000 casks, and some of the maturing stock at Glencadam is up to 30 years old.

Mellow spirits

The distillery is equipped with a single pair of stills, as it was when first constructed, and unusually, their lyne arms run upward at an angle of 15 degrees, rather than sloping downward as in most Scotch whiskey distilleries. This helps to produce comparatively delicate and mellow "new make" spirits. Process water is sourced from springs at The Morans, 9 miles (14.5 km) from Glencadam, giving it one of the longest water supply lines of any distillery in Scotland.

Glencadam is one of those relatively rare Scottish distilleries to have an urban location, and it boasts one potentially noisy neighbor and another very quiet one. The Brechin City soccer field is close to the distillery, while the site also borders the municipal graveyard.

Changing regimes

Glencadam was established in 1825 by George Cooper, and after changing hands several times the distillery was purchased by Gilmour Thomson & Co. Ltd. in 1891. That Glasgow blending company owned it until 1954, when it was acquired by Canadian distillers Hiram Walker & Sons (Scotland) Ltd., which undertook a major reconstruction program five years later. Through

GLENCADAM 14-YEAR-OLD

GLENCADAM 21-YEAR-OLD

The pretty South Esk River *meanders gently past the town of Brechin and is superb for sea trout fishing.*

a series of takeovers, Glencadam came into the possession of Allied Lyons in 1987, with Allied Lyons later becoming Allied Domecq.

Under Allied Domecq and previous ownership regimes, Glencadam had been confined to a blending role, but in 2005 Angus Dundee offered the first generally available bottling of Glencadam, namely a 15-year-old. Today that has been joined by 10- and 21-year-old variants, along with a port wood-finished 12-year-old and an Oloroso sherry-finished 14-year-old. Additionally, a single cask 32-year-old bottling was undertaken in 2010.

TASTING NOTES

GLENCADAM 10-YEAR-OLD
single malt, 40% ABV
A delicate, floral nose with soft fruit, vanilla, and a slightly nutty note. Citrus fruit, malt, and spicy oak on the smooth palate. The finish is relatively long and fruity.

GLENCADAM 14-YEAR-OLD
single malt, 46% ABV, finished in Oloroso sherry casks
Vanilla and spice on the sweet nose, while the palate exhibits floral, spicy notes, and sweet sherry, giving extra body and resonance. White pepper and mixed spices in the medium-length finish.

GLENCADAM 21-YEAR-OLD
single malt, 46% ABV
The nose is floral, with citrus fruit notes, principally Jaffa oranges. The palate is elegant, with more orange and contrasting black pepper and oak. The finish is lengthy and drying.

GLEN ORD 12-YEAR-OLD "THE SINGLETON"

GLEN ORD

OWNER Diageo PLC
FOUNDED 1838 **CAPACITY** 1.3m gal (5m liters)
ADDRESS Muir of Ord, Ross-shire IV6 7UJ
WEBSITE www.discoveringdistilleries.com

Now little known in the UK and mainland Europe, Glen Ord has become something of a cult single malt in East Asia and especially Taiwan, thanks to reformulation and rebranding as "Singleton of Glen Ord" in 2006. The "Singleton" name, first used in relation to Auchroisk Distillery during the 1980s, is now applied to Diageo's Glen Ord for markets in East Asia, and to Glendullan for the United States.

Glen Ord distillery is located in fertile farmland to the west of Inverness and dates back to 1838, when it was established by Thomas Mackenzie. Through a number of owners, Glen Ord came into the possession of John Dewar & Sons Ltd. in 1923, and when Dewar's joined the Distillers Company Ltd. (DCL) two years later, the distillery was one of the assets transferred to DCL's Scottish Malt Distillers subsidiary.

Spirit of the Sixties

Along with many other DCL malt distilleries, Glen Ord was virtually rebuilt during the 1960s, when the complement of stills was increased from two to six, all housed in one of the distinctive glass-fronted stillhouses that make a DCL plant from the period instantly recognizable today.

Glen Ord is an important component of the Johnnie Walker range of blends, and from a blending perspective, the distillery produces spirits that are green, grassy, fruity, waxy, and oily in character. The stills are run slowly but very hot in order to capture pure, intense, grassy spirits.

GLEN ORD 12-YEAR-OLD "THE SINGLETON"

TASTING NOTES

GLEN ORD 12-YEAR-OLD
single malt, 43% ABV
Fragrant nose, with toffee apples, sherry, and barley notes. Sherry and spice on the silky palate, with a hint of smoke. Medium-length in the spicy, gently oaky finish.

GLEN ORD 12-YEAR-OLD "THE SINGLETON"
single malt, 40% ABV, matured in 50% ex-Bourbon casks and 50% ex-sherry wood
Milk chocolate orange, honey, and malt on the floral nose. Sweet on the palate, soft and smooth, with sherry, ripe orange, and graham crackers. Spicy, dry finish.

GLEN ORD "MANAGERS' CHOICE"
single malt, 59.2% ABV, single cask, cask strength, ex-Bourbon barrel (204 bottles)
Initially sweet on the nose, with vanilla and lemonade. Malt loaf and faint aniseed develop. Full, rich palate, with raisins and chocolate. Long and gingery finish.

GLEN ORD 12-YEAR-OLD

LOCH LOMOND

OWNER Loch Lomond Distillery Company Ltd. **FOUNDED** 1965

CAPACITY 2.6m gal (10m liters) grain spirit,

660,000 gal (2.5m liters) malt spirit

ADDRESS Lomond Estate, Alexandria, Dunbartonshire G83 OTL

WEBSITE www.lochlomonddistillery.com

Despite the romance associated with the Loch Lomond name, the eponymous distillery is very much a no-nonsense whiskey-making facility tucked away in an industrial park in Alexandria, about 5 miles (8 km) from the western shore of the famous loch itself.

Converted from a dye works during the mid-1960s, the distillery is now owned by the Loch Lomond Distillery Co. Ltd., which also operates the Glen Scotia distillery in Campbeltown. Loch Lomond is unique among Scottish distilleries in producing both malt and grain spirit, with the latter stillhouse being commissioned in 1994.

The distillation regimen is remarkably diverse and complex, as in addition to a pair of traditionally designed copper pot stills, Loch Lomond is also equipped with four stills with rectifying heads, which can be used to produce different styles of spirits by replicating varying lengths of still neck. There is also a Coffey still that has been used to produce Rhosdhu malt whiskey, thereby causing category-related confusion within the ranks of the Scotch Whisky Association.

Loch Lomond distillery *lies to the south of the popular loch, which is justifiably renowned for its beauty.*

Eight distinct styles of single malt are produced at the Loch Lomond distillery, ranging from heavily peated through Speyside and Highland to a more Lowland-like spirit. The permanent range includes Loch Lomond "Single Malt" (no age statement), Loch Lomond "Peated" (no age statement), as well as Loch Lomond "Single Highland Blend," a highly unusual product that is blended from a range of malts all distilled in one distillery and grain spirit from the same plant. Additionally there is an Inchmurrin 12-year-old and single cask bottlings are released from time to time under the Distillery Select Scotch Single Malt banner.

TASTING NOTES

LOCH LOMOND "SINGLE MALT"
single malt, 40% ABV
Feints on the slightly smoky nose, which sweetens into an oatmeal-like aroma. Medium-bodied, grassy, nutty, with unripe bananas. The finish is sweet, with raisins, bread pudding, and oak.

INCHMURRIN 12-YEAR-OLD
single malt, 40% ABV
Cereal, herbs, and floral notes on the relatively full nose. Pine nuts, honey, spice, and freshly planed wood on the palate, while the finish is quite short and spicy.

LOCH LOMOND 44-YEAR-OLD "1966"
single malt, 40% ABV
Newly mown grass, oak, nuts, and a hint of mint on the nose. Toffee, gentle spice, and vanilla, with wood tannins. Barley, malt, wood spice, and coffee in the lengthy finish.

LOCH LOMOND "SINGLE MALT"

INCHMURRIN 12-YEAR-OLD

LOCH EWE

OWNER John Clotworthy

FOUNDED 2004 **CAPACITY** 264 gal (1,000 liters)

ADDRESS Drumchork Estate, Aultbea, Wester Ross IV22 2HU

WEBSITE www.lochewedistillery.co.uk

The smallest legal distillery in Scotland and quite possibly in the world, Loch Ewe was developed in a former garage at Drumchork Lodge Hotel in the remote northwest Highlands of Wester Ross by proprietors John Clotworthy and Frances Oates. Clotworthy's practical knowledge of whiskey making came from time spent at the Bladnoch Distillery Whisky School, and from learning about the illicit distilling methods passed down through generations of local families living around the beautiful sea loch after which the distillery is named.

According to Clotworthy, however, their whiskey-making setup draws on a heritage of distilling technology that can be traced even farther back, into the ancient past.

"We are using an alembic pot still of the sort which was used by the ancient Egyptians to produce perfumes and aromas as far back as 200BC. Around 200AD European monks were using this design of still to make pot ales and their fortified wines."

The smallest still

The stills in question have a capacity of just 32 gallons (120 liters), though the minimum legal size of still for whiskey distillation in the UK is usually 476 gallons (1,800 liters). Loch Ewe operates on the right side of the law as it was the first Scottish distillery to be granted a private license in 190 years, thanks to a rapidly closed loophole in the law. Once distilled, the spirit is filled into casks with a capacity of no more than 6 gallons (23 liters) and optimum maturation is measured in months rather than years as a result of the small casks and thus the amount of contact the spirit has with the oak.

Drumchork Lodge Hotel offers more than 700 single malts and has won numerous whiskey bar awards. An open cask of "Spirit of Loch Ewe" is available for visitors to purchase by the dram, and "Whisky Experience" vacations are offered, giving practical insight into what are essentially 18th-century whiskey-making techniques.

TASTING NOTES

"SPIRIT OF LOCH EWE"
spirit drink, 54.3% ABV
Sweet and fruity on the nose with pears and peaches in evidence. Water brings out a mild note of honey. Fresh and clean on the palate, with gentle smoke, and, again, very fruity. Short in the finish.

ROYAL BRACKLA 1991
(GORDON & MACPHAIL)

DEWAR'S "WHITE LABEL"

ROYAL BRACKLA

OWNER John Dewar & Sons Ltd.

FOUNDED 1812 **CAPACITY** 1m gal (4m liters)

ADDRESS Cawdor, Nairn, Inverness-shire IV12 5QY

WEBSITE www.dewars.com

An identity as one of only two distilleries entitled to carry the "Royal" prefix might seem to offer huge promotional opportunities, but sadly for Brackla it has been one of the unsung backroom boys of the Scotch whiskey world for as long as anyone can remember.

Now part of Bacardi's John Dewar & Sons Ltd. portfolio, Brackla's attractive whiskey is starting to receive more attention, but inevitably the bulk of the distillery's output will always be destined for the blending vats to satisfy demand for Dewar's "White Label," its best-seller in the US.

Fit for a king

Just three distilleries were ever given permission to claim royal association in their title: the now demolished Glenury Royal in Stonehaven, Diageo's Royal Lochnagar, and Brackla, the first of the trio to be granted a Royal Warrant, with King William IV bestowing the honor in 1834 for the brand named "The King's Own Whisky." Brackla had been founded more than two decades before gaining official royal approval and was the creation of Captain William Fraser, who at times seems to have fought a losing battle against the many illicit distillers located in the area south of the coastal town of Nairn.

The distillery today largely dates from a major reconstruction program undertaken by then-owners Distillers Company Ltd in 1966, and four years later the number of stills was doubled from two to four. Brackla was one of many DCL distilleries to fall victim to the company's cull of the 1980s, closing in 1985, but unlike fellow casualties of that year, including Glenury Royal, it reopened in 1991. DCL's successor company United Distillers & Vintners invested in a $3 million upgrade in 1997, but a year later it was sold to Bacardi.

"House" bottlings include 10- and 25-year-old expressions, while Gordon & MacPhail continues to keep the flag flying, currently offering 1991 and 1995 vintages in its Connoisseur's Choice range.

TASTING NOTES

ROYAL BRACKLA 1991
(GORDON & MACPHAIL)
single malt, 46% ABV, refill sherry casks
Earthy and herbal on the nose, with citrus fruits and sherry. Spicy sherry, licorice, and fresh leather on the relatively full palate, which also features caramel. Slowly drying to gentle char in the medium-length finish.

TEANINICH

OWNER Diageo PLC
FOUNDED 1817 **CAPACITY** 1.2m gal (4.4m liters)
ADDRESS Alness, Ross-shire IV17 0XB

This distillery may be seen as the less glamorous relation of nearby Dalmore—the latter visually a very traditional Scottish distillery located on the shores of a firth, with its output acknowledged as one of the great single malts of the world, certainly in terms of its ultra-exclusive bottlings with price tags to match.

By contrast, only the most dedicated whiskey fans have tasted Teaninich single malt, and the distillery itself is a relatively characterless early-1970s structure, situated in an industrial park. In fact, of the two, Teaninich has greater provenance, dating back to 1817, more than two decades before Dalmore. The difference is that at Teaninich virtually all traces of the old distillery have been obliterated.

Established by Captain Hugh Munro, Teaninich has belonged to Distillers Company Ltd. and its successors since 1933. After an additional pair of stills was installed in 1962, a new production area was built in 1970, equipped with six more stills and known as 'Side A.' Both sides were shut down during the 1980s, and while Side A reopened in 1991, the old distillery was demolished in 1999.

Green and oily spirit

At Teaninich the aim is to produce spirit with a green and oily profile for blending purposes, and this is facilitated by the presence of a mash filter, rather than the usual mash tun. Commonly used in the brewing industry, Teaninich is the only Scotch whiskey distillery operating such a filter.

Diageo's Process Development Manager Douglas Murray says, "The spirit from Teaninich will principally be used by blenders to ramp up Johnnie Walker output. It's got smoothness; it's to do with mouthfeel. It's a very complementary whiskey in the blending process."

TASTING NOTES

TEANINICH 10-YEAR-OLD
single malt, 43% ABV
Fresh and grassy on the initial nose, with developing pineapple and spicy vanilla. Cereal notes on the palate, nutty and spicy, slightly herbal, and a suggestion of coffee. Drying in the finish, with cocoa powder and pepper.

TEANINICH "MANAGERS' CHOICE"
single malt, 55.3% ABV, single cask, cask strength, matured in a rejuvenated American oak hogshead
Fragrant, rounded, and sweet on the nose, with a palate of melon, ripe bananas, and background parma violets; banoffee pie with a sprinkling of ginger. The finish is medium in length, spicy, with oak and black bananas.

TEANINICH "MANAGERS' CHOICE"

TEANINICH 10-YEAR-OLD

TOMATIN

OWNER Tomatin Distillery Company Ltd.
FOUNDED 1897 **CAPACITY** 1.3m gal (5m liters)
ADDRESS Tomatin, Inverness-shire IV13 7YT
WEBSITE www.tomatin.com

Just as you should never judge a book by its cover, so you should never judge a single malt by the appearance of its distillery. Some very average whiskeys are made in picture-postcard distilleries, while a number of extremely fine malts are turned out from facilities that bear more than a passing resemblance to Soviet-era tractor factories.

While not wishing to compare Tomatin with the latter, the most fervent admirers of this distillery, set amid the bleakly beautiful moorland scenery of the Monadhliath Mountains, will surely concede that it is less than architecturally appealing.

Japanese giant

The three decades following World War II can be blamed for the rather industrial appearance of Tomatin. Expansion began in 1956, and by 1974 no fewer than 23 stills were in place, theoretically able to produce about 3.17 million gallons (12 million liters) of spirits per year, making it by far the largest distillery in Scotland in terms of capacity. However, Tomatin entered receivership in 1985, becoming the first Scottish distillery to be wholly owned by Japanese interests a year later.

Today, the focus is on developing a range of quality single malts. In 2011 Tomatin "Decades" was released to commemorate 50 years of service at the distillery by Tomatin-born Master Distiller and Brand Ambassador Douglas Campbell.

TOMATIN 30-YEAR-OLD

TASTING NOTES

TOMATIN 12-YEAR-OLD
single malt, 40% ABV, matured first-fill Bourbon barrels, refill American oak casks, and Spanish sherry butts, married in Spanish sherry butts prior to bottling
Barley, spice, oak, and floral notes on the nose, along with a hint of peat. Candy apples, cereal, malt, spice, and herbs on the reasonably full and nutty palate. Sweet fruitiness in the medium-length, oily finish.

TOMATIN 30-YEAR-OLD
single malt, 49.3% ABV, matured ex-Bourbon casks, finished Spanish Oloroso sherry casks, non-chill-filtered
A sophisticated nose with apricots, raisins, and spicy leather notes. Big and very fruity on the palate, with oranges and delicate spice. The finish dries through fruit and bubblegum notes to acceptable oakiness.

TOMATIN "DECADES"
single malt, 46% ABV, refill sherry casks (1967, 1976, 1984) and first-fill Bourbon barrels (1990 and 2005)
Vanilla, stewed fruits, raisins, dates, and caramel on the nose. More vanilla on the palate, with sherbet, cinnamon, apples, ginger, and toffee. Spicy oak in the drying finish.

TOMATIN 12-YEAR-OLD

TOMATIN "DECADES"

ISLAY & THE ISLANDS

The Highlands may be geographically the largest region for single malt whiskey production, but Islay and the Islands are the most disparate in terms of distillery locations. Whiskey is distilled on no fewer than seven Scottish islands, ranging from Arran in the southwest via Islay, Jura, Mull, Skye, and Lewis to Orkney, north of the mainland. The Hebridean Isles share a Gaelic heritage and culture, reflected in the place names and sometimes still in the speech of the people who live there. These are beautiful and often rugged places. In contrast to the Hebrides, Orkney's heritage is largely derived from Scandinavia, with place names reflecting the strong Norse influences that have shaped the story of this austere yet compelling group of islands.

Regional Styles

Single malts from Islay are often categorized as peaty and medicinal, but distilleries such as Bruichladdich and Bunnahabhain have long made whiskeys with low peating levels. Each island distillery has a distinctive style, from the smoky, heathery, sherried malt of Highland Park to the fruity, floral offerings of Arran.

Author's Choice

BOWMORE Located at the heart of Islay and dating back to the 18th century, Bowmore still operates floor maltings and produces a range of medium-peated single malts that are highly respected all over the world.

HIGHLAND PARK Another historic distillery, also malting on site, using sherry casks for single malt maturation and with a globally revered portfolio of expressions.

Regional Events

Islay boasts an extremely well-attended annual late-spring festival that goes by the name of Feis Islay, also known as the Islay Festival of Malt and Music (www.theislayfestival.co.uk). All of Islay's working distilleries participate, plus neighboring Jura, with each having a designated day to showcase their operations. There are also many associated events and attractions offered during festival week, with tours of Diageo's Port Ellen Maltings, not normally open to the public, and visits to Islay Ales, makers of "Ales from the Isle of Malts."

The economies of relatively small island communities always have a sense of vulnerability about them, and the presence of distilleries on so many Scottish islands provides welcome regular and relatively well-paid employment, as well as bringing in "whiskey tourists" eager to visit the places where their favorite drams are made.

Island distilleries such as Tobermory on Mull, Talisker on Skye, and Highland Park in the Orkneys are all long-established ventures, rooted in their local communities, while Arran is a relative newcomer, and Abhainn Dearg on Lewis a positive whiskey-making babe in arms. Potential new island distilleries have been mooted for Barra and Shetland, but neither has come to fruition. In terms of new-build distilleries, choosing an island location adds significantly to production and transportation costs, making survival during those early years with little income even more difficult.

Of all island distilleries, those on Islay have the greatest collective cachet. The "whiskey island" has eight productive distilleries at present, and during the past couple of decades the peaty, medicinal style widely associated with Islay single malts has developed an international cult following. The island's distilleries struggle to match supply to demand, and unless the world suddenly falls out of love with the Islay whiskey character, which seems unlikely, the economic future of Islay's distilleries looks very promising.

Located in the island's tiny "capital," Isle of Jura *malt is notably less peated than its Islay neighbors'.*

GETTING AROUND

Be prepared for lengthy drives and ferry trips, or take the option of a flight where available. Edinburgh and Glasgow airports serve many Scottish islands, with Glasgow being the mainland terminus for flights to Islay. Ferries to the Western Isles are operated by Caledonian Macbrayne (www.calmac.co.uk) and those to Orkney are run by NorthLink Ferries (www.northlinkferries.co.uk). The Isle of Skye is now linked to the mainland by bridge.

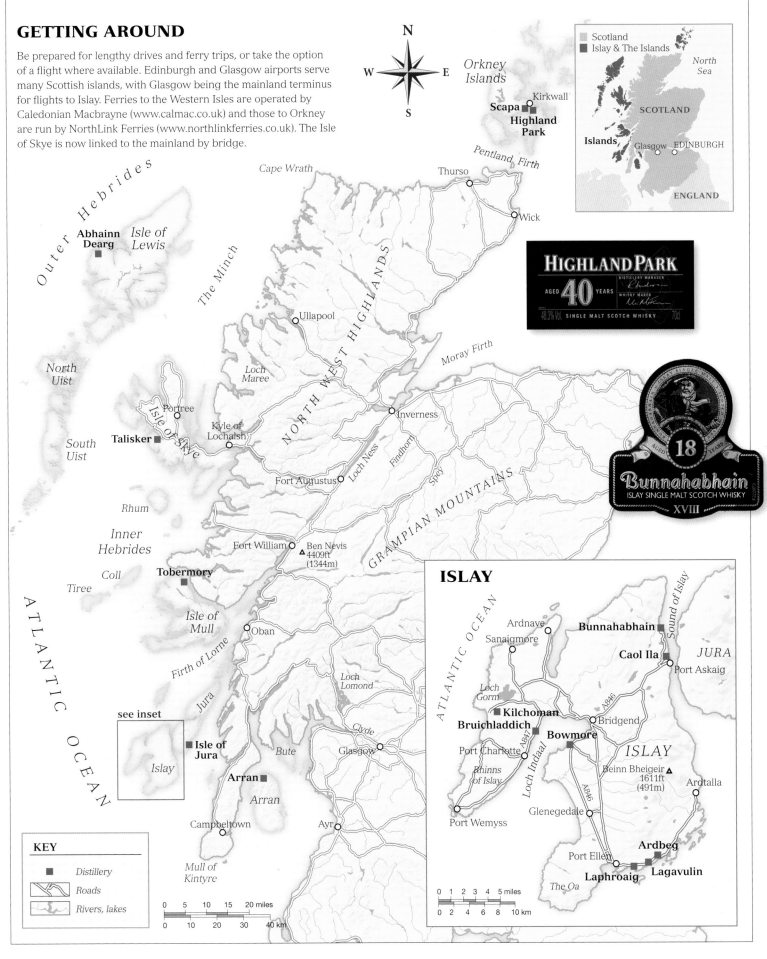

KEY

■	Distillery
	Roads
	Rivers, lakes

ARDBEG

OWNER The Glenmorangie Company Ltd.
FOUNDED 1794 **CAPACITY** 304,000 gal (1.15m liters)
ADDRESS Port Ellen, Isle of Islay, Argyll PA42 7EA
WEBSITE www.ardbeg.com

Distilleries do come back from the dead, and sometimes the experience can make them even stronger; Ardbeg is living proof of that. Long regarded as something of a cult whiskey, even before Islay single malts became fashionable, the heavily peated Ardbeg is now one of the most highly regarded whiskeys in the world. Yet as recently as the mid-1990s, the future of Ardbeg, both as a distillery and as a single malt, was in doubt.

A checkered history

The story begins in 1794, when a distillery was first recorded at Ardbeg, though the current plant was actually established by John MacDougall in 1815. It operated in private ownership until 1959, when Ardbeg Distillery Ltd. was formed, then in 1973 Ardbeg was jointly purchased by Hiram Walker & Sons Ltd. and the Distillers Company Ltd., with the former assuming full control in 1977.

However, when blended whiskey was truly king, a little of the powerful, assertive Ardbeg malt went a long way and with the Scotch whiskey industry facing a glut of maturing spirits, Ardbeg was silent between 1982 and 1989, during which period it became part of Allied Distillers Ltd. when Hiram Walker was taken over by that company in 1987. Ardbeg reopened two years later, but production was limited and Allied finally closed the distillery once again during 1996. The future looked less than rosy for the run-down plant, but in 1997 it was acquired by Glenmorangie PLC, who invested over $1.5 million in the purchase and refurbishment.

Ardbeg in action

The year 2000 saw the introduction of the Ardbeg 10-year-old, now the principal core offering. Along with the 10-year-old, Ardbeg embarked on an imaginative release program, with many products being exclusively previewed by the Ardbeg Committee, an organization for aficionados of the brand, established in 2000.

In 2004 the distillery took what was then the relatively bold step of releasing a six-year-old Ardbeg under the name "Very Young Ardbeg." The aim of this, and subsequent "Still Young" and "Almost There" bottlings, was to illustrate the changes that took place as spirits distilled in one particular year (1997) matured, and was intended to engage consumers in the ongoing process that led to the release of the new 10-year-old variant, initially issued at cask strength as "Renaissance."

ARDBEG 10-YEAR-OLD

ARDBEG "BLASDA"

ARDBEG "ALLIGATOR"

Peat-freak portfolio

Ardbeg has also brought out bottlings at opposite ends of the phenolic spectrum, with the lightly peated Ardbeg "Blasda" appearing in 2008, followed in 2009 by Ardbeg "Supernova," which boasted a phenol level in excess of 100 ppm. "Blasda" came as something of a shock to committed Ardbeg fans, being peated to around one-third of the whiskey's normal level and offered chill-filtered at 40 percent ABV. Glenmorangie's Head of Distilling and Whisky Creation, Dr. Bill Lumsden, says of "Blasda" that "we wanted to offer consumers the chance to taste more of the fruity and floral flavor congeners in Ardbeg, and to show that it is not all about peat."

The following year, "Supernova" served to reassure the diehard "peat freak" fans that all was well with Ardbeg. As Lumsden explains: "In "Supernova" there were even more of the chewy, peat smoke flavors usually associated with the brand." In addition to the 10-year-old and "Blasda," the permanent portfolio includes the cask strength "Uigeadail," named after one of the lochs supplying water to the distillery and introduced in 2003.

Also permanently available are "Corryvreckan" and "Alligator." "Corryvreckan" was launched in 2008 and takes its name from an infamous whirlpool close to Islay. It carries no age statement but principally comprises spirits distilled during the period 1998–2000, along with some younger Ardbeg. A proportion of the total has been matured in new French oak casks.

Cask strength "Alligator" joined the lineup in 2011 and employs some re-charred American oak casks for maturation. "Alligator" is a style of cask charring in which the burned wood staves take on the appearance of an alligator's scales. The heart of "Alligator" is spirits matured in Level Four casks—the most intense type of charring possible.

TASTING NOTES

ARDBEG 10-YEAR-OLD
single malt, 46% ABV, non-chill-filtered
Sweet on the nose, with soft peat, carbolic soap, and smoked fish. Intense yet delicate palate, with burning peat, dried fruit, malt, and licorice. Long, smoky finish.

ARDBEG "UIGEADAIL"
single malt, 54.2% ABV, cask-strength, matured ex-Bourbon barrels and ex-Oloroso sherry butts, non-chill-filtered
Peat, coffee, barley, raisins, sherry, and asphalt on the complex nose; citrus fruits, malt, peat, treacle, and honey on the substantial palate. Caramel and peat in the finish.

ARDBEG "ALLIGATOR"
single malt, 51.2% ABV, non-chill-filtered
Beach bonfires, ozone, and a savory note on the nose. The palate is sweet and smoky, with chili, ginger, and tea. Long and gently spiced in the sweetly smoky finish, with a final citric and medicinal tang.

ARDBEG "UIGEADAIL"

TALKING HEADS

Mickey Heads has been distillery manager at Ardbeg since moving there from Jura distillery in 2007. An Ileach born and bred, Heads started his distilling career at nearby Laphroaig in 1979. "Ardbeg has had a lot of positive publicity since Glenmorangie took over," he says, "and the timing has been good. It's gone with the growth in single malts. I've always liked the spirit itself. It's got lightness and fruit and floral notes, then smoke, and finally a big explosion in the mouth. People are looking for flavor in their whiskey, not just knocking it back any more."

THE ARRAN "100° PROOF"

THE ARRAN 10-YEAR-OLD

ARRAN

OWNER Isle of Arran Distillers Ltd.

FOUNDED 1993 **CAPACITY** 198,000 gal (750,000 liters)

ADDRESS Shore Road, Lochranza, Isle of Arran KA27 8HJ

WEBSITE www.arranwhisky.com

Most of Scotland's whiskey distilleries came into being thanks to favorable changes in legislation and improving trading conditions. Hence a great number of distilleries were established in the years following the liberalizing Excise Act of 1823, while the late-Victorian whiskey boom produced another spike on the distilleries graph during the 1880s and 1890s. The next spike came in the 1960s and 1970s as global demand for blended Scotch whiskey rose once more.

Since then, most entirely new distilling operations have tended to be relatively small in scale and independent in operation. One of the first of these ventures was the Isle of Arran distillery, established in 1993 by former Chivas Brothers managing director and whiskey industry veteran Harold Currie, who had long associations with the island and was attracted to the idea of restoring legal whiskey-making after a gap of more than 150 years. Currie chose a site in Lochranza in the north of the island, although most of the 19th-century distilleries had been based in the south. The principal reason for the new distillery's location was the discovery of an ideal water source. The project was partly funded by the sale of 2,000 bonds, each of which entitled the bondholder to an amount of whiskey once the distillery was in operation.

Arran in action

Arran is a small, two-still distillery, designed from the outset to be aesthetically pleasing, with mock pagodas and whitewashed buildings that blend well with the island's older architecture. As all the production processes take place within one room, it is also ideal for the reception of visitors.

Although no longer owned by the Currie family, the distillery remains in independent hands, with Euan Mitchell serving as Managing Director of Isle of Arran Distillers Ltd. The company strategy is to develop a permanent range, embracing 10-, 14-, and 18-year-old expressions, with the 14-year-old having a greater Bourbon wood maturation influence than the 10-year-old. However, the very first release from Arran was of one-year-old spirits, back in 1996, designed to whet the appetite of consumers and remind them that Arran was up and running.

The first bottling which could legally be called Scotch whiskey appeared as a three-year-old in 1998, followed by a four-year-old, several single cask editions, and a 1996 vintage, along with an

THE ARRAN "SINGLE CASK SHERRY"

THE ARRAN "MACHRIE MOOR"

expression without an age statement, marketed as "The Arran Malt." A milestone came in 2006 with the launch of the distillery's first 10-year-old.

The finished product

By this time, the distillery had gained a reputation for its energetic cask finish program, mirroring the likes of BenRiach and Tullibardine, which sought to broaden their range and shelf presence by finishing spirits in a variety of secondary casks.

"Finishes did us a huge favor at the time," states Euan Mitchell. "They opened the brand up to a lot of people who perhaps thought Arran was too young to be taken seriously." The first raft of finishes appeared in 2003, starting with Calvados, and for a time up to six different finishes were released each year, though that has subsequently been scaled back, with Amarone, port, and Sauternes finishes now part of the permanent portfolio.

That portfolio also includes "Arran Original," a variant that does not carry an age statement but comprises principally five-year-old spirits, a five-year-old "Robert Burns Single Malt," and "Machrie Moor," named after a peat bog in the west of Arran. "Machrie Moor" is released in batches, starting in 2010, and contains whiskey dating back to 2004 and 2005, peated to a level of 14 ppm, so this is not a peat monster up there with the Ardbegs and Laphroaigs of the whiskey world. However, more recently the peating level has been increased to 20 ppm, and having initially made 2,600 gallons (10,000 liters) of peated Arran each year, the company has now doubled that amount. "We deliberately went for a medium peating level to ensure the Arran character was not obliterated in the process," says Euan Mitchell.

SCOTLAND IN MINIATURE

The Isle of Arran is one of the most southerly of Scotland's islands, situated between Ayrshire and the Kintyre peninsula. It is often referred to as "Scotland in miniature," since it embraces so many aspects of Scottish geography and topography, including pretty coastal villages, rugged mountains in the north, and soft, rolling hills and woodlands in the south. Although Arran is less than 20 miles (32 km) long and 10 miles (16 km) wide, it's thought that as many as 50 distilling ventures were active during the 19th century. While most ran without the formality of licenses, three were officially sanctioned, with the last of these, in Lagg, operating until 1837.

TASTING NOTES

THE ARRAN 10-YEAR-OLD
single malt, 46% ABV, 70% from second-fill sherry casks, balanced mixture of ex-Bourbon and some first-fill sherry casks
Vanilla, apples, pears, malt, and gentle spice on the nose. Medium-bodied, with citrus fruits, soft cinnamon notes, graham crackers, and gentle oak on the palate. The fruity, malty finish fades slowly.

THE ARRAN "SINGLE CASK SHERRY"
single malt, 56.3% ABV, ex-sherry butt
Figs, chocolate caramels, and a little sweet smoke on the nose. More fudgelike in time. Full-bodied, with sherry, dates, and raisins on the fruitcake palate. The finish is mellow and warming.

THE ARRAN "MACHRIE MOOR"
single malt, 46% ABV
Nutty peat, spicy malt, and lemon on the nose. Vibrant on the palate, with lots of citrus fruit. Developing bonfire smoke, with spice, nuts, and dark chocolate. The lengthy finish features citrus fruits.

BOWMORE

OWNER Morrison Bowmore Distillers Ltd.
FOUNDED 1779 **CAPACITY** 581,000 gal (2.2m liters)
ADDRESS School Street, Bowmore, Isle of Islay,
Argyll PA43 7JS **WEBSITE** www.bowmore.com

Bowmore is not only the oldest licensed distillery on the island of Islay but also one of the oldest surviving distilleries in Scotland. Built by farmer and distiller David Simson, the distillery passed through various hands before coming into the possession of whiskey brokers Stanley P. Morrison Ltd. in 1963. During 1989 Suntory Ltd., Japan's largest distiller, took a 35 percent share in what was by then known as Morrison Bowmore Ltd., and in 1994 Suntory assumed full ownership of Bowmore distillery, along with Auchentoshan and Glengarioch.

Bowmore is notable for being one of very few distilleries still making malt "in house," and about 40 percent of the plant's requirements are produced on its three malting floors, with the remainder being sourced from the mainland and peated to the same level of 25ppm. This places Bowmore in the middle ground of Islay single malts in terms of peating, though it is sometimes described as the smokiest of all the Islays.

At Bowmore, tradition blends with innovation, and a significant amount of time, energy, and money have been plowed into making the distillery more environmentally friendly. A process was developed to macerate and bake peat into

Bowmore stands on the shores *of Loch Indaal, with the salty sea breeze blowing right into its warehouses.*

BOWMORE 40-YEAR-OLD

"caff" for burning in the floor maltings, which generates increased peat flavor in the malting barley yet requires up to 75 percent less peat than was previously the case. In 1990, a warehouse was donated to the local community to create an indoor swimming pool, which is heated by hot water from the still house condensers.

On-site maturation

Maturation is key to creating fine whiskeys, and in particular, the type and quality of casks used and the location in which they are stored are vitally important when their contents are to be bottled as single malt.

Bowmore currently fills around 20 percent of its output into ex-sherry casks, and the remainder into former Bourbon casks, with the entire make now being destined for single malt bottling rather than blending. Some of the fresh spirit is transported to the mainland, but the majority is matured on site, where a total of around 27,000 casks are stored in three warehouses.

Bowmore's Head Warehouseman is Willie MacNeill, universally known as "Ginger Willie" and one of the true characters of the whiskey industry on Islay. "I'm an Ileach born and bred and very proud of it," he declares. "My grandfather and great-grandfather both worked at Ardbeg distillery and my mother's family were all born there. My first distillery job was at Ardbeg."

MacNeill contends, "You don't get the same whiskey when it's not matured on the island. There's a heavy sea air and no pollution. We have galvanized hoops on casks here because

the old mild steel ones rusted—the salt air affected them. Those sorts of conditions are bound to have a little effect on the whiskey.

"Number 1 warehouse was the first warehouse to be built when the distillery was established. It's partly below sea level and you get very little temperature change in it. During the winter, when it gets down to minus eight degrees [18°F] outside, it's appreciably warmer in the number 1 warehouse. It mainly houses sherry butts.

"To me, the ideal warehouse has thick, old walls and is slightly below sea level. You get damp salt air. Evaporation is slower than in the big modern ones. You don't lose as much spirit through evaporation as you do in the middle of the mainland. At Bowmore during the last 20 years we've gotten into spending lots of money on wood. All wood now is ex-first fill. You get the benefit at the beginning."

Rising sales

Sales of Bowmore have increased significantly since the entire range was revamped in 2007, and in percentage terms the brand has started to catch up with peaty Islay competitors, such as Ardbeg and Laphroaig. In 2010, a 40-year-old limited release was added to the portfolio and received high praise.

The core Bowmore range comprises "Legend," a 12-year-old, "Darkest 15 Years," an 18-year-old, and a 25-year-old, while the increasingly important duty-free sector has several dedicated expressions, including "Surf," 12-year-old "Enigma," and a "Cask Strength." "Darkest 15 Years" is the only "finished" whiskey in the principal Bowmore lineup and has spent 12 years maturing in former Bourbon barrels before a final period of three years in ex-Oloroso sherry butts, while the 25-year-old has been matured in a marriage of ex-Bourbon and ex-sherry casks.

BOWMORE 12-YEAR-OLD

TASTING NOTES

BOWMORE 12-YEAR-OLD
single malt, 40% ABV
An enticing nose of lemon and gentle brine leads into a smoky, citric palate with notes of cocoa and hard candy appearing in the lengthy, complex finish.

BOWMORE 40-YEAR-OLD
single malt, 44.8% ABV, single cask, ex-Bourbon cask, 43 bottles, non-chill-filtered
Medicinal, maritime, and smoky, backed up by vanilla and oranges in syrup on the nose. Rich stewed fruits on the palate, becoming progressively peatier. Long and consistent in the firm finish, no negative wood impact.

BLACK BOWMORE 42-YEAR-OLD
single malt, 40.5% ABV, cask strength, from five Oloroso sherry casks, 804 bottles, non-chill-filtered
Ginger, cinnamon, toffee, figs, and dark chocolate on the rich nose. The palate is notably full, with more toffee and chocolate notes, plus worn leather, coffee, and wood smoke. The finish is very long and satisfying.

BLACK BOWMORE

There are certain expressions of single malt whiskey that cause a frisson of excitement among collectors and connoisseurs just at the mention of their names. One such expression is "Black Bowmore." The initial release of this 1964 spirit, filled into Oloroso sherry casks, took place in 1993, and the notably dark color imparted during maturation led to the expression's name. It was soon considered a classic and bottles have been known to change hands for four-figure sums, having initially retailed for £100 ($150)each. In 2007 "Black Bowmore" appeared again, with five casks from the same batch yielding 804 bottles of what was now 42-year-old single malt.

BLACK BOWMORE 42-YEAR-OLD

BRUICHLADDICH
3-YEAR-OLD "X4+3"

BRUICHLADDICH 21-YEAR-OLD

BRUICHLADDICH

OWNER	The Bruichladdich Distillery Company Ltd.
FOUNDED 1881	**CAPACITY** 396,000 gal (1.5m liters)
ADDRESS	Isle of Islay, Argyll PA49 7UN
WEBSITE	www.bruichladdich.com

Without Bruichladdich, the world of Scotch whiskey would be an infinitely duller place. Marketing themselves as "progressive Hebridean distillers," the Bruichladdich team takes pride in a defiantly independent stance and an ability to seize opportunities for quirky product development and run with them. The distillery was somewhat unconventional from the start, being designed by 23-year-old engineer Robert Harvey and built in 1881 for the Glasgow-based Harvey distillers. Unlike many other Islay distilleries, Bruichladdich was a modern "courtyard" distillery, made with a new product called concrete, rather than being an extension of an existing agricultural enterprise, and it was designed with tall, narrow-necked stills to produce a relatively pure, elegant style of spirits.

Decline and revival
The Harveys operated Bruichladdich until it fell silent in 1929, a victim of the interwar Depression along with the nearby Port Charlotte distillery. Bruichladdich, however, was revived in 1936, then sold by the Harveys in 1938 to Ben Nevis distillery owner Joseph Hobbs and his associates. It was ultimately bought in 1968 by Invergordon Distillers Ltd., who doubled the stills from two to four.

After Whyte & Mackay Ltd. won a fierce takeover battle for Invergordon, Bruichladdich was closed as surplus to requirements. The distillery remained almost entirely dormant from 1993 to December 2000, when a private company headed by Mark Reynier of independent bottler Murray McDavid bought it for around $10 million. Reynier and his team, including veteran Islay distiller Jim McEwan and distillery manager Duncan McGillivray, inherited what was effectively an unreconstituted Victorian operation, with an open-topped, cast-iron mash tun and wooden washbacks, while one of the two wash stills, now renovated, dates from the distillery's founding and is the oldest in Scotland.

A different approach
From the start, the new Bruichladdich regimen decided to be different, with Mark Reynier declaring the venture "free from corporate industry control. Bruichladdich (a Scottish company) is now operated, managed, and directed on site, producing Scotland's purest single malt whiskey from an unlikely marriage of manual 19th-century equipment, preindustrial techniques, wine trade influences, and state-of-the-art telecommunications."

While distilling their own spirits, the company released a sometimes bewildering variety of often limited editions from existing stocks. Today there are two core ranges of unpeated and peated expressions, while eye-catching innovations include the high-strength, quadruple-distilled "X4," based on a legendary Gaelic drink known as *usquebaugh-baul* or "perilous whiskey."

Pugnacious peat

When distillation resumed in May 2001, the first batch of spirits produced was heavily peated, to around 40ppm. This variant was called "Port Charlotte" and was released as a limited edition on an annual basis, now part of the core range. There are plans to revive small-scale distillation at the old Port Charlotte site. Bruichladdich has also been producing "Octomore" spirit, described as "the most heavily peated whiskey in the world," with phenolic levels of at least 80ppm.

In 2003, Islay's only bottling line was installed at the distillery, which means that some Bruichladdich is made with Islay-grown barley and is also bottled on the island. Along with the two pairs of conventional pot stills, the distillery now boasts the last fully functioning Lomond still in Scotland, rescued from Inverleven distillery at Dumbarton in 2004. "Ugly Betty," as the still was christened, now produces "The Botanist" gin.

In 2011, Mark Reynier celebrated 10 years at the helm, and the first bottling of 10-year-old distilled on his watch was released as "The Laddie Ten." In typically pugnacious style, Mark Reynier declares, "The packaging carries no flags, no crests, no little woodcut illustrations of Highland glens or oak casks, no Victorian engravings, no Gaelic typefaces. No fake heritage to hide behind, just our aqua, and our progressive, modern typography."

TASTING NOTES

BRUICHLADDICH 10-YEAR-OLD "THE LADDIE TEN"

single malt, 46% ABV, non-chill-filtered
Fruity and floral, with gentle peat and brine, plus honey and vanilla notes on the nose. Malt, vanilla, honey, soft peat, and brine on the palate, with spice and tea. Citrus fruit, ginger, oak, and delicate smoke in the finish.

BRUICHLADDICH 21-YEAR-OLD

single malt, 46% ABV, Oloroso sherry butt, non-chill-filtered
Ripe banana, nuts, brittle toffee, mango, and raisins on the nose. Full, rich sherry on the palate, with tropical fruits and caramel. Long, plump, sherried finish.

BRUICHLADDICH 3-YEAR-OLD "X4+3"

single malt, 63.5% ABV, non-chill-filtered
Cereal and floral notes on the somewhat spirity, phenolic nose. The palate is fresh, clean, intense, salty, and drying. Short in the powerful finish.

UNDER SURVEILLANCE

Bruichladdich is one of those distilleries just begging to be visited, due in part to its superb location on the shores of Loch Indaal. If you are unable to make the trip in person, the distillery website offers a range of webcams, so you can take a virtual tour and watch whiskey-making take place. On one occasion the webcams were almost the distillery's undoing when it was discovered that the CIA was spying on the site via its webcams, having been convinced that the equipment was so old it must be manufacturing some sort of chemical weapon.

BRUICHLADDICH 10-YEAR-OLD "THE LADDIE TEN"

BUNNAHABHAIN 10-YEAR-OLD "TOITEACH"

BLACK BOTTLE BLEND

Bunnahabhain Distillery is closely associated with the Black Bottle blend of Scotch whiskey, which was launched by the Graham brothers of Aberdeen in 1879. Originally, the characteristic peaty style of Black Bottle would have come primarily from malts made in northeastern Scotland, but after passing out of family ownership, Black Bottle became just another blended Scotch whiskey. Then, in 1995, the original and singular identity of Black Bottle was restored when the bold decision was made by The Edrington Group, then the brand owner, to include malt from each of Islay's working distilleries, with Bunnahabhain at its heart.

BUNNAHABHAIN

OWNER Burn Stewart Distillers Ltd. (CL World Brands)	
FOUNDED 1881 **CAPACITY** 660,000 gal (2.5m liters)	
ADDRESS Port Askaig, Isle of Islay, Argyll PA46 7RP	
WEBSITE www.bunnahabhain.com	

Bunnahabhain was established in the same year as fellow Islay distillery Bruichladdich, with production beginning two years later in 1883. Although all of Islay's distilleries, with the exception of Bowmore, are isolated in location, Bunnahabhain takes remoteness to a whole new level, situated at the end of a long, unclassified road just outside the northern ferry terminal of Port Askaig. Views across the Sound of Islay to neighboring Jura with its distinctive Paps are exquisite.

The distillery's spectacular site was chosen by founders William and James Greenlees and William Robertson for the availability of pure water and high-quality peat, along with its sheltered coastal location, which was important in the days when Islay's distilleries were served directly by sea.

It became part of Highland Distilleries Company Ltd. in 1887 and remained in its control until 1999, when The Edrington Group took over. Edrington decided to concentrate its energies on a small number of high-profile single malt brands, such as The Macallan, and sold off Glengoyne and Bunnahabhain in 2003. Bunnahabhain was bought by Burn Stewart Distillers plc, along with the popular Black Bottle blended Scotch whiskey brand.

The power of the island

Burn Stewart's Distilleries Manager and Master Blender, Ian Macmillan, says, "When we bought the business in 2003, Black Bottle was one of the most important aspects of the purchase. The power of the big, peaty Islays is calmed by the considerable Bunnahabhain influence."

Bunnahabhain distillery is noted for the large size of its four stills, and Macmillan explains, "Because of their size you get a great deal of copper contact and we run the stills very slowly. This allows for lots of reflux—the heavy, oily stuff falls back into the stills instead of passing over into the condensers. This, plus all the copper contact, makes for a gentle style of spirit, flavorful and sweet."

There is an ongoing debate about whether the location where whiskey is matured has an influence on its character. Macmillan declares, "We have some stocks of Bunnahabhain distilled under the Edrington regime that have been entirely matured on the mainland, and there is definitely a difference between these and the same whiskey matured on Islay. It becomes noticeable as the whiskey ages. At 20 to 25 years, you get a lovely saltiness that's not there in casks matured on the mainland."

Piling on the peat

Known as the "gentle spirit of Islay," Bunnahabhain single malt has been lightly peated during the past half-century, but since Burn Stewart took over, the distillery has also produced heavily peated batches of spirits on an annual basis.

"There is great demand for it," says Macmillan. "Lots of our customers want to fill peated Islays, and they want the Bunnahabhain because they are finding it harder to get hold of some of the others. In future we may well be doing more peated Bunnahabhain, and the amount we have distilled varies from 20 percent of total production up to as much as 80 percent. In 2014 we will bring out a 10-year-old expression of "Moine," the Gaelic word for "peat" and the name we give to our peated Bunnahabhain.

"The peating level is much the same as Laphroaig and Lagavulin, but because the stills are large and onion-shaped, giving lots of reflux, it's not as medicinal as some other Islays. The 'cut' points are totally different from when we are making 'standard' Bunnahabhain, because the rich, phenolic flavors come out later in the run, so you run longer at the end. You also get more oiliness."

New releases

In 2004, a six-year-old version of "Moine" was released, followed four years later by "Toiteach," Gaelic for "smoky." This comprises proportions of young "Moine" and 20-year-old heavily sherried standard Bunnahabhain. "Cruach-Mhona" ("peat stack") was launched into travel retail outlets in 2010, and contains youthful, heavily peated spirits and sherry butt-matured Bunnahabhain upwards of 20 years old. The permanent range includes 12-, 18-, and 25-year-old expressions. Since 2010 these have been offered at a higher strength of 46.3 percent. All whiskeys are non-colored and non-chill-filtered.

TASTING NOTES

BUNNAHABHAIN 12-YEAR-OLD
single malt, 46.3% ABV, non-chill-filtered
Fresh on the nose, with light peat and discreet smoke. More overt peat on the nutty and fruity palate, but still restrained for an Islay. The finish is full-bodied and lingering, with a hint of vanilla and some smoke.

BUNNAHABHAIN 25-YEAR-OLD
single malt, 46.3% ABV, non-chill-filtered
Sweet and floral on the nose, with developing spices. The palate is sherried and elegant, with baked apple. The sherry lingers and dries in the long, pleasing finish.

BUNNAHABHAIN 10-YEAR-OLD "TOITEACH"
single malt, 46% ABV, non-chill-filtered
Subtle peat, spice, and mild medicinal notes on the nose. Warm peat and sherry on the palate, with citrus fruit and white pepper. Long and spicy in the finish.

BUNNAHABHAIN 12-YEAR-OLD

BUNNAHABHAIN 25-YEAR-OLD

CAOL ILA

OWNER Diageo PLC	
FOUNDED 1846	**CAPACITY** 1.7m gal (6.4m liters)
ADDRESS Port Askaig, Isle of Islay, Argyllshire PA46 7RL	
WEBSITE www.discovering-distilleries.com	

In terms of capacity, Caol Ila was already far and away the largest distillery on Islay before Diageo's announcement during November 2011 that it was to spend $5.5 million making it even larger. Work during 2012 saw potential output increase from its previous level of 1.5 million gallons (5.7 million liters) to 1.7 million gallons (6.4 million liters) per year, and upgrading included the installation of a new full lauter mash tun and two new wooden washbacks, taking the complement to 10.

Discussing the investment at Caol Ila, Diageo's Knowledge & Heritage Director Dr Nick Morgan says that "We are first and foremost a blending company. We make the best single malts in the world to help us make the best blended Scotch whiskies, like Johnnie Walker or Bell's."

Master Blender Jim Beveridge adds that "Caol Ila provides a rich, smoky character, perfect for blending with our malts and grains," and Nick Morgan explains that "One of the trademarks of Johnnie Walker is a rich smokiness, and it's obviously critical that our malt distilling regime is geared to ensure we can maintain that character as sales continue to expand. So we look on Caol Ila both as an important part of our overall malts business, but also as a 'must-have' component for many of our blends. That's the thinking that led to the expansion there."

As a single malt, Caol Ila has also been enjoying increasing popularity since the brand was re-launched during 2002, coinciding with the apparently never-ending thirst for Islay whisky among consumers in a wide range of countries.

Between cliff and Sound

The distillery in its original form dates from 1846, when it was established by Hector Henderson, who also owned Glasgow's Camlachie Distillery. The location between a steep cliff and the Sound of Islay may seem an unusual choice, but it was close to an extremely good water supply, rising through limestone in Loch nam Ban and entering the sea at Caol Ila, and coastal locations were important for transportation when the needs of island distilleries were serviced by small vessels known as "puffers."

Caol Ila ultimately passed into the hands of Glasgow blender Bulloch Lade & Company in 1863, with rebuilding taking place 16 years later, but the most dramatic reconstruction at Caol Ila

CAOL ILA 25-YEAR-OLD

CAOL ILA 12-YEAR-OLD

occurred during 1972 and 1974. The distillery, owned by the Distillers Company Ltd. since 1927, was totally rebuilt in somewhat stark, modernistic style, and the complement of stills was increased from two to the present six.

The characteristic 1960–70s style of the DCL stillhouse, with a significant amount of glass, means that the Caol Ila stillman enjoys a superb view across the Sound of Islay to the neighboring Isle of Jura. Only the warehouse of the 19th-century distillery remains intact and in use, though today all the spirit produced at Caol Ila is transported by road tanker to the mainland for cask filling and maturation.

Although Caol Ila's spirit, peated to 30–35ppm, is now in great demand, there was a time not too long ago when Diageo had a potential over-capacity of it and accordingly an annual batch of unpeated "Highland-style" Caol Ila was made for some years. This was intended primarily for blending purposes, but in 2006 an unpeated eight-year-old expression was released in the annual Special Releases lineup, and 10- and 12-year-old variants subsequently followed.

Core Caol Ilas

The core range comprises 12-, 18-, and 25-year-olds, along with a "Natural Cask Strength" expression (with no age statement) and a "Distillers Edition" bottling, which has undergone secondary maturation in Moscatel casks. In 2011 Caol Ila "Moch" (Gaelic for "Dawn") with no age statement was introduced, initially only available to the "Friends of the Classic Malts." Releasing a whisky that's defined by taste rather than age, strength, or finish is a new departure for Caol Ila.

TASTING NOTES

CAOL ILA 12-YEAR-OLD
single malt, 43% ABV
Iodine, fresh fish, and bacon on the nose, plus delicate, floral notes. Smoke, malt, lemon, and peat on the slightly oily palate, plus vanilla and a dash of mustard. Peppery peat in the drying finish.

CAOL ILA 25-YEAR-OLD
single malt, 43% ABV
The nose is fresh and fruity, with band-aids, brine, and bonfire smoke. Relatively sweet on the palate, with more fruit notes, plus wood smoke, pepper, and some oak. The finish dries steadily, with mild smokiness.

CAOL ILA UNPEATED 12-YEAR-OLD 1999 (SPECIAL RELEASES 2011)
single malt, 64% ABV, cask strength, matured in first-fill ex-Bourbon casks (fewer than 6,000 bottles)
Discreet rolling tobacco, banana oil, vanilla, and a hint of cocoa powder on the nose. Sweet and lively on the palate, with summer berries, honey, and intense, spicy fruitiness. Lingering spices in the finish.

CAOL ILA 18-YEAR-OLD

CAOL ILA "NATURAL CASK STRENGTH"

CAOL ILA UNPEATED 12-YEAR-OLD 1999 (SPECIAL RELEASES 2011)

DRAFF AND ALE

The Scotch whiskey industry takes its environmental responsibilities very seriously. The "draff" residue of malted barley husks left over after mashing is usually sold to farmers as cattle feed, while "dark grain" feeds are produced by evaporating pot ale left over after distillation and incorporating it with the dried draff to form cubes or pellets. On Islay it's not economically viable to process by-products, so while wet draff is fed to cattle, disposal of pot ale is by way of a long sea outfall pipe close to Caol Ila distillery. Liquid waste from a number of the island's distilleries is transported by road tanker to Caol Ila for disposal. This may be about to change, however, as Bruichladdich distillery has recently invested in an anaerobic digester to deal with its pot ale waste.

HIGHLAND PARK 40-YEAR-OLD

HIGHLAND PARK

OWNER	The Edrington Group
FOUNDED 1798	**CAPACITY** 660,000 gal (2.5m liters)
ADDRESS	Holm Road, Kirkwall, Orkney KW15 1SU
WEBSITE	www.highlandpark.co.uk

The Orkney Isles, to the north of mainland Scotland, have a character all their own; more Norse than Scottish in heritage, and closer to the Arctic Circle than to London. The islands actually belonged to Norway until 1472. Given the individualistic nature of the place and its independent-minded people, it is appropriate that the whiskey made in Orkney's best-known distillery is equally individualistic.

Gerry Tosh, the distillery's Global Marketing Manager, declares, "There are five reasons why we make great whiskey: traditional floor maltings, the use of Orcadian peat and sherry oak casks, cold maturation, and cask harmonization. Most distilleries will use two or three of these methods but only Highland Park uses them all together."

Unique character

The peat burned in the Highland Park kilns is notably aromatic, and very different in character from that of Islay. Orcadian peat derives from heather, dried grass, and plants, rather than from trees, as there were no trees on Orkney 3,000 years ago, just as there are very few today, as a result of the frequent strong winds. The distillery owns about 2,000 acres (809 hectares) of peat land on Hobbister Moor, annually cutting around 200 tons to fuel the distillery furnace and impart its unique flavor. Some 20 percent of the distillery's requirements are served by its own maltings, which produce malt peated to approximately the same level as that at Bowmore, while the balance of malt required is unpeated and is imported from the mainland.

About $15 million per year is spent on casks, with all spirits destined for single malt bottlings being matured in ex-sherry wood. Nineteen of the 23 warehouses on site are of the old-fashioned "dunnage" variety, allowing for a relatively even and cool maturation. Each batch of Highland Park single malt is the product of a vatting of a combination of cask types. After vatting, the whiskey is returned to casks for a "marrying" period of about six months, though this period may be longer for some of the older expressions.

Highland Park's heritage

The northernmost distillery in Scotland, Highland Park stands on the southern outskirts of Kirkwall, the largest settlement on Mainland island and the capital of the Orkneys. The distillery was constructed by David Robertson during the last

HIGHLAND PARK "NEW MAKE SPIRIT"

HIGHLAND PARK 12-YEAR-OLD

decade of the 18th century, though the precise date of establishment has proved elusive, as is the case with so many of Scotland's older distilleries.

From 1826, various members of the Borthwick family ran Highland Park, and in 1895 James Grant purchased the distillery. Three years later he doubled capacity by adding two more stills alongside the existing pair. In 1937 Highland Distilleries acquired Highland Park, and in 1979 the first official bottling of the brand took place, with the company investing heavily to promote it, carving out an international profile for their prized single malt. Highland Distilleries was subsequently renamed Highland Distillers, and in 1999 became part of The Edrington Group.

Under the stewardship of Edrington, sales of Highland Park increased by 175 percent during the decade from 2000, and Gerry Tosh says, "We look at 2005 as a turning point, as two major events in the brand's history took place. First, we opted for new, more authentic packaging, where we took an old sample bottle from circa 1860 and blew it up to full size to create the template for the new bottle. Just weeks after launching the bottle we won the accolade of 'The Best Spirit in the World,' catapulting our 18-year-old to the top of the tree."

The whiskeys

The heart of the permanent Highland Park range is formed by 12-, 15-, 18-, 25-, and 30-year-olds, while 40- and 50-year-old expressions are also available. Five single-cask "Ambassador Cask" bottlings were released between 2005 and 2008, and a trio of natural strength "Earl Magnus" limited editions appeared from 2009 to 2011. The distillery also pays a great deal of attention to the whiskey-buying traveler, creating unusual limited vintages exclusive to the travel market.

HIGHLAND PARK 18-YEAR-OLD

HEAVENLY SPIRITS

By 1798, Highland Park distillery had been established on the site of a bothy previously used by local beadle and smuggler/illicit distiller Magnus Eunson. According to legend, Eunson stored illicit whiskey beneath a church pulpit, on one occasion moving it to his house in anticipation of a raid by excise officers. When the excisemen arrived at the house, they found Eunson and his family solemnly gathered around what looked like a bier but was actually the offending kegs of whiskey, covered with a cloth. Eunson intimated to the officers that there had been a death, and utterance of the word "smallpox" was enough to send them scurrying away.

TASTING NOTES

HIGHLAND PARK "NEW MAKE SPIRIT"
new make spirit, 50% ABV
Fresh on the nose, with cereal, bladderwrack, and a whiff of cocoa. Intense fruits, graham crackers, and smoke on the palate. Unsurprisingly short in the finish, with nuts and ash.

HIGHLAND PARK 12-YEAR-OLD
single malt, 40% ABV, ex-sherry casks
The nose is fragrant and floral, with hints of heather and some spice. Smooth and honeyed on the palate, with citric fruits, malt, and wood smoke in the warm, lengthy, slightly peaty finish.

HIGHLAND PARK 18-YEAR-OLD
single malt, 43% ABV, ex-sherry casks
Floral and aromatic on the nose, with heather, honeycombs, wood smoke, salt, and oak. The palate is sweet, with peat, nuts, honey, and stem ginger. The finish is spicy, drying, and long.

JURA 10-YEAR-OLD "ORIGINS"

JURA "PROPHECY"

ISLE OF JURA

OWNER Whyte & Mackay Ltd.	
FOUNDED 1810 **CAPACITY** 581,000 gal (2.2m liters)	
ADDRESS Craighouse, Isle of Jura PA60 7XT	
WEBSITE www.isleofjura.com	

Although separated from the Isle of Islay by only a narrow stretch of sea, in stylistic terms the single malt from the Isle of Jura distillery in the island's tiny capital of Craighouse is generally much closer to the mainland whiskeys of the Highland and Speyside regions. This is due to a conscious decision made at the time of the distillery's creation in the early 1960s to produce a single malt that would have wider appeal than the heavily peated drams of Islay, which at the time were a long way from having the sort of cult status they enjoy today. Accordingly, tall stills were installed and a lightly peated malt regimen was put in place.

Whiskey once more
The style of spirits produced when Jura's pair of stills was first fired up in 1963 was very different from that of the original Jura distillery, which was probably established in 1810 and was first licensed during 1831 to William Abercrombie. Distilling continued under a number of different licensees until James Ferguson & Company took over in 1876, but the operation ceased in 1901, due to a dispute between Ferguson and his landlord, Colin Campbell. Ferguson stripped the distillery of its equipment, and Campbell removed the roofs of the buildings in 1920 to avoid having to pay tax.

Distilling appeared to have been lost to Jura forever, but in 1960, as part of an attempt to stem depopulation and introduce new employment opportunities, Leith blenders and bottlers Charles Mackinlay & Company set out to restore whiskey-making to the island. The designer of Tullibardine distillery, William Delmé-Evans, was recruited to head the project to build a new Jura distillery in Craighouse, and some of the existing buildings were incorporated into the design.

By the time the distillery came on line in 1963, Mackinlay & Company had been taken over by Scottish & Newcastle Breweries Ltd., which ran the distillery until it was purchased by Invergordon Distillers Group PLC in 1985. In 1993, Invergordon was acquired by Whyte & Mackay Ltd. after a hostile takeover, and the Glasgow-based distiller continues to operate Jura today.

Jura style
Although stylistically and geographically separated from Islay, the Jura distillery participates fully in the annual Feis Ile, or Islay Festival of Malt & Music, and its visitors' center, imaginatively upgraded in

2011, attracts an increasing number of people. The whiskey itself is also becoming more popular and well regarded, with inspired limited edition releases, such as the 2008 quartet of vintage "Elements" bottlings and 2010's trio of "Boutique Barrels."

Master Blender Richard Paterson says, "Jura is a light island whiskey; it's very individual in style and has lots of complexity. For the last 10 years we have been involved in an ongoing wood program to recask younger whiskeys into fresh Bourbon casks. We started with some that were three years old and have been doing it ever since. This has brought the liquid to a new level, imparting lovely buttery, honeyed notes. American white oak is key to Jura, as it really doesn't like ex-sherry wood until it is at least 16 years old."

David Robertson, Director of Rare Malts for Whyte & Mackay, adds, "Sales of Jura have been phenomenal, and it is now the fastest-growing malt brand in the world. This is due to a number of PR and marketing initiatives, including link-ups with Visit Scotland to run a worldwide photography competition, and the reintroduction of our Writers in Residence program, where we have famous authors pen a story set on the island, and of course it helps that our whiskey has a diverse portfolio."

Peat now plays a part within that portfolio, as Jura "Superstition" has been in existence since 2002, comprising heavily peated younger spirits and some older "standard" Jura, and the warmth of its reception encouraged the distillers to add "Prophecy" to the lineup in 2009. "Prophecy" is non-chill-filtered and the peating level has been cranked up so that you could be forgiven for thinking that it was made on the other side of the Sound of Islay. Away from peated expressions, the core Jura range includes a 10-year-old ("Origins") and 16-year-old ("Diurach's Own").

WRITERS' RETREAT

George Orwell wrote his futuristic novel *Nineteen Eighty-Four* while living in a remote cottage at Barnhill, in northern Jura, during 1946–48. Although his favorite drink was dark rum, the Jura Malt Whisky Writers' Retreat program now gives authors the opportunity to spend a month living and writing on the island, based in the restored Jura Lodge. Literature and Jura single malt whiskey had already been linked with the release of a limited edition sherry cask-finished 19-year-old "Jura 1984" bottling.

JURA 16-YEAR-OLD "DIURACH'S OWN"

TASTING NOTES

JURA 10-YEAR-OLD "ORIGINS"
single malt, 40% ABV
Resin, oil, and pine notes on the delicate nose, light-bodied in the mouth, with malt and drying saltiness. The finish is malty and nutty, with more salt and a wisp of smoke.

JURA 16-YEAR-OLD "DIURACH'S OWN"
single malt, 40% ABV
The nose offers malt, cinnamon, cedar, and citrus fruits. The palate is rounded and sweet, with almonds, honey, buttered scones, and mild spice. Marzipan, more spice, and oak are in the finish.

JURA "PROPHECY"
single malt, 46% ABV, non-chill-filtered
A nose of smoked fish, brine, and butter. Textured and mouth-coating, with flavors of luscious fruit, peat smoke, spice, and licorice sticks. Peat lingers in the spicy finish, which becomes drier and more ashy.

LAGAVULIN

OWNER Diageo PLC	

FOUNDED 1816 **CAPACITY** 594,000 gal (2.25m liters)

ADDRESS Port Ellen, Isle of Islay, Argyllshire PA42 7DZ

WEBSITE www.discovering-distilleries.com

The most evocative way to arrive on Islay is by ferry into the southern ferry terminus of Port Ellen. That way you sail past the three distinctive white-washed Kildalton distilleries of Ardbeg, Lagavulin, and Laphroaig—the big-hitting trio of the island. From the mainland, Lagavulin distillery boasts views across Lagavulin Bay to the ruins of Dunyvaig Castle.

Lagavulin is of similar vintage to its two distilling neighbors, first being licensed to John Johnston in 1816, when the area was a haven for illicit distillers. A year later another distillery was constructed close by, carrying the Ardmore name and operated by Archibald Campbell. Ardmore survived for just four years before closing, at which time it was acquired by John Johnston, who ran it in tandem with Lagavulin until 1835.

Lagavulin's long and ongoing association with the White Horse blend of Scotch whiskey effectively began in 1867, when the distillery was bought by James Logan Mackie & Company. Mackie's nephew, Peter, joined the company in 1878, and in 1889 he inherited the distillery on the death of his uncle.

Restless Peter

Peter Mackie has been described as "one-third genius, one-third megalomaniac, one-third eccentric," earning the nickname "Restless Peter" because of his enormous enthusiasm and appetite for innovation and the pursuit of excellence.

A year after he took over the distillery he launched White Horse into export markets; somewhat unusually, the brand didn't appear in the domestic arena until 1901. Lagavulin was a major component of the blend, and to this day White Horse betrays a much greater Islay influence than most of its competitors. The name was taken from the White Horse Cellar Inn, located on Edinburgh's Canongate, and it in turn was named after the white palfrey ridden by Mary, Queen of Scots to and from the Palace of Holyrood.

Peter Mackie died in 1924, having been knighted for services to whiskey, and in that year the company was renamed White Horse Distillers Ltd. in recognition of its best-known product. In 1927 it became part of Distillers Company Ltd.

In 1988 a 16-year-old Lagavulin was chosen as the Islay representative in what had by then become United Distillers' Classic Malts portfolio. Diageo's Georgie Crawford says, "Sales have

LAGAVULIN 12-YEAR-OLD

LAGAVULIN "DISTILLERS EDITION"

Although you would never know it from looking at the distillery buildings today, the Lagavulin site once boasted a second, smaller-scale working distillery by the name of Malt Mill, which operated between 1908 and 1960; one of several lost distilleries from Islay's past. This partner plant was developed by Peter Mackie to produce a long-lost illicit style of "small still" spirits and he made liberal use of peat rather than coal in his new facility. Malt Mill utilized some of the buildings of the erstwhile Ardmore Distillery, which had closed in 1835. In 1962 the pair of stills from Malt Mill were transferred into Lagavulin and today the maltings of Malt Mill serve as the Lagavulin visitors' center, where tours of the distillery end with a welcome dram.

Lagavulin enjoys a beautiful location *on the shores of the bay after which it is named.*

gradually increased and Lagavulin remains very much in demand, and therefore sometimes hard to get hold of. The quality of liquid, reputation, and availability means the brand continues to command ever-higher prices, and we are seeing growing demand and sales outside the established European market, including in Asia."

Making Lagavulin

Since the opening of DCL's large-scale commercial Port Ellen Maltings in 1974, Lagavulin has sourced its peated malt from that facility, and slow fermentation of between 55 and 75 hours allows the full peaty character to shine through.

Lagavulin is equipped with four stills, two of which are in the same pear-shaped style as those transferred from Malt Mill back in the early 1960s. The same slowness of processing that characterizes fermentation continues in the stills, with the first run lasting for some five hours and the second for nearly twice that duration. Unusually, the spirit stills are filled almost to their full capacity in order to ensure minimal contact between spirit and copper, leading to the whiskey's distinctively robust character.

Once distilled, Lagavulin is now transported to the mainland for maturation, though around 16,000 casks are currently maturing on Islay, in warehouses at Lagavulin, Caol Ila, and the former distillery of Port Ellen. The stone warehouses at Port Ellen date back to the founding of the

distillery in 1825 and, along with the listed malt kilns, are almost the only surviving structures.

A decade after Lagavulin 16-year-old was selected as one of the founding whiskies of the Classic Malts range, it was joined by a "Distillers Edition" expression. A cask-strength 12-year-old was added to the lineup in 2002, and many subsequent editions at that age have followed in Diageo's "Special Releases." Until 1987, a 12-year-old was the principal Lagavulin variant available.

TASTING NOTES

LAGAVULIN 12-YEAR-OLD (SPECIAL RELEASES 2011)
single malt, 57.5% ABV, cask strength, matured in refilled American oak casks
A big hit of Islay on the nose—salt, seaweed, and iodine. The palate is fruity, with developing wood smoke, spice, mixed herbs, bonfire embers, and carbolic soap. Citrus fruit, sweet peat, pepper, and medicine chests in the finish.

LAGAVULIN 16-YEAR-OLD
single malt, 43% ABV
Peat, iodine, sherry, and vanilla come together on the rich nose. The peat and iodine theme continues onto the big, spicy, sherried palate, with brine and raisins. Peat embers in the long, full, spicy finish.

LAGAVULIN "DISTILLERS EDITION" (VINTAGE 1994)
single malt, 43% ABV, finished in ex-Pedro Ximénez sherry butts after principal period of maturation
Smoky and mildly fishy on the nose, with big, sherried, stewed fruit, and raisin notes. Full-bodied and rounded, with peat smoke and sherry. The finish is long, softly smoky, and gently spiced.

LAGAVULIN 16-YEAR-OLD

LAPHROAIG

OWNER Beam Global
FOUNDED 1815 **CAPACITY** 766,000 gal (2.9m liters)
ADDRESS Port Ellen, Isle of Islay, Argyll PA42 7DU
WEBSITE www.laphroaig.com

LAPHROAIG 10-YEAR-OLD

It could be said that Laphroaig is the Limburger cheese of the whiskey world, since few consumers are noncommittal about its hardcore peaty, medicinal charms. Indeed, the marketing team behind the brand chose to make a virtue of this polarization several years ago with a campaign that declared "Laphroaig—love it or hate it." There was even a rather brave tagline to the effect that "Your first taste may be your last." High-profile aficionados of the distinctive style include HRH The Prince of Wales, who bestowed his Royal Warrant on the distillery in 1994.

John Campbell has been Distillery Manager at Laphroaig since stepping into the shoes of the legendary Iain Henderson in 2006, when he became the youngest distillery manager on Islay and the first Ileach (native of Islay) to hold the position in living memory. For Campbell, the continuation of in-house malting plays a significant part in the unique style of Laphroaig, and around 15 percent of the distillery's total malt requirements are made on the four malting floors. The overall phenolic level of all malt used at Laphroaig is around 60 ppm.

According to Campbell, "Some of the unique salty, medicinal character we want in Laphroaig comes from the floor maltings. For one thing, we peat the malt before we dry it, whereas everybody else peats and dries at the same time. That gives

you a smaller range of peat flavors. We peat at a low temperature and then dry the barley, which gives our spirits a wider range of phenol flavors."

The original two stills at Laphroaig were augmented by a second pair in 1923, with another pair added in 1968–69 and the seventh still going in during 1974 to increase capacity further. The spirit distillation boasts the longest foreshots run of any Scottish distillery, a practice designed to eliminate the sweet esters that flow early from the spirit still and are not part of the Laphroaig character profile.

The owners of Laphroaig

Laphroaig is the world's best-selling Islay single malt and the distillery that produces it was first licensed in 1815, to brothers Alexander and Donald Johnston, though it is thought that the Johnstons may have been distilling at Laphroaig for several years prior to receiving their license.

The distillery was operated by the Johnston family until the death in 1954 of Ian Hunter, the last family member to be involved. Hunter was famously succeeded at the Laphroaig helm by the redoubtable Elizabeth "Bessie" Williamson, who had worked as Ian Hunter's personal assistant and became one of the very few women at that time to have a distillery role that extended beyond making tea or typing correspondence.

Bessie Williamson ran Laphroaig until she retired in 1972, though during the previous decade, ownership of the distillery had passed

As one of the few *distilleries to retain its floor maltings, the rich aroma of peat smoke is common around Laphroaig.*

FINE MALT FRIENDS

In 1994, Laphroaig devised a marketing innovation in the shape of the "Friends of Laphroaig," which now boasts around half a million members worldwide. Each Friend is given a lifetime's lease on a tiny portion of land at the distillery and the annual "rent" takes the form of a dram of Laphroaig. The scheme commemorates the Johnston brothers' struggle, after founding the distillery at the beginning of the 19th century, to secure the distillery's water supply. The brothers eventually purchased the land that the water flows through. In addition, the distillery offers a number of varied visitor experiences, including the Hunter's Hike, during which participants enjoy a dram at the distillery water source, cut peat, and then return to the distillery to tend the barley on the malting floors.

to Seager Evans & Company. The famous brewer Whitbread & Company Ltd. bought Seager Evans in 1975 and in 1989 Allied Distillers Ltd. took over Whitbread's spirits division. When the Allied empire was split up in 2005, Laphroaig, along with Ardmore distillery in Aberdeenshire and Teacher's blended Scotch whiskey, was purchased by Fortune Brands. Today, that organization's Scotch whiskey interests are controlled by its Beam Global Spirits & Wine subsidiary.

Laphroaig releases

Compared to fellow Islay distilleries Ardbeg and Bruichladdich, Laphroaig has adopted a restrained releases policy, with a "Quarter Cask" expression being bottled under the Allied Distillers' regime in 2005 to keep the standard 10-year-old company. "Quarter Cask" draws its inspiration from the small casks often used to transport whiskey on horseback during the 19th century, and as the smaller casks provide up to 30 percent more contact between the wood and its contents, the maturation process is intensified.

Subsequently, the principal additions to the core range have been a 25-year-old in 2007, an 18-year-old in 2009, and "Triple Wood" (previously exclusive to travel retail outlets) in 2011. Like "Quarter Cask," "Triple Wood" is bottled at 48 percent ABV and carries no age statement. Initial maturation takes place in ex-Bourbon barrels, before spirit of varying ages is transferred into quarter casks for a period of secondary aging, with a final spell of maturation in European oak ex-Oloroso sherry casks.

LAPHROAIG "QUARTER CASK"

TASTING NOTES

LAPHROAIG 10-YEAR-OLD
single malt, 40% ABV
Old-fashioned adhesive bandages, peat smoke, and seaweed leap off the nose, followed by sweeter and fruitier notes. Massive on the palate, with fish oil, salt, and plankton, though the finish is surprisingly tight and increasingly drying.

LAPHROAIG 25-YEAR-OLD "CASK STRENGTH"
single malt, 50.9% ABV, matured in a mix of ex-Bourbon and ex-Oloroso sherry casks, non-chill-filtered
Sherry, sweet peat, and soft spices on the nose, with antiseptic cream, smoke, and new leather. Full-bodied, with restrained sherry, more peat, spices, and apples. The finish is lengthy, with gentle smoke, sustained fruit notes, licorice, and iodine.

LAPHROAIG "QUARTER CASK"
single malt, 48% ABV, initially matured in ex-Bourbon barrels, transferred into 125-liter quarter casks for a final period, non-chill-filtered
Sweet barley and profound smoky, medicinal notes, coal, and spice on the nose. Toffee, hazelnuts, powerful peat, and cigarette ash on the palate. The lengthy finish features graham crackers and chimneys.

LAPHROAIG 25-YEAR-OLD "CASK STRENGTH"

TALISKER

OWNER	Diageo PLC
FOUNDED 1830	**CAPACITY** 687,000 gal (2.6m liters)
ADDRESS	Carbost, Isle of Skye, Inverness-shire IV47 8SR
WEBSITE	www.discovering-distilleries.com

Talisker distillery was established in 1830 by brothers Hugh and Kenneth MacAskill, who had arrived in Skye just a few years previously from their native island of Eigg, purchasing agricultural land and the mansion of Talisker House, which had played host to Dr. Johnson and James Boswell during their famous 1773 tour of the Hebrides.

Subsequent owners of Talisker distillery included Anderson & Company, whose principal, John Anderson, was jailed in 1880 for selling nonexistent whiskey to customers who assumed it was safely maturing in the Talisker warehouses. In the same year, ownership passed to Alexander Grigor Allan and Roderick Kemp, though Kemp was later to sell his shares and invest instead in a Speyside distillery by the name of Macallan.

"King o'drinks"

At a time when single malt whiskey was a relative rarity outside the Highlands, Talisker was already highly regarded, with the novelist Robert Louis Stevenson writing in the same year that Anderson was imprisoned, "The King o'drinks, as I conceive it, Talisker, Isla or Glenlivet!"

In 1894 The Talisker Distillery Company Ltd. was founded, and four years later, Talisker merged with Dailuaine-Glenlivet Distillers and Imperial Distillers to create the Dailuaine-Talisker Distilleries Ltd. In 1916 that company was taken over by a consortium including W P Lowrie & Company, John Walker & Sons Ltd., and John Dewar & Sons Ltd., and Talisker was one of the assets which passed into the hands of The Distillers Company Ltd. in 1925.

Three years later the practice of triple-distillation was abandoned at Talisker, though the stillhouse configuration of two wash stills and three spirit stills that persists to this day harks back to the time of triple-distillation.

Talisker aflame

Those five stills were at the center of the most dramatic episode in Talisker's history, when, on November 22, 1960, a valve on the coal-fired No.1 spirit still was inadvertently left open during distillation. Spirit escaped from the still and caught fire, and the entire stillhouse burned down. A reconstruction program was instigated, and the new stillhouse was equipped with five stills that were exact copies of the originals.

TALISKER 10-YEAR-OLD

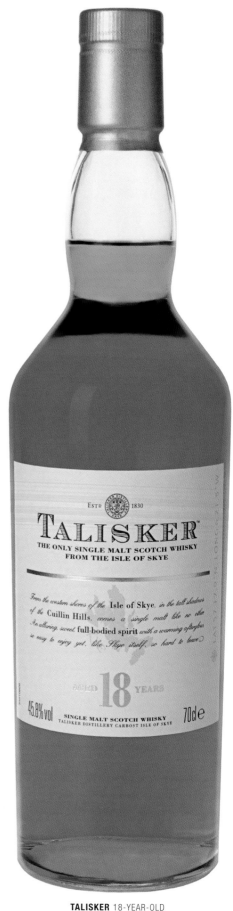

TALISKER 18-YEAR-OLD

Many Scottish distilleries are blessed with beautiful surroundings, but few can match the sheer grandeur of Talisker's setting in the northwest of the Isle of Skye. The distillery stands on the shores of Loch Harport, in the shadow of the mighty Cuillin Hills, a dramatically jagged range of hills that were formed from volcanic eruptions at least 70 million years ago. Indeed, Talisker is sometimes referred to as "The lava of the Cuillins" and one dram of this smoky and characterful single malt is enough to reveal the aptness of the saying. The only distillery located on Skye (so far as Her Majesty's Revenue & Customs knows, at any rate) is quite modern and even utilitarian in appearance, contrasting with the ancient grandeur of its setting.

The hills of Skye *were formed out of lava flows, making the hot-and-smoky style of Talisker whiskey most apt.*

It is sometimes claimed that the fire actually saved the distillery, since it would have been an obvious candidate for closure during owner DCL's 1980s program of cutbacks due to its isolated location. Only the fact that so much money had been spent on it two decades previously meant that it was not a victim of the cutbacks, or so the argument goes.

In 1972 the replacement stills were converted to steam heating, and at the same time floor malting was abandoned, with malted barley being shipped in from the recently-constructed Glen Ord Maltings in Inverness-shire. Talisker's malt is peated to 18–20ppm.

A 10-year-old Talisker was included in the new Classic Malts line up in 1988, and a visitors' center was created. Despite its geographical remoteness, Talisker is Diageo's most-visited distillery, playing host to around 50,000 people per year.

Today's Talisker

This interest in the distillery reflects the level of appreciation of the individualistic whiskey made there, and sales have risen dramatically during the past few years. Today's core range comprises 10- and 18-year-olds, along with a "Distillers Edition" and Talisker "57° North" (a cask-strength expression with no age statement), while 25- and 30-year-old limited edition bottlings have regularly appeared as part of Diageo's annual Special Releases program. Additionally, a 12-year-old cask strength Talisker is available exclusively at the distillery.

Mark Lochhead of Diageo explains the effects of Talisker's distilling regime, noting that "Talisker's two wash stills are unique. The lye pipes leading off from the main neck are U-shaped, to trap vapors from the first distillation before they reach the outside worm tubs, while a small secondary copper pipe carries the vapors so-trapped back to the wash stills for a second distillation. Faithfully following the original design, it is believed that this double distillation ensures that all of the rich, deep character of Talisker is captured first time."

TASTING NOTES

TALISKER 10-YEAR-OLD
single malt, 45.8% ABV
Pungent peat, brown sugar, and lots of spice on the nose. More peat and spice on the full, confident palate, with malt and pepper notes. The finish is very long, with hot peat and chili pepper.

TALISKER 18-YEAR-OLD
single malt, 45.8% ABV
A powerful yet mellow nose, sweet and slightly smoky. The palate opens with sweet, fruity notes that deepen, with hints of a smoldering peat fire. The finish is rich, with a classic Talisker peppery kick.

TALISKER "DISTILLERS EDITION" (2000)
single malt, 45.8% ABV, finished in
ex-Amoroso sherry casks
A nose of warm leather, pipe tobacco, black pepper, toffee, and prunes. Mouth-coating and luscious, with a palate of treacle, sherry, malt, and nutmeg. Slowly drying in a fruity, buttery finish, with pepper at the close.

TALISKER "DISTILLERS EDITION"

TOBERMORY

OWNER Burn Stewart Distillers (CL World Brands Ltd.)
FOUNDED 1798 **CAPACITY** 264,000 gal (1m liters)
ADDRESS Tobermory, Isle of Mull PA75 6NR
WEBSITE www.tobermorymalt.com

Tobermory distillery is located close to the harbor in the eponymous fishing and tourist port that serves as the capital of the Inner Hebridean Isle of Mull. The town is characterized by its many brightly painted properties and gained wide recognition internationally thanks to the children's television series *Balamory*, filmed among its primary-colored houses and shops.

The distillery is one of Scotland's oldest surviving whiskey-making facilities, dating back to 1798, when it was founded by local merchant John Sinclair. He christened the new venture Ledaig, which translates from the Gaelic as "safe haven." However, during the ensuing two centuries, Ledaig was to be far from a safe haven for whiskey-making, as the distillery has actually been silent for more than half of its entire existence. It was first closed between 1837 and 1878, and then from 1930 until 1972, having been bought by the Distillers Company Ltd. in 1916. Prior to its next bout of whiskey production, the site served as a canteen for sailors and even as a power station.

In 1972 production began again, this time under the auspices of the Ledaig Distillery Ltd., formed by a Liverpool shipping operator and the Spanish sherry firm of Domecq. However, that company went bankrupt three years later. Yorkshire-based Kirkleavington Property Company Ltd. bought Tobermory in 1979, but they also found profits elusive, committing the cardinal sin of selling the distillery's one warehouse for redevelopment into apartments, and then closing the plant by 1989. Happily for Tobermory, Burn Stewart Distillers saw potential in the only licensed distillery on Mull, and in 1993 spent $900,000 buying it, devoting a further $300,000 to maturing stock.

The complexities of maturation

Burn Stewart uses Tobermory and Ledaig in its "Scottish Leader" and "Black Bottle" blends and has striven to raise the profile and improve the image and quality of Tobermory single malt, turning a former tun room into a small warehouse during 2007 so that at least some of the spirits being made could be matured in their place of origin.

This initiative draws on the idea that there are subtle differences between the way whiskey matures in varying microclimates, and Burn Stewart's Distilleries Manager and Master Blender Ian Macmillan is a firm believer in the phenomenon. "Five years ago I took a filling of Ledaig, tankered it to our Deanston distillery in Perthshire, filled it into refill hogsheads there, and then left one-third of the casks at Deanston to mature, took one-third back to Mull, and the other third went to Bunnahabhain on Islay. So we are now five years into that experiment to see what the differences are, and I reckon it will soon be time to sample and analyze the three batches. Maybe when the whiskey is 10 years old we will produce a three-bottle pack so that consumers can judge the differences for themselves."

Tobermory's picture-postcard *harbor front is famed for its row of brightly colored houses.*

LEDAIG 10-YEAR-OLD

In from the cold

Along with Bunnahabhain and Deanston, since 2010 Tobermory and Ledaig's principal single malts have been offered at a strength of 46.3 per cent ABV and are no longer subject to chill filtration, designed to ensure that lower-strength whiskeys do not become cloudy at lower temperatures.

"As a blender you always work with non-chill-filtered samples, so I knew that those samples and the chill-filtered whiskey that we bottled were totally different animals," says Macmillan. "Tobermory and Ledaig were crying out to be non-chill-filtered, and now you have increased depth, weight of flavor, and complexity. They are much more structured and textured. The 'before' and 'after' were like two different liquids.

"When I took the sheets from the filter plates after chill filtration, they were oily and greasy; they left a great intensity of aroma and texture on my hands. This was part of the DNA of my single malts. Making the whiskey "pretty" by chill-filtering it was at the expense of aroma and flavor. There was a part of the whiskey missing, in effect. What was once seen as a flaw by marketing people is now being seen as a sign of integrity and quality. We were the first company to take our entire range, across all our distilleries, to non-chill-filtered status, and it's been very well received."

At present, the lineup embraces 10- and 15-year-old Tobermory single malts and a 10-year-old Ledaig, with a significant number of limited editions of the latter brand having also appeared over the years. In 2005 a 32-year-old bottling of Tobermory was released, while 2012 saw 40-year-old variants of both Tobermory and Ledaig hit the shelves.

TASTING NOTES

TOBERMORY 10-YEAR-OLD
single malt, 46.3% ABV, non-chill-filtered
Fresh and nutty on the nose, with citrus fruit and brittle toffee. Medium-bodied, textured, quite dry on the palate, with malt and nuts. The finish boasts a hint of mint and a slight citric tang.

LEDAIG 10-YEAR-OLD
single malt, 46.3% ABV, non-chill-filtered
The nose is peaty, sweet, and full, with butter and smoked fish. Bold, yet sweet on the palate, with iodine, soft peat, and heather, developing spices. The finish reveals pepper, ginger, licorice, and peat.

TOBERMORY 32-YEAR-OLD
single malt, 49.7% ABV, finished in Oloroso sherry casks, 902 bottles, non-chill-filtered
A rich and fragrant nose, with dry sherry, raisins, and peat smoke. The rounded palate presents powerful sherry, smoke, chocolate, stewed fruit, and some tannins. The finish is medium in length, drying, with coffee.

A PEATY PRESENCE

While some distilleries producing unpeated or lightly peated single malt whiskey also make occasional batches of more heavily peated spirits, 50 percent of Tobermory's annual output is now heavily peated spirits, bearing the Ledaig name. Ledaig was first introduced in 1996 and is peated to at least 35–40ppm. "You get a very different style of peated whiskey because of the unique Tobermory stills," says Burn Stewart's Ian Macmillan; the stills in question are equipped with "S"-shaped lyne arms, designed to give heavy reflux. "There is a lot of smoke and lots of sweetness, too," says Macmillan. "We are effectively recreating the original style of whiskey."

TOBERMORY 10-YEAR-OLD

ABHAINN DEARG

OWNER Mark Tayburn
FOUNDED 2008 **CAPACITY** 6,600 gal (25,000 liters)
ADDRESS Carnish, Isle of Lewis HS2 9EX
WEBSITE www.abhainndearg.co.uk

Scotland's westernmost distillery, and the only licensed distillery in the Outer Hebrides, Abhainn Dearg is situated on the ruggedly beautiful Atlantic coast of the island of Lewis. This is one of the remaining Gaelic heartlands and the name translates as "Red River."

The distillery started production in September 2008, and in 2011 just 2,011 bottles of three-year-old Abhainn Dearg "Single Malt Special Edition" were released. No more whiskey will be bottled until it is five years of age.

An idiosyncratic distillery
Abhainn Dearg's founder is one-time construction worker turned recycling merchant Mark Tayburn, who constructed his distillery on the site of a former salmon hatchery. The pair of steam-heated stills are truly idiosyncratic and reminiscent of old-fashioned domestic hot water tanks, with necks like elongated witches' hats, linked to lyne arms that twist dramatically before descending into a pair of wooden worm tubs. The distillery also boasts a genuine former illicit still, which takes a 21-gallon (80-liter) charge and is used from time to time, with the make filled into Oloroso sherry casks.

Additionally, around five tons of peated malt is distilled each year, with a peating level of 35–40ppm. "While 90 percent of everything we distill goes into ex-Bourbon casks, we also experiment with sherry, red, and white wine casks, Madeira, and virgin oak," says Tayburn. "We've got some interesting stuff maturing in the warehouses!

"The three-year-old single malt received very positive feedback, and I hope we will be able to release a 'standard' bottling of between seven and ten years old, with limited releases along the way."

ABHAINN DEARG "SINGLE MALT"

TASTING NOTES

ABHAINN DEARG
"SINGLE MALT SPECIAL EDITION"
single malt, 46% ABV
The nose exhibits ginger, candied citrus peel, and apricots, while in the mouth there is lively spice, vanilla, honey, and toffee. The finish is relatively short and nutty.

ABHAINN DEARG "SPIRIT OF LEWIS"
spirit drink, 40% ABV, new spirit filled into ex-Pedro Ximénez sherry casks for a three-month maturation
Grass and canned pears on the nose, with sweet cereal and a mildly herbal note. Quite voluptuous in the mouth, with plump barley. The finish is gently spicy, with a final note of fruit-and-nut chocolate.

KILCHOMAN

OWNER Kilchoman Distillery Company Ltd.
FOUNDED 2005 **CAPACITY** 30,400 gal (115,000 liters)
ADDRESS Rockside Farm, Bruichladdich, Isle of Islay PA49 7UT
WEBSITE www.kilchomandistillery.com

Kilchoman has established such a high-profile position among the ranks of Islay distilleries, it's easy to forget the first casks were only filled in 2005. This is partly a result of Kilchoman's welcoming visitors right from the start. Perhaps more significantly, however, Kilchoman was one of the first distilleries to offer miniature bottles of its new-make spirit for sale, thereby embedding the Kilchoman name in the consciousness of Islay whiskey aficionados. Since the first spirits distilled at Kilchoman reached three years of age, there has been a stream of limited edition releases charting the progress of this enjoyably precocious whiskey.

Islay from barley to bottle
Kilchoman was established at Rockside Farm, 4 miles (6.5 km) from Bruichladdich, by Anthony Wills, and when it opened for business it was the first new Islay distillery to come into being since the long-defunct Malt Mill plant was set up at Lagavulin in 1908. The distillery malts a percentage of its own barley (usually to 20–25ppm), some of which is grown on Rockside Farm, with the rest of the malt coming from Port Ellen maltings and being peated to 50ppm. Since the installation of a bottling line, Wills's original dream of being able to boast that his operation embraces everything from barley to bottle has come to fruition, and accordingly in 2011 Kilchoman "100% Islay" was released.

TASTING NOTES

KILCHOMAN 5-YEAR-OLD "2006 VINTAGE"
single malt, 46% ABV, matured 80% fresh and 20% refill Bourbon barrels, non-chill-filtered
Grist and peat embers, citrus fruit, and vanilla on the nose. More peat on the palate, with Weetabix and a sprinkling of black pepper. Medium finish, spicy, and ashy.

KILCHOMAN "100% ISLAY"
single malt, 50% ABV, peated to 10–20ppm and matured first-fill Bourbon barrels from Buffalo Trace Distillery, non-chill-filtered
Lots of brine, peat smoke, and overt citrus notes on the nose. Lemon pith and beach bonfires. Sweet, fruit notes on the early palate, then antiseptic and ashy peat. Relatively lengthy in the finish, with smoldering peat.

KILCHOMAN 2-YEAR-OLD "NEW SPIRIT"
new-make spirit, 63.5% ABV
Fresh and cereally on the nose, with mild antiseptic notes. Quite sweet, peaty, and fruity. Big and smoky-sweet on the palate, with pears, mangoes, and oranges. The finish is long, warming, and delicately smoky.

KILCHOMAN "NEW SPIRIT"

SCAPA

OWNER Chivas Brothers Ltd. (Pernod Ricard)
FOUNDED 1885 **CAPACITY** 396,000 gal (1.5m liters)
ADDRESS St. Ola, Kirkwall, Orkney KW15 1SE
WEBSITE www.scapamalt.com

A very fine single malt in its own right, Scapa has played second fiddle to its older and much better known Orcadian neighbor, Highland Park, for as long as anyone remembers. Today, however, after benefiting from a $3 million upgrade in 2004, and with a well-regarded 16-year-old expression now being offered, Scapa enjoys a higher profile than ever before.

A tradition maintained

The distillery is notable for its extremely long fermentation times (up to 160 hours), which tend to give a distinctly fruity character to the spirit when distilled, and for the fact that its wash still is of the "Lomond" type. This was installed at Scapa in 1959 in order to give the then-owners Hiram Walker a heavier and oilier style of spirit for blending purposes. Suitably modified for standard distillation, with its rectification plates removed, this idiosyncratic still is the only one of its kind making whiskey in Scotland today.

Scapa dates back to 1885, when it was established on the shores of the famous anchorage of Scapa Flow by Glasgow-based Macfarlane & Townsend. Until recently, the owner to do most with Scapa was Hiram Walker & Sons (Scotland) Ltd., which acquired it in 1954 and largely rebuilt it in 1959.

Further modernization followed in 1978 and a decade later Hiram Walker merged with Allied Vintners to become Allied Distillers. Then, in 1994, Scapa was mothballed, with sporadic production introduced three years later. It was thus a surprise when Allied decided on a program of much-needed investment, but the present Chivas Brothers regime is grateful to them for the money and effort they spent on Orkney's "second" distillery.

TASTING NOTES

SCAPA 16-YEAR-OLD

single malt, 40% ABV, finished for
two years in first-fill ex-Bourbon casks
The nose offers apricots and peaches, nougat, and mixed spices. Medium-bodied, with caramel and spice notes in the mouth. The finish is medium in length and gingery, with fat, buttery notes emerging at the end.

SCAPA 25-YEAR-OLD (1980)

single malt, 54% ABV, cask strength
Cinnamon, honey, and cereal notes on the nose, balanced by a smattering of sea spray. Full-bodied, rich in the mouth, with honey, Jaffa oranges, and sweet oak. Long and spicy in the finish.

SCAPA 16-YEAR-OLD

SCAPA 25-YEAR-OLD

CAMPBELTOWN AND THE LOWLANDS

A port and former royal burgh located on the Kintyre peninsula in Argyllshire, Campbeltown is the historic capital of Scotch whiskey. Whiskey-making thrived here during the 19th century and it retains its identity as a classification of single malt, though today the streets are mainly filled with the ghosts of past distillers. The designated Lowlands region encompasses mainland Scotland below the theoretical "Highland Line," taking in many of the country's principal population centers. However, the distilleries of the Lowlands tend to enjoy unspoiled rural locations to rival anything the Highlands and Islands can offer.

During the late 19th century, Campbeltown was home to more than 20 distilleries, but today that number has dwindled to just three, with the Speyside region having usurped Campbeltown as the principal center of Scotland's whiskey-making industry. However, the remaining Campbeltown distilleries are in responsible hands, and the old herring port's whiskey heritage looks to be secure.

From the point of view of scale, the Lowlands region once far outstripped the Highlands in whiskey-making capacity and output. The establishment of a major commercial Lowland distilling industry dates from the 1770s and 1780s, with no fewer than 23 distilleries being built in the

A new take on an old-fashioned farm distillery, *Daftmill began distilling with home-grown barley in 2005.*

Lowlands during those two decades. The area boasted ready supplies of high-quality malting barley, coal to fire the kilns and stills, and a comparatively good transportation infrastructure; hence the prevalence of distilling operations in the region. As with Campbeltown, however, whiskey history has not been kind to the Lowlands, and at present just five malt distilleries are in operation there, with only three of these offering single malts for retail sale.

However, due to its transportation links and population density, the area classified as the Lowlands malt whiskey-producing region is still at the very center of the Scotch whiskey industry, being home to four of the country's six grain distilleries, as well as most of its blending and bottling operations and administrative functions.

GETTING AROUND

Ideally, make the most of a visit to remote Campbeltown by taking in some of the spectacular coastal scenery in the area, and perhaps even making the short ferry trip from Claonaig to Lochranza on Arran. Road access to Campbeltown is via the A83 from the Glasgow area. In the Lowlands, Glenkinchie is close to Edinburgh via the A68 and Auchentoshan is accessed from Glasgow by the A82, while in Galloway, Bladnoch enjoys a location almost as remote as Campbeltown.

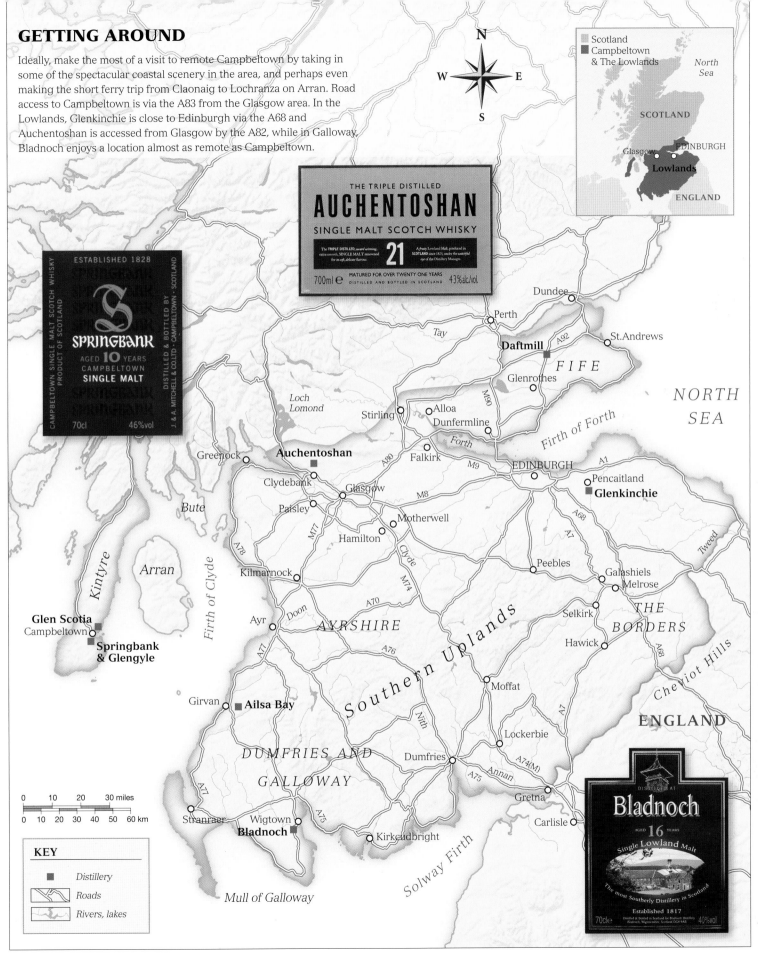

Scotland
Campbeltown
& The Lowlands

North Sea

SCOTLAND

Glasgow EDINBURGH

Lowlands

ENGLAND

THE TRIPLE DISTILLED
AUCHENTOSHAN
SINGLE MALT SCOTCH WHISKY

The TRIPLE DISTILLED, award-winning, extra smooth, SINGLE MALT renowned for its soft, delicate flavour. **21** A fruity Lowland Malt, produced in SCOTLAND since 1823, under the watchful eye of the Distillery Manager.

700ml e   MATURED FOR OVER TWENTY ONE YEARS   43%alc/vol.
DISTILLED AND BOTTLED IN SCOTLAND

ESTABLISHED 1828
SPRINGBANK
AGED **10** YEARS
CAMPBELTOWN
SINGLE MALT

70cl   46%vol

Dundee
Perth

Tay

Daftmill   A92   St.Andrews

FIFE

Glenrothes

NORTH SEA

Loch Lomond

Stirling   Alloa
Dunfermline   *Forth*   *Firth of Forth*

M90

Greenock

Auchentoshan

Clydebank   Glasgow   Falkirk   M9   EDINBURGH   A1   Pencaitland
Paisley   M8   **Glenkinchie**

Bute

Motherwell   A68   A7

Hamilton   *Clyde*   Peebles   Galashiels
                                                    Melrose

A78   Kilmarnock   M74

Arran   A77   Ayr   *Doon*   A70   **AYRSHIRE**   *Tweed*

Kintyre   *Firth of Clyde*

Glen Scotia
Campbeltown   A76   Selkirk   **THE BORDERS**
Springbank & Glengyle   *Nith*   Hawick   A7   A68

Southern Uplands

Moffat

Girvan   **Ailsa Bay**   **ENGLAND**

Lockerbie

DUMFRIES AND   Dumfries   A74(M)
GALLOWAY   A75   *Annan*   Gretna

A77   Carlisle
Stranraer   Wigtown   A75
Bladnoch   Kirkcudbright

Solway Firth

Mull of Galloway

0   10   20   30 miles
0   10   20   30   40   50   60 km

KEY

■   Distillery
    Roads
    Rivers, lakes

DISTILLED AT
Bladnoch
AGED **16** YEARS
Single Lowland Malt
The most Southerly Distillery in Scotland
Established 1817
70cl   40%vol

Cheviot Hills

AUCHENTOSHAN

OWNER Morrison Bowmore Distillers Ltd.
FOUNDED 1823 **CAPACITY** 462,000 gal (1.75m liters)
ADDRESS By Dalmuir, Clydebank, Glasgow G81 4SJ
WEBSITE www.auchentoshan.com

AUCHENTOSHAN "THREE WOOD"

AUCHENTOSHAN 18-YEAR-OLD

AUCHENTOSHAN 21-YEAR-OLD

Every single malt needs a point of difference, something unique to mark it out from the competition as special and worthy of note. In the case of the single malt from Auchentoshan Distillery, the marketing team at owner Morrison Bowmore Distillers Ltd. is gifted with the fact that their whiskey is the only one in Scotland to be fully triple distilled.

Triple distillation is principally associated with Ireland but was also a traditional characteristic of the Lowland Scottish style of production. So how does the process work in practice and what differences in character result from it?

Three times distilled

According to Kirsteen Beeston, Head of Brands Marketing for Morrison Bowmore, "Auchentoshan uses three stills—a wash still, an intermediate still, and a spirit still. Triple distillation results in a new-make spirit that starts life at 81.5 percent ABV; most other distilleries settle for a new-make spirit of 70 percent ABV, through double distillation.

"As a result of triple distillation, a lighter, cleaner, and more delicate new-make spirit is produced and it then matures inside fine oak casks." And the end product is "one of the smoothest, most delicate-tasting malts."

Starting out

That malt was first made at Auchentoshan in 1823—or, to be more precise, the first license to distill was taken out in 1823 by a Mr. Thorne, though it is thought that distilling may have been taking place on the site since around 1800.

Auchentoshan passed through various hands during the 19th century, being substantially rebuilt in 1875. In 1903 the distillery was acquired by John Maclachlan, better known as a Glasgow brewer. The distillery remained in the hands of the Maclachlans until 1960, when Maclachlans Ltd. was bought out by its high-profile brewing rival J. & R. Tennent. However, Auchentoshan had been seriously damaged during the Clydebank Blitz of March 13–14, 1941, when the equivalent of a million bottles of whiskey was lost, with contemporary reports describing a burn of flaming whiskey stretching to the Clyde River. During the Luftwaffe's devastating attack on Clydebank, around 1,200 people lost their lives, with a further 1,100 suffering serious injuries, and of the 12,000 houses in the borough it is said that only eight escaped damage.

AUCHENTOSHAN 50-YEAR-OLD "1957"

If the postwar period saw some dramatic changes in distillery and whiskey-brand ownership, this was nothing compared to the rate of consolidation prevalent in the British brewing industry, and Tennent's lost its independence to Charrington & Company in 1964, with Charrington morphing into Bass Charrington Ltd. three years later.

Ownership today

Auchentoshan was bought out of the brewer's ownership by Eadie Cairns Ltd. in 1969, and an extensive program of modernization followed. The distillery then passed to Stanley P. Morrison in 1984, for slightly more than three times the previous sale price, and a decade later, Morrison Bowmore was acquired by the Japanese distilling giant Suntory Ltd.

Investment in a $1.5 million visitors' center followed in 2004, and this stylish, modern facility now attracts about 20,000 people annually. That year also saw the eye-catching release of a 42-year-old expression, the oldest ever to be offered by the distillery. The core range was expanded significantly, and a number of vintage bottlings have been a comparatively recent feature.

Principal bottlings in the core range now include Auchentoshan "Classic," a non-age-statement variant introduced in 2008, 12-, 18-, and 21-year-olds, and "Three Wood," which appeared in 2002 and has proved notably popular.

According to Kirsteen Beeston, "Auchentoshan has been enjoying double-digit growth in recent years. Emerging markets like Russia and Taiwan are quickly challenging our established markets with growing consumption of all expressions."

TASTING NOTES

AUCHENTOSHAN "CLASSIC"
single malt, 40% ABV
Initially, intensely sweet on the nose, with peaches and Madeira, vanilla, and coconut. Smooth and fruity on the palate, with vanilla ice cream. The finish is fresh and floral, with a lingering note of ripe peaches.

AUCHENTOSHAN "THREE WOOD"
single malt, 43% ABV, matured principally in American oak ex-Bourbon casks, then finished in Spanish Oloroso sherry wood, and finally Pedro Ximénez sherry casks
Butterscotch, dates, hazelnuts, and sherry on the nose. Sweet and sherried on the rich palate, with developing citrus fruits and almonds. Quite lengthy in the fruity finish, with a tang of oak.

AUCHENTOSHAN 50-YEAR-OLD "1957"
single malt, single cask, cask-strength, 46.8% ABV, matured in Oloroso sherry butt #479 (171 bottles)
Green fruits, honey, old leather, and pipe tobacco on the complex nose. The palate is relatively dry, with initial oak followed by developing Jaffa oranges, caramel, and cloves. The medium-length finish features a menthol note.

GLASGOW MALTS

Just as Glenkinchie in the east is promoted as "the Edinburgh malt," so Auchentoshan is sometimes known as "Glasgow's malt whiskey," since the distillery is situated just 10 miles (16 km) from the center of Scotland's largest city. Auchentoshan once had a distilling neighbor in the shape of Littlemill on the north bank of the Clyde River at Bowling, until its closure in 1992 and demolition in 2006. Meanwhile, about 6 miles (9 km) west of Auchentoshan, the vast Dumbarton grain distillery complex operated from 1938 until its closure in 2002, when owners Allied Distillers switched grain production to their Strathclyde plant in Glasgow's Gorbals district.

AUCHENTOSHAN "CLASSIC"

BLADNOCH

OWNER	Coordinated Development Services Ltd.
FOUNDED 1817	**CAPACITY** 26,400 gal (100,000 liters)
ADDRESS	Bladnoch, Dumfries & Galloway DG8 9AB
WEBSITE	www.bladnoch.co.uk

BLADNOCH 16-YEAR-OLD

Located in the village of the same name, near Wigtown in Dumfries and Galloway, Bladnoch is the most southerly operational distillery in Scotland. It was founded between 1814 and 1817 by Thomas McClelland, remaining in the family's hands until 1930, when it was acquired by the Belfast distilling company of Dunville.

Since then, Bladnoch has experienced a somewhat checkered history, characterized by numerous changes of ownership and two decades of silence between 1936 and 1956. Historically, triple distillation has been a common feature of many Lowland distilleries, and Bladnoch was a triple-distilled single malt until the 1960s.

Bladnoch's owners have included Inver House Distillers, who acquired the site in 1973 and operated the plant for a decade before selling it to the expanding empire of Arthur Bell & Sons Ltd. Another decade on, and now part of United Distillers, Bladnoch's remoteness in the far south-western corner of Scotland counted against it, and the company decided to concentrate its Lowland energies on Glenkinchie, handily located within easy reach of Edinburgh. The last spirits flowed from Bladnoch's stills in June 1993. In the same year, United Distillers closed its fellow Lowland distillery of Rosebank, at Falkirk, along with the Speyside duo of Pittyvaich and Balmenach.

The restoration of Bladnoch

That could well have been the end of Bladnoch as a productive distillery but for the arrival of Raymond Armstrong, a partner in the family construction business in Banbridge, County Down. Armstrong had first come across the closed distillery while vacationing in nearby Dalbeattie, and he saw the potential for converting the principal buildings into tourist apartments while running the existing visitors' center, which had survived the distillery's closure.

Raymond Armstrong approached United Distillers, and after some rigorous negotiations Bladnoch returned to Northern Irish hands for the second time in its history in November 1994. A restrictive covenant prevented Armstrong from distilling, but by 1998 the vacation apartment venture had been put on ice, and he was eager to explore the possibility of making whiskey at Bladnoch once more. United Distillers finally agreed that a maximum of 26,400 gallons (100,000 liters) of spirits could be distilled each year.

RENAISSANCE IN THE LOWLANDS

When the Victorian journalist and author Alfred Barnard toured Scotland during the mid-1880s researching his book *The Whisky Distilleries of the United Kingdom*, he visited no fewer than 28 operational Lowland distilleries. Just a few years ago, however, the region boasted only two working distilleries in the shape of Auchentoshan and Glenkinchie, with St. Magdalene in Linlithgow having closed in 1983, followed a decade later by Rosebank, Littlemill, and Bladnoch. Happily for this sometimes underrated region, Bladnoch was revived during 2000, while Daftmill in Fife came on stream in 2005, and Annandale distillery is being restored to working order after falling silent in 1921.

BLADNOCH 8-YEAR-OLD

Home to Scotland's *first whiskey school, Bladnoch is more than just a pretty distillery in an idyllic setting.*

By the end of 2000 the distillery had been reequipped and restored, and distilling recommenced on December 18, 2000. "I was determined the year 2000 would not go out without Bladnoch distilling," says Armstrong.

Since taking over the distillery, Armstrong has marketed a wide variety of Bladnoch expressions, most of which comprised whiskey made under the previous United Distillers regime. However, in 2008, three different cask-strength six-year-old expressions of whiskey distilled under Armstrong's ownership were released. Another milestone was reached in 2009–10 with the launch of a trio of eight-year-olds, one of which was matured in ex-Bourbon casks and another in former sherry casks, with a lightly peated, ex-Bourbon cask variant making up the trio. Also released in 2010 were two single-cask, cask-strength 20-year-olds, while a quirky offering is Bladnoch "Dew Peated New Make" spirit.

TASTING NOTES

BLADNOCH 8-YEAR-OLD
single malt, 46% ABV, refill American oak hogsheads
Bright, fresh, and citric, with lemon, cereal, soft toffee, and nuts on the nose. Medium in body, the palate is gingery and very lively, with vanilla, hot spices, and hazelnuts. The finish offers persistently fruity spice.

BLADNOCH 20-YEAR-OLD
single malt, 52.9% ABV, single cask #5338, American oak hogshead, non-chill-filtered
Eating apples, freshly mown grass, roses in bloom, and caramel on the nose. Spicy citrus fruit, becoming more stewed, on the lively palate, with plain chocolate in the relatively lengthy finish.

BLADNOCH "DEW PEATED NEW MAKE"
new make spirit, 46% ABV
Cereal and yeast notes on the oily nose, earthy, with quite subtle peat. Sweet and cereal-like on the palate, with cookie notes and soft peat. The finish is short and intense.

BLADNOCH 20-YEAR-OLD

BLADNOCH "DEW PEATED NEW MAKE"

GLENKINCHIE

OWNER	Diageo PLC
FOUNDED 1825	**CAPACITY** 621,000 gal (2.35m liters)
ADDRESS	Pencaitland, Tranent, East Lothian EH34 5ET
WEBSITE	www.discovering-distilleries.com

Although Glenkinchie is situated in rolling East Lothian farmland some 17 miles (27 km) southeast of Edinburgh, its proximity to Scotland's capital has led to its being known as "The Edinburgh Malt." The city has its very own "Edinburgh Grain," produced in the historic North British Distillery, which operates in the western outskirts and is co-owned by Diageo PLC and The Edrington Group.

Now one of just five working Lowland malt distilleries, Glenkinchie was founded under the name of Milton Distillery in 1825 by the farming brothers John and George Rate, who grew their own malting barley. Glenkinchie's agricultural connection continued until relatively recent times, with the distillery manager running the distillery's own farm himself during the 1940s and 1950s, winning many prizes with his herd of pedigree Aberdeen Angus cattle.

The Glenkinchie name was first adopted in 1837, but after the Rates sold their distillery to a local farmer in 1853, he chose to use the premises as a sawmill and cow shed rather than a place to make whiskey. However, in 1880, with blended whiskey firmly in fashion, a consortium of Edinburgh businessmen purchased the site and subsequently began to distill again under the auspices of the Glen Kinchie Distillery Company, which became a limited company in 1890.

The distillery was refurbished and upgraded over the next few years, then in 1914 it was one of five Lowland distilleries (along with Clydesdale, Grange, Rosebank, and St. Magdalene) which merged to form Scottish Malt Distillers (SMD). Membership of SMD almost certainly ensured Glenkinchie's survival during the harsh economic climate of the next two decades. In 1925 SMD was acquired by Distillers Company Ltd. While in the ownership of DCL, Glenkinchie was licensed to John Haig & Company Ltd, and to this day the distillery provides malt for the Haig blend.

The Haig connection

From the 1930s to the 1970s the Haig brand was Scotland's leading whiskey, and by 1939 Gold Label had become the biggest seller in the DCL stable. The blend's origins lie in the 17th century, and claims have been made that Haig's is the oldest whiskey distilling company in the world. During the 18th and 19th centuries, various members of the Haig family were at the very heart of large-

GLENKINCHIE "DISTILLERS EDITION"

GLENKINCHIE 20-YEAR-OLD

GLENKINCHIE 12-YEAR-OLD

A MODEL DISTILLERY

All of the Diageo distilleries that open their doors to the public offer a highly professional visitor experience, but at Glenkinchie they really do go the extra mile. The standard tour offers the opportunity to sample two malts, plus two more for an extra fee, and visitors also have the opportunity to purchase a bottle of the distillery-exclusive cask strength variant of Glenkinchie. Additionally, the former floor maltings has served as a museum since 1969, and is now officially the Museum of Malt Whisky Production. It houses an absorbing array of distilling plant and memorabilia, which includes a scale model distillery built for the 1924–25 British Empire Exhibition, at the time the largest exhibition that had ever been held in the world.

Self-styled as the Edinburgh distillery, *Glenkinchie's proximity to the capital helps it attract many visitors.*

scale Scotch whiskey distillation. Most famously, Cameronbridge Distillery at Windygates in Fife was established by John Haig in 1824, and the plant is credited with being the first in Scotland to produce grain whiskey. Cameronbridge became one of the six founding distilleries of DCL in 1877, and today is Diageo's flagship grain-producing facility, with a capacity of more than 26 million gallons (100 million liters) of spirits per year.

Classic Lowland

In 1986 Glenkinchie was selected as the Lowland representative in the Classic Malts portfolio, and this choice may have played a major part in the subsequent closure of Rosebank at Falkirk in 1993. There are connoisseurs who claim that Rosebank was the superior single malt, but the distillery's situation on the outskirts of an industrial town were no match for the lush pastures of rural East Lothian when it came to creating a visitor-friendly environment. Rosebank's loss was Glenkinchie's gain, and today the latter plays host to more than 40,000 visitors each year.

Glenkinchie is equipped with a pair of notably large stills, providing a relatively low level of copper contact for the spirit being distilled. Glenkinchie is known for producing clear wort, and Diageo's Sarah Burgess says, "This is achieved by not back-stirring in the mash tun, but I wouldn't say that clear wort alone is responsible for the spirit character that we produce. It is the

combination of the wort, the length of fermentation, our distillation process, and the fact that we have a worm, that all contribute to create Glenkinchie."

The drams

A 12-year-old was selected as the core expression in 2007 and sits alongside a 14-year-old "Distillers Edition," introduced in 1998. In 2009 a 1992 single cask was bottled in the "Managers' Choice" collection, and the following year a 20-year-old appeared as part of the "Special Releases."

TASTING NOTES

GLENKINCHIE 12-YEAR-OLD
single malt, 43% ABV

Fresh and floral nose, with spices and citrus fruits, plus a hint of marshmallow. Medium-bodied, smooth, sweet, and fruity, with malt, butter, and cheesecake. The finish is comparatively long and drying, initially rather herbal.

GLENKINCHIE "DISTILLERS EDITION" (1992 VINTAGE)
single malt, 43% ABV, finished in ex-Amontillado sherry butts after its principal period of maturation

Rich and complex on the nose, with honey, vanilla, sherry, and new leather. Full-bodied palate, with stewed fruit and molasses, contrasting with drier, slightly smoky notes. The finish features toffee apples and nuts.

GLENKINCHIE 20-YEAR-OLD ("SPECIAL RELEASES" 2010)
single malt, 55.1% ABV, cask strength, matured in ex-Bourbon refill casks (6,000 bottles)

A sweet nose, with heather, malt, vanilla, and subtle spice. Rich and very fruity on the rather floral palate, with toffee, honey, oak, and mild licorice. The finish is medium in length and steadily drying.

SPRINGBANK & GLENGYLE

OWNER J. & A. Mitchell & Company Ltd.

FOUNDED 1828 (Springbank); 2004 (Glengyle)

CAPACITY 198,000 gal (750,000 litres) (each)

ADDRESS Springbank: Well Close, Campbeltown, Argyll PA28 6ET; Glengyle: 85 Longrow, Campbeltown, Argyll PA28 6EX

WEBSITE www.springbankdistillers.com; www.kilkerran.com

SPRINGBANK 18-YEAR-OLD

Campbeltown stands close to the southern end of the remote Kintyre Peninsula, and was once as notable for its herring fleet as it was for its whiskey-making. The fishing industry in Scotland is a shadow of its former self and Campbeltown has suffered along with most other ports, while the great whiskey industry that flourished there in the 19th century was dramatically diminished during the 20th. By 1925, only 12 Campbeltown distilleries were working and 1935 saw just Glen Scotia and Springbank operational.

Heritage and survival

When it comes to whiskey, Springbank Distillery is one of the great survivors, due in part to the fact that it is privately owned by members of the Mitchell family, with Chairman Hedley G. Wright being a passionate advocate of Campbeltown's continuation as a center for whiskey-making.

Such is his passion that in 2000 he acquired the site and structures of the town's former Glengyle Distillery, and four years later, after almost eight decades of silence, it was back in production, becoming the first "new" whiskey-making facility in Campbeltown for over 125 years. Glengyle is now quietly amassing stocks of single malt for a 12-year-old bottling under the "Kilkerran" name, as "Glengyle" is registered for a blended malt.

Springbank and Glengyle distillery manager Gavin McLachlan reports, "The whiskey itself is coming on well. It's sweet, floral, lightly peated, and maturing well. We bottle it as work in progress for people to try, and the current one is our third such bottling. It's seven years old and the component whiskeys come from sherry, rum, and port casks as well as Bourbon wood."

Glengyle's big brother, Springbank, was the 14th distillery to be established in Campbeltown, founded in 1828. It was founded by the Reid family, whose in-laws, the Mitchells, purchased it from them during a period of financial difficulty in 1837. It has remained with the Mitchells ever since and is the oldest family-owned distillery in Scotland.

Idiosyncratic

Long-standing Director of Production Frank McHardy first joined Springbank in 1977, and apart from a decade spent working at Bushmills

SPRINGBANK 18-YEAR-OLD "LONGROW"

in Northern Ireland, has been in Campbeltown ever since. McHardy is the ultimate sage on all things Springbank and Campbeltown, and he explains, "One of the factors that make Springbank unique is that it is effectively two-and-a-half-times distilled. It's a lightly peated and very sweet spirit. The sweet, fruity character comes in part from long fermentations—up to 110 hours. Springbank is also unique in that we do 100 percent of the whole process from malting to bottling here, and the place is almost a working museum. We employ a lot of people compared to most distilleries these days, in effect to handcraft the whiskey."

In addition to making two-and-a-half-times-distilled Springbank in its one wash still and pair of spirit stills, the distillery has produced a double-distilled, heavily peated single malt by the name of "Longrow" since the mid-1970s, with a 10-year-old variant being released in 1985. Batches of unpeated, triple-distilled Hazelburn single malt are also made, while the wash still in which all these whiskeys are created is singular in being both heated by internal steam coils and direct-fired by oil.

Springbank was silent from 1979 to 1987, and closed again during 2008–09 when fuel and barley costs were high. Production has resumed since then, though on a relatively modest scale, with Springbank making up an average of 60 percent of annual output, while the remainder is split between "Longrow" and "Hazelburn." Each of the three single malts is also presented in a CV variant, with no age statement. Frank McHardy promises, "We will be bottling quite a lot of Longrow CV, as younger peated whiskeys give you a good hit of peat, which fades as they get older, so Longrow works well in CV format."

TASTING NOTES

SPRINGBANK 10-YEAR-OLD
single malt, 46% ABV, matured in a mix of ex-sherry and ex-Bourbon casks
Fresh and briny on the nose, with citrus fruit and barley. Sweet on the palate, with developing brine and vanilla toffee. Long and spicy in the finish, with more salt, coconut oil, and peat.

SPRINGBANK 18-YEAR-OLD
single malt, 46% ABV, matured 80 percent ex-sherry and 20 percent ex-Bourbon casks
The nose is rich, with sweet sherry, angelica, and apricots, while the big, creamy palate is rounded and confident, offering fresh fruit, smoke, molasses, and licorice. The finish dries slowly and elegantly.

SPRINGBANK 18-YEAR-OLD "LONGROW"
single malt, 46% ABV
Sweet and savory on the nose, with vanilla, ripe bananas, fall berries, and linseed oil. Waxy mouth feel; vanilla, banana, and berries carry over from the nose, and peat notes develop. Smoky in the long finish.

WHISKEY CITY

Although only three distilleries operate in Campbeltown today, whiskey-making has actually taken place on approximately 35 sites in the Kintyre borough, with the first written reference to whiskey in relation to the area occurring in 1591. When the writer Alfred Barnard visited Campbeltown in 1885, researching his epic tome *The Whisky Distilleries of the United Kingdom*, he toured no fewer than 21 distilleries and proclaimed Campbeltown to be "Whisky City." Among those he graced with his presence was Springbank, which had been built during the great distillery construction boom that saw a remarkable 24 new distilleries appear in Campbeltown between 1823 and 1835.

SPRINGBANK 10-YEAR-OLD

SPRINGBANK 15-YEAR-OLD

AILSA BAY

OWNER William Grant & Sons Ltd.
FOUNDED 2007 **CAPACITY** 1.65m gal (6.25m liters)
ADDRESS Grangestone Industrial Estate, Ayrshire KA26 9PT
WEBSITE www.williamgrant.com

William Grant & Sons Ltd. is not a company that likes to make a fuss about its activities, and so it was that when the Ailsa Bay malt whiskey distillery began producing spirit in September 2007, many people did not even know that the facility had been under construction.

Ailsa Bay is the latest addition to the sadly depleted ranks of Lowland distilleries, but from a stylistic viewpoint the spirit it produces is pure Speyside, so only geography really makes this a Lowland distillery. It is located within Grant's vast Girvan grain distilling, blending, and bonding complex, close to the Ayrshire coast, and is the second malt whiskey plant to have existed on the site, as Ladyburn operated there from 1966 to 1975.

Freedom to experiment

The new distillery was developed within an existing structure that had previously housed a plant making glucose syrup for the confectionery industry until 2003, and took just nine months to build. It is equipped with eight stills, similar in shape and size to those in place at the company's Balvenie distillery on Speyside. One wash still condenser is made of a metal alloy, rather than copper, and is intended to allow the production of a sulfur-rich spirit. Experimentation with the style is ongoing, and Master Blender Brian Kinsman also notes the intention to install a stainless steel condenser on a spirit still, too, allowing for further experimentation.

"The whole place was set up to let us be experimental in ways we can't be with our more traditional distilleries," he explains. "Some 95 percent of the Ailsa Bay output is standard style, peated to less than 2ppm, while up to 5 percent comprises spirit that is lightly peated to 5–8ppm or heavily peated to 15ppm plus."

The plant is geared toward making whiskey for Grant's portfolio of blends. Kinsman describes the template blend, "Family Reserve," as "a Speyside-style blend with a sweet base of grain. Our own three malts of Glenfiddich, Balvenie and Kininvie give it its essential fruity and floral style. A tiny amount of peated whiskey is also used, helping to add complexity, but it's not overly smoky."

The portfolio also includes the first two cask-finished blended Scotch whiskeys to be introduced to the market, "Ale Cask Finish" and "Sherry Cask Reserve," together with aged blends, which all still reflect the flavor profile of "Family Reserve."

GRANT'S "SHERRY CASK RESERVE"

GRANT'S "ALE CASK FINISH"

DAFTMILL

OWNER The Cuthbert family
FOUNDED 2003 **CAPACITY** 17,200 gal (65,000 liters)
ADDRESS By Cupar, Fife KY15 5RF
WEBSITE www.daftmilldistillery.com

Most fledgling whiskey-distilling operations are in a hurry to make a financial return on their investments. Not so the Cuthbert family of Daftmill, who are in the relatively luxurious economic position of being able to fill spirit into casks and put them away in their two traditional dunnage warehouses until they feel the spirit has reached its optimum age for release.

Down on the farm

This is not to say that the Cuthberts could ever be classed as members of the idle rich. Brothers Ian and Francis combine distilling duties with the demands of farming beef cattle, barley, and potatoes, as well as a quarrying business. Indeed, it's surprising that they ever find time to make any whiskey at all, but make it they do, and it is mostly filled into first-fill ex-Bourbon casks, along with a few sherry butts from time to time.

Daftmill distillery is the ultimate farm-based distillery, since it's located in previously unused traditional stone agricultural buildings at the heart

An old stone mill at the heart *of Daftmill Farm was converted to house the distillery operation.*

of the farmstead itself. The pair of stills was commissioned from leading coppersmiths Forsyth's of Rothes, on Speyside, but all other equipment and specialist skills were sourced as close to home as possible. Barley grown on the Cuthberts' own land is sent away for malting and then used for distillation, and the first spirit ran from the Daftmill stills on December 16, 2005. The distillation regimen is set up to produce what should be a classic Lowland style of whiskey. The projected date for an initial bottling is 2015.

GLEN SCOTIA

OWNER Loch Lomond Distillery Company Ltd.
FOUNDED 1832 **CAPACITY** 198,000 gal (750,000 liters)
ADDRESS 12 High Street, Campbeltown, Argyll PA28 6DS
WEBSITE www.glenscotia-distillery.co.uk

Although it has long played second fiddle to its slightly older Campbeltown brother Springbank, Glen Scotia has given aficionados of its distinctive single malt some hope that things might be starting to change. An ongoing program of upgrades to the distillery facilities has been put in place and there are plans to extend the range of expressions available.
The distillery is just four years younger than Springbank, but its fortunes since the 19th-century heyday of Campbeltown distilling have been precarious, with ominous periods of silence. However, the distillery established by Stewart, Galbraith & Company Ltd. still exists, despite being closed between 1928 and 1933, after which production resumed under the ownership of Bloch Brothers (Distillers) Ltd., who sold the distillery to Hiram Walker (Scotland) Ltd. in 1954.

Hiram Walker soon disposed of Glen Scotia to the Glasgow blenders A Gillies & Company, which became part of Amalgamated Distillers Products (ADP) in 1970. Between 1979 and 1982 more than $2 million was spent refurbishing Glen Scotia, but another period of silence was just two years away. Whiskey making restarted in 1989 under ADP's new parent Gibson International, but a further change of ownership saw the distillery mothballed once more by Glen Catrine Bonded Warehouse Ltd. in 1994. However, distilling began again five years later under the current owners Loch Lomond Distillers, initially with modest annual volumes of spirits being distilled, and the future for this historic Campbeltown survivor now looks brighter than it has for many years.

TASTING NOTES

GLEN SCOTIA, 12-YEAR-OLD
single malt, 40% ABV
Floral on the nose, with citrus fruits and a mildly phenolic note. Quite full-bodied, peaty, nutty and fudgy on the palate. Lengthy in the gently herbal, spicy finish.

GLEN SCOTIA 17-YEAR-OLD
single malt, 43% ABV
Brine, ginger, and delicate peat notes on the nose. Oily on the palate, malty and smooth and spicy. The finish is long, elegant and drying, with salted peanuts.

GLEN SCOTIA "HEAVILY PEATED" 1999
single malt, 45% ABV, cask #518
Soft peat and hazelnuts on the nose; sweet marzipan, caramel and vanilla on the relatively mouth-coating palate. The finish dries slowly with persistent peat.

GLEN SCOTIA 12-YEAR-OLD

IRELAND

IRELAND

Where whiskey is concerned, no country in the world has turned its fortunes around more dramatically and successfully than Ireland. It could be likened to a boxer who, nine rounds into a 12-round fight, has been sprawled against the ropes, taking a pounding from both a weighty and bullish American whiskey industry and a spritely and quick-punching Scotch one. Yet, incredibly, it has dragged itself back onto its feet and has come out of its corner fighting—and indeed since 2010 has become imperious, matching any other territory on the planet for world-class whiskey, despite the fact that it only has three-and-a-bit distilleries making it.

Regional Styles

Traditionally, Ireland has been known primarily for two styles of whiskey: the triple-distilled smooth and fruity Irish blend best represented by Jameson, and the rarer, rugged pot-still style such as Redbreast. Today, though, there is more variety to choose from.

Author's Choice

Once upon a time, Ireland had dozens of small distilleries due to the moderate climate and the abundance of grain, water, and peat, but now few remain. BUSHMILLS Located near the spectacular Giant's Causeway on the beautiful Northern Irish coast, Bushmills is the oldest licensed distillery in the world and offers lots of old-world charm, with an emphasis on heritage, and a very warm welcome.

Regional Events

Irish Distillers, owned by Pernod Ricard and producer of Jameson, has visitors' centers in Dublin and Midleton near Cork. You can also visit Bushmills in Northern Ireland, and Kilbeggan and Tullamore Dew are open to the public, too, though neither of these are working distilleries in the conventional sense. In 2011, Whisky Live (www.whiskylive. com) came to Ireland for the first time, offering whiskey tasting and the chance to meet producers and distillers from all over the world.

At the turn of the century, Irish whiskey in any abundance consisted of Jameson and a couple of underfunded Irish blends from the south, Bushmills blended and single malt whiskeys in the north, and a smattering of small-batch bottlings from Midleton and Cooley. Now the country is increasingly ditching the triple-distilled, unpeated, blended straitjacket and turning to lip-lickingly exciting whiskeys that are winning awards around the world.

There are many more brands in Ireland than there are distilleries, and for credibility's sake Irish whiskey's next task is to dispense with the smoke and mirrors and be honest about its origins. Two examples come to mind: Tullamore Dew distillery is a museum and no whiskey is made there. Tullamore Dew, the whiskey, is made at Midleton—for the time being at least. And while Inish Turk

The Old Midleton distillery *has been converted into a state-of-the-art visitors' center telling the story of Jameson.*

Ireland's remote west coast *isn't home to any distilleries, but Inish Turk Beg whiskey is partly matured at Clew Bay.*

Beg is a fine premium whiskey, it isn't made on the island of Inish Turk Beg.

The year of 2011 was a game changer. With William Grant joining Diageo and Irish Distillers in the Irish market with the purchase of Tullamore Dew, and the sale of Cooley to Beam Global, the next few years are set to be highly exciting for the Irish sector. There's no doubt about it—Ireland has the swagger of a heavyweight champion.

GETTING AROUND

Developments in Irish road networks mean it's now easy to base yourself in Dublin and reach out to all the island's distilleries. The best highway links Dublin to Belfast, with Bushmills a little farther on, while Midleton can be reached by the road or train down to Cork. A new cross-country highway to the west coast passes Kilbeggan, so getting there and to nearby Tullamore is a much quicker and easier experience than it once was.

KEY

■ Distillery

Roads

Rivers, lakes

0 10 20 30 40 miles
0 20 40 60 80 km

BUSHMILLS

OWNERS Diageo	
FOUNDED 1608	**CAPACITY** 925,000 gal (3.5m liters)
ADDRESS 2 Distillery Road, Bushmills, County Antrim	
BT57 8XH	**WEBSITE** www.bushmills.com

The way Diageo bought up the Bushmills distillery a few years ago, and its subsequent treatment of it since, can be compared to a football team snapping up a hot new quarterback and then leaving him on the bench save for an occasional appearance in an exhibition game.

Diageo's strategy for the Northern Irish distillery has been at best baffling and some whiskey fans feel Bushmills has been let down. True, investment was made and capacity increased, but while many Irish whiskey stars have been shining brightly of late, Bushmills hasn't been among them.

A deal is done

The distillery had been part of the Irish Distillers Group, which in turn is owned by Pernod Ricard. When the Allied Domecq estate was up for sale a few years ago, Pernod was eager to buy up some of its distilleries. So Diageo made the French company an offer: let us buy Bushmills and we won't stand in your way or compete with you to buy any of the other distilleries.

At the time the move looked perfectly logical, particularly as Diageo is formed around Irish beer giant Guinness. Since then, though, the company has done very little with its purchase beyond some activities to celebrate the distillery's 400th anniversary in early 2009. Not its finest moment either, because the 400th anniversary was in 2008.

What makes the lack of any serious activity even more surprising is the fact that over the same period of time there has been a massive resurgence in Irish whiskey and every other player has upped its game. All of which is a great pity, because if ever a distillery was due its place in the sun, it's this one. It's one of the prettiest and friendliest of distilleries you'll find anywhere in the world, it makes fine whiskey with dedication and care, and it combines innovation and tradition seamlessly and with panache. It is every bit the world-beater that Diageo no doubt wants it to be, and it has the potential to play a leading role in the Irish renaissance if given the chance.

One of a kind

If Diageo isn't quite sure what to make of its purchase, then it wouldn't be the first not to understand it. Bushmills has always been something of an anomaly. It's in Northern Ireland, for a start, so although it was part of Irish

BUSHMILLS "BLACK BUSH"

BUSHMILLS 21-YEAR-OLD

Distillers, it wasn't strictly Irish, but rather part of the United Kingdom. In whiskey terms, however, Ireland has long been united.

And even within Irish Distillers, the distillery stood out, for while the likes of Jameson, Paddy, and Powers produced pot-still and pot-still-based blended whiskey, Bushmills produced triple-distilled single malt and blended whiskey, putting it head to head to some extent with its neighbors over the water to the east. Perhaps for this reason the distillery boasts some of the most impressive cask management and wood policy anywhere in Ireland.

Bushmills has something else unusual in Ireland, too—visitor facilities on a distillery site that is really and truly making whiskey. Irish Distillers can't offer that, and Cooley barely can, because the amount of whiskey coming from Kilbeggan is minuscule.

Today Bushmills makes a range of whiskeys, none of which is anything less than excellent. Indeed, the rich and sherried "Black Bush" has given Jameson a run for its money in the past. Drinking any Bushmills in the warmth of the distillery is one of the whiskey world's greatest pleasures. It's charm personified and it would be a shame if the Irish whiskey boom passed it by. Perhaps Diageo has a bigger, longer-term plan for Bushmills. Let's hope so. It deserves all the love we can give it.

TASTING NOTES

BUSHMILLS "BLACK BUSH"
blend, 40% ABV
As soft and silky as a jazz crooner, and as fruity as whiskey gets, "Black Bush" is a classic mix of sherried berry fruits, stewed apple and pear, and some citrus notes, all delivered in an ordered, pleasant, and smooth package.

BUSHMILLS 16-YEAR-OLD
single malt, 40% ABV
Maintaining the sweet, fruity triple-distilled character of many Irish whiskeys with 16 years of maturation as a single malt is a hard trick to pull off, but this does it. A world-class whiskey, it is a complex stepping sequence between oak, spice, gooseberry, and apple, both sweet and drying at the same time. Delightful.

BUSHMILLS 21-YEAR-OLD
single malt, 40% ABV
Twenty-one years is a lifetime for most Irish whiskeys, but this is by no means drowned in oak; far from it. It's beautifully ordered with rich, juicy raisin and black currant notes, a depth from the oak but no nasty sharpness, and some grape and citrus flourishes to make the overall experience a rewarding and complex one.

A GREAT PLACE TO VISIT

Bushmills is some distillery to visit. One of the greatest ironies about Northern Ireland is that while it was known for little else but the violence and terror of "The Troubles" for many, many years, to the north it boasts some of the prettiest shorelines in Europe, is an unspoiled delight, and has next to zero crime. Here the Giant's Causeway is a natural phenomenon, and little villages nestle in a rural idyll. And it's here that you'll find the warmest of welcomes befitting an Irish distillery. This is the oldest licensed distillery in the world, and the staff make a point of maintaining some of its old-world charm and focusing on the site's heritage and provenance as a renowned whiskey-maker.

BUSHMILLS 10-YEAR-OLD

BUSHMILLS 16-YEAR-OLD

KILBEGGAN

OWNER Beam Global

FOUNDED 1757 **CAPACITY** Unknown

ADDRESS Kilbeggan, County Westmeath

WEBSITE www.kilbegganwhiskey.com

Kilbeggan is an example of those one-street Irish towns comprising a couple of pubs, a couple of shops, and not much else—the sort of place where most of the time nothing happens and which you tend to pass through without stopping.

Yet Kilbeggan has something that sets it apart from most small-time Irish towns and villages; it is home to Locke's Distillery, a stunning wood and wrought-iron piece of history in pristine condition. For many years it was part of the strange inverted Southern Irish whiskey world, which dictated that if you could visit the distillery, it wasn't making whiskey, and if it was making whiskey, you couldn't visit it.

Stunning as the distillery is, a visit, like visits to Tullamore or Old Midleton, was like visiting a mausoleum, bereft of the aroma of malt and grain production, its cold, damp, wooden, and dusty interior more like the main deck of the *Marie Celeste* than a whiskey distillery.

Locke's comes back to life

All that has changed now. Cooley's John Teeling had a dream to bring whiskey back to this amazing and must-see distillery, and he has done it. The big water wheel turns once more, pistons shudder, and wheels whir, and while most of the main distillery's activity is for show only, you will find a fully operational micro-distillery producing all sorts of wacky, weird, and wonderful takes on what we know as Irish whiskey.

"It's wonderful that there's whiskey coming from the site again," says Cooley's marketing director, Stephen Teeling. "We're able to try all sorts of new whiskeys, some of which will never see the light of the day but some which will help continue the trend to more diverse Irish whiskey. We have found original Locke's recipes from the past and we're trying them out. There's a pot-still recipe using malted and unmalted barley but also some oats. You can definitely taste the oats and the spirit is lovely.

"But there are other, stranger things being done, too, with wine cask and other spirit cask finishes. One which isn't totally to my taste is a whiskey finished in a green-tea cask. It's weird, but it's taking the category to new and exciting places."

For Cooley, the Locke's distillery isn't just a picturesque focal point for the company; it's allowing it to make whiskeys in a way that the Cooley distillery just isn't equipped for. Cooley Distillery lies to the north of Dublin and is an old industrial alcohol plant; it isn't

The distillery lies at the heart of Ireland's horse country, and it was the Locke family who, in 1879, provided the field for the first official meeting at Kilbeggan Racecourse.

KILBEGGAN 18-YEAR-OLD

visitor-friendly and adds nothing to the romantic Irish whiskey story. It contains pot and column stills and is the production center for Cooley's extensive range of whiskey, but one missing whiskey style from the Cooley range is the one most associated with Ireland: single pot-still whiskey—that is, whiskey made in a pot still using a grist of mixed malted and unmalted barley.

"The mix gets very gloopy and clogs up our equipment," says Teeling. "It causes quite a bit of damage, is difficult to work with, and the guys at Cooley didn't care for it. At Kilbeggan we can make pot-still and the oats actually help with filtration."

A renaissance in Irish whiskey

For many years it was Cooley that set the pace for Ireland's whiskey industry, bringing peated whiskey, cask finishes, double distillation, and single malts to the attention of the world. But with four big companies now making Irish whiskey and with Irish Distillers producing top-notch spirits and Tullamore Dew receiving substantial backing, competition is as fierce as it has been in generations. "That can only be a good thing," says Teeling.

"It brings more focus on Irish whiskey in general, and that will bring in new drinkers. Irish whiskey is enjoying a true renaissance and I think it's great that there is much good whiskey coming from here. We welcome the new whiskeys, but are confident that we can continue to produce exciting and innovative whiskeys into the future."

STILL QUEUING

When businessman John Teeling floated the idea of launching an Irish whiskey company when the category was struggling, more than a few people thought he was crazy. For many, that view was reinforced when he decided to transport a huge copper pot still along rural roads. Kilbeggan used to be on the main thoroughfare from Dublin to the West Coast, and every weekend the *nouveau riche* of the city headed west for some sailing. It was a Friday afternoon when Teeling and his team made the move, with a still so heavy the lifting crane nearly collapsed. For many hours the still blocked the route, causing a traffic jam stretching back miles.

TASTING NOTES

KILBEGGAN
blend, 40% ABV
This is not distilled at Locke's in Kilbeggan and is a blend, but it is an Irish blend in the best sense, with a gutsy fruity baseline, powerful malt at its heart, and sparkling sweet apple and vanilla as its lead melody.

KILBEGGAN 15-YEAR-OLD
aged blend, 40% ABV
Impressive, with overripe berry and green fruit, an array of spice including nutmeg, cinnamon, cayenne, and paprika, and enough tannin to steer clear of cloying sweetness. There's some apple seed and dark chocolate in the mix, too.

KILBEGGAN 18-YEAR-OLD
aged blend, 55.3% ABV
The extra age means that tannin and a big wave of savory spice turns typical Irish whiskey on its head. It starts off with apple, pear, peach, and berries, but then the spices and tannins slash like a sword across the taste buds.

KILBEGGAN

KILBEGGAN 15-YEAR-OLD

MIDLETON

OWNER Irish Distillers	
FOUNDED 1780	**CAPACITY** Not given
ADDRESS Midleton, County Cork	
WEBSITE www.jamesonwhiskey.com	

Irish whiskey finds itself in a very good place right now, but it wasn't always thus. From its glory days in the 18th and 19th centuries, Irish whiskey suffered a long and undignified fall from grace. Its fate was in part self-inflicted, in part a consequence of social, economic, and political upheaval, and in part due to the merciless business practices of its rivals, particularly in Scotland.

By the 1960s, the small number of surviving distilleries in Ireland had banded together as Irish Distillers and defined themselves as a distinct entity from Scotch, stressing their characteristics as unpeated, triple-distilled, sweet fruity blends. The tactic worked, and Jameson in particular managed to excel even when Irish whiskey had to take a back seat as first Scotch, then Japanese whiskey and finally a resurgent American whiskey industry cast it into the shadows.

The flourishing of Irish Distillers

Midleton became the base first for the entrenchment of Irish Distillers and then for its charge back into battle. The move to a new state-of-the-art plant is the most obvious manifestation of the flourishing of Irish Distillers, but the fact that land around the distillery has been occupied by an increasing number of warehouses is another clue.

Today, Irish whiskey is growing faster than pretty much any other whiskey category in the world, and after a somewhat belated entry into the new wave of innovation and diversity, Irish Distillers is firmly center stage. From 2011, it has made one of the most telling contributions to the resurgence of Irish whiskey with the launch of three new pot-still whiskeys and a pot-still-dominated Jameson blend.

Irish pot still whiskey

Pot still whiskey is unique to Ireland; it's made by taking malted barley and mixing it with another grain or grains, often unmalted barley, at the grist or flour stage—that is, before water is added and the wash fermented into beer.

"It's a difficult trick to pull off because the mix becomes very gloopy and can block up the fermenting equipment," says one Irish whiskey expert. "It requires considerable time and effort to get right, and demands a great deal of care and attention, but when it's done correctly the results can be outstanding." Indeed they can.

MIDLETON 12-YEAR-OLD "REDBREAST"

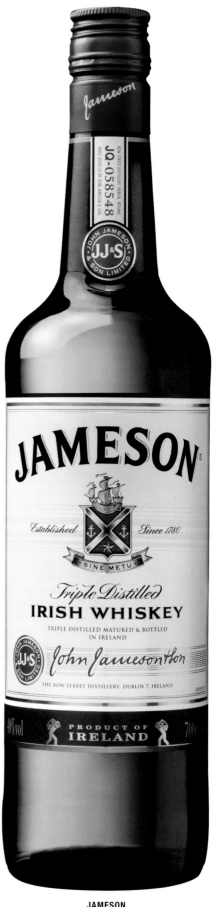

JAMESON

Pot-still whiskey survived through the odd bottling of Midleton, through Green Spot—distilled by Irish Distillers for Dublin wine and spirits merchant Mitchell & Son—and through Redbreast, which was given periodic support by Irish Distillers and is bottled as a 12-year-old and 15-year-old. But in 2011 Irish Distillers launched a cask-strength version of the 12-year-old "Redbreast" as well as Midleton "Barry Crockett Legacy" and Powers "John's Lane."

With all sorts of unusual casks holding Midleton spirit in the distillery's warehouses, there's a true frisson of excitement among Irish whiskey lovers these days, and they're relishing the battle between the experienced Midleton mob and the relatively new upstarts at Cooley. The winner? The Irish whiskey drinker, undoubtedly.

Midleton old and new

If you pay a visit to Midleton, a short drive out of Cork, you are guaranteed to end up seeing double, though not necessarily because of a glass too many at the tasting session. For the site is, in fact, home to two distilleries sitting almost side by side. One is the new Midleton plant, which isn't open to the public but is the powerhouse of the current distilling operation of Irish Distillers, producing not only the globally known Jameson brand but a number of other leading Irish whiskeys too, including Paddy,

The Old Midleton distillery is now a visitors' center, the Jameson Experience, which tells the story of John Jameson.

Midleton Very Rare, and Powers, as well as other spirits such as Cork Dry Gin. The other is Old Midleton, which is no longer in operation but offers visitors as good a tour of a historic distillery as you will be able to find anywhere. Its solid, beautifully restored Victorian stone buildings lie alongside the Dungourney River, which still turns the giant waterwheel that once powered the distillery, and whose waters continue to be used in the production of whiskey at the new plant.

TASTING NOTES

JAMESON
blend, 40% ABV
Defines classic quality Irish whiskey at its best, with a healthy dose of oily, big-flavored fruity pot-still whiskey, some red berry sherry notes, and lots of fruit with milk chocolate in the mix.

JAMESON SELECT RESERVE "BLACK BARREL"
blend, 40% ABV
A sharper, fiercer, feistier version of Jameson made up of older pot-still whiskey and rare grain whiskey than is normal. There are lots of dark berry notes, some sharper green fruit flavors, and delicious woody, spicy, and dark chocolate notes.

MIDLETON 12-YEAR-OLD "REDBREAST" CASK STRENGTH
single pot still, 57.7% ABV, non-chill-filtered
As fine as Irish whiskey gets, this is rich, full, oily and sherried, with fruitcake, bitter orange, an array of berries and kitchen pantry spices, and some oak.

JAMESON SELECT RESERVE "BLACK BARREL"

COOLEY

OWNERS Beam Global
FOUNDED 1987 **CAPACITY** 859,000 gal (3.25m liters)
ADDRESS Riverstown, Cooley, County Louth
WEBSITE www.cooleywhiskey.com

They're not big on visitors at Cooley. If you drive north from Dublin, you'll find the Cooley peninsula but, once there, chances are you won't find the distillery. It's hidden off the road, an ugly factory-style building concealed for many years behind forbidding barbed-wire fencing.

The folks at Cooley aren't quite as defensive now, but Marketing Director Stephen Teeling tells how in early 2012 the new American owners from Beam Global paid a subdued visit to the plant, clearly ill at ease in the less-than-salubrious surroundings when they thought they had bought a friendly "top o' the morning to you" stereotypical Irish whiskey distillery. That treat awaited them the next day down the road at Kilbeggan.

Alcohol powerhouse

However it might look, though, Cooley Distillery is the powerhouse of Irish whiskey. It's an old industrial alcohol factory with column and pot stills, and the spirits it has produced in the last three decades have turned the Irish whiskey industry on its head. So threatened was the existing establishment by a small independent, which refused to operate by conventional rules and set about playing with Irish whiskey styles, that it tried to close it down.

But the Teelings—chairman John and sons Stephen and Jack—survived on cheap own-brand contracts for supermarkets, and slowly but surely set about establishing new whiskeys in the struggling Irish sector. Now many of those names are becoming as famous as the likes of Midleton, Powers, and Paddy, and as the Irish category in general flourishes, Cooley can take a lot of credit.

In addition to the Locke's distillery in Kilbeggan, Cooley produces a range of whiskeys, of which Connemara is unusual because it is single malt whiskey made with peated barley. In addition to a core range, which includes an outstanding cask-strength version, Cooley has experimented with innovative finishes and limited edition bottlings such as "Turf Mor" and "Bog Oak." The Tyrconnell high-quality premium single malt whiskeys are finished in a variety of casks including sherry and port, while Greenore is a range of grain whiskeys. The sweet, vanilla-tinged whiskeys are sold as 8, 15, and 18 years old, the latter being the oldest Irish grain ever bottled.

Cooley whiskey matures in the former Locke's Distillery warehouses.

TASTING NOTES

CONNEMARA "CASK STRENGTH"
single malt, 57.9% ABV, aged in American oak
The traditional sweet green fruit and soft vanilla tones normally associated with the category are mixed here with growling, smoky notes that tease the taste buds.

THE TYRCONNELL 10-YEAR-OLD "SHERRY FINISH"
single malt, 46% ABV, finished in ex-sherry casks
The alcoholic strength gives a bite to this rich, toffeed single malt, and the sherry adds a depth of berry fruits and some orange citrus notes. There are some gentle spices at work here, too, preventing it from becoming too cloying. Very impressive.

GREENORE 15-YEAR-OLD
grain whiskey 43% ABV
This single grain whiskey is a treat, its sweet corn, candy, vanilla, and honey sweetness all in evidence, but the age allows woody tannins to add a bite that holds it in check.

GREENORE 15-YEAR-OLD

CONNEMARA "CASK STRENGTH"

INISH TURK BEG

OWNER Nadim Sadek

CAPACITY None **ADDRESS** Clew Bay, County Mayo

WEBSITE www.inishturkbeg.com

Inish Turk Beg stands apart from many artificially created Irish whiskeys because the island of Inish Turk Beg does actually exist off Ireland's west coast. Owner Nadim Sadek has brought water and electricity to the island, provided vacation accommodations, opened a riding school with Connemara ponies, introduced an artists-in-residence program, recorded Irish music with top musicians, started an upmarket tuna, mackerel, and herring business, and launched a premium whiskey.

Buy a bottle of Inish Turk Beg and you will be drinking whiskey matured partly in ex-*poitín* (or poteen) barrels on the island. It comes in a bottle made of glass forged using a handful of the island's sand, and it will have been brought down to bottling strength using rainwater collected on the island. But the whiskey was neither distilled on the island nor matured for the better part of its life there.

The whiskey was actually produced at Cooley Distillery in County Louth, north of Dublin, and has aged for at least 10 years. It's packaged in a bottle designed to look like a sea buoy, and might appear to be a case of style over substance if the whiskey didn't taste so good.

INISH TURK BEG "MAIDEN VOYAGE"

The largest of numerous islands in Clew Bay, Inish Turk Beg translates as "small island of the wild boar."

TASTING NOTES

INISH TURK BEG "MAIDEN VOYAGE"
*single malt, 44% ABV, matured for a period
in ex-poitín barrels*
Rich, full, and very fruity Irish whiskey, with melon, pear, gooseberry, and grape in the mix, but with some discernible salt and pepper notes, and some notable tannins and cereal undertones. The Irish notes are set off by some attractive maltiness.

TULLAMORE

OWNERS William Grant & Sons

CAPACITY None **ADDRESS** Bury Quay, Tullamore,
County Offaly **WEBSITE** www.tullamoredew.com

Dating from the 1820s, Tullamore Distillery is a real distillery in a real town, but it isn't where the Tullamore Dew range of whiskeys is made. The distillery ceased production in the 1950s and the old bonded warehouses exist these days as a whiskey museum, a sad and silent totem to a once-great industry.

Tullamore Dew has been distilled under license at Midleton, home of Jameson, for several years. Until 2010 it belonged to Campbell & Cochrane, who own Magners cider, but it has now been bought by Scottish family company William Grant & Sons and that purchase has secured it a new lease on life.

In 2012 the Tullamore Dew range was extended, repackaged, and given substantial financial backing. Plans to extend warehousing and bottling facilities were actioned, and there was talk of building a new Tullamore distillery. Whether it materializes or not, chances are we'll see a lot more of Tullamore Dew in the future.

The standard Tullamore Dew is very typical of fruity Irish blends, while a 12-year-old version provides more weight and body.

TULLAMORE DEW

TASTING NOTES

TULLAMORE DEW
blend, 40% ABV
Almost stereotypically Irish in flavor, this is a whiskey which is improving in quality and, with major financial support, is set to become a big player. There's a mix of green, yellow, and red fruits, and some oily pot still characteristics, along with a pleasant, easy-drinking sweetness throughout.

**TULLAMORE DEW 12-YEAR-OLD
"SPECIAL RESERVE"**
*aged blend, 40% ABV, matured in ex-Bourbon
and ex-Oloroso sherry casks*
If Tullamore Dew errs on the cautious and therefore slightly unchallenging and bland side, the extra years in cask make this a Jameson taste-alike, the wood adding some depth and bringing a sharper, less flabby aspect to the fruit. The softness and smoothness of the blend raises it up a division.

TULLAMORE DEW "BLACK 43"
*triple distilled blend, 43% ABV, includes pot still
whiskey aged in ex-Oloroso sherry casks*
The extra strength gives this limited release whiskey a sharp bite often lacking in many Irish whiskeys. Oloroso sherry casks have been used to intensify the flavor, and somewhere in the process an extra spiciness has appeared, making for a grown-up, impressive release.

UNITED STATES

UNITED STATES

Historically, whiskey has been a fringe player in the United States, and although the distilleries here are very large, traditionally there have been very few of them. In fact, not long ago, American whiskey outside of the Bourbon producers of Kentucky consisted of only a couple of important distilleries in Tennessee, a few bit players in Portland, Oregon, and another two in the San Francisco area. Why whiskey making has had such a limited impact is something of a mystery. Perhaps it's partly because the indigenous whiskey is so far removed from the much-sought-after Scotch and Irish whiskeys that the American middle class has tended to give it a wide berth over the generations, condemning local liquor to the bottom shelf as an inferior blue-collar drink.

Regional Styles
Bourbon remains the dominant whiskey style and is unique to the US. It must be made of at least 51 percent corn, though the proportion is normally far higher, with the mash bill topped off by other grains, usually malted barley and wheat or rye. The law dictates new white oak barrels must be used for maturation.

Author's Choice
BUFFALO TRACE The distillery offers one of the best hard-hat tours in the world.

HEAVEN HILL The diversity of whiskey produced and an excellent visitors' center make this Bardstown distillery a must.

Regional Events and Trails
Tourist authorities have helped drive the Bourbon renaissance with an official Kentucky Bourbon Trail, as well as an urban one that links prime Bourbon-serving restaurants in Louisville (www.kybourbontrail.com). For a celebration of local whiskey, the Kentucky Bourbon Festival (www.kybourbonfestival.com) held in September in Bardstown, the "Bourbon capital," is an absolute must. Elsewhere, WhiskyFest is held in New York, Chicago, and San Francisco (www.maltadvocate.com/whiskyfest).

All that has changed, though, and since the start of the new millennium's second decade, there has been a microdistilling revolution that was still in full flow at the time of writing. Yet even before then, the distillers of Kentucky had already turned the image of Bourbon on its head and won for it a new respect. Premium Bourbons and limited-batch annual releases have won acclaim at international competitions across the world.

Much is made of the need to use soft water for great Scotch, but in Kentucky the opposite is true. The water is hard and calcium-rich, great for breeding strong racehorses and making fine Bourbon. Kentucky has long, hot summers and very cold winters, ideal for the accelerated maturation of Bourbon.

Buffalo Trace is older *than most Scottish distilleries; little wonder that it has filled over 6 million barrels.*

Of course, Bourbon isn't the country's only whiskey. Rye whiskey, wheat whiskey, and corn whiskey are all popular in pockets, and even before the new wave of whiskey-makers there were other whiskey styles produced in the US, including single malts. But while the American picture is changing massively, it remains the case that, just as with single malt whiskey and Scotland, if you discover American whiskey anywhere, you will eventually be drawn to Kentucky, where traditional big-name Bourbons are now being joined by exciting and innovative new products.

With its distinctive dark wood and red shutters, *Maker's Mark cuts a neat figure among distilleries.*

GETTING AROUND

Louisville, Kentucky is the perfect place to base yourself—it's a vibrant and stylish city with some stunning modern restaurants where Bourbon is spotlighted. You'll need to rent a car to follow the Kentucky Tourist Bureau's Bourbon Trail farther afield. Jack Daniel's and George Dickel can be accessed from Nashville, Tennessee, which has an international airport. Other distilleries are spread across the country.

COLORADO WHISKEY
Stranahan's
ORIGINAL & HANDMADE

N
W E
S

CANADA

Seattle
WASHINGTON · Dry Fly
Clear Creek
Portland · Rogue
OREGON

Lake Superior

St. Lawrence

Missouri

Mississippi

Lake Huron

Lake Michigan

Lake Ontario
NEW YORK
Tuthilltown

Boston
MASS.

Lake Erie

New York

Triple Eight

Great Salt Lake
Salt Lake City
Anchor
San Francisco
St. George Spirits
UTAH
CALIFORNIA

Denver
Leopold Bros.
COLORADO

NEBRASKA
Stranahan's

Arkansas

IOWA
Templeton Rye

Chicago

WASHINGTON, D.C.
see inset
Copper Fox
A. Smith Bowman
VIRGINIA
KENTUCKY
Piedmont
NORTH CAROLINA

UNITED STATES

SMALL BATCH
BERNHEIM ORIGINAL
KENTUCKY STRAIGHT WHEAT WHISKEY

TENNESSEE
Nashville
Jack Daniel's
George Dickel

PACIFIC OCEAN

Rio Grande

MEXICO

New Orleans

ATLANTIC OCEAN

Gulf of Mexico

SINGLE BARREL BOURBON
WILD TURKEY
KENTUCKY SPIRIT
HAND SELECTED BY OUR MASTER DISTILLER

INDIANA
Ohio River
Louisville
Heaven Hill
Buffalo Trace & Old Rip Van Winkle
Frankfort
I-75
Woodford Reserve
Lawrenceburg
Four Roses · Wild Turkey
Lexington
Beam
Bardstown
Kentucky Bourbon Distillers
Elizabethtown
Loretto · Maker's Mark
KENTUCKY
I-65
Kentucky River
I-75

0   10   20 miles
0   20   40 km

KEY
■ Distillery
Roads
Rivers, lakes

0   200   400 miles
0   200   400   600   800 km

BEAM

OWNER	Beam Inc.
FOUNDED 1933	**CAPACITY** 10.6m gal (40m liters), both sites
ADDRESS	149 Happy Hollow Road, Clermont, Kentucky 40110
WEBSITE	www.jimbeam.com

There are two types of distilleries in Kentucky: pretty little ones and big factory ones. Jim Beam is made at two sites, one of which is in Kentucky in a place called Clermont, and without doubt this distillery is very much of the second type. Situated on the main road from Bardstown to Louisville, it's a factory-like monster of a place.

Proper Bourbon, monster scale

Indeed, Jim Beam is the world's biggest Bourbon brand, and in addition to the two core whiskeys there are several other products also made here. But that doesn't mean it isn't making proper Bourbon or that the quality isn't very high.

The statue of Booker Noe *at the Jim Beam distillery shows him in a typically relaxed and welcoming mood.*

"We make it by the same strict rules as everyone else but just on a bigger scale," says Beam's "whiskey professor" Bernie Lubbers, originally a professional comedian and now a respected Bourbon and Beam ambassador.

Until recently, many of the distillery's secrets had been kept hidden under lock and key. Although the site was open to visitors, the distillery itself was out of bounds. That changed in September 2012 when a visitor walkway through the distillery allowed tours to take place. "That is important," says Lubbers, "because the modern whiskey-lover has an increasing thirst for information on the technicalities of making Bourbon."

Small batch spirit

In addition to the core Beam brands, Clermont also makes the "small batch" range of Knob Creek, Baker's, Booker's, and Basil Hayden's. It has been said that "small batch" doesn't really exist, but

KNOB CREEK 9-YEAR-OLD

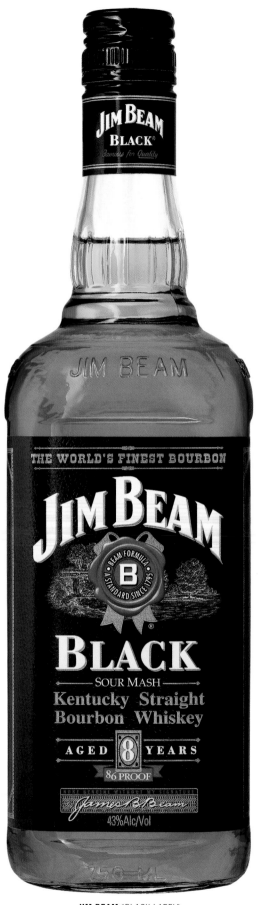

JIM BEAM "BLACK LABEL"

Lubbers is quick to take issue with that, too. "The spirit used in those whiskeys comes off the same still as Beam and is taken from the same basic Beam recipes," he says, "but the cut points are different and the whiskey is taken off for maturation in a different way. When we ran out of Knob Creek a few years back, records show that we had plenty of 'none-year-old' Bourbon, but we didn't use it because it wasn't Knob Creek."

Sweating hard for innovation

Jim Beam is the world's biggest-selling Bourbon, and you'd forgive the brand's owners for not fixing what's not broken. But these are exciting times for American whiskey and Beam isn't dropping behind when it comes to innovation and new products either, says Master Distiller Fred Noe.

"We launched a cherry-infused Bourbon called 'Red Stag' in 2011 and it became one of our biggest launches," he says. "And we followed that with a honey-infused Bourbon. People seem to love this stuff and it's bringing new people to the category."

That doesn't mean serious whiskey drinkers are seeing their favorites replaced, however, and in the meantime Beam is busy trying to create new favorites for the future, too.

"We are looking at new ways of making great whiskey," says Noe. "For instance, "Devil's Cut" is a Bourbon where we've sweated the empty barrels by adding water and agitating them to bring Bourbon out of the wood. It's called the 'Devil's Cut' as opposed to the 'Angel's Share,' And we released a rye version of Knob Creek; rye matured for a longer period of time."

TASTING NOTES

JIM BEAM "BLACK LABEL"
Bourbon, 43% ABV
Everything you'd expect from a good Bourbon is here, the extra years in the barrel giving it a weightier, oakier, and spicier delivery than the standard "White Label" version, but there's plenty of vanilla, honey, saddle leather, and stewed fruits. Honeycomb at its heart, too.

KNOB CREEK 9-YEAR-OLD
Bourbon, 50% ABV
Although there are older Bourbons than this, nine years is a long, long time for Bourbon to mature and this lets fly with both barrels. There's oak, spice, and a delightful nuttiness, plus overripe apricots, and red berries in the mix, combined with a woozy weaving rye trail to make it utterly irresistible. Outstanding.

BASIL HAYDEN'S 8-YEAR-OLD
Bourbon, 40% ABV
This proves that subtlety and softness have a place in Bourbon production. This is a light, sophisticated, and aperitif-like Bourbon with more lemon, lime, and orange in its makeup than virtually any other Bourbon. Lacks the punch of many of its siblings, but offers variety instead.

BOOKER NOE

A number of Jim Beam's "Small Batch Bourbon Collection" whiskeys take their names from legendary Bourbon characters, including Booker Noe, Master Distiller at Jim Beam for more than 40 years and father of current Master Distiller Fred Noe. Booker lends his name to the distillery's first-ever cask strength Bourbon and was well known for his generous hospitality. One visitor was told that if he were to turn up at Booker's house unannounced he would be offered food, drink, and a place to stay. Amazed, he hesitated at first but was eventually persuaded to go. When he returned, the visitor was asked whether he had indeed been offered food, drink, and somewhere to stay. "No," he replied. "Booker offered me the drink first."

BOOKER'S TRUE BARREL BOURBON

BASIL HAYDEN'S 8-YEAR-OLD

BUFFALO TRACE

OWNER Sazerac

FOUNDED 1787 (as Lee's Town)

CAPACITY 11.9m gal (45m liters)

ADDRESS 113 Great Buffalo Trace, Franklin County, Frankfort, Kentucky 40601

WEBSITE www.buffalotrace.com

You could search the world over but find few distilleries that have such a great sense of history as the massive Buffalo Trace Distillery in Frankfort. Occupying a site on the side of a hill that sweeps down to the Kentucky River, a tributary of the mighty Ohio River, the distillery feels significant in every way. Its history stretches back to the beginning of white settlement and, incredibly for an American whiskey-making facility, it is older than most Scottish distilleries.

In the earliest days of settlement, several European pioneers who formed the garrison of Frankfort lost their lives in battles with American Indians as they fought to establish ownership of the land. The prize they were fighting for—an abundance of water and arable land and access to rivers that would provide transportation—guaranteed prosperity for the white settlers. The Kentucky River quickly became associated with whiskey making, from moonshiners upstream to licensed distilleries in the bluegrass pasture area, and in 1787 the distillery at Buffalo Trace, then known as Lee's Town, began shipping whiskey down the river

BUFFALO TRACE BOURBON

to New Orleans. The whiskey business was brisk, and by 1810 there were no fewer than 2,000 distilleries in Kentucky.

Distillery ups and downs

Buffalo Trace Distillery has been home to some of the greatest names of distilling, and in 1904 was named after one of them, George T. Stagg, who had bought it in 1878. It survived the days of Prohibition by gaining a permit to produce medicinal whiskey, which was evidently of such benefit that one million bottles were produced in 1925. After the end of Prohibition in 1933, capacity steadily increased and by 1939 the distillery employed 1,000 staff. By the early 1990s, however, as a result of the vicissitudes of the Bourbon industry, the number of employees had fallen to only 50 and closure threatened.

This is a distillery that has survived a lot of the difficulties that come with a long history, however, and with extensive renovations and the bestowal in 1999 of its present name, Buffalo Trace is back on top, producing a range of world-famous and iconic Bourbons including George T. Stagg, Eagle Rare, W. L. Weller, and Van Winkle, as well as the flagship brand Buffalo Trace. Legendary distiller Elmer T. Lee, who at the time of writing was in his early nineties, still oversees production of the Bourbon named after him from this site.

The water towers of the distillery *are an iconic landmark in the heartland of Bourbon Country.*

A place to visit

If all of that history doesn't take your breath away, as you stand overlooking the distillery when the early morning dew hangs in the air and the first of the day's Kentucky heat caresses your head, then walk down to the visitors' center. Here you will find old black-and-white pictures of the distillery staff—a surprisingly mixed group of black and white workers given the region's racial history—and of the old paddle steamers that opened up the interior of North America and ensured the future of Bourbon.

If you're lucky, a staff member will point out his great-grandfather in one of the pictures, and here more than anywhere else you realize that whiskey making is a conveyor belt that is in constant motion. We step onto it and then one day we step off again, but it keeps slowly moving on from generation to generation.

The sprawling Buffalo Trace site is just a tad ramshackle, but if you get the chance, clear the day and go on the hard-hat tour. The guides here are part of the Buffalo Trace story and will surprise and delight you with fact after fact of incredible information about the distillery. The tour takes you into the heart of the distillery, through the maturation warehouses, and on to the roof with stunning views across the Kentucky countryside. You will also see the small still where the distillery is carrying out microdistilling experiments with a view to competing with the new wave of American whiskeys. Quite possibly there isn't a finer distillery on the planet.

TASTING NOTES

BUFFALO TRACE BOURBON
Bourbon, 45% ABV
This is a beauty of a Bourbon; it starts off sweet and light, with citrus and vanilla, then builds to a crescendo with a touch of oak, a dollop of rye, and banoffee pie in the mix. Superb.

EAGLE RARE
SINGLE BARREL 17-YEAR-OLD
Bourbon, 45% ABV
Released annually in a unique batch, so there will be some variation. Seventeen years is an immense age for a Bourbon but the oak doesn't overwhelm, providing a drying and spicy box for the toffee, rye, grain, and honey to bounce off each other.

GEORGE T. STAGG 15-YEAR-OLD
Bourbon, varies around 70% ABV,
cask strength, non-chill-filtered
Another batch whiskey, and you'll have to move fast to get it because this really is much in demand, with good reason—it's among the best whiskeys in the world. Take at least a sip at the full strength: dark chocolate, candied cherries, some licorice, and the sexiest rye imaginable will coat your throat and leave the taste evolving for hours.

BUFFALO CROSSING

The distillery's name is a reference to the fact that the original settlement of 1775 was sited on a trail, or "trace," called the Great Buffalo Trace. This was a path carved in the land by one of the massive herds of American bison, or buffalo, which used to migrate by the hundreds of thousands across the great plains of North America, their numbers so large that it took hours for them to pass. The bison would slow to cross the relatively narrow and shallow section of the Kentucky River here, making it an ideal location for American Indians to hunt them. White settlers found these wide, clear paths forged by the bison to be extremely useful transportation routes, and the crossing an ideal place to found a settlement, laying the groundwork for a violent clash of cultures.

EAGLE RARE SINGLE BARREL 10-YEAR-OLD

ELMER T. LEE BOURBON

FOUR ROSES "SMALL BATCH"

FOUR ROSES "YELLOW"

FOUR ROSES

OWNER Kirin Brewery Company	
FOUNDED 1910 **CAPACITY** 4.76m gal (18m liters)	
ADDRESS 1224 Bond Mills Road, Lawrenceburg, Kentucky 40342	
WEBSITE www.fourroses.us	

A whiskey-making facility out on a limb and standing apart from its competitors, Four Roses has always enjoyed the reputation of being a slightly oddball distillery in Kentucky. With more than 100 years of history behind it, the distillery building was built in Spanish Mission Revival style and has the appearance more of a Spanish Colonial hacienda than a whiskey distillery, an incongruous but atmospheric site surrounded by dark and broody Bourbon warehouses. For this reason alone it's worth making the effort to travel to the site and join the distillery tour.

The way the distillery operates is also different from what happens in Bourbon distilleries elsewhere. And there's another factor here as well: Four Roses has been an American enigma because very little, if any, of its Bourbon was sold in the US, and those who had heard of it tended to assume it was a very different product from the one that was actually being made. This is partly for historical reasons and partly because its owner is the Japanese beer giant Kirin, and it has always operated in its own bubble.

Rescued from its reputation

Many years ago there was a cheap blend known as Four Roses, and it was an average-quality, big-selling whiskey. It was originally launched in 1888, and as a result of its success it moved to what was then a state-of-the-art distillery in Lawrenceburg. The whiskey made today at Four Roses is a very different proposition and is as good as anything else from the state of Kentucky, but until recently Kirin exported the Bourbon to Japanese and selected European markets and at home it struggled to shake off the old negative reputation.

What reputation it did enjoy at home stemmed from the tireless work of Master Distiller Jim Rutledge, who is an ambassador not just for the distillery but also for Bourbon in general. He has been involved with the Kentucky Bourbon Festival for years, resulting in the somewhat bizarre situation of hundreds of overseas visitors flocking to the distillery while it remained relatively unknown at home.

Rutledge was supposed to have retired by now, but he can't keep away from the distillery and he's still a high-profile figure in Kentucky. He's loving the fact that having been launched into the domestic market, Four Roses is starting to turn heads in all sorts of places.

"We've continued to grow our markets in the United States and, in addition, last year Four Roses successfully introduced our Bourbon into Turkey and also into the second-largest province of Canada—Ontario," he says with relish. On the back of this success, "One or two additional

The striking distillery building was built in a Spanish Mission Revival style popular at the time of its foundation.

Canadian provinces are now being targeted. The year 2011 was very successful, with global case sales increasing 42 percent over 2010. A Four Roses 'Limited Edition Single Barrel Bourbon' was introduced to the US market in April 2012, with 35 percent rye grain and our 'K' yeast, which generates spicy characters."

The Four Roses lineup

The reference to yeast is an important one for Four Roses, because the distillery operates in the same way that a Japanese distillery might. The Bourbon is marketed as three core products, with a number of special releases being put out for different markets and for different occasions. Several whiskeys are made with various recipe and yeast combinations, and these are combined to produce the standard Four Roses offering. The best four whiskeys are selected for Four Roses "Small Batch," and the rest of them are used for the "Single Barrel" offering. The distillery also produces other well-known Bourbon brands under license, including Bulleit and I.W. Harper "President's Reserve."

Rutledge is proud of the distillery's progress and seems unconcerned by the rise of new distilleries across the country. "I believe we'll continue to see 'boutique' distilleries entering the American whiskey market for several years," he says. "Some will be successful in creating niche markets for specialty whiskeys, but the overall impact on the American whiskey market will be minimal. I believe that the future for the eight major Kentucky Bourbon distilleries is very bright and that sales will continue to grow domestically and globally."

TASTING NOTES

FOUR ROSES "YELLOW"
Bourbon, 40% ABV
True to its mellow-yellow name, this is a less aggressive Bourbon than most, and with a softer, more feminine taste. It's a sophisticated one with vanilla, oak, and orange fruit, with a honeyed core. Some rye spice arrives later on.

FOUR ROSES "SMALL BATCH"
Bourbon, 45% ABV
Not dissimilar to the standard bottling but with a more intense and bolder offering of fruit and spice. The honey and spice dominate toward the finish, while the citrus fruit weaves in and out.

FOUR ROSES "SINGLE BARREL"
Bourbon, approx. 50% ABV (variable)
Four Roses unleashed! Far and away the best version of the standard range. The taste varies from batch to batch but this has full fruit, candy, vanilla, and oak pulling together to create a taste sensation. The finish is decidedly long.

FOUR ROSES "SINGLE BARREL"

GEORGIA MOON
CORN WHISKEY

HEAVEN HILL

OWNER The Shapira family	
FOUNDED 1934 **CAPACITY** 5.94m gal (22.5m liters)	
ADDRESS 1311 Gilkey Run Road, Bardstown,	
Kentucky 40004 (Bourbon Heritage Center)	
WEBSITE www.heavenhill.com;	
www.bourbonheritagecenter.com	

Although Heaven Hill might not be the most familiar Bourbon name to many, it is a massive distillery that has grown significantly in recent years and seems to be going from strength to strength.

Independently owned and run by the Shapira family, the company has two significant parts: the large production site in Louisville, which it moved into after the original distillery was destroyed by fire in November 1996, and where the spirit is distilled; and a custom-built and very stylish visitors' center close to some of its maturation warehouses near Bardstown. The visitors' center is relatively new and includes a comprehensive exhibition telling the story of Bourbon, as well as a shop and a barrel-shaped tasting room where visitors can attend tastings of some of the distillery's best whiskeys.

The visitor experience also includes tours and highly informative walks through the huge stack warehouses in the neighboring fields. Although they may be tired of talking about it, the staff will tell you about the great fire that took most of the warehouses here and burned for days.

Famous Bourbon brands

While the company may not be familiar to many whiskey enthusiasts outside the United States, its brands are: Heaven Hill counts the legendary Bourbon names of Evan Williams and Elijah Craig among its portfolio. But, says Larry Kass, Director of Corporate Communications, there is much more to Heaven Hill, and the company is in great shape to ride the American whiskey wave into the future.

"Heaven Hill is the only major American whiskey producer that makes all styles—Bourbon, rye, wheat, corn—and since we're the world's second-largest Bourbon producer, we are in a unique position," he points out. "There is no doubt that young, affluent male consumers, both here in the United States and internationally, are interested not only in Bourbons but in other styles of American straight whiskey as well. You can see this in the fact that those of us who make traditional straight rye have been bought out, and new entrants on the rye market include non-traditional, non-straight ryes that were formerly blending components for Canadian and American blended whiskeys.

ELIJAH CRAIG 12-YEAR-OLD

EVAN WILLIAMS BOURBON

"The increasing popularity of brands such as Bernheim Original Kentucky Straight Wheat Whiskey and Mellow Corn Bottled In Bond Corn Whiskey is further evidence of the diversity of tastes now being sought by American whiskey consumers. Those of us who are devoted Bourbon producers and marketers will continue, within the tight parameters allowed by law, to experiment with barrel finishes, grains, aging regimens, and other ways to differentiate products."

Looking to the future

Take a close look at the recent track record of the distillery, which is overseen by father and son team Craig and Parker Beam, and you'll see it's a heady combination of all the benefits of an independent family-run business and all the economies that giant size can bring. Heaven Hill is second only to Beam in size and has warehouse space for more than a million barrels.

And while single-cask and special bottling releases are now commonplace across the distilleries of Kentucky, Heaven Hill has been doing it for years; in 2012 the 18th Evan Williams Single Barrel Vintage was released. But the business hasn't been slow to respond to new challenges either, and includes cinnamon- and cherry-flavored Bourbons in its repertoire.

"There have been many highlights for us in recent years, almost too many to summarize," says Kass. "With new products set to be released, the future is looking very bright."

TASTING NOTES

EVAN WILLIAMS SINGLE BARREL VINTAGE BOURBON
Bourbon, 43.3% ABV
No-nonsense, big-hearted, and simple Bourbon with an emphasis on candy and vanilla and with oak and rye very much in the background. The finish is relatively short, but it's a perfectly palatable and easy-drinking whiskey.

ELIJAH CRAIG 12-YEAR-OLD
Bourbon, 47% ABV
Now made from whiskey distilled at Bernheim, this whiskey has its critics, and indeed, doesn't taste as if it's been matured for 12 years—long for Kentucky. But shake off the age and judge it on its own merits and it's a good Bourbon, with a balance of candy, fruit, oak, and rye.

BERNHEIM ORIGINAL KENTUCKY STRAIGHT WHEAT WHISKEY
wheat whiskey, 45% ABV
Arguably the best whiskey to come out of Heaven Hill, though the ryes in the Rittenhouse range are pretty wonderful, too. There is a rounded softness to this whiskey from the wheat, and the palate offers a delightful lemon, orange, and honey mix with a delicious spiciness at its heart. Excellent.

BEST OF THE BARRELS

The annual single-barrel vintage Bourbon releases of Evan Williams have become something of a Kentucky institution, but in recent years a second annual release has been introduced by the company. The "Parker's Heritage Collection" range gives Master Distiller Parker Beam the opportunity to release some of his rarest and most unusual whiskey; recent years have seen a cask strength high-wheat mash release and one barrel finished in Cognac casks. To the company's credit, however, in the light of a major downturn in the US economy, the 2011 release was deliberately priced down to ensure it was still accessible to the distillery's legion of fans. In the last few years the company has balanced affordable releases with aged, award-winning Bourbons—a heady combination.

RITTENHOUSE RYE "100 PROOF"

BERNHEIM ORIGINAL WHEAT WHISKEY

JACK DANIEL'S

OWNER	Brown Forman
FOUNDED 1866	**CAPACITY** 39m gal (150m liters)
ADDRESS	182 Lynchburg Highway, Lynchburg, Tennessee 37352
WEBSITE	www.jackdaniels.com

Whiskey lovers tend at best to take Jack Daniel's for granted and, at worst, to distance themselves from it and condemn it for not being a "proper whiskey." This is insultingly simplistic and grossly unfair on a brand that has done more than any other to keep the world whiskey flag flying over the many years when it wasn't in vogue.

A good ol' success story

In fact, the brand's owners have pulled off three marketing feats that deserve our total respect. One, they convinced young people that it could be cool to drink whiskey; two, they succeeded in making a brown spirit a success story when hardly any other dark spirit was selling very well at all; and three, they managed to convince drinkers that it was a small, good ol' boy brand when actually it's a commercial monster.

Pay a visit to the distillery and they're working overtime to protect that impression. Lynchburg itself is a dry town, so you can't actually buy the drink, but it is a shrine to the distillery, and when you wander through shop after shop selling "JD" merchandise from lapel badges to Harley-Davidson motorcycles, you get a sense of how big a brand it is—up there with Coca Cola and, indeed, Harley. Not bad for a hard liquor.

The "JD" experience

The distillery itself is akin to a whiskey version of a Disney theme park. If you stop off for something to eat, you'll find the staff dressed in appropriate Southern casual style, while the food is all home cooking this and granny's apple pie that.

There's a little train that runs around the vast site, but a lot of the bigger production facilities—the bottling plants, for instance—are kept well away from the tourist part of the facility. The production areas you are shown are nowhere near adequate to produce the huge volumes of liquid, and you never really get the sense that more than 264,000 gallons (1 million liters) of whiskey spirits are maturing. A walk around the site along pathways crossing well-cultivated lawns takes you to little monuments to "Mr. Jack" and one or two of his successors, and to a little shack where you can see the safe Jack Daniel kicked, causing an eventual foot infection that would kill him. But that's not to knock the JD distillery experience—Jack Daniel's

JACK DANIEL'S "SINGLE BARREL"

JACK DANIEL'S "OLD NO.7 TENNESSEE WHISKEY"

Lem Motlow was Jack's nephew *who inherited the business and whose name remains on the distillery sign.*

is made to the same exacting standards as other whiskey from Tennessee and neighboring Kentucky, and the distillery is beautifully presented and will not disappoint.

Lincoln County Process

Jack Daniel's is a Tennessee whiskey and not a Bourbon, and perhaps the best part of the distillery is the area that demonstrates this in unforgettable fashion. Tennessee whiskey is made using the Lincoln County Process, which disqualifies it from being a Bourbon. In Kentucky they will tell you that the process dumbs down the whiskey, but in Tennessee they will argue that it is there to mellow and improve the whiskey, and if it didn't it would be cheaper to dispense with it.

According to this process, Tennessee whiskey must be poured down a wall of charred maple wood, which is burned on site. This is the charcoal-mellowing process referred to with great pride by Jack Daniel's and fellow Tennessee whiskey maker George Dickel. There are some Bourbon bottles that refer to charcoal filtering, but this is not the same: the whiskey is filtered through charcoal after it has been matured in a cask, and the process is mainly carried out to remove floating impurities from the wood.

The "JD" range

The whole thrust of the marketing of the whiskey is that Jack got it right the first time and you don't fix what ain't broke. As a result, there are only three brand extensions of the basic Jack Daniel's "Old No.7"—"Tennessee Honey," "Gentleman Jack," and Jack Daniel's "Single Barrel Tennessee Whiskey." At one time you could pretty much only find these at the distillery, but they're distributed a lot farther now. While "Tennessee Honey" is a whiskey liqueur and "Gentleman Jack" is a muted version of "Old No.7," both aimed at the non-whiskey-drinker, if anybody tells you that Jack Daniel's isn't real whiskey, introduce them to the "Single Barrel" expression—as good as many fine Bourbons, without a doubt.

TASTING NOTES

JACK DANIEL'S "OLD NO.7 TENNESSEE WHISKEY"

Tennessee whiskey, 40% ABV

Burnt toffee, nut brittle, and overripe stewed fruit, with a challenging, plummy, rich candy and corn heart. Most people mix it, but try throwing it over some ice one hot summer day and drinking it straight. It's a lot better than it's given credit for.

JACK DANIEL'S "GENTLEMAN JACK"

Tennessee whiskey, 40% ABV

Jack Lite, anybody? This is for people who don't much care for whiskey but want to have the Jack experience—so there's sweet mellow corn, some citrus notes, a hint of oak and spice, and a short finish. Blink and you could miss it.

JACK DANIEL'S "SINGLE BARREL TENNESSEE WHISKEY"

Tennessee whiskey, 45% ABV

Now you're talking—first introduced in 1997, each barrel differs from the next and you may get sharp citrus fruits, toffee, vanilla, dark cherries, dark chocolate, praline, coffee, hickory, and licorice. Well worth seeking out.

JACK DANIEL'S "GENTLEMAN JACK"

MAKER'S MARK

OWNERS Beam Inc.

FOUNDED 1954 **CAPACITY** 2.1m gal (8m liters)

ADDRESS 3350 Burk Spring Road, Loretto, Kentucky 40037

WEBSITE www.makersmark.com

There's something distinctly kooky about Maker's Mark and the region of Kentucky it's situated in, and the Samuels family—who still run the company, albeit now within the fold of global drinks conglomerate Beam—would have it no other way. Certainly there's no whiskey experience anywhere in the world quite like the one this distillery offers.

Kentucky has a sizable Catholic population, and as you approach the distillery you'll see dozens of shrines to the Virgin Mary housed in what appear to be bathtubs. That's because they *are* bathtubs. The story goes that a bathtub salesman unable to interest the local population in the value of regular bathing struck upon an ingenious idea, bought a few hundred statues of Our Lady, and reversed his fortunes overnight.

Illusions of scale

The distillery itself is as well kept as any distillery anywhere, so much so that you'd be forgiven for thinking no whiskey is made here. Actually, make that "whisky," as another of the family quirks is to recognize its Scottish ancestry and spell the word the Scottish way.

You enter the distillery through gardens with an assortment of trees from around the world, the pathways lined with old fire engines and outbuildings. The whole site is neat and tidy, and the distillery is all dark wood, red-painted colonnades, and picket fences.

But looks can be deceptive, and while the owners might like to give you the impression that this is a small-batch distillery with a boutique whiskey, it's an illusion. This distillery has the capacity to produce more spirits than all but three or four of the Scottish malt distilleries. It's probably gotten as big as it's ever going to get now, though, because after two or three expansions the water source at the back of the distillery has reached its limit.

You don't need to look very far around the distillery to see evidence of the brand's worldwide success. Enter the visitor facilities and style is the order of the day. It's a bit unnerving, though. Pictures of the Samuels family have eyes that follow as you pass through, and if you're a Maker's Mark "ambassador"—for which you can sign up online—they will make a song and dance about you when you introduce yourself. There's a stylish and hyper-modern bar on site, a shop, and a station where you can put your own label on a bottle of the Bourbon and then dip it in the trademark red wax to make it unique to you.

The Samuels family

The illusion of small scale stretches as far as the distillery's ownership, because while it's part of the Beam empire now, it still plays on the Samuels family connection. It was originally built by Bill

MAKER'S MARK

Samuels bought the Burks' Distillery, *the oldest Kentucky distillery site still in use, to make his new whiskey.*

Samuels, a legendary figure in the world of Bourbon who had retired from the business following World War II but had become restless. So, after taking advice from the great producers in Louisville's whiskey row, including Pappy Van Winkle, he set about making a new Bourbon. His aim was to make a whiskey that people who didn't like whiskey would drink, one that appealed to a larger audience than the traditional blue-collar working man, and he did so by using a higher proportion of wheat in his recipe.

Legend has it that Bill Samuels' wife came up with the name Maker's Mark, taking the idea from the silver and gold industry and arguing that what the world did not need was another Bourbon bearing the surname of the maker. Bill Samuels Jr., who oversaw production of his father's brand until retiring as President and CEO in 2011, has also said that the logo bearing the numeral "IV" is a mistake and should read "VI"—an interesting twist given that the current Bill Samuels is dyslexic. Possibly dyslexia explains Samuels' ability to think outside of the box and constantly come up with new ideas.

Bill Junior's legacy

That capacity for innovation didn't stretch to whiskey, however—or at least it didn't for more than 50 years. Maker's Mark was one product made with one recipe and matured to the same age. But as Bill Samuels Jr. approached retirement age, he was overwhelmed by the thought that he would be remembered for no more than being a caretaker for his brand and that he would leave no legacy.

The result of this soul-searching was "Maker's 46." Launched in August 2010, this is a fabulous toasty, oaky take on the standard bottling. The name derives from the reference number to the toasting and charring of special staves added into the production.

TASTING NOTES

MAKER'S MARK
Bourbon, 46% ABV
Sweet, easy-to-drink whiskey of the highest order, with a soft and rounded wheat palate, lots of flavorsome grain, and a late hit of white pepper spice to keep everything in check. Quite weighty, too, with candy and saddle leather mixing it up with corn, fruit, and honey.

MAKER'S MARK "MAKER'S 46"
Bourbon, 47% ABV
Sharpens up the trademark Maker's Mark flavors and dollops syrup, toasted oak, burnt treacle toffee, and dark chocolate onto them. It's like a grown-up version of the standard bottling, the whiskey equivalent of dark chocolate compared to the standard bottling's milk chocolate.

MAKER'S MARK "MAKER'S 46"

AN INDIVIDUAL APPROACH

It may be a big distillery these days, but Maker's Mark still does things a little differently from its competitors. The grain is ground on a mill that uses a roller system rather than a hammer system, because the distillery believes that the heat from hammering makes for a more bitter taste. Also, the barrels are rotated in the warehouse for consistency, important for a Bourbon that uses relatively few barrels in each batch and should not vary enormously in taste—something hard to avoid in Kentucky because of the huge temperature variations in the large, multi-floored warehouses.

WILD TURKEY "KENTUCKY SPIRIT"

RUSSELL'S RESERVE 10-YEAR-OLD

WILD TURKEY

OWNER Gruppo Campari
FOUNDED 1869 **CAPACITY** 13m gal (50m liters)
ADDRESS 1525 Tyrone Road, Lawrenceburg, Kentucky 40342
WEBSITE www.wildturkey.com

If ever you wanted proof that American whiskey in general and Bourbon in particular is in a good place, it's at Wild Turkey. One of the more traditional Kentucky distilleries, it never quite had the size and presence of the likes of Jim Beam or Buffalo Trace, but neither did it have the prettiness and small batch feeling of Woodford Reserve or Maker's Mark. In fact, truth be told, until recently it was crumbling and looking pretty tattered around the edges. And the brand wasn't in much better shape, either.

Campari investment

Legendary Master Distiller Jimmy Russell, who at 90-plus has more energy than many men half his age and still travels the world, reminisces about the happy years mixing with Booker Noe and a generation of friends which includes Julian Van Winkle, Elmer T. Lee, Parker Beam, and Jim Rutledge. But now there's plenty to look forward to as well, because in 2011 new owners Campari, who bought the distillery from Pernod Ricard in 2009, unveiled a $50 million distillery plant capable of upping production of the Bourbon from 6 million gallons (23 million liters) to 13 million gallons (50 million liters), making it one of the biggest whiskey-making plants in the world. The unveiling was marked with an event featuring retired staff, local dignitaries, and both Jimmy Russell and his Assistant Master Distiller, son Eddie.

"This company displays its Kentucky roots proudly, and its investment in Kentucky has reaped great success and respect worldwide," said Kentucky Governor Steve Beshear at the time. "This expansion will not only bring the potential of more jobs to our Kentucky families but will also bring continued stability and longevity to this remarkable business."

Commenting on the opening of the new distillery, Campari Chief Executive Bob Kunze-Concewitz said: "This project reflects the confidence we have in the growth prospects of the iconic Wild Turkey family of brands."

New distillery, new image

The new distillery couldn't be more different from the old one, incorporating the latest in energy efficiency and environmental protection facilities. New features include improved emissions controls, water recycling, and a renewable fuel system. Distilling began at the new plant in 2011 and the first stocks of aged Wild Turkey Bourbon distilled under the new regime will be available to whiskey fans in 2016.

Campari intends to update Wild Turkey's slightly tired image, too. It's said that if a Kentucky bar patron ever asks you what you are drinking, you just have to say "101" and buy him a shot to have a friend for life. The trouble is that the old redneck image of Bourbon isn't a profitable one these days, and since the turn of the millennium many of the key brands have been reinventing themselves by launching into the premium category.

Wild Turkey fell off the page for a while, though in the early part of the millennium it dipped its feet into the premium market in the United States. Now a new mixable Wild Turkey brand called Wild Turkey "81 Proof," created by Eddie Russell, has been launched successfully. The rest of the range is set for a facelift and has already been repackaged and rebranded in the United States and Australasia.

The turkey flies

Even before the Campari purchase, the Wild Turkey range had been expanded, but the brand is expected to enjoy a much higher profile from now on. Commenting on the changes, a spokesman for Campari said, "These are exciting times for the distillery, which can now offer visitors a proper Bourbon experience in a modern and functional environment. People who know whiskey know what a strong brand Wild Turkey is. Now is the time to make the brand fly again."

TASTING NOTES

WILD TURKEY "101 PROOF"
Bourbon, 50.5% ABV
Now lives up to its billing as the daddy of blue-collar bar-drinkin' Bourbon, with a feisty rye spice and honeyed oak combination going on and some dark chocolate and cherry notes.

WILD TURKEY "81 PROOF"
Bourbon, 40.5% ABV
Firmly aimed at the younger drinker and the cocktail craze, this whiskey is unashamedly light on the corn, oak, and spice, and has a gentle, rounded taste. It's Bourbon's answer to blended Scotch. Short finish, pleasant and sweet.

RUSSELL'S RESERVE 10-YEAR-OLD
Bourbon, 45% ABV
Stablemate Bourbon to the Russell's Reserve Rye in a small batch range launched in 2007 and named after the father-and-son distilling team. This one goes off-piste, with grape and raisin, some big oily notes, and some dusty oak and pepper on the one hand, and syrup and caramel on the other, giving a sugar and spice combination that is complex, rich, deep, and rewarding.

TALKING TURKEY

Wild turkey shooting is a big sport in the American South, as is the sport of turkey calling—impersonating a female turkey to attract a male one so that you can shoot it. Competitions featuring turkey impersonators are even televised and attract good prize money. The "Wild Turkey" brand was conceived in 1940 and took its inspiration from an annual Kentucky turkey shoot. It was traditional for the local distiller to bring along a cask of special Bourbon to the festivities. Thomas McCarthy, president of Austin, Nichols, the New York-based company that owned the distillery at the time, chose a quantity of 101-proof straight Bourbon from company stocks to take along on the shoot. After a few years, people began to ask for the "wild turkey Bourbon" and from there the brand was born.

WILD TURKEY "81 PROOF"

WILD TURKEY "101 PROOF"

WOODFORD RESERVE

OWNER	Brown Forman
FOUNDED 1994	**CAPACITY** Not given
ADDRESS	7855 McCracken Pike, Versailles, Kentucky 40383
WEBSITE	www.woodfordreserve.com

If you're looking for a quaint distillery set in a stunning rural location and steeped in the past, then Brown Forman's Woodford Reserve is the place for you. The old Labrot & Graham distillery is as historic as American whiskey gets, occupying a site where whiskey legends Elijah Pepper and James Crow fine-tuned the Bourbon-making process, not exactly inventing the drink but bringing to it a consistency and quality that ensured a bright future.

Brown Forman own Jack Daniel's and the big Early Times Distillery in the city of Louisville, Kentucky, but Woodford Reserve couldn't be more different from them. To reach it, you travel through some of the prettiest parts of the state, passing the huge stud farms where some of the world's finest racehorses are bred, and where the likes of the British monarch and various sheikhs own stock. The horses are here for the same reason that the whiskey is: a water supply drawn from calcium-rich hard-water basins that both produces great Bourbons and enriches the grassland that the horses graze on, helping to raise strong animals.

Pushing the boundaries

The distillery itself seems almost like a model rather than a working establishment. Lovingly restored by its owners in an area of verdant natural beauty, it has a stylish visitors' center, great views, and a comprehensive and highly informative tour—not the longest one, though, because the distillery really is "small batch," its facilities tiny. In the visitors' center the ghosts of the past are never far away and, unsurprisingly, tourists are constantly reminded of the distillery's place within the story of American whiskey.

But don't make the mistake of thinking that the distillery is backward-looking, for in Chris Morris, Brown Forman has a feisty, inquisitive, and not uncontroversial distiller who is prepared to push at the boundaries of whiskey. Just look at the annual "Master's Collection" releases, which have included Bourbon matured in Sonoma-Cutrer American wine barrels, a "sweet mash" whiskey, a four-grain expression, and Bourbon matured in seasoned oak. In the warehouses there are experimental maple and hickory casks, and whiskeys made using oats. Many of the experiments won't see the light of day, but they're proof that Morris and his team are continuing a long tradition of thinking outside of the box

WOODFORD RESERVE "DISTILLER'S SELECT"

WOODFORD RESERVE "MASTER'S COLLECTION FOUR GRAIN"

when it comes to Woodford Reserve. "People question whether we should be messing around with Bourbon, but there's a long history here of doing just that," says Morris. "We are leaving the core whiskey unchanged, and it's great whiskey, but it's good to see what happens when we change one part of the process or introduce something new."

Pot still Bourbon

The principal production innovation that sets Woodford Reserve apart from other Bourbon distilleries is the fact that in the still room are pot stills similar to those used to make single malt whiskey in Scotland. Bourbon is normally produced in column stills with doublers, the mash passing through the columns with a consistency as thick as oatmeal. Using pot stills hasn't been without its problems because in malt whiskey production, the grain is removed so that just liquid enters the still. The Bourbon mash led to scalding in the still, so Brown Forman brought in Scottish distiller Ed Dobson, who was working at Glen Moray at the time, and the problem was eventually ironed out by adapting the stills to keep the grain moving.

"We are very proud of the Bourbon we're making here," says Morris. "It's different from anything else available and has a quality to it that far outweighs its price." Woodford Reserve is indeed a special Bourbon, with a rye spiciness and a sophisticated and rounded taste.

TASTING NOTES

WOODFORD RESERVE "DISTILLER'S SELECT"
Bourbon, 45.2% ABV
Big, full, rich, and plush Bourbon, stylish and packed with flavors including burnt toffee, raisins, stewed peaches and apricots, and an array of spice from ginger and nutmeg through to cinnamon and chili pepper. There's a toasty heart to this Bourbon, too, and traces of hickory and red licorice.

WOODFORD RESERVE "MASTER'S COLLECTION SEASONED OAK FINISH"
Bourbon, 45.2% ABV
Brittle toffee crisp, dark chocolate, rich honey, and caramel, and a great big dollop of oak and spice. This is a rich, mouth-coating, beautiful Bourbon with traces of green fruits and some red berries in the mix.

OLD FORESTER "BIRTHDAY BOURBON"
Bourbon, 47% ABV
Chunky, chewy, right-on-the-money Bourbon, with sweet candied fruits, saddle polish, floral talcum powder, and mahogany cigar box with a trace of tobacco. The fruit here is rich and bright, the rye zipping and zinging across the palate like a bouncing waterskier. Fresh, bright, and perfectly balanced between sugar and spice and sweet and sour.

FOUR-GRAIN WONDER

Bourbon whiskey is normally made up of three different grains, of which corn is predominant, and matured in new white oak barrels. At Woodford Reserve, however, they use a mash with a higher-than-normal rye content, giving it a licorice spiciness. But distiller Chris Morris and his team were eager to see what happened when four grains were used. Combining corn, malted barley, and rye with wheat, they created "Four Grain" in the "Master's Collection" range, an oily, full-flavored whiskey that astounded many Bourbon aficionados.

OLD FORESTER "REPEAL BOURBON 75TH ANNIVERSARY"

A. SMITH BOWMAN

OWNER Sazerac

FOUNDED 1935 **CAPACITY** Not given

ADDRESS One Bowman Drive, At Deep Run, Fredericksburg, Virginia 22408

WEBSITE www.asmithbowman.com

The tornado that is plowing through the American whiskey industry is sucking up everything in its path, and that includes the older distilleries. Founded after the repeal of Prohibition, A. Smith Bowman is the only full-scale distillery in Virginia, a state that used to make more whiskey than Kentucky, and it has been producing "Virginia Gentleman" Bourbon for decades. Currently owned by New Orleans–based Sazerac Group, the distillery is being gripped by the changes elsewhere in the industry, as new distiller Truman Cox explains.

"The crew at A. Smith Bowman has been working diligently to refocus as a microdistillery, putting more craft and effort into our products," he says. Evidence of this new focus can be seen in the "Pioneer Spirit" range of limited edition small batch and single barrel expressions.

"With the recent retirement of 33-year-veteran Master Distiller Joe Dangler, the reins have been passed to me," says Cox. "Before the micro-distillery boom we were the Bourbon distillery outside of Kentucky. The Bowman family has a great tradition in the Bourbon industry and I hope to add honor to the tradition of A. Smith Bowman and his sons.

"We are unique as a microdistillery. Most of the new distilleries are starting from the ground up. We were a big distillation company but we lost our craft focus during the 1990s. Now we have streamlined our footprint and product offerings so we can center on quality and providing premium and ultra-premium spirits.

"Unfortunately, whiskey moves at a glacial pace compared to beer and vodka, and experiments take time to mature. I understand the need to put out younger whiskeys to keep profit flowing, but when some of these whiskeys on the shelf are allowed to reach maturity in a barrel, I think that is when we will really see some fine products and excitement from the public."

TASTING NOTES

VIRGINIA GENTLEMAN
Bourbon, 40% ABV
Undergoing a facelift, so it may become considerably different, but this is a light Bourbon with lemon and blood-orange flavors, some caramel, and a big dollop of chili spice. The modest strength and subdued flavors make it a little thin and underwhelming.

VIRGINIA GENTLEMAN

ABRAHAM BOWMAN "RYE WHISKEY"

BOWMAN'S BOURBON

ANCHOR DISTILLING COMPANY

OWNER The Griffin Group
FOUNDED 1993 **CAPACITY** 8,320 gal (31,500 liters)
ADDRESS 1705 Mariposa Street, San Francisco,
California 94107
WEBSITE www.anchordistilling.net

Fritz Maytag is a legendary figure in the world of American craft brewing and microdistilling, and part of that status is due to the fact that he set up a boutique distillery that makes some of the world's most respected and sought-after whiskeys in such small quantities that they are virtually impossible to get hold of. Maytag ran San Francisco's historic Anchor Steam Brewery from 1965, but it wasn't until the early 1990s that he added a small-scale distillery.

"Old Potrero 18th Century Style Whiskey" and "Old Potrero Hotaling's" recreate original American whiskeys by means of distillation on a small copper pot still. They're an acquired taste, but boy, do they have tastes worth acquiring. "Hotaling's" is named after a tenacious whiskey warehouse that survived the 1906 San Francisco earthquake and fire, which devastated the city. Arguably the star of the show, though, is "Old Potrero Straight Rye Whiskey," made with 100 percent rye—one of the toughest whiskeys to make. All these whiskeys are world-class and have won countless awards across the world.

In 2010 Anchor was sold to a San Francisco-based investment company The Griffin Group, but the new owners have experience in the alcohol industry, and they are ambitious about whiskey and are importing some of Scotland's finest malts. They have added an exciting portfolio of other spirits and, in David King, have a president with a big reputation in whiskey in the UK. Exciting times, then, for a distilling company on the move.

TASTING NOTES

OLD POTRERO "STRAIGHT RYE WHISKEY"
single malt rye whiskey, 45% ABV
The nose on this is all over the place, with oily, sappy youthfulness that isn't altogether pleasant. But this tastes fantastic, with chili, fruit, and wood. Licorice and hickory flick in and out, and the overall whiskey is as complex as it gets. Getting to grips with the taste is like trying to control a kite in a gale.

OLD POTRERO "18TH CENTURY STYLE WHISKEY"
single malt rye whiskey, 62.55% ABV, cask strength
Distilled in a copper pot still from a mash of 100% rye malt, then aged for one year in new, lightly toasted oak barrels, this displays a floral, nutty nose, with vanilla and spice. Oily and smooth on the palate, with mint, honey, chocolate, and pepper in the lengthy finish.

OLD POTRERO "STRAIGHT RYE WHISKEY"

OLD POTRERO "18TH CENTURY STYLE WHISKEY"

COPPER FOX

OWNER Rick Wasmund

FOUNDED 2000 **CAPACITY** 18,500 gal (70,000 liters)

ADDRESS 9 River Lane, Sperryville, Virginia 22740

WEBSITE www.copperfox.biz

This distillery is the home of Wasmund's Single Malt Whisky, made by Rick Wasmund, who is something of a distilling legend. He had long cherished the idea of making a single malt in the Scotch style, and a magical trip overseas to Scotland to observe whiskey making and distilling at first hand gave him the impetus to launch his own business back home.

In 2000 he founded the Copper Fox Distillery, purchasing an existing Virginia distillery as a springboard for launching his eponymous whisky on the world—and it is "whisky," not "whiskey," in recognition of its Scotch inspiration. Wasmund malts barley in the traditional Scottish manner, and he produces his spirit on a small double pot still in single cask batches.

But Wasmund didn't want to just copy long-established Scottish methods—he brought his own twist to production, using creativity and innovation in the distilling process.

"We are the only distillery in North America to hand malt our own barley and the only distillery on the planet to use apple and cherry wood smoke to flavor the malted barley," he says. "We put great emphasis on flavor and we produce one barrel at a time. The spirit is non-chill-filtered to preserve the complete flavor."

Copper Fox also employs innovative techniques in its aging process by maturing the spirits using an original "chip and barrel" method, which dramatically speeds up maturation and which, for now, Wasmund is keeping tightly under wraps. The end product is, as Wasmund says, "Not Scotch-like, not Bourbon-like, just American whiskey on a path of our own."

The dinky distillery, which moved to its newly built site at the foot of the Blue Ridge Mountains in 2005, offers a tour of the operation and the chance to pick up your own barrel kit in order to mature the Wasmund spirit yourself—another first from this innovative distiller.

TASTING NOTE

WASMUND'S SINGLE MALT WHISKY
single malt, 48% ABV, non-chill-filtered
This is distilled for a relatively short period of time, and while the floral and spicy flavor might not show it, the feisty, sappy nose is a giveaway and so is the slight finish and lack of complexity. What flavor there is on the palate, though, includes elderberry, raisin, and a delightful sweet smokiness.

WASMUND'S SINGLE MALT SPIRIT

WASMUND'S SINGLE MALT WHISKY

CLEAR CREEK

OWNER Stephen McCarthy

FOUNDED 1986 **CAPACITY** Not given

ADDRESS 2389 NW Wilson Street, Portland, Oregon 97210

WEBSITE www.clearcreekdistillery.com

Set up by Steve McCarthy in 1986, Clear Creek Distillery is part of the original wave of microdistilleries and stands apart from many other whiskey making establishments in the United States because it not only makes single malt whiskey but makes it using heavily peated barley.

The distillery lies at the foot of the impressive Mount Hood near Portland, Oregon, in the Pacific Northwest, and was originally set up to make fruit liqueurs, brandies, and *eaux de vie* using the abundant produce from the family orchards in the region. Using a traditional European pot still, McCarthy draws on skills that he learned in Austria and Switzerland.

The whiskey made here is called McCarthy's Oregon Single Malt Whiskey, and it is a heavily peated one that uses peated barley imported from Scotland.

"Of Scotland's malt whiskeys, the nearest I would compare it to is Lagavulin," McCarthy says. "It's very peaty and very full-flavored. The present bottling is only three years old, but we think it is remarkably smooth for such a young whiskey. The result is a smooth whiskey with a surprisingly clean finish. Production is very limited because what we put in the barrel doesn't come out for years."

In fact, distribution is so limited that whenever stock becomes available, it tends to sell out very quickly, so much so that there is a waiting list for each new batch. Nevertheless, attempts are made to ensure that some of McCarthy's can be found across much of the United States and some is also now exported to Europe.

The whiskey is initially matured in former sherry casks for two or three years, then for six to 12 months in barrels made from air-dried Oregon oak. Despite the uniquely Oregon flavor imparted by the local oak, McCarthy is of the opinion that, since it is made from peat-malted barley brought in from Scotland, "our whiskey would be a single malt Scotch if Oregon were Scotland."

TASTING NOTE

MCCARTHY'S OREGON SINGLE MALT WHISKEY
single malt, 42.5% ABV
The nose has pencil shavings and delicate citrus, and the bitter lemon and orange, sharp, clean taste gives way to a wave of peat. Not particularly complex but balanced, tasty, and very well made.

MCCARTHY'S OREGON SINGLE MALT WHISKEY

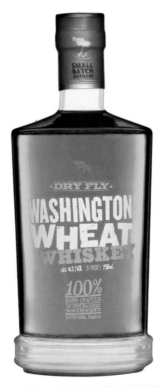

DRY FLY "WASHINGTON WHEAT WHISKEY"

DRY FLY

OWNER Dry Fly Distilling Company

FOUNDED 2007 **CAPACITY** 35,700 gal (135,000 liters)

ADDRESS 1003 E Trent Avenue #200,
Spokane, Washington 99202

WEBSITE www.dryflydistilling.com

With its stylish bottles, ultra-cool red "dry fly" branding, and irrelevant and irreverent name, Dry Fly is one of several indicators that American microdistilling is on the same page as its microbrewing industry a few years back. Whether it's a case of style over substance here remains to be seen because the distillery—the first legal distilling operation in Washington State since the Prohibition era—is still very young, but the signs are good. Kent Fleischmann, Don Poffenroth, and Patrick Donovan, the three-man team behind Dry Fly, have already been winning awards for their spirits and earning particular praise for a Bourbon that defies its young age in complexity and bodes very well for the future. As well as Bourbon and wheat whiskey, the Dry Fly team produces vodka and gin using a custom-designed 119-gallon (450-liter) pot still imported from Germany.

The name stems from the trio's love of fishing and the idea for the distillery was conceived while on a trip in the Pacific Northwest, casting their rods in a location that they describe as one of the prettiest places on earth. Distributing the spirits from the distillery is, they say, a way to share their home with others. And this isn't simply clever marketing: the trio are using only locally sourced raw ingredients grown on sustainable farms. The chance to share all this Washington grain, though, is very limited—the team plans to sell only 12,000–15,000 cases of 12 bottles each year. They are helping to spread the microdistilling style, too, offering would-be distillers training at their own distilling school.

TASTING NOTES

DRY FLY "WASHINGTON WHEAT WHISKEY"
wheat whiskey, 40% ABV
Very soft on the palate as you would expect with wheat whiskey, but the flavor is completed with freshly baked orange scones, cinnamon toast, white pepper, and peppermint notes.

DRY FLY "WASHINGTON BOURBON 101"
Bourbon, 40% ABV
Aged for only three years, and distilled from corn, unmalted wheat, and barley, this 101-proof Bourbon— the first from Washington State—is undoubtedly young but packs an unusual degree of complexity, with strong spice aromas that continue on the palate, balanced by vanilla warmth and caramel sweetness.

GEORGE DICKEL "BARREL SELECT"

GEORGE DICKEL

OWNER Diageo PLC	
FOUNDED 1870 **CAPACITY** 3.9m gal (15m liters)	
ADDRESS 1950 Cascade Hollow Road,	
Tullahoma, Tennessee 37388	
WEBSITE www.dickel.com	

It's tough to be referred to as the "other distillery" in Tennessee, but in recent years the presence of George Dickel has indeed been patchy. That might well be changing now, and if so, it's to be welcomed, because this is a distillery with a good story to tell and a whiskey to match.

George Dickel founded the distillery using the pure local water nearly 150 years ago, and by the time of his death in 1894, his establishment was Tennessee's oldest surviving business to have retained its own name. The name still stands, even though the arrival of Prohibition in Tennessee in 1910 saw the Dickel operation move states to Kentucky. Acquired by Schenley Distilling Company in 1937, it wasn't until 1958 that Dickel returned to Tennessee, in a new distillery built close to the location of the old one, instigating a new regimen where recipes from Dickel's own notes were revived.

The company follows the Lincoln County Process of pouring new-make spirit through a wall of charcoal, but Dickel also discovered that whiskey made during the winter is smoother than that made in the summer. Consequently, George Dickel is the only Tennessee whiskey to chill the whiskey to filter out oils and fatty acids before it goes into the charcoal mellowing vats.

There's another little aberration, too: George Dickel declared that because his product was as smooth as the finest Scotch, he would always spell it "whisky" without an "e" in keeping with Scotch.

TASTING NOTES

GEORGE DICKEL "NO.8"
Tennessee whiskey, 40% ABV
Easy-drinking smooth, sweet, and rounded whiskey with caramel, nuts, light spice, and some charcoal and oak to give it some character. Perfectly acceptable and solid corn-style whiskey.

GEORGE DICKEL "NO.12"
Tennessee whiskey, 45% ABV
The nose is aromatic, with fruit, leather, butterscotch, and a whiff of charcoal and vanilla. The palate is rich, with rye, chocolate, fruit, and vanilla. The finish offers vanilla toffee and drying oak.

GEORGE DICKEL "BARREL SELECT"
Tennessee whiskey, 43% ABV
Aromas of rich corn, honey, nuts, and caramel lead into a full body with soft vanilla, spices, and roast nuts. The long, creamy finish boasts almonds and spices.

GEORGE DICKEL "NO.8"

GEORGE DICKEL "NO.12"

KENTUCKY BOURBON DISTILLERS

OWNER	Kentucky Bourbon Distillers Ltd.
FOUNDED	1935 (as the Willett Distilling Company)
CAPACITY	Not given
ADDRESS	1869 Loretto Road, Bardstown, Kentucky 40004
WEBSITE	www.kentuckybourbonwhiskey.com

WILLETT "POT STILL RESERVE"

JOHNNY DRUM

In one sense this could be said to be the newest distillery in Kentucky, though there have been whiskey products coming from this company for more than 75 years. Founded by Thompson Willett as the Willett Distilling Company, the firm was an independent bottler until 2010, putting out its own range of high-grade and aged Bourbon. Among the many whiskeys on its list are Johnny Drum, Willett, the Bardstown Collection, and Noah's Mill. What it wasn't doing, since the early 1980s, was distilling on the site, so those whiskeys all contain spirits bought in from elsewhere.

The company also made its bread-and-butter money from bottling for other people. The company is responsible for scores of whiskey brands in existence flaunting the words "Bottled in Bardstown, Kentucky" and many claim to have been distilled there as well—so it's likely the company used whiskey bought from down the road at the Barton distillery.

The game-changer came with the decision a few years back to build a new distillery on the site. Construction progressed as and when the company could afford it, determined that there was to be no running up of big costs. This was clever thinking, given what happened to the American economy around the year 2009.

The company completed the work in time to be part of the resurgent American whiskey market and at the time of writing had just started bringing its new whiskey spirit to trade shows such as the Nth Show in Las Vegas—a statement of intent from the fledgling distillery, because that show is arguably the world's most lucrative and extravagant.

Expect some progressive whiskeys at some point in the not-too-distant future—early samples were very exciting and encouraging indeed. Restoration is underway of the original distillery building on the site, dating from 1935, and when it is complete, visitors will be made welcome.

TASTING NOTES

NOAH'S MILL 15-YEAR-OLD
Bourbon, 57.15% ABV
Hand-bottled and made only in small batches, this is very old wheated Bourbon, with a softness and roundness beautifully complemented by a spicy oakiness. Hominy and corn give the whiskey a sweet note, too. An excellent Bourbon.

NOAH'S MILL 15-YEAR-OLD

LEOPOLD BROS.

OWNER Scott and Todd Leopold	
FOUNDED 1999 **CAPACITY** Not given	
ADDRESS 4950 Nome Street, Denver, Colorado 80239	
WEBSITE www.leopoldbros.com	

Colorado has a surprising number of distilleries producing a variety of different spirits, some of which are making whiskey. Leopold Bros. was set up by Scott and Todd Leopold when the latter sold his successful brewpub and relocated with his family to Denver. Scott has a manufacturing background, focusing on environmentally sustainable processes, while Todd gained a diploma in brewing followed by experience at German breweries and distilleries; together, they developed a distillery that benefits from their respective skills.

Leopold is building a reputation for the quality of its drinks and has won awards across the board, particularly for its high-quality vodka. The distillery branched out into whiskey production a few years ago and now makes several, specializing in small batch blends and, with their 48-gallon (180-liter) copper pot still, taking inspiration from traditional 19th-century whiskey-making techniques. In addition to the core brand there's a range made from fruits including apples, raisins, peaches, and plums, and there are plans for rye and Tennessee-style whiskeys, too.

Although Leopold whiskey is produced on a relatively small scale, it's available across the United States and increasingly in the United Kingdom, having benefited from the current microdistilling boom. The distillery isn't open to the public, though tours are organized through local liquor stores.

TASTING NOTES

LEOPOLD BROS. "SMALL BATCH WHISKEY"
American corn and rye whiskey, 40% ABV
This is young, with corn and rye dominating, but it's a soft and gentle spirit with pear, vanilla, rock candy, sandalwood, and overripe apple and pear.

LEOPOLD BROS. "NEW YORK APPLE"
flavored whiskey, 40% ABV
Blended with apples grown in New York State, this whiskey is racked into used Bourbon barrels for additional aging. The barrels add the oak, raisin, and vanilla finish, while the mix of the sweet and tart apples balances perfectly with the charred-oak finish.

LEOPOLD BROS. "GEORGIA PEACH"
flavored whiskey, 30% ABV
Peach juice is blended with small-batch whiskey, and matured in Bourbon barrels. The result is a peachy-sweet spirit with oak, vanilla, and raisins.

LEOPOLD BROS. "NEW YORK APPLE"

CATDADDY "CAROLINA MOONSHINE"

PIEDMONT

OWNER Piedmont Distillers	
FOUNDED 1997 **CAPACITY** Not given	
ADDRESS 203 East Murphy Street, Madison, North Carolina 27025	
WEBSITE www.piedmontdistillers.com	

In his youth, former New York resident Joe Michalek traveled regularly down to the Southern states for music festivals and to follow NASCAR racing. On one trip he was offered some peach moonshine and was so impressed that he started studying the whole subject of illicit distilling and its links to NASCAR—the hugely popular sport in which the cars are based on the customized super-engined vehicles that moonshiners drove to race their stock to the borders, as made famous by the TV series *The Dukes of Hazzard*.

Moonshine whiskey is made with a corn recipe and has a reputation for being young and rough, but it needn't be, and the moonshine Michalek tried was, he says, surprisingly smooth and rounded. When he eventually went into distilling and founded Piedmont in 2005, the only licensed distillery in North Carolina and the first since before Prohibition, he went for a premium spirit, calling it Catdaddy, a name reserved for the very finest illegally produced spirits. It's distilled in a traditional copper pot still using a corn-dominated recipe that also includes other secret ingredients.

Most recently the company has been joined by Junior Johnson, a star of NASCAR racing from the 1950s and '60s who learned his driving skills delivering moonshine. Johnson brought his own family recipe and now makes Midnight Moon triple-distilled moonshine and a range of moonshine flavored with fruit, packaged in glass jars that resemble the containers in which moonshine was originally sold. Both Catdaddy and Midnight Moon are 40 percent ABV and triple-distilled. The distillery plans tours in the future; currently there's a shop for souvenirs, but the whiskey has to be bought from a liquor store around the corner.

TASTING NOTES

CATDADDY CAROLINA MOONSHINE
corn whiskey, 40% ABV
Sweet and dominated by corn, this has an assortment of other flavors including some overripe apple, vanilla, and spices including cinnamon, clove, and ginger.

JUNIOR JOHNSON'S MIDNIGHT MOON
corn whiskey, 40% ABV
Triple distilled in a copper still, Johnson's family recipe is smooth and well-rounded, subtle on the corn and with a surprising cotton-candy sweetness.

OLD RIP VAN WINKLE

OWNER Julian Van Winkle	
FOUNDED 1896	**CAPACITY** None
ADDRESS 113 Great Buffalo Trace, Frankfort, Kentucky 40601	
WEBSITE www.oldripvanwinkle.com	

VAN WINKLE "FAMILY RESERVE RYE"

There's no Old Rip Van Winkle distillery these days but you can't tell the story of the modern Bourbon industry without including the Van Winkle family, and third- and fourth-generation team Julian and Preston occupy a unique position in Kentucky's whiskey output.

They are releasing whiskey at the super-premium end of the spectrum, Bourbon in excess of 20 years old in some cases, and the stock is extremely limited. Originally the releases came from stock made by the now silent Old Hoffman Distillery and laid down by Julian's grandfather, but these days Van Winkle whiskey is made at Buffalo Trace in extremely small quantities to the original wheated Bourbon Van Winkle recipes.

It's a source of great frustration to the Van Winkles that they spend all their time firefighting due to lack of stock. "We'll give a bar some stock here and a whole load of other bars will ask why they can't have the same," Preston says. "Make one guy happy and a whole bunch of others get upset."

It's a cause of endless frustration, and while the distillery is no doubt trying to lay down more stock for future demand, the only positive the Van Winkles take from it is that you need patience to make fine Bourbon—and this is very fine Bourbon—and the whiskey boom isn't going away.

"The sky is the limit," says Preston. "There seems to be unlimited interest in premium spirits in the United States, so premium American whiskey has plenty of room to grow, and there is huge potential in Europe and Asia. I don't see this train slowing any time soon. I just wish we had some extra barrels with which to capitalize on all this potential."

Amen to that—and if you get the chance to taste this incredible liquid, take it.

TASTING NOTES

PAPPY VAN WINKLE'S "FAMILY RESERVE' 15-YEAR-OLD
Bourbon, 53.5% ABV
Classic aged Bourbon with sharp and astringent wood and chili spice battling it out with softer toffee nut sundae, stewed peach, cinnamon, and sandalwood flavors. Full, spicy, and oaky.

OLD RIP VAN WINKLE 10-YEAR-OLD
Bourbon, 45% ABV
Caramel and molasses on the big nose, then honey and rich, spicy fruit on the profound, mellow palate. The finish is long, with coffee and licorice notes.

OLD RIP VAN WINKLE 10-YEAR-OLD

PAPPY VAN WINKLE'S 20-YEAR-OLD

ROGUE

OWNER Rogue
FOUNDED 2006 **CAPACITY** None given
ADDRESS 1339 NW Flanders, Portland, Oregon 97209
WEBSITE www.rogue.com

Perhaps more than any other, the Rogue distillery draws the line between the American microbrewing revolution of a few years back and the microdistilling one that has marked the new millennium. Rogue makes great beers, markets them with a youthful enthusiasm, and since 2006 has made spirits on its own stills at its Flanders Street pub in Portland.

"Dead Guy Ale" was created in the early 1990s to celebrate the Mayan Day of the Dead (November 1 or All Souls' Day) and, in 2008, the

Rogue's flagship brewpub is wonderfully situated on the historic Bay Front in Newport, Oregon.

Oregon-based producers launched their "Dead Guy Whiskey." Using the "Dead Guy" name is more than just clever marketing, however, as the whiskey is distilled using the same four malts that go into creating "Dead Guy Ale." Fermented wort from the brewery is taken to the nearby Rogue House of Spirits, where it is double distilled in a 150-gallon (570-liter) copper pot still. Maturation is very brief, in charred American white oak casks.

"Dead Guy" is young and still has some way to go; the "Oregon Single Malt Whiskey" is aged for a little longer and holds out more promise. The still is also used for rum, vodka, and gin, so it's hard to estimate how much whiskey is made, but it could be around 6,870 gallons (26,000 liters) a year.

TASTING NOTE

ROGUE "DEAD GUY WHISKEY"
single malt, 40% ABV
With very little maturation and at a relatively low strength, this is sappy, reedy, feisty, and thin. There is some pepper and lemon, as well as green salad, but it's hard to love this. More style than substance.

ROGUE "DEAD GUY WHISKEY"

ROGUE "OREGON SINGLE MALT WHISKEY"

STRANAHAN'S

OWNER Stranahan's Colorado Whiskey Company

FOUNDED 2004 **CAPACITY** 44,900 gal (170,000 liters)

ADDRESS 200 South Kalamath Street,
Denver, Colorado 80223

WEBSITE www.stranahans.com

The brainchild of enthusiasts George Stranahan and Jess Graber, Stranahan's Denver distillery was founded in 2004 and was at the forefront of the microdistilling revolution. It was also the first-ever licensed distillery in the state of Colorado. Priding itself on its mainly Colorado-sourced grain and water derived from the Rocky Mountains, Stranahan's Colorado Whiskey is distilled using a four-barley fermented wash produced by the neighboring Flying Dog Brewery. The distillation takes place in a still made by the famous Vendome Copper Company of Louisville, Kentucky, and the spirit is put into new, charred American oak barrels. Each batch bottled comprises the contents of between two and six barrels.

The distillery is also thinking beyond just making its core Colorado Whiskey and is expanding into experimental and unusual whiskeys, too. In 2011, for instance, it released the tenth whiskey in its "Snowflake" series. It reflects the growing confidence of microdistilleries that have a few years under their belts and are determined to keep moving forward, staying ahead of the competition.

"It's called the 'Conundrum Peak Snowflake,'" says George Stranahan. "It's aged from two to five years in new white oak barrels with a Number 4 char. We refilled three whiskey casks with the finished batch, aging it two months before transferring to a white oak Syrah wine barrel. We then aged it for another three months for a bright, wine-cask finish. Then, just before bottling, we flash-aged it in a second, fresh Syrah barrel for a rich, dark fruit, wine oak finish. The end result is Christmas in a bottle."

With just 12 barrels of whiskey made each week, a lot of thought goes into such matters. With whiskey in such a good place these days, though, the distillery is ambitious, installing new stills and other equipment with the aim of quadrupling its output for bottling by 2014. Undoubtedly a distillery to watch.

STRANAHAN'S COLORADO WHISKEY

TASTING NOTE

STRANAHAN'S COLORADO WHISKEY
single malt, 47% ABV
A lovely balanced mix of sugar and spice, with an almost plummy, liqueur-like burnt banana and caramel mix combined with polished wood and pepper. Unusual, but it works extremely well.

BREAKING & ENTERING BOURBON

ST. GEORGE SPIRITS

OWNER St. George Spirits

FOUNDED 1982 **CAPACITY** Not given

ADDRESS 2601 Monarch Street, Alameda, California 94501

WEBSITE www.stgeorgespirits.com

Long before there was an English whiskey distillery under the name of St. George's there was one in the United States, and making single malt whiskey, too. St. George Spirits was founded by Bavarian-born Jörg Rupf in 1982 who, naturally enough given his German background, began by distilling fruit liqueurs. While the distillery now produces a range of spirits, from absinthe to rum, it's the single malt whiskey that has a special place in the company's heart—and a lot of this can be put down to the passion of co-owner Lance Winters, who first came to Rupf seeking advice for his small still whiskey-making experiments.

"Making whiskey is what drew Lance Winters to distillation in the first place," says a spokesperson for the company. "Before starting at St. George, Lance had spent five years working as a brewer. When he realized that making beer was halfway to making whiskey, he turned in his brewer's card and dedicated himself to the craft of distillation."

The distillery has been making whiskey since 2000, before the current wave of microdistillers as it proudly asserts. The whiskey is made in batches each year, numbered by lot, and it's well into double figures. Each batch is slightly different from the last, since they're able to draw from older barrels with every new batch they put out, and the goal is to blend for "positive inconsistency," increasing flavor and expressiveness with every lot released. It's clear this distillery takes whiskey making very seriously. As Winters says, "Alcohol is secondary, almost incidental to our work. Alcohol merely carries the heart of what we're crafting— the scent, the nuances, the flora we incorporate."

TASTING NOTES

ST. GEORGE SINGLE MALT WHISKEY "LOT 11"
single malt, 43% ABV, matured in ex-Bourbon casks, French oak, and ex-port and ex-sherry barrels
The distillery uses different woods rather than peat to dry the barley, so there's a smoky nuttiness to this. The spirit is matured in port barrels as well as sherry and Bourbon, giving dried fruit, nutmeg, cinnamon, some lemon, and soft cocoa.

BREAKING & ENTERING BOURBON
Bourbon, 43% ABV
Not actually distilled at St. George, this is a bottling of Kentucky Bourbon selected from 80 different barrels that's still full of California surprise. Banana and a hint of corn on the nose lead to spice and smoke on the not-too-sweet palate, with a lively marmalade finish.

TEMPLETON RYE

OWNER Lawrenceburg Distillers, Indiana

FOUNDED 2001 **CAPACITY** Not given

ADDRESS 209 East 3rd Street, Templeton, Iowa 51463

WEBSITE www.templetonrye.com

One of the quirkiest and most respected whiskeys you'll find anywhere. Since coming on the market in 2006, Templeton Rye has built up a reputation for quality—though it's hard to obtain and seems to revel in its obscurity.

While the modern version of Templeton Rye is a premium whiskey distilled in a 300-gallon (1,150-liter) copper pot still before being aged in new, charred-oak barrels, its history as a staple whiskey in Al Capone's speakeasies guarantees it a romantic back-story.

The tale goes that the original Templeton Rye whiskey was produced illegally during the Prohibition era by the residents of the small town of Templeton, Iowa. Owing to its smoothness, the whiskey gained the moniker "The Good Stuff" and became one of the premium whiskeys of the era, commanding high prices and attracting the attentions of notorious mobster Al Capone. It was said to be his favorite whiskey, and he added it to his bootlegging operation, selling Templeton Rye in speakeasies across the country.

Even after the repeal of Prohibition, the whiskey continued to be produced in secret and remained illegal until the turn of the millennium, when an entrepreneur named Scott Bush heard about it from his grandfather and became enamored of the whole story. Bush saw an opportunity to recreate it and sought help, eventually making contact with the Kerkhoff family, who had historical links with the illicit distilling business and were initially wary of sharing their knowledge and recipes. Ultimately, however, Keith Kerkhoff, grandson of Prohibition-era distiller Alphonse Kerkhoff, went into partnership with Bush and passed on the recipe.

Today's Templeton Rye is actually made in the state of Indiana and transported to Iowa for bottling. The duo have built a new distillery in Templeton but it is, as yet, only focused on producing limited edition experimental whiskeys. The distillery is open to visitors and tours are available if you make a reservation in advance.

TASTING NOTE

TEMPLETON RYE
rye whiskey, 40% ABV
This well-made small-batch rye whiskey is gaining a good reputation. There's the expected spiciness and rich, full, mellow flavor, but also Bourbon-like leather and dried dark fruits. Clean, spicy finish.

TRIPLE EIGHT DISTILLERY LOGO

TEMPLETON RYE

TRIPLE EIGHT

OWNER Cisco Brewers

FOUNDED 2000 **CAPACITY** 3,960 gal (15,000 liters)

ADDRESS 5 Bartlett Farm Road, Nantucket, Massachusetts 02554

WEBSITE www.ciscobrewers.com

Although classed as a microdistillery and grouped with the current explosion in such establishments, Massachusetts-based Triple Eight Distillery is one of a handful of independent producers that predate the current wave, having been set up as a brewery in the late 1990s by Randy and Wendy Hudson with Dean and Melissa Long.

Whiskey is just one of a number of products made by the microdistillery, which also distills vodka, gin, and rum, and is named after its water source, well #888. The partners met when the Longs were trying to grow grapes for wine-making before eventually deciding that importation from California was their best bet. They turned their attention to making spirits around the time of the new millennium and now produce a range that includes some award-winners, as well as a feisty absinthe.

Most recently they have made a single malt whiskey, which they call The Notch because it's Not (quite) Scotch, but it definitely is a Scotch-style whiskey, for which distilling began in 2000. To achieve an authentic approximation of Scotch, they called on the distilling expertise of George McClements, former production manager with Glasgow-based Morrison Bowmore Distillers, owners of Islay's Bowmore distillery, among others, who worked alongside the Triple Eight team to advise them in the ways of Scotch. Inevitably, though, local conditions help to produce a single malt that is Nantucket's own, not least because the foggy air and summer heat of the island help to speed up the maturation process.

The first non-illicit whiskey ever produced on Nantucket, The Notch is distilled from beer made at the brewery on a small copper still before being matured for a minimum of eight years in Bourbon and American whiskey barrels. Tours of the plant and tastings can be arranged by appointment.

TASTING NOTE

THE NOTCH SINGLE MALT WHISKEY
single malt, 44.4% ABV
This is serious whiskey and considerably more advanced than a lot of recent American releases. Very different from the West Coast Scottish single malt whiskey it's influenced by, it's an easy-drinking whiskey with lots of vanilla, crisp fruit, and some deeper oak notes from the time spent in the cask.

HUDSON "FOUR GRAIN BOURBON"

HUDSON "SINGLE MALT"

HUDSON "MANHATTAN RYE"

HUDSON "BABY BOURBON"

TUTHILLTOWN

OWNER	William Grant & Sons
FOUNDED 2001	**CAPACITY** 9,250 gal (35,000 liters)
ADDRESS	14 Grist Mill Lane, Gardiner, New York 12525
WEBSITE	www.tuthilltown.com

Ask Peter Gordon of William Grant & Sons how the company constantly seems to be in the right place at the right time and he'll say it's luck. He's being modest.

Having started the Scotch malt whiskey craze, invested in its own grain distillery, launched groundbreaking products such as Monkey Shoulder and Hendrick's gin, and become the first Scottish company to buy into Irish whiskey in generations, it should come as no surprise that the company has entered the American microdistilling market. It says much about this distillery that Grant chose it for its first foray into the rapidly expanding American microdistilling scene. Tuthilltown is the first whiskey maker in New York since Prohibition, but at one time there were scores of farm distilleries, and it's to these that the distillery looks for inspiration. Marketed under the name Hudson, Tuthilltown's whiskeys are succeeding in bringing a fashionable new generation of drinkers into the category.

Tuthilltown makes a range of innovative whiskeys, including a baby Bourbon, rye, and an intriguing four-grain whiskey, all excellently packaged in fashionable bottles. A high proportion of the distillery's ingredients are produced locally. With substantial backing and a growing market, this is definitely one to watch.

TASTING NOTES

HUDSON "BABY BOURBON"
Bourbon, 46% ABV, matured in small American oak barrels
This represents two firsts for New York: the first Bourbon ever distilled in the state and the first legal pot-distilled whiskey since Prohibition. It is exactly what it says it is—a sappy, corny Bourbon that isn't anywhere near as rich and developed as its Kentucky cousins but has a delightful grainy sweetness, making an excellent cocktail ingredient. Very well made but needs some time to grow up.

HUDSON "MANHATTAN RYE"
rye whiskey, 46% ABV
This was the first whiskey to be distilled in New York State for more than 80 years. The palate offers floral notes and a smooth finish, though there is a very recognizable rye edge.

HUDSON "NEW YORK CORN"
corn whiskey, 40% ABV
Made with 100 percent New York State corn, this unaged corn whiskey is a mildly sweet, smooth spirit with subtle hints of vanilla and caramel. The foundation spirit for the "Baby Bourbon."

CANADA

CANADA

How huge is Canada? Spending roughly 80 hours behind the wheel from Shelter Point, British Columbia, in the west to Glenville in Nova Scotia nearly 4,000 miles (6,400 km) to the east would convince you of this country's massive size. Between the two oceans you would cross a coastal delta, two gigantic mountain ranges, the flattest of prairies, rolling hills, rich, lush farmland, and the comparatively barren Canadian Shield, which stretches north from the Great Lakes to the Arctic Ocean and covers about half of the country's land mass. Driving from one Canadian distillery to the next often means traveling a greater distance than the entire length of Scotland. That's why, in Canada, talking "whiskey regions" is impossible.

Regional Styles

The Canadian style is sweet and spicy, finishing in citrus pith. For a symphony of variation on this style, there's one memorable source: Hiram Walker's distillery in Windsor, Ontario. Canada's longest-operating distillery produces three distinct house styles: for black fruit it's Canadian Club, for creaminess it's Gibson's, and for crisp oak and candied spices it's Wiser's. Still, each reflects the signature Canadian style.

Author's Choice

HIRAM WALKER This Ontario distillery has plenty of history attached: its Detroit River waterfront, frequented by Prohibition-era rum runners, later afforded a berth for the Royal Yacht Britannia when Queen Elizabeth II and Prince Philip stopped by for a visit.

Regional Events

Canada's whiskey season begins on the third weekend of January with the three-day Victoria Whisky Festival (www.victoriawhiskyfestival.com), held annually at the Grand Pacific Hotel in Victoria. It's the only place in Canada where you'll see spring flowers in January. In mid-May, Toronto's Roy Thomson Hall is alive with whiskey people at a gala evening of whiskey and jazz called the Spirit of Toronto, Canada's longest-running whiskey show (www.spiritoftoronto.ca). Then, to kick off the Christmas season, October brings Whisky Live to Toronto (www.whiskylive.com). Smaller festivals in British Columbia, Alberta, New Brunswick, and Newfoundland fill out the rest of the whiskey calendar.

Distance would make Canadian distillery tourism impractical and, in fact, anti-terrorism legislation renders it impossible. Foodstuffs entering the US by truck must be made in secure plants, and since the US buys nearly 70 percent of Canada's whiskey, it's too risky to invite a visitor into a distillery. So the whiskey aficionado must make do with reading and tasting.

At all Canadian distilleries except Valleyfield, finished whiskey is made by mingling a variety of whiskeys, all made in one distillery. In Canada that product is called simply "Canadian whiskey," though more commonly "rye." Confusingly, the first use of the word "rye" to describe Canadian whiskey dates back to the time when most of it was made from wheat. Someone decided to add a small amount of rye grain to his wheat mash

As well as mountains, snow, and ice, *Canada is also a land of fertile farmland perfect for growing hardy grain.*

Hiram Walker distillery is an imposing presence *facing Detroit on the riverfront in Windsor, Ontario.*

and a new whiskey style was born. Customers soon demanded "rye" to be sure their whiskey was made with a dash of rye grain.

In the 1950s, distillers in the US decided their rye whiskey needed at least 51 percent rye grain in the mash. That makes sense. American rye is matured in new charred oak barrels; anything less than 51 percent gets lost in the rich oak flavors. But as Canadian distillers reuse their barrels, rye grain flavors shine through even at very low concentrations.

GETTING AROUND

Known colloquially as the "Great White North," much of Canada is indeed cold in winter and so snowy that from October to April mountain passes are open only to vehicles equipped with tire chains. Maritime influences moderate the Atlantic and Pacific coasts. Across the land, though, spring is warm and summer hot. The Windsor-Montreal corridor, a 550-mile (885-km) hard day's drive, encourages travel by car; for the rest of the country, traveling any distance means boarding a plane.

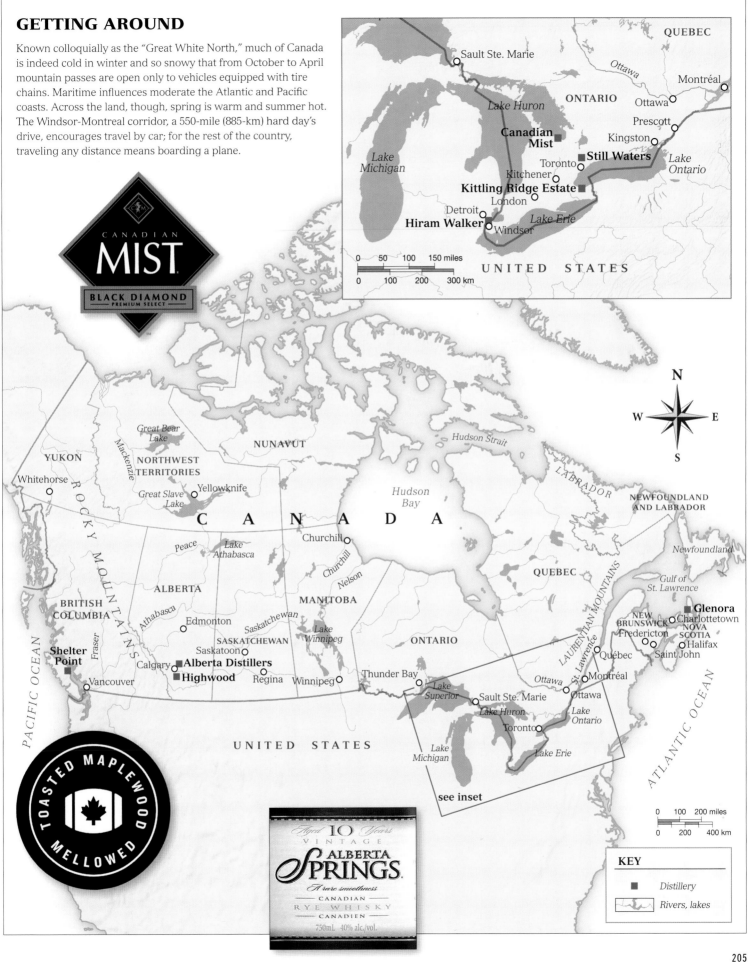

Inset map (upper right):

QUEBEC

Sault Ste. Marie

Ottawa

Montréal

Lake Huron

ONTARIO

Ottawa

Prescott

Canadian Mist

Kingston

Still Waters

Lake Ontario

Toronto

Lake Michigan

Kitchener

Kittling Ridge Estate

London

Detroit

Hiram Walker

Windsor

Lake Erie

UNITED STATES

0 50 100 150 miles
0 100 200 300 km

Main map:

Great Bear Lake

NUNAVUT

NORTHWEST TERRITORIES

YUKON

Mackenzie

Whitehorse

Great Slave Lake

Yellowknife

Hudson Strait

LABRADOR

NEWFOUNDLAND AND LABRADOR

ROCKY MOUNTAINS

C A N A D A

Hudson Bay

Newfoundland

Peace

Lake Athabasca

Churchill

Churchill

Nelson

QUEBEC

Gulf of St. Lawrence

ALBERTA

Athabasca

MANITOBA

LAURENTIAN MOUNTAINS

Glenora

BRITISH COLUMBIA

Edmonton

Saskatchewan

Lake Winnipeg

NEW BRUNSWICK

Charlottetown

NOVA SCOTIA

SASKATCHEWAN

ONTARIO

Fredericton

Halifax

Shelter Point

Fraser

Saskatoon

St. Lawrence

Québec

Saint John

Calgary

Alberta Distillers

Regina

Winnipeg

Thunder Bay

Ottawa

Montréal

Highwood

Lake Superior

Ottawa

Vancouver

PACIFIC OCEAN

UNITED STATES

Sault Ste. Marie

Lake Huron

Lake Ontario

Toronto

Lake Erie

ATLANTIC OCEAN

Lake Michigan

see inset

0 100 200 miles
0 200 400 km

KEY

■ Distillery

▭ Rivers, lakes

ALBERTA DISTILLERS

OWNER	Beam Inc.
FOUNDED 1946	**CAPACITY** 5.3m gal (20m liters)
ADDRESS	1521 34 Avenue Southeast, Calgary, Alberta T2G 1V9

There are whiskey-lovers whose enjoyment is increased just by the knowledge that they are drinking whiskey made from rye; perhaps its reputation prompts them to spend more time savoring its eccentricities. What makes rye so special is that certain flavor elements that are much subdued in other grains abound in it, and skilled whiskey-makers know just how to highlight this distinctive rye flavor profile.

"We produce a controlled but wide range of whiskeys based on the rye profile," says Alberta Distillers' Distillery Manager Rob Tuer. "We separate the alcohols to mature separately, then blend them more specifically later." And just what is this rye profile? Tasting the newly distilled spirit is instructive. While Alberta Distillers' corn spirits reveal woody, musty, corn-cob flavors, the rye spirits are lavishly grainlike. After three years in new oak, both smell like whiskey, but on the palate the rye now sports its characteristic cloves, ginger, and hot, blistering pepper, the corn its creamy softness.

Curiously, whiskeys that declare a high percentage of rye tend to draw more favorable reviews than whiskeys whose high content of rye grain is kept secret. The people at Alberta Distillers, the only major distillery in the world to make much of its whiskey from 100 percent rye, recognize that response. Their declared high-rye whiskeys earn endless praise while others, such as Alberta Springs and Windsor Canadian, simply fly under the connoisseur's radar.

Mashing rye grain

When the distillery was built in 1946 on Calgary's ragged fringe, rye was the most commonly grown local grain, and the plant was designed specifically to process it. Alberta Distillers uses plain, unmalted rye only. But wouldn't sticky mashes grind operations to a halt without malt? Alberta's Master Distiller, Rick Murphy, explains: "Mash viscosity is the reason other distillers avoid rye. We use commercial enzymes when we distill corn, but we grow our own enzymes for rye, barley, and wheat." These are grown in three enzyme reactors over a staggered 7–10 day period to ensure that ample fresh enzymes are always available.

Commercial enzymes made specifically for mashing corn are highly purified and are much less effective for rye, while Alberta Distillers' homegrown enzymes are a mix of many other enzymes. Along with the starch, these other enzymes break down cell walls, other carbohydrates, and, most importantly, sticky glucans. While distilling rye grain is messy enough that other distillers will often shut down the plant for a thorough cleaning afterward, at Alberta Distillers making rye is a routine process. This is one of the reasons why the distillery can bottle nearly three times as much high-rye whiskey as all other distilleries in North America combined.

The Canadian west *boasts rye-friendly prairies and clear water flowing down from the Rocky Mountains.*

WHISKY OR REAL ESTATE?

Forty acres (16 hectares) is a lot of land in the hot Calgary real estate market. Cement silos across the road and other complexes throughout the area ensure that the neighborhood will remain industrial—for now. But how long can a foreign parent company resist an easy profit? Alberta Distillers is a homegrown distillery, but it is owned by the multinational company Beam Inc. Whiskey-lovers everywhere should cross their fingers that the suits in Beam's headquarters in Deerfield, Illinois, will resist any temptation to create quick bonuses. If Beam is crafting spirits that stir the world, Alberta Distillers' spirit is most certainly one of its most stirring.

Straight rye whiskey

A so-called "rye renaissance" has led American producers to ramp up their production of straight rye whiskey. But whiskey does not materialize overnight, and until that rye is mature enough to bottle, American distillers are looking to Canada to meet their growing demand. What better place than Alberta Distillers? Indeed, one of the finest of these Canadian straight ryes, Masterson's Rye, is a careful mingling of various ryes produced at the Calgary plant.

Straight rye can be overly flavorful and a little roughshod sometimes, so it is a very pleasant surprise to find that the people at 35 Maple, the California company bottling Masterson's, have maintained its power while smoothing out both its attack and its finish.

ALBERTA SPRINGS 10-YEAR-OLD

The bustle of whiskey-making

Walking around the plant site with Rick Murphy does wonders for the whiskey writer's soul. Workers wrestle barrels in nine-rank rack warehouses that effuse the potent musty aromas of maturing whiskey. Huge stacks of empty barrels sit waiting to be filled with promising new spirits. Custom-built carriers lift and cart barrels around the site while mature whiskey emptying from creaking barrels gushes into a stainless steel dump trough, ready for blending. Overhead, long gangways bring whiskey and spirits to a pumping station where tanker trucks and shipping containers are filled and then dispatched abroad.

Inside, workers on two bottling lines pack 640,000 cases of whiskey each year, much of it for Canadians and more than one-third of it made from 100 percent rye grain. Yes, Canada loves its rye, and Alberta Distillers' is one of its favorites.

TASTING NOTES

WINDSOR CANADIAN
single distillery blended Canadian whiskey, 40% ABV
Clean oak, rye spices, white chocolate, and creamy caramel balance fiery cinnamon and a peppery burn. Simple, yet richly mouth-filling.

ALBERTA SPRINGS 10-YEAR-OLD
single distillery blended Canadian whiskey, 40% ABV
Aromatic spices, sour pickles, and dusty rye on the nose become vanilla, butterscotch, maple syrup, and black licorice on the palate. A solid crisp Canadian oak backbone supports waves of heat and a vague fruitiness. Finishes with cleansing citrus pith.

MASTERSON'S 10-YEAR-OLD
Canadian straight rye, 45% ABV
Dry grain, gunny sacks, and damp blue clay engage fragrant tobacco and sweet, floral vanilla pods. Its fruitiness, licorice, and toffee offset gingery hot pepper. This is a very complex whisky and masterfully composed.

WINDSOR CANADIAN

MASTERSON'S 10-YEAR-OLD

COLLINGWOOD LABEL DETAIL

CANADIAN MIST

OWNER Brown-Forman Corporation	
FOUNDED 1967 **CAPACITY** 3.3m gal (12.5m liters)	
ADDRESS 202 MacDonald Road, Collingwood, Ontario L9Y 4J2	
WEBSITE www.canadianmist.com	

The scenery of Ochos Rios in Jamaica may be spectacular, but when David Dobbin vacationed there in the winter of 2010, what caught his eye was something distinctly Canadian: a bottle of Canadian Mist. Back home in Canada, Dobbin had recently taken the helm of the Ontario-based Canadian Mist distillery. It was an auspicious sign that shortly thereafter a bottle of this whiskey appeared on the bar at his vacation resort.

The making of a whiskey man
In 1967, Canada marked its first century as a nation. Canadians waved flags, built community centers, and hosted a full-fledged world fair—Expo 67. In Collingwood, the celebration took quite a different turn: in addition to official events, somebody built a distillery. It is in this very distillery that Dobbin eventually found his whiskey calling.

A degree in chemistry and biochemistry had led him into a successful career in the food and beverage industry, but after 30 years of that, he was ready for a completely new challenge. The long-time manager of Canadian Mist was about to retire, and Dobbin was surprised to learn that there were many commonalities between making spirits and making food and beverages. He realized that although making whiskey was new for him, he had a wealth of experience to draw on. How could he say no?

A town gets its own whiskey
Canadian Mist is hugely popular in the US, and with Dobbin's arrival in Collingwood, anticipation was in the air. The distillery team was still celebrating the introduction of Canadian Mist "Black Diamond," a fruity, toothsome dram that brings Canadian Mist to the connoisseur's table.

Plans to further expand the product line, already well underway, soon became the Canadian whiskey story of 2011—a whiskey itself called Collingwood. Of course, whiskey takes many years to mature, meaning that Collingwood was already in the pipeline when Dobbin arrived. The handiwork of 35 experienced staff, Collingwood turned out to be a resounding success.

Local pride
Collingwood is an unusual Canadian whiskey. It begins with rye and corn, like so many others, but after the rye and corn spirits have matured and have been blended together, they are left to

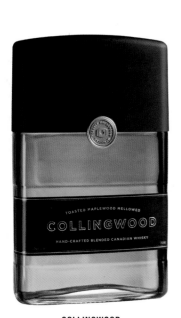

COLLINGWOOD

CANADIAN MIST "BLACK DIAMOND"

Lake Huron provides fresh water *for Canadian Mist as well as great fishing opportunities around Collingwood.*

rest in a huge "marrying vat," with staves of toasted maple wood. What could be more Canadian than a whiskey finished with maple wood?

It is a great whiskey, and if you live in this pretty little tourist town just an hour north of Toronto, where it is made, it is also a great story. "Collingwood has had a fantastic impact on the whole community," Dobbin enthuses. "People can really identify with it. It has done wonders for local pride." Seventeen local businesses felt the same way and joined the festivities that accompanied the day-long launch. It was all smiles when Her Worship The Mayor dropped by with an official proclamation.

Dobbin describes moving to Collingwood as a wonderful adventure. "We get a lot of visitors in the community, so there are many amenities, yet it's peaceful enough that every now and then a deer wanders into our yard. My wife just loves it. From our front door it's a two-minute walk to the lake in one direction and two minutes to skiing in the other." A short drive away are some of the farms that grow the corn that will become Canadian Mist.

But it's the whiskey that has him most excited. "There's something wonderful about the heritage in this industry that you just don't get in any other— the artisan's touch. There's something almost spiritual," he continues, the pun deliberate, "about going out in a warehouse with thousands of barrels of whiskey and just breathing the air—something timeless that I haven't come across before. People want to know how the whiskey is made and I get to tell them. It's an opportunity that I really enjoy."

The long ride home

By Canadian standards, Canadian Mist is a medium to small distillery. It mashes the grain, distills the fermented beer, ages the whiskey, and blends it on site, but it does not have a bottling line. Although the local liquor store is only 1½ miles (2.4 km) away, the whiskey must take a long, circuitous route from the distillery to get there. In between is a 650-mile (1,000-km) trip by stainless-steel tanker truck to Louisville, Kentucky, for bottling, another 600 miles (970 km) north to Toronto for distribution, and then a final 100 miles (160 km) home to Collingwood.

TASTING NOTES

CANADIAN MIST
single distillery blended Canadian whiskey,
40% ABV
Dry grass, nutty malt, fresh orchard fruit, cola, tingling pepper, and earthy rye. Fresh lager, toffee-sweet vanilla, and lemon zest.

CANADIAN MIST "BLACK DIAMOND"
single distillery blended Canadian whiskey,
40% ABV
Dusty rye, fall fruits, coconut, rose water, caramel, and hard candy. Fruit, mash, and cola dominate. Intense white pepper complements chocolate-covered ginger. Creamy, almost waxy mouth feel cleansed by citrus pith. Fuller, rounder, weightier, and much more expressive than the original.

COLLINGWOOD
single distillery blended Canadian whiskey,
40% ABV, maple wood finish
Fragrant roses, dried fruits, Concord grapes, dark cherries, and sweet pipe tobacco on earthy rye. The lusty round body tingles with chili peppers, which offset tugging tannic peach pits. Unique.

CANADIAN MIST

HIRAM WALKER

OWNER Pernod Ricard **FOUNDED** 1858	
CAPACITY 14.5m gal (55m liters)	
ADDRESS 2072 Riverside Drive East, Windsor, Ontario N8Y 4S5	
WEBSITES www.canadianclubwhisky.ca;	
www.gibsonsfinest.ca; www.wisers.ca	

When Detroit grain broker, vinegar-maker, and whiskey-rectifier Hiram Walker decided in 1858 to distill whiskey, prohibition sentiments in the US made such a venture very risky there. As a grain broker, Walker knew that the Windsor area, which lay just across the Detroit River from his home but over the border into Canada, did not have a proper flour mill of its own. And that's how Walker, an American citizen, gained his toehold in Canada.

Within months, grinding imported American corn for whiskey accounted for half his milling business. Corn that would grow and thrive in Canada's climate was still more than a century of experimentation away, so at that time, most distillers made whiskey from wheat. Walker knew the American grain market well and became one of the first distillers in Canada to make whiskey primarily from corn. Copying Canada's wheat distillers, he added small amounts of rye to increase the flavor, and his distillery eventually became the only one in Canada to use malted rye. As Master Brewer Don Livermore explains, "Rye malt imparts a unique spicy quality to the spirit, yet provides a smooth finish on the palate."

Barrel blending
From the beginning, Walker established a reputation for a high-quality product. He "rectified" his whiskey by filtering it through tall wooden columns packed with charcoal; soon he switched to maturing it in white oak barrels, as many other Canadian distillers were already doing. Rather than using a mixed-grain mash, Walker experimented with adding newly distilled rye spirit to his corn spirit before filling barrels with the mixture. He felt that distilling the spirits separately, then barrel-blending them improved the flavor as the spirits married during maturation. To this day, Hiram Walker's best-known whiskey, "Canadian Club," is still barrel blended.

Consolidations in Windsor
Walker was far from being the first commercial-scale distiller in Canada; he joined J. P. Wiser, Gooderham and Worts, and Henry Corby, among others. There is a certain irony, then, that it's Walker's distillery that remains. With

GIBSON'S FINEST 18-YEAR-OLD "RARE"

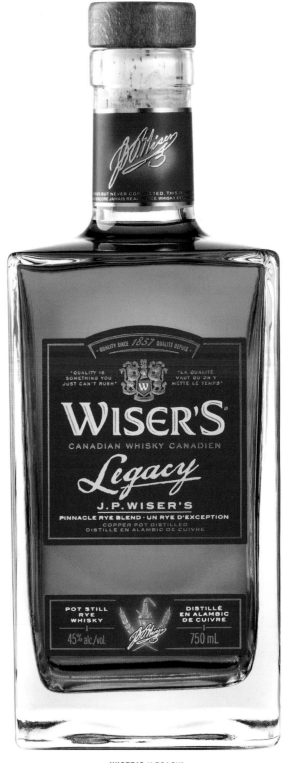

WISER'S "LEGACY"

these competitors gone, production of their famed whiskeys has now been moved to Hiram Walker's. Though his chest might swell with pride to know that his distillery is the last of Canada's historic distilleries to survive, his pride might turn to dismay were he to learn that his plant is now run not by his successors, but by Corby's, and their key brand is Wiser's.

Walker's rye

It is not without some effort that Hiram Walker's still maintains the tradition of using malted rye in its whiskeys. Distilling from rye grain is notoriously difficult and many distillers limit production to the bare minimum required for blending. It's in the mashing that things begin to get tricky, since sticky glucans in the rye grain can really gum up the equipment. Don Livermore uses a mix of malted and unmalted rye to overcome this stickiness.

"Since malted rye produces a cocktail of enzymes including glucanases and proteases, it can break down the glucans inherent in the rye kernel. The addition of malt improves the 'flowability' of the mash during cooking, fermentation, distillation, and drying processes," says Livermore.

There are other benefits, too. He adds, "It is far easier to mill malted rye as the grain kernel is more friable and easier on the hammer mills that grind the grain."

Hard, unmalted rye, which is often described as "glassy," is more difficult to mill. For Livermore, though, the biggest challenge in using rye is sourcing the malted grain itself, since so few distillers use it—but tradition and the unique characteristics with which it imbues his whiskey ensure it will always have a place at the Hiram Walker distillery.

Pennsylvania rye made in Canada?

The Prohibition Act truly devastated the American distilling industry, and one of the most sorely lamented losses was Pennsylvania's famed Monongahela rye. Of these ryes, one of the most popular was Gibson's, and when Prohibition forced John Gibson's distillery to close its doors, Lewis Rosensteil, an American whiskey entrepreneur, bought the Gibson brand name. He would later use it for an ultra-premium whiskey that he was distilling at a safe distance in the Schenley Distillery near Montreal.

The final irony in the Hiram Walker story is that after a succession of corporate moves, the present owners of the Gibson brand found themselves without a distillery. Corby's to the

The former town of Walkerville, *where the distillery sits, is now a preserved, heritage precinct of Windsor city.*

rescue! The Gibson's Finest brands, some of the most sought-after of Canadian whiskeys, are now distilled at the Hiram Walker plant and an originally American whiskey transplanted to Canada is now distilled in a Canadian distillery started more than a century and a half ago by... an American.

TASTING NOTES

WISER'S "LEGACY"
pot still Canadian rye, 45% ABV
Malted rye exemplified. Fragrant lilacs and spicy cinnamon on the nose ripen into stewed dark fruits, mild sawdust, and leathery Kahnawake Rainbow tobacco. A peppery hot, ultra-complex synthesis of menthol, dairy barn, sour rye bread, and citrus zest follows.

CANADIAN CLUB 12-YEAR-OLD "CLASSIC"
barrel-blended, single distillery Canadian whiskey, 40% ABV
Toffee, white pepper, and sweet dark fruits forestall murmurs of sour rye. Herbs and flowers melt into rum-soaked fruitcake.

GIBSON'S FINEST 18-YEAR-OLD "RARE"
single distillery blended Canadian whiskey, 40% ABV
Crisp clean Canadian oak rich in butterscotch and fresh sweet corn. Spicy rye with hints of pepper transform a burst of cedar into a rich and nectarous smorgasbord.

FROM LEADER TO LODGER

Watching Canada's whiskey brands ride the ownership rodeo can be a dizzying experience: Hiram Walker built the original distillery, where he created the Canadian Club brand. During the Prohibition era, Harry Hatch, who already owned the Gooderham and Worts distillery based in Toronto, also acquired the Hiram Walker plant. In 1932, Wiser's Prescott distillery closed, Henry Corby's distillery took over production of Wiser's brands, and Harry Hatch in turn bought out Corby's distillery. Consolidation of Wiser's, Corby's, and Gooderham & Worts' brands under Hiram Walker's roof became inevitable. In 1994, Allied-Lyons acquired Walker's, then in 2005 Pernod Ricard took over, selling Canadian Club to Beam Inc., handing the reins of management to Corby's, and making Canadian Club suddenly a tenant in its own distillery.

CANADIAN CLUB 12-YEAR-OLD "CLASSIC"

KITTLING RIDGE ESTATE

OWNER Kittling Ridge Estate Wines & Spirits **FOUNDED** 1971 as eau-de-vie; 1992 as Kittling Ridge **CAPACITY** Not given **ADDRESS** 297 South Service Road, Grimsby, Ontario L3M 1Y6 **WEBSITES** www.kittlingridge.com; www.fortycreekwhisky.com

John Hall brought his Forty Creek whiskeys to market about a decade ago and rapidly became the best-known Canadian whiskey-maker in the country. He struggled at first to have his whiskey recognized, but today anyone who knows Canadian whiskey knows of John Hall.

"There is no doubt that I have gone beyond my wildest dreams with Forty Creek whiskey. Yet the dreaming hasn't stopped. My dreams unfold with passion, patience, and creativity. I believe my whiskey journey has just begun. There are many more good things still to come."

Growing up near the Hiram Walker distillery in Windsor, and fascinated by chemistry and microbiology, Hall always assumed he'd end up making whiskey there. But fate intervened; he embarked on a career as a winemaker. "As it turned out, I loved winemaking and I was good at it. Being a winemaker was a perfect blend of science and art."

Hockey, maple syrup, and Canadian whiskey

"The idea of being a whiskey-maker didn't come back to me until 1992, after 22 successful years in the Ontario wine business," explains Hall. "Over the years I had moved away from actually making wine and into corporate management. I was looking to get back to my creative roots. Canadian whiskey is one of our country's iconic products—enjoyed internationally, just like maple syrup and hockey. I couldn't wait to bring back creativity and passion to our country's spirit."

This combination of creativity and passion characterizes the man himself. As a student, he paid his way through school playing saxophone with various bands. Now he scratches his creative itch by making whiskey.

"There is much in my wine making background that influences my whiskey style and has led to the Forty Creek signature flavor profile. There are also lots of interesting ideas that can be found when looking at cocktail and food trends. I try not to look at what other Canadian distilleries are doing, though, because I think that limits your options."

While John Hall still has plenty of whiskey dreams, he's often surprised by the ones that come true. As so much depends on how the spirit develops in the barrel, it's often the whiskey itself that decides.

FORTY CREEK "JOHN'S PRIVATE CASK NO. 1"

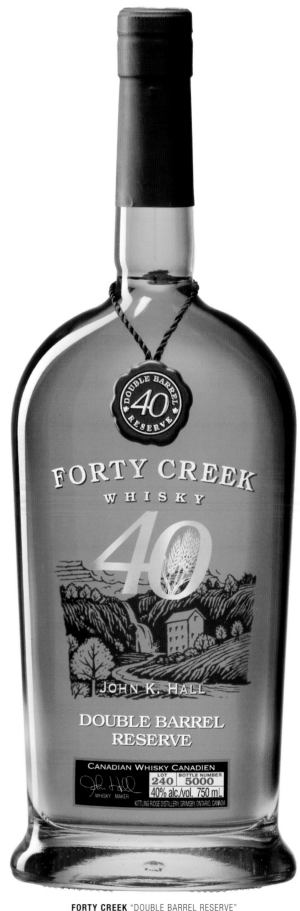

FORTY CREEK "DOUBLE BARREL RESERVE"

Annual pilgrimage

Each September Canadian whiskey-lovers flock to Grimsby, Ontario, to sample John Hall's latest whiskey dream. This pilgrimage began in 2007 with the release of "Small Batch Reserve," a one-time selection of whiskeys finished in Kittling Ridge sherry barrels. When Hall decided to invite people to visit his distillery for tours and tastings, he didn't quite know what to expect. Visiting distilleries is not common in Canada. However, the response to his invitation was overwhelming and an annual tradition was born. Collectors now sign up months in advance to select the number their bottle will bear.

Possibly the most interesting of these special releases is a whiskey called "Confederation Oak." When Hall learned that a local oak forest was being culled to allow new growth, he promptly bought several of the giant trees and had them shipped to Missouri to be made into barrels. The extra thick staves mellowed over two years of outdoor air drying. Hall then used these uniquely Canadian barrels to finish selected whiskeys, producing the creamiest yet of his special releases. And why call it "Confederation Oak"? It seems those oak trees grew from little acorns that sprouted right about the time of Canadian Confederation in 1867.

What's next for John Hall and Kittling Ridge Estate Wines and Spirits? He wants us to think he's not sure, but his record speaks for itself. We can be confident that new taste expressions and unique Forty Creek offerings will soon find their way to market. "Creating new whiskeys brings me great pleasure. I know Forty Creek fans have come to expect innovation and excitement. I will try my hardest not to disappoint them!"

TASTING NOTES

FORTY CREEK "BARREL SELECT"
single distillery blended Canadian whiskey, 40% ABV
Rich caramel, cream sherry, creamy corn, dusty rye, and zesty, pithy citrus peel. Rye spices, white pepper, cinnamon, and ginger.

FORTY CREEK "DOUBLE BARREL RESERVE"
single distillery blended Canadian whiskey, 40% ABV
Hot spice and soothing vanilla caramel, then lemon cream, oranges, and whispers of coconut. Sweet dry grain and fresh-cut lumber. Ends hot and spicy, with vanilla toffee and citrus zest.

FORTY CREEK "JOHN'S PRIVATE CASK NO. 1"
single distillery blended Canadian whiskey, 40% ABV
A spice monster, loaded with ginger, pepper, and cloves. Creamy fruits and crispy wood: cedar and balsam. A campfire in a muggy redwood forest. Hot candied ginger engulfs surging butterscotch.

A 10-YEAR OVERNIGHT SENSATION

It's a typically Canadian story. By tradition, anyone creative—writers, actors, artists, musicians—must first find validation abroad, usually in the US, before being recognized at home. It seems the same is true of whiskey-makers. Today, John Hall is Canada's best-known distiller, but his whiskeys didn't take off at home until they were recognized in Texas. Rapid and widespread approval in the Lone Star State made him an "overnight success" back in Canada. Indeed, his "John's Private Cask No. 1" was voted Canadian Whisky of the Year for 2011 at the annual Canadian Whisky Awards.

FORTY CREEK "BARREL SELECT"

GLENORA

OWNER Glenora Distillers **FOUNDED** 1990
CAPACITY 13,200 gal (50,000 liters) **ADDRESS** 13727 Route 19,
Glenville, Cape Breton, Nova Scotia; PO Box 181, Mabou,
Nova Scotia B0E 1X0 **WEBSITE** www.glenoradistillery.com

Twenty freshwater springs surging out of red Cape Breton granite and Mabou Highlands marble feed the maze of burns that bring their crystal waters to MacLellan's Brook. This is picture-postcard Canada when autumn's golden-purples and fiery crimsons emblazon the rugged crags, a natural fireworks display announcing the start of another winter's distilling season. The rest of the year you could well be in the Scottish Highlands.

Although the locals speak English with a brogue and Gaelic with alacrity, they are 2,500 miles (4,200 km) from the motherland. For this is Nova Scotia—New Scotland, named in 1622 by King James VI of Scotland. Here, Scottish Canadians began distilling not whiskey but rum and applejack soon after their arrival in 1773.

There is a claim that the Scots invented Canada. If they did, why did they wait 220 years to make their first whiskey here in Nova Scotia? That aside, when Glenora's first drops flowed in 1990 it was sweet, pure, malt spirit, distilled, in fact, from barley imported from "old" Scotland. And the water used to mash that barley was drawn from MacLellan's Brook.

Donnie Campbell, the Nova Scotia–born former food and beverage manager at Toronto's Royal York Hotel, came home to Cape Breton to manage the distillery with its upscale inn and rustic chalets. It's a whiskey-lover's idyll and the only place to sample many of its flavorful single malt whiskeys. It's as different from Toronto as is, well, Scotland.

TASTING NOTES

GLEN BRETON 10-YEAR-OLD "RARE"
single malt, 40% ABV
Bowmore-like perfume fades to creamy vanilla, caramel, and burnt fenugreek. Overripe apples and sweet marshmallow dominate an undefined fruitiness. Typical Glenora nutty barley peeks through hot lemon pepper sauce.

GLEN BRETON 17-YEAR-OLD "ICE"
single malt, 54.6% ABV, ice wine barrel finish
Fresh orchard fruit, autumn leaves, and roasted grain. Sweet, salty, and slightly pulling with glowing pepper and brisk green fruit.

GLEN BRETON "BATTLE OF THE GLEN"
single malt, 43% ABV
Sweet apple sauce, apricots, yellow plums, and rose petals. Damp soil, dry grass, fresh-cut hay, nutty grain, and pulling tannins, then hot pepper. A robust nose and round voluptuous body.

HIGHWOOD "CENTENNIAL"

GLEN BRETON 10-YEAR-OLD "RARE"

HIGHWOOD

OWNER Highwood Distillers Limited
FOUNDED 1974 **CAPACITY** 660,000 gal (2.5m liters)
ADDRESS 114 10th Avenue South-East, High River,
Alberta T1V 1M7 **WEBSITE** www.highwood-distillers.com

The latest vogue word for organizations that react quickly to changing situations is "nimble." Among Canadian distillers, tiny Highwood may be the most nimble of all. Ample stocks of well-aged whiskey and complete local control allow the whiskey-makers at Highwood to be real innovators. Nothing, however, can match their response to a growing trend in the US.

Desperate for cash flow, some American micro-distillers have begun selling newly distilled spirits while they wait for their whiskey to mature. They call this product "white whiskey." It's not legally whiskey in Canada, but American regulations allow it to be labeled as such south of the border.

Clear as vodka, white whiskey can be flavorful and has been making successful incursions into the cocktail scene. The Highwood approach is different: they filter fully mature whiskey, as much as 10 years old, through charcoal and have succeeded, after many trial runs, in removing the color while retaining key elements of the rye whiskey flavor profile. The resulting White Owl Whisky has been such a success that they can barely keep up with the demand. A new, spiced version of White Owl takes this innovative experiment to yet another level.

Highwood has not abandoned its traditional whiskey base, though. It distills whiskey daily from rye or wheat for the popular "Centennial." For their high-end Century products, single batches of corn whiskey are bought and aged on site.

TASTING NOTES

WHITE OWL WHISKY
single distillery white Canadian rye, 40% ABV
Lemon custard, citrus fruit, slight licorice root, soft rye spices, caramel, hot pepper, and citrus pith, with crisp, woody hints of oak tannins. Arguably the tastiest white whiskey ever made.

CENTURY RESERVE 21-YEAR-OLD
single distillery Canadian whiskey, 40% ABV
The creamiest, sweetest corn, richly nuanced and suggestive. Complex and ever-changing, although subtle. Red cedar, vague floral notes, and dry grain in a cow barn. Peppery with cleansing citrus pith.

HIGHWOOD "CENTENNIAL"
single distillery blended Canadian whiskey, 40% ABV
Creamy caramel and blistering hot pepper lead into lemon peels and fireworks. Oily and mouth-coating, with a tart finish.

SHELTER POINT

OWNER Patrick & Kimm Evans

FOUNDED 2011 **CAPACITY** 39,600 gal (150,000 liters)

ADDRESS 4650 Regent Road, Campbell River, British Columbia V9H 1E3 **WEBSITE** www.shelterpointdistillery.com

Making whiskey, they say, gets in your blood. After 30 years as a distiller in some of Scotland's revered distilleries (Lagavulin, Blair Athol, Caol Ila, Dalwhinnie), Mike Nicholson retired to Canada's Vancouver Island—or so he thought. But it didn't take long for the partners in a newly founded local distillery to get wind of Nicholson's arrival, nor did it take much arm-twisting to convince him to join them in their new adventure. Aptly named, Shelter Point is about three Canadian wilderness hours "up Island" from Victoria. This lovely spot to make whiskey is nestled in a grove of trees on the edge of acres of barley fields; owners Patrick and Kimm Evans have plans to malt their own barley.

From its inception, the distillery was planned as a tourist destination and features a comfortable still-side lounge where visitors can watch operations while relaxing in leather armchairs. For now, though, the only whiskey the visitor can take home is a scrumptious 5-year-old Canadian rye the proprietors have brought in from another distillery. "We bottle this on site," says Patrick, "but it's hard to get excited about someone else's work."

Nicholson is making fruity spirits in the two copper pot stills Shelter Point's owners had custom-crafted in Scotland. After their long sea voyage to Shelter Point, Nicholson finally fired up those stills in June 2011. Whether the whiskey will taste like Scotch is not certain yet, but with Nicholson overseeing the stills you know it will be exceptional.

TASTING NOTES

SHELTER POINT NEW SPIRIT
malt spirit, 65% ABV
Creamy malt, the essence of roasted grain, banana oil, and a generic fruitiness point hopefully to a fruity, malty future.

SHELTER POINT FOUR-MONTH-OLD SPIRIT
malt spirit, 65% ABV
Hope becomes promise as the barrel turns malt to malty, and grain to nutty. A fruity harshness will soon be fruit.

SHELTER POINT FIVE-YEAR-OLD RYE
single distillery Canadian rye whiskey, 40% ABV
Aroma of fresh-pressed apple juice. Peppery hot Canadian rye with a sweet estery fruitiness. Creamy butterscotch smothers dusty dry rye, while a hint of spirit melds into menthol. Overtures of Concord grapes, then sweetened cream of wheat with a dash of rose water and hot pepper. Finishes in refreshing citric pith.

STILL WATERS SINGLE MALT

SHELTER POINT FIVE-YEAR-OLD RYE

STILL WATERS

OWNER Barry Bernstein and Barry Stein

FOUNDED 2009 **CAPACITY** 9,500 gal (36,000 liters)

ADDRESS 150 Bradwick Drive, Unit #26, Concord, Ontario L4K 4M7 **WEBSITE** www.stillwatersdistillery.com

In Concord, Ontario, on the northern edge of Toronto, partners Barry Stein and Barry Bernstein smile broadly as they point to their gleaming copper pot and column stills. Surrounding them is their growing collection of maturing barrels of whiskey. Several years ago, when the two single malt aficionados and best friends opted out of the corporate rat race to pursue their dream to make whiskey, their wives feared the worst.

Recently, the team has added an old Canadian whiskey tradition to their operation. In addition to single malt, they have begun to distill corn—the creamiest of Canadian whiskey grains—as well as Canada's spicy signature grain: rye. After some initial headaches, the results are very promising. Making corn whiskey is pretty straightforward and the partners had no problems mashing corn, then distilling it in the Carl brand stills they imported from Germany and assembled themselves. Rye, though, proved quite a challenge.

As Bernstein recalls, "We came in the morning after we put our first rye mash to ferment and the place was flooded. There was rye mash everywhere." The reputation of rye as a difficult, foamy, sticky grain led them to conclude at first that they had underestimated its challenges. They soon found the culprit: a clogged valve on the closed fermenter had allowed pressure to build up. The fermenting mash simply sprayed out onto the floor. Lesson learned, these adventurous distillers now triple-check everything.

TASTING NOTES

STILL WATERS "CORN NEW SPIRIT"
new spirit, about 63% ABV
Creamy, slippery, and surprisingly grainy, this newly distilled corn spirit hints at musty sweet corn cobs and caramel corn.

STILL WATERS "RYE NEW SPIRIT"
new spirit, about 63% ABV
Faint but real Canadian rye spices, pepper, and burnt sweet toffee await shaping by charred white oak. A promising beginning.

STILL WATERS "MALT NEW SPIRIT"
new spirit, about 63% ABV
This creamy new spirit already showcases barley mash, barley sugar, red licorice, and white pepper with murmurs of orchard fruits. A year in ex-Bourbon barrels delivers mouthwatering tropical notes of coconut and pineapple, while new oak aging emphasizes orchard fruit.

JAPAN

JAPAN

While Ireland has been enjoying a renaissance in the last five years and the US has become a hotbed for new distilleries, no other country has made such an indelible stamp on the world of whiskey recently as Japan. Although whiskey making there stretches back decades, it has a checkered history. Japan originally set out to emulate Scotland and much effort was made to replicate the great distilleries there. In recent years, though, it has gathered a momentum of its own and, backed by whiskey writers and malt lovers discovering its charms and with countless awards under its belt, Japanese whiskey has truly joined the major leagues. Even now, though, it has been struggling, a victim of its own success.

Regional Styles

The nature of Japanese whiskey production is that every conceivable style is made in a very small number of distilleries. Both Suntory and Nikka, the principal producers, go to great lengths to make sure they have a range of whiskeys of a wide variety of ages, peated and unpeated, and available matured in both sherry and Bourbon barrels. Japan is even bringing new woods to the whiskey party and, in its older whiskeys, seems to have developed a natural characteristic, a sort of mushroomy note.

Author's Choice

YOICHI Located on the northern island of Hokkaido, Yoichi is difficult to get to but well worth the effort for the beautiful coastal scenery, pretty distillery buildings, and fascinating museum exploring the life of the distiller who brought whiskey-making to Japan.

Regional Events

Whisky Live Tokyo (www.whiskylive.com) is the oldest Whisky Live event, organized by *Whisky Magazine* in the UK, and has grown into a total celebration of all things whiskey, attracting the cream of the Scotch whiskey contingent and the most enthusiastic whiskey fans in the world.

It could be said that the modern era of whiskey-making began with the financial crisis of 1997, which swept across Asia and forced many Japanese whiskey makers to give up in favor of local spirits. But the few that remained—and really, there were just two companies of any note—got serious. Japanese whiskey, long shunned in its homeland in favor of Scottish malts, began to attract attention overseas. By 2003 a Japanese whiskey had topped the poll in a worldwide hunt for the "Best of the Best" conducted by *Whisky Magazine*.

Miyagikyo's high-tech operation contrasts with its tranquil location in the foothills of Miyagi prefecture.

Surrounded by forest trails *in the Southern Japanese Alps, Hakushu is Japan's highest distillery.*

So all's well that ends well? Not quite. Japanese whiskey is still difficult to find. Its success has meant that older whiskey is hard to find and very expensive—mainly because the producers could not have predicted the future demand and did not lay down enough malt for long maturation.

With countries such as Taiwan, India, and to some extent Australia positioning themselves as premier Asian whiskeys, the heat is on for Japan—but the high quality and decades of experience should be enough to keep the country at the forefront of the world whiskey boom.

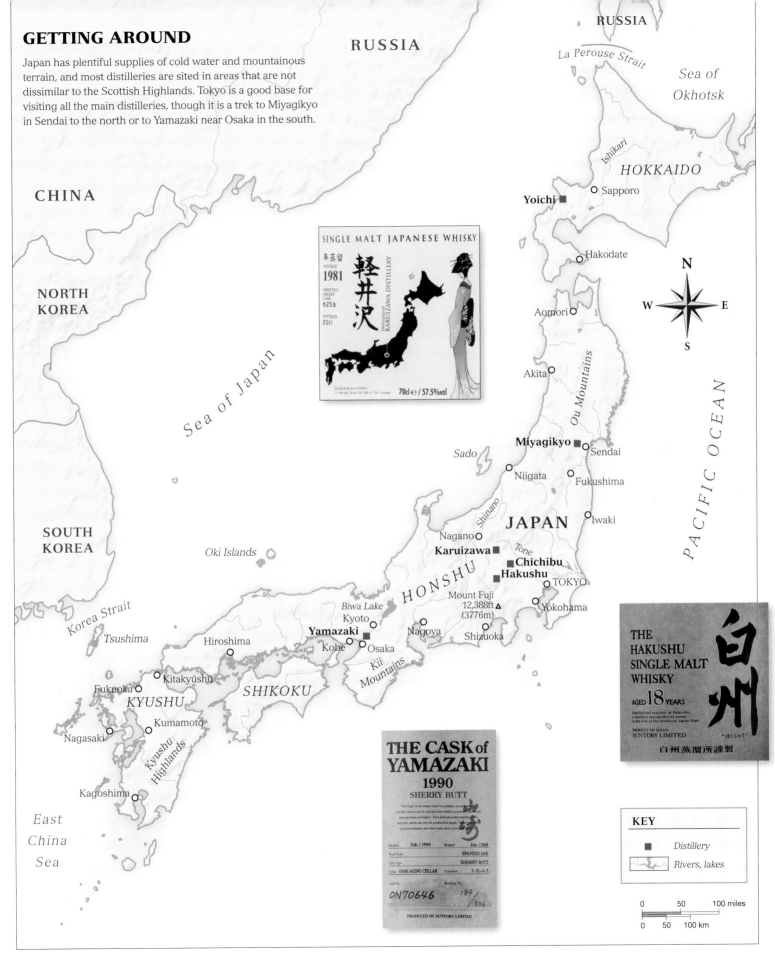

GETTING AROUND

Japan has plentiful supplies of cold water and mountainous terrain, and most distilleries are sited in areas that are not dissimilar to the Scottish Highlands. Tokyo is a good base for visiting all the main distilleries, though it is a trek to Miyagikyo in Sendai to the north or to Yamazaki near Osaka in the south.

RUSSIA

RUSSIA

La Perouse Strait

Sea of Okhotsk

Ishikari

HOKKAIDO

CHINA

Yoichi ■   ○ Sapporo

○ Hakodate

NORTH KOREA

Aomori ○

Sea of Japan

Akita ○

Ou Mountains

Miyagikyo ■   ○ Sendai

Sado

○ Niigata   ○ Fukushima

SOUTH KOREA

Oki Islands

Shinano

JAPAN

Nagano ○   ○ Iwaki

Korea Strait

Tsushima

Hiroshima ○

Biwa Lake
Kyoto ○

HONSHU

Tone

Karuizawa ■

■ **Chichibu**
■ **Hakushu**

○ TOKYO

Mount Fuji
12,388ft △
(3776m)

○ Yokohama

Yamazaki ■
Kobe ○   ○ Osaka

Nagoya ○

Shizuoka ○

Kii Mountains

Fukuoka ○   ○ Kitakyūshū

SHIKOKU

Kumamoto ○

KYUSHU

Nagasaki ○

Kyushu Highlands

Kagoshima ○

East China Sea

PACIFIC OCEAN

N
W   E
S

SINGLE MALT JAPANESE WHISKY

年蒸留
VINTAGE
1981

FIRST FILL
SHERRY
CASK
6256

BOTTLED
2011

軽井沢

DISTILLED AT
KARUIZAWA DISTILLERY

Distilled & Bottled in JAPAN
for Speciality Drinks Ltd. NW10 7SD / London

70cl ℮ / 57.5%vol

THE CASK of YAMAZAKI
1990
SHERRY BUTT

The "Cask" is our dream come true product, as each is
carefully chosen one by one and then bottled to preserve the
character from each barrel. Each malt advocates exquisite aroma
and taste, which can only be produced in Japan. Subtle yet
prominent balance, and other malts show a profound experience.

Distilled	Feb. / 1990	Bottled	Jun. / 2008
Wood Type			SPANISH OAK
Cask Type			SHERRY BUTT
Cellar	OHMI AGING CELLAR	Location	3-N-4-5

Cask No.
0N70646   Bottling No.   184/506

PRODUCED BY SUNTORY LIMITED

THE HAKUSHU SINGLE MALT WHISKY
AGED **18** YEARS

白州

Distilled and matured at Hakushu,
a distillery surrounded by forest
at the foot of the Southern Japan Alps

PRODUCT OF JAPAN
SUNTORY LIMITED

"はくしゅう"

白州蒸溜所謹製

KEY

■ Distillery

Rivers, lakes

0   50   100 miles
0   50   100 km

CHICHIBU

OWNER Ichiro Akuto	
FOUNDED 2007	**CAPACITY** 31,700 gal (120,000 liters)
ADDRESS 49 Midorigaoka, Chichibu-shi, Saitama	
WEBSITE www.one-drinks.com	

When Ichiro Akuto opened his own distillery in Japan, it wasn't just a realization of a dream; it was the fulfillment of a personal promise. Ichiro has a long association with drinks production in Japan—nearly 400 years, in fact. When the family association with distilling came to an end early in the 21st century, Ichiro vowed that he would bring it back to life.

"My family has been making sake in Chichibu since 1625," he says. "It made sense for me, therefore, to build my new distillery in this place that has meant so much to the Akuto family for 21 generations. My grandfather built Hanyu Distillery in the 1940s, and when it was closed in 2000 and demolished in 2004, I was determined that should not be the last chapter for our distilling history. Work began at Chichibu in late 2007 and we were granted a distilling license in early 2008. In 2011, I was very proud to release Chichibu "The First," a three-year-old single malt from my new distillery."

Ichiro's releases

Ichiro didn't sit around wasting time in the intervening years; he sought out and bought up old Japanese whiskey stock. In the process, he earned cult status for a series of award-winning and stimulating new releases, including heavily sherried and intensely peated bottles of very rare Karuizawa vintage malt.

Ichiro is also responsible for the much-sought-after "Card" series, in which each bottling features a different playing card on the label—launched, he says, because he wanted to make it possible for people to recognize their favorite malts on the back bar shelf without having to study labels, age statements, vintages, and so on. The whiskeys were drawn from 400 casks of Hanyu single malt that Ichiro managed to obtain after the distillery was closed down.

Another series of releases is known as Ichiro's Malt, and if you're fortunate to find any of them, the advice is to buy, because they are both rare and uniformly excellent to drink. One of these, "MWR" (Mizunara Wood Reserve), is described as pure malt whiskey and was matured, vatted, and bottled at Chichibu. Another, known as "Double Distilleries," was again vatted and bottled at Chichibu and is presumably made up of small quantities of Japanese malt bought from independent sources by Ichiro.

ICHIRO'S "MALT & GRAIN"
Advertised as a worldwide whiskey, this non-chill-filtered blend uses a mix of Hanyu and Chichibu single malts with other malts from around the world.

ICHIRO'S MALT "DOUBLE DISTILLERIES"

CHICHIBU "THE FIRST"

The plant features equipment imported from Scotland and what may be the only Japanese oak washbacks in the world.

The Chichibu arrives

"The First" arrived in late 2011 and the transformation from the spirit in three years is quite remarkable. The first whiskey proper was unpeated but amazingly full, rich, and confident. Its astonishing maturity is attributed not just to climatic conditions but also to the care and attention Ichiro put into every stage of the process. It's abundantly obvious that he is a major distilling talent who will make a huge impact on Japanese whiskey in the years to come.

Looking to the future

The first release was bottled at cask strength, but the follow-up three-year-olds will be bottled at 46 percent. A peated whiskey at 46 percent, released at the end of 2012, is something else again. It's not unusual for Japanese distilleries to mix up house styles to give themselves as many whiskey options as possible, but will there be a house style at Chichibu?

"That's an excellent question," says Ichiro. "It's a small distillery and I wanted flexibility, albeit in a heavier style. That's why the stills are small, with a straight head and downward lyne arm. We create three different types of spirits: non-peated medium-light body, non-peated heavy, and heavily peated (50–55ppm) medium-light body. I have experimented with cooling temperatures to create the different spirit weights. Of course, most whiskey flavor comes

from maturation casks and we have mostly ex-Bourbon and some Japanese oak."

Recent years haven't been without their problems for Japan. Just as the world was starting to take serious interest in its whiskey, a triple whammy of stock shortages, the problems created by the tsunami and subsequent radiation concerns, and the emergence of many New World whiskeys all threatened Japanese success. But Ichiro is upbeat.

"I'm excited by the positive international reception for my whiskey," he says. "I'll keep on making the very best single malt I can. As long as whiskey experts and fans of single malt continue to like what I do, then I remain optimistic!"

TASTING NOTES

CHICHIBU "THE FIRST"
single malt, 61.8% ABV
aged in ex-Bourbon barrels
This is only three years old but it's surprisingly rich and full. Strictly limited, it's a vatting of malt matured in ex-Bourbon barrels, and with water it is nuanced and sophisticated, with lemongrass, Thai spices, lime, and lemon.

CHICHIBU "NEWBORN BOURBON BARREL"
new make, 62.5% ABV, cask strength,
aged in fresh Bourbon barrels
Just 262 bottles—almost certainly one barrel's worth—of this six-month-old version of Chichibu was released. Too young legally to be called whiskey, not only is the spirit newborn but the barrel was too—a fresh Bourbon barrel was used. It's understandably sappy and raw, but water releases a great wave of lime chocolate dipped in pepper sauce. You can just about find a sweet vanilla note trying to climb out from behind the barley.

ONE HUNDRED PERCENT EFFORT

Ichiro Akuto isn't content with just producing a new whiskey in the way whiskey has always been produced in Japan. He has a dream that's bigger than that: to produce a whiskey that can truly be called Japanese born and bred. Both Nikka and Suntory, the two giants of Japan's whiskey industry, use either Australian or Scottish malt or barrels imported from elsewhere. Ichiro aims to do things differently. "My dream is to create the first 100 percent Japanese whiskey. We have planted barley, I have found a source of Japanese peat, and we already have washbacks and casks made from Japanese oak, so this may become a reality. I am thinking of the future and I hope one day to have a 20-year-old Chichibu or an all-Japanese-made whiskey!"

CHICHIBU "NEWBORN BOURBON BARREL"

MIYAGIKYO

OWNER Nikka	
FOUNDED 1969	**CAPACITY** 1.3m gal (5m liters)
ADDRESS Sendaishi, Miyagiken	
WEBSITE www.nikkawhisky.eu	

Founded in 1969, Miyagikyo was designed to help Nikka extend its production output and was the result of three years' research. The story goes that Master Distiller Masataka Taketsuru had spent about three years looking for the perfect place to build a second distillery and as soon as he tasted the local water he declared the site fit for the purpose. This may be the case, but it's only part of the story; today the folks at Nikka will tell you that the high humidity levels and pure air are also significant contributors to a site ideal for making high-quality single malt whiskey.

The distillery is located on the island of Honshu to the west of the city of Sendai, two hours northeast of Tokyo by high-speed train. It is also known as Sendai Distillery for this reason, but the site is very much a rural one in the foothills of the Miyagi prefecture.

The region is beautiful, rich in green woodlands, and famous for its waterfalls and many hot springs, and the distillery itself is surrounded by mountains. However, the peaceful environment is in stark contrast to the high-tech and highly automated distillery, where most of the production process is controlled by state-of-the-art computers.

Left-field whiskey

As with all Japanese distilleries, Miyagikyo makes malt in a variety of ways, including one or two that could be considered pretty left-field. Malt is imported from Scotland and Australia, and on one level at least, the aim has been to emulate Scotch malts. The distillery has eight stills to produce conventional single malt whiskey, while the barrels are stored in traditional cellars with just two floors—mainly because the distillery is situated in the middle of an earthquake zone, but also partly because this emulates Scottish maturation methods. The most commonly produced spirit at Miyagikyo is rich and fruity with elegant aromas, using large stills.

So far so conventional, but that isn't the end of the story. The distillery also boasts Coffey (column) stills which are normally used to make Bourbon or grain whiskey, but there are all sorts of more unusual creations going on. For instance, Coffey stills are used here to make whiskey from corn, malted barley, and a mixture of both.

This practice was quite common in Scotland once upon a time but is now very uncommon. Indeed, the practice is frowned upon by the

MIYAGIKYO 15-YEAR-OLD

MIYAGIKYO 10-YEAR-OLD

Scotch Whisky Association (SWA); it was the use of Coffey stills for making single malt whiskey that got Loch Lomond distillery into so much trouble with the SWA. Nikka "Single Coffey Malt," aged for 12 years, is made with malted barley from Miyagikyo. Nikka's "Pure Malt" series of blends also draws on Miyagikyo's output.

New Nikka releases

The distillery has also been the center for some of the new range of Nikka whiskeys that have started to appear on the world stage. Nikka Whisky Brand Manager Didier Ghorbanzadeh is unfazed by the perceived problems caused by the tsunami and radiation issues and points to the new bottlings, including three single cask Miyagikyo releases and two vintage ones.

"As knowledge of Japanese whiskey is only now beginning to reach the general public, it is expected that its reputation will continue to increase in the near future," he says. "There is still much room to grow, especially considering that its inherent quality is widely recognized by specialists and connoisseurs internationally. We also intend to put more focus on local innovators in the field of gastronomy who incorporate Nikka whiskey in their artisanal products. Finally, the third edition of the European Nikka Perfect Serve bartender competition will introduce a new Japanese concept which continues to build on the notion of perfect service."

Fittingly, Miyagikyo also has a huge visitors' center with a typical Japanese restaurant and a bar offering tastings of all Nikka group whiskeys, where tourists can ponder on the niceties of whiskey and gastronomy combined.

TASTING NOTES

MIYAGIKYO 10-YEAR-OLD
single malt, 45% ABV
The nose isn't the greatest, a little inconsequential and floral, but on the palate there's green fruit, a touch of oak, some feisty spice notes, and traces of vanilla and creamy toffee. Easy-drinking and pleasant.

MIYAGIKYO 15-YEAR-OLD
single malt, 45% ABV
The age when this malt hits its stride, with fruit and flowers on the nose and a fat and juicy palate feel, with currants, plums, grapes, vanilla, and mocha. The finish is a sherry-trifle delight.

NIKKA 12-YEAR OLD "SINGLE COFFEY MALT"
malted barley mash, 55% ABV
Whiskey well and truly off-piste and outside the box. It's got Bourbon-like polished oak, tropical fruits, dark chocolate, bitter coffee, and red berries to the front and softer Bourbon vanilla, toffee, and nut-sprinkled vanilla ice cream in the finish. Great.

NIKKA 12-YEAR-OLD "SINGLE COFFEY MALT"

MIZUWARI STYLE

So big is the trend for drinking Japanese whiskey long with water—known as *mizuwari* style—that Nikka has released a younger expression of Miyagikyo specifically for that market. There is a growing view that the trend will spread elsewhere, and whiskey is being drunk increasingly with fancy carved ice, with ice balls, and as a highball—the way it was first consumed by the British.

NIKKA "PURE MALT RED"

YAMAZAKI

OWNER Suntory Ltd.

FOUNDED 1921 **CAPACITY** 1.85m gal (7m liters)

ADDRESS 5-2-1 Yamazaki, Shimamoto-cho, Mishima-gun, Osaka

WEBSITE www.suntory.com

The distillery at Yamazaki, between Kyoto and Osaka towards the south end of Japan's main island of Honshu, is where it all started for Japanese whiskey. Not just the physical production of malted barley spirits, either, but the philosophy that Japanese whiskey should experiment, challenge the existing parameters and create and develop new tastes, practised from the 1920s at Yamazaki right up to the present day at Japan's latest distillery, Chichibu.

The birthplace of Japanese whiskey

Japan's first whiskey distillery was built on land bought by Shinjiro Torii, who employed scientist and whiskey-making expert Masataka Taketsuru—equipped with distilling experience gained in Scotland—and set about creating Japanese whiskey. Since then, Yamazaki has grown into one of the biggest malt whiskey–making institutions in the world and also one of the most fascinating.

Japanese distillers don't share their malts for making blends and in the pursuit of excellence that means creating the ability to make many different whiskeys for variety. The still room at Yamazaki, then, has stills of all shapes and sizes. There are six of them in all, and two different fermentation tanks. Various combinations of stills working in tandem and using different yeasts produce plenty of diversity in the new-make spirit. Throw in an assortment of casks seasoned by a wide range of spirits, wines, fortified wines, and liqueurs, as well as charred and toasted virgin casks, and you're looking at an almost overwhelming selection of whiskeys. There have been any number of estimates as to how many different whiskeys are made here—often as high as 120 or 125—but it's a secret and nobody outside the distillery really knows, except that it's a lot, and that Yamazaki produces non-peated, lightly peated, and heavily peated malts.

This means that every single malt whiskey from Yamazaki is a vatting of whiskeys from the distillery prepared in totally different ways, and while this is true of most single malts, the variations in flavor are more pronounced in this distillery than almost anywhere else. Unsurprisingly, therefore, the whiskey is extremely good, but it is only recently that the rest of the world has caught on.

The rise of Yamazaki

Master Distiller Mike Miyamoto says that you can almost pinpoint the time when Suntory's whiskeys began their meteoric rise to the top. "Ever since the International Spirits Council awarded the Yamazaki 12-year-old with a gold medal in 2003, Japanese whiskey has earned recognition from around the world," he says. "In Japan itself, demand for whiskey has been growing in the past three years; this includes demand from younger

The imposing appearance *of the red-brick structure has led the villagers to liken it to a giant radio.*

THE YAMAZAKI "BOURBON BARREL"

people due to the popularity of the whiskey soda highball. This trend allows newcomers to have their first experience of whiskey, and because of this the demographic of whiskey-lovers is expanding.

"We also hope to expand from the predominant Japan-centric market to overseas markets. Whiskey has traditionally been perceived as a pre- or post-meal drink. With the increased interest in Japanese cuisine, and the fact that Suntory whiskeys go extremely well with food, we hope that whiskeys can be established as a drink to have during your meal, like wine."

Worldwide interest

The wide variety of malts isn't just to provide sophistication and variety in the single malt output—it provides the perfect platform for creating world-class blended whiskeys, too. Yamazaki is owned by Suntory and the parent company has enjoyed as much success for its blends, which make use of different malts made at Yamazaki and sister distillery Hakushu. The results are impressive. The company's flagship blend Hibiki has picked up a large cache of awards, including the title of the "World's Best Blend" on more than one occasion in the World Whisky Awards.

The growing interest in Japanese whiskey has in turn led to a large number of visitors, and the distillery's facilities for them have developed accordingly. Comprehensive guided tours are held and visitors can participate in seminars and events, as well as taste samples from the huge collection of whiskey varieties showcased in the adjacent whiskey museum. Consequently, the distillery has earned a good reputation in the international whiskey community.

TASTING NOTES

THE YAMAZAKI 10-YEAR-OLD
single malt, 40% ABV, aged in American oak puncheon
Soft and comfortable mix of squidgy banana, fluffy apple, sweet vanilla, and soft barley. It's a light, moreish, easy-drinking whiskey with toffee and vanilla in the finish.

THE YAMAZAKI 18-YEAR-OLD
single malt 43% ABV, aged in American, Spanish, and Japanese oak casks
Up there with the world's great 18-year-olds, it's a complex mix of mango, kiwi, and other tropical fruits, sweeter than expected and with oak and spice. The finish is a bit oddball but with hints of the unique Japanese flavors that develop in older whiskey.

THE YAMAZAKI "BOURBON BARREL"
single malt, 48.2% ABV, aged in Bourbon barrels, non-chill-filtered, limited to 1000 bottles
One of two Bourbon barrel offerings from Suntory in 2011—the other was a peated Hakushu—this is a truly fantastic whiskey. It's soft and sublime, a rich vanilla ice cream in caramel sauce that's utterly moreish.

NATIVE TREND

If it took a long time for Japanese whiskey to be fully appreciated across the world, it took even longer for Japan's own fashion-conscious youth to accept it, even though the country is generally whiskey-crazy. Japan's main cities specialize in small, intimate whiskey bars where the finest Scotch is on sale, but it was only as recently as 2010 that trendy Japanese youths began to adopt their own home-grown versions, mixing Yamazaki 10-year-old in particular into highballs. Whiskey also has a domestic spirit competitor in Japan—shochu.

THE YAMAZAKI 18-YEAR-OLD

THE YAMAZAKI 10-YEAR-OLD

NIKKA YOICHI 20-YEAR-OLD

YOICHI

OWNER Nikka	
FOUNDED 1934	**CAPACITY** 28,000 gal (2m liters)
ADDRESS 7–6 Kurokawacho, Yoichimachi, Yoichigun, Hokkaido	
WEBSITE www.nikkawhisky.eu	

Situated 30 miles (50 km) west of Sapporo on the island of Hokkaido, Yoichi Distillery is striking and impressive, with a bright-red tile roof and large stone walls. It's the only distillery on the island, which is in the north of Japan, and of all the Japanese distilleries is said to have the climate most like that of Scotland. It is also regarded by many as the prettiest in Japan, Yoichi being a small fishing village with mountains on three sides and the sea in front of it. This is the distillery that Masataka Taketsuru, the first distiller at Yamazaki, built upon the formation of his company Dainipponkaju Company Ltd. in 1934, renamed Nikka Whisky Distilling in 1952.

Mission for malt
Taketsuru is a hugely influential figure in the story of Japanese whiskey, bringing his knowledge of distilling to Yamazaki and effectively starting the journey that would transform Suntory into the country's most important whiskey producer. And with Nikka he established the only other major player in Japanese whiskey.

Born into a sake-brewing dynasty, Taketsuru was packed off to Scotland while still a university student, tasked with discovering the secrets of Scotch whiskey and bringing the knowledge back to Japan. He enrolled in a chemistry course at the University of Glasgow, then struck out for Speyside, eventually turning up at the door of Longmorn Distillery, near Elgin, where he received his first, week-long crash course in whiskey-making. After perfecting his skills with an apprenticeship at Hazelburn Distillery in Campbeltown—and falling in love with a Scottish girl named Jessie Roberta "Rita" Cowan—Taketsuru returned to Japan in 1920 with his new wife and hard-earned whiskey expertise. He was soon recruited by Suntory founder Shinjiro Torii, and so began a partnership that would firmly set Japan on the whiskey-making map.

Hokkaido matures into Yoichi
Originally called Hokkaido Distillery, the plant was making whiskey by 1940 and had a capacity of a modest 40,000 gallons (150,000 liters) per year, though it has been expanded considerably since. Yet it wasn't until the 1980s that a single malt was released, and the name Nikka Whisky didn't come into use until the company was taken over in 2001 and the distillery was renamed Yoichi. In addition

NIKKA YOICHI 10-YEAR-OLD

NIKKA YOICHI 15-YEAR-OLD

Founder Masataka Taketsuru *and his Scottish wife, Rita, lived in one of the distillery's neat stone buildings.*

to producing some of Japan's most respected single malts, Yoichi is also a key component in some of Nikka's blended malt whiskeys and blends.

Like all Japanese distilleries, Yoichi makes a range of different malts, but if it has a house style it is for rich, oily, full-bodied, peaty, and smoky whiskeys. Water is sourced from an underground water table and drawn up through peat beds—the only ones that exist in Japan, though the peat isn't used for drying barley. The distillery has its own malting kiln and traditional pagoda-style chimneys, but these are no longer in use.

The Yoichi character

With its coastal location, the distillery produces whiskeys that have been compared to those of Islay and the west coast distilleries of Scotland, not least because the geography is said to contribute to the salty and medicinal notes that can be found in the spirits. Another contributing factor is the stills, which are squat and onion-shaped.

However, the key point of difference for Yoichi comes from its use of wood. It has its own cooperage, and it includes in its inventory barrels made at the distillery from Japanese new oak. Known as mizunara, Japanese oak is more porous than European or American oak and therefore imparts more color and flavor to the spirits than some other oak types—so much so that the spirits are transferred from mizunara casks to traditional ones during the maturation process.

The whiskey has enjoyed huge success in recent years and is a regular award-winner. Yoichi, like other older Japanese expressions, has been a victim of its own success. Prior to the early part of the new millennium Nikka's owners, unaware of the huge success that was to follow, didn't put aside enough stock for long aging. Hence older expressions have been hard to come by.

The distillery isn't the easiest to visit if Tokyo is your base, but it's worth the effort because apart from being in an area of outstanding natural beauty, it also boasts a visitors' center and museum telling the story of Taketsuru-San and his Scottish wife.

TASTING NOTES

NIKKA YOICHI 10-YEAR-OLD
single malt, 45% ABV
Quite full and oily, with some smoke and canned fruits. Pleasant, rounded, easy-drinking, and with a controlled amount of the gutsy, oily house style. There is a dustiness to it later on.

NIKKA YOICHI 15-YEAR-OLD
single malt, 45% ABV
Wispy, smoky, floral, and understated nose, but that is more than compensated for by the tangy taste, with rich salt and pepper bursts, toffee notes, stewed apricot, and pear. There are touches of hickory in this, too. A treat.

NIKKA YOICHI 20-YEAR-OLD
single malt, 52% ABV, cask strength
One of the world's greatest whiskeys. The nose is grungy, earthy, robust, and with a whiff of industrial oil, while the taste kicks off in all directions, mixing in autumn forest, sea-sprayed beach, barbecued trout, spice, oak, and dark chocolate. It ebbs and flows and tantalizes the taste buds. It's all here and then some.

HAKUSHU

OWNER Suntory Ltd.
FOUNDED 1999 **CAPACITY** 793,000 gal (3m liters)
ADDRESS 2913-1 Torihara, Hakushu-cho, Hokuto-shi,
Yamanashi **WEBSITE** www.suntory.com

While it may be the lesser known of Suntory's two distilleries, Hakushu is a fascinating one. It is Japan's highest distillery and its most remote, situated as it is in the Southern Japanese Alps, about two and a half hours by fast train from Tokyo, surrounded by natural forests with walking and cycling trails for the energetic. Apart from the wonderful location, Hakushu also offers a museum and visitors' center.

The distillery itself is effectively two distilleries close together, though only one, Hakushu East, is used, and many of the stills here stand idle.

Fueling the "salaryman" boom

Hakushu was built in 1973, in the 50th anniversary year of Suntory's whiskey-making operation, when the company was riding a Japanese whiskey boom that was in part its own creation. Suntory's success was built on satisfying the hard-drinking habits of Japan's white collar business class, or "salarymen," who drove the country's postwar economic expansion and tended to let their hair down over *mizuwari*-style drinks of whiskey mixed with two parts water. The blends Suntory developed were designed to keep their distinctive flavor even when diluted to such an extent.

Beginning with the "Shirofuda" or "White Label" blend in 1929, "Kakubin" followed in 1937, "Torys" in 1946, and "Suntory Royal" in 1960. The company sought to secure its dominance of the market and further fuel demand by launching a chain of bars in the 1950s, offering what was then a new concept in after-work drinking for men. Dubbed "Torys" bars they became a phenomenal success and at their peak numbered more than 1,500. By the 1980s, "Suntory Royal" was the biggest-selling whiskey brand in the world, selling more than 15 million cases in Japan alone.

Premium future

The huge stillhouses of Hakushu were built primarily to satisfy this demand for easy-drinking blends, and when that boom ended in the 1990s, Hakushu West was forced to close its doors. But Keizo Saji, son of Suntory founder Shinjiro Torii, who became president of his father's company in the 1960s, also believed in a future for premium blends and single malts. To that end, Hakushu was crucial in the development of Suntory's Hibiki range of premium aged blends, launched in 1989, and in 1994 the distillery added its own single malt

Nestled high up in the Japanese Alps, *Hakushu was once the world's largest malt distillery.*

offering to sit alongside Yamazaki's in the Suntory profile. With its cooler mountain location and soft water source drawn from a mountain spring, the standard style of Hakushu is very much its own: fresh, clean, and fruity. There has, however, been a trend in recent years to limited edition bottlings in different styles, along with a beautiful honeyed treat of a whiskey, Hakushu "Bourbon Barrel," and one called Hakushu "Heavily Peated."

TASTING NOTES

THE HAKUSHU 12-YEAR-OLD
single malt, 43.5% ABV
A light and fluffy nose, with some pine and fresh-cut grass. The taste is fresh and clean, with spearmint. Sweet and palate-cleansing, with fresh barley. As easy-drinking as Japanese whiskey ever gets.

THE HAKUSHU 18-YEAR-OLD
single malt 43% ABV
The nose is still shy here, with wet forest paths and damp leaves. The palate is all toasted oak, fresh green fruit, fluffy apples, sweet barley, and then more oak. A medium-long finish.

THE HAKUSHU "HEAVILY PEATED"
single malt, 48% ABV
An utter delight, though the name is a little misleading. Other flavors hold up well here so the peat has to dip in and out like a frustrated boxer stabbing smoky punches at a complex repertoire of lemon, lime, and sweet melon. No knockout blows here, and the peat possibly wins on points. Lots of grounds for a rematch, though.

THE HAKUSHU 18-YEAR-OLD

THE HAKUSHU 12-YEAR-OLD

KARUIZAWA

STOCK OWNER Ichiro Akuto
FOUNDED 1955 **CLOSED** 2000
WEBSITE www.one-drinks.com

It's unusual to write about a closed distillery, but a substantial amount of big-hearted, quality whiskey from Karuizawa is making its way to world whiskey markets, and whiskey lovers constantly ask to know more about it. In addition, the owners of the remaining stock are planning new releases.

Built in 1955 on an active volcano, Karuizawa had the highest altitude of any Japanese whiskey distillery at 2,788 ft (850 m) above sea level. The microclimate affected maturation of the spirits in that the average humidity of 80 percent resulted in high evaporation of water. The alcoholic strength of the whiskey made at the distillery remained high, but the whiskeys have a fantastic concentration of aromas and flavors.

Stout like a soldier

The distillery was built to make whiskey in the most traditional style; 100 percent Golden Promise barley imported from Scotland, small stills, and European sherry oak casks. Sadly, distillation ceased at Karuizawa in 2000.

"The house style is defined as being 'stout like a soldier,'" says Ichiro Akuto, who bought the remaining stocks of Karuizawa. "The whiskey is broad in the shoulder, high in strength, and very bold in the sherry style. It's amazing whiskey.

"Our intention is to bring the whiskey of Karuizawa to as wide an audience as possible while stocks last. We will continue to release single casks as previous examples have won many awards. In addition, we are creating "Spirit of Asama," made in small batches from hand-selected casks of the final vintages of Karuizawa, 1999 and 2000. The whiskey has been put together by a very distinguished Japanese master distiller. These whiskeys are part of Japan's liquid history."

TASTING NOTES

KARUIZAWA 1971 CASK NO. 6878
single malt, 64.1% ABV
An assault on the senses, with so much going on it's hard to take it all in. Exotic fruits, jammy plum and prune, stewed peach, and waves of sherry and oak are all part of the oral attack. Not for the faint-hearted, but a treat nevertheless.

KARUIZAWA 1986 CASK NO. 7387
single malt, 60.7% ABV
Fragrant smoke and scented candle on the nose, then a dusty, drying, musty, and fruity palate with figs and fruit jam. Some nuts, sherry notes, a touch of sulfur, and a delightfully spicy conclusion.

KARUIZAWA 1986 CASK NO. 7387

KARUIZAWA 1971 CASK NO. 6878

KARUIZAWA 1981 CASK NO. 6256

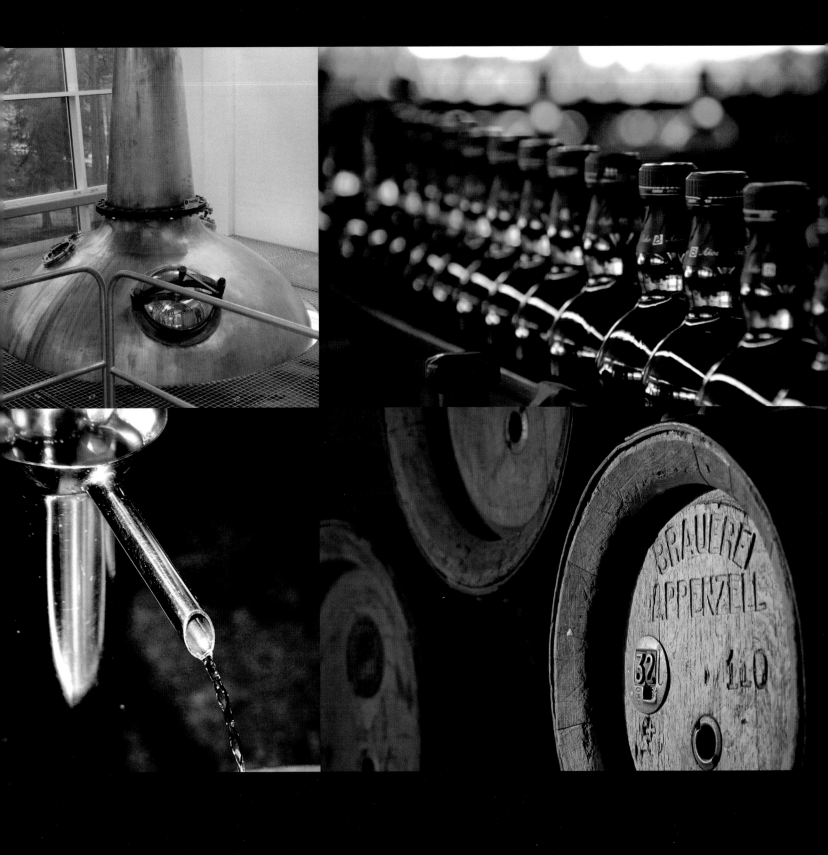

EUROPE

EUROPE

When it comes to making whiskey, no region is met with more skepticism than Europe. In some ways that's understandable, because outside Scotland and Ireland there would seem to be no discernible whiskey-making culture. Considering the matter, though, you can't help wondering why not. After all, Europe can boast an abundance of the vital ingredients required for making whiskey: grain, yeast, and water. In countries such as Belgium, the Netherlands, England, and Germany, and in some regions of France, they make great beer, the starting point for whiskey. Many European countries also excel at distilling, making everything from genever and brandy to any number of fruit liqueurs. So in view of this, why does whiskey seem not to feature much on the agenda?

Regional Styles

There is no typical regional style across Europe, and malts vary from sweet and fruity to heavily peated and spicy. Some of the whiskeys from the Germanic countries are radically different from Scotch and are an acquired taste.

Author's Choice

GLANN AR MOR in France, THE BELGIAN OWL in Belgium, BLAUE MAUS in Germany, and PENDERYN in Wales all make delightful clean, sweet, dessert whiskeys.

ST. GEORGE'S in England produces (somewhat ironically) Scotch-style peated and unpeated whiskey.

MACKMYRA makes distinctive whiskey with Swedish peat and oak and local grain, sometimes dried over juniper twigs.

Regional Events and Tours

Whiskey festivals are common across Europe, with Limburg and Den Haag boasting big events and Whisky Live (www.whiskylive.com), organized by *Whisky Magazine*, staged in various places including Paris and London. Nordic whiskey enthusiasts can join whiskey cruises including the Viking Whisky Festival, which departs from Stockholm in Sweden. A long-weekend camp called Maltstock (www.maltstock. com) is held in the Netherlands each September, and a young person's whiskey and music event called Pure (www.purefestival.com) takes place in London in the same month.

Of course, whiskey is indeed made in Europe, but it has been highly regionalized and produced in relatively small quantities. European whiskey enthusiasts, spoiled by the abundance of Scotch and Irish whiskey, have seen little incentive to seek out whiskey elsewhere on the Continent. Now, though, with the demand for premium spirits at its highest-ever level and set to grow even further, some European whiskey is ready to take its place in the sun. Perhaps just as pertinently, some distillers feel they have learned enough about quality whiskey making to market their whiskeys outside their national borders.

As with New World whiskey, European distillers fall into two broad categories: those who seek to emulate Scotch by making single malt and blended whiskey in the same way, and those who are trying new grains, new recipes, new wood types, and new ways of drying their malted barley to produce radically different styles of whiskey. And with greater interest in whiskey generally, the support of an increasingly diverse number of whiskey publications, and a larger number of routes to market, European whiskeys are finding their way to new territories across the world.

Many of us would not be surprised to find Japanese or even Indian whiskey on the shelves. Increasingly, though, we're seeing Welsh, English, Swedish, French, Belgian, and Dutch whiskey up there, too. It makes for exciting times.

State-of-the-art Slyrs distillery *benefits from pure spring water from the Bavarian mountains.*

GETTING AROUND

Europe's whiskey distilleries tend to be in colder climes, in rural locations near plentiful sources of grain and cold water. Europe's whiskey has traditionally been made by fruit liqueur makers or brewers and in France most of the distilleries come from the cider making region of Brittany. Europe is perhaps uniquely well connected by road and, often, high speed rail, making whiskey tourism a comfortable prospect.

mackmyra
SVENSK WHISKY

MACKMYRA BRUKSWHISKY

I VÅRT DESTILLERI PÅ MACKMYRA BRUK HAR VI AV UTVALDA LOKALA RÅVAROR SKAPAT DENNA SVENSKA MALTWHISKY, EN LÄTT RÖKIGHET MED ENRISDOFT MÖTER FRUKTIG CITRUS I EN WHISKY ATT NJUTA AV.

Lagrad i Bockis Grunlager, Alkoholsyreka. 41.4%

The **Belgian Owl**

Barley raised in Belgium
Whisky made

WHISKY

BELGIAN
SINGLE MALT

50 cl   HANDCRAFTED   46% vol

DYC

COLECCIÓN BARRICAS

10 AÑOS   SPECIAL WHISKY SINGLE MALT

WHISKY 100% DE MALTA DESTILADO EN SEGOVIA, ESPAÑA

SINGLE MALT

R K

WHISKY CASTLE
SWITZERLAND

RARITAS DIABOLI

SWEDEN

Mackmyra

Vänern

Stockholm

Vättern

North Sea

Baltic Sea

The Lakes Distillery

Dublin

IRELAND

UNITED KINGDOM

Spirit of Hven

Malmö

Penderyn   St George's   Us Heit

Hamburg

Adnams   NETH.

Amsterdam   Berlin

Cornish Cyder Farm   London   Rhine   Zuidam   Hammerschmiede
St Austell Brewery

Brussels   Het Anker

Wambrechies   Birkenhof

The Belgian Owl   Ziegler

Warenghem   BELGIUM   Frankfurt

Distillerie   Paris   GERMANY   Blaue Maus
des Menhirs

Glann ar Mor   Reisetbauer

Loire   Weidenauer
Roggenhof

FRANCE   Bosch   Vienna
Coillmór   Finch
Käser's Whisky Castle   Munich   Slyrs
Langatun   Locher   AUSTRIA
Bern   LIECH.
Etter   SWITZ.   Telser
Bordeaux   Rhône   ALPS

ATLANTIC OCEAN

Bay of Biscay

Ebro

Douro   Corsica

Segovia   DYC
Madrid   Sardinia

SPAIN

Guadalquivir

Liber   Granada

Mediterranean Sea

KEY

■ Distillery

▱ Rivers, lakes

0   50 100 150 200 miles

0   100 200 300 400 km

233

SWEDEN

Sweden is whiskey-crazy, so it came as no surprise when Mackmyra gave the country its own distillery. Since then several small independent distilleries have been set up, but it's early days for the fledgling producers. Meanwhile, Mackmyra took another major step up the malt whiskey rankings in 2012 when it moved into a new distillery with the capacity to produce a seriously large volume of whiskey.

MACKMYRA

OWNER Mackmyra	
FOUNDED 1999	**CAPACITY** 317,000 gal (1.2m liters)
ADDRESS Kolonnvägen 2, 80267 Gävle	
WEBSITE www.mackmyra.com	

Mackmyra has gone from a twinkle in the eyes of a group of friends to one of the biggest malt-producing facilities outside Scotland and Ireland. It was born of a skiing trip when the friends rented a mountain lodge and brought a bottle of Scotch each to stock the bar. Over drinks they started musing about why there was no Swedish whiskey, given the ideal environment.

From that evening, a trial malt was made and the company has grown and grown, often in the strangest of ways. The spirits are matured in several locations, for instance, including in a mine and on an island.

Mackmyra has for some time been a key player in the production of whiskey outside the traditional whiskey-making nations, but even by its lofty standards the start of 2012 was special. After 10 years of successfully serving whiskey to its domestic market and developing a unique but exceptionally well-made Swedish version of malt whiskey, it reaped the benefits of its efforts with a stock market listing and the opening of a brand new distillery capable of quadrupling its former output.

The company, which was set up at the start of the millennium, began operating out of a converted mill and cattle shed in a rural part of Sweden, 98 miles (157 km) north of Stockholm.

Sweden has state-controlled alcohol distribution and, like all beverages with more than 3.5 percent alcohol, new Mackmyra releases have to be sold through government-owned liquor stores. Such is the distillery's reputation that lines regularly form outside shops on the day of a new malt's release, and many bottlings sell out within hours. For this reason—and in common with many New World whiskeys—only a limited amount of Mackmyra had been exported up until 2011.

Mackmyra lies west of Gävle *on the Gulf of Bothnia, a pristine coastline of pine forests and traditional villages.*

Mackmyra expands worldwide

The new facilities, officially opened at the end of December 2011, mean that Mackmyra has been able to increase production and take the next step up the ladder to worldwide success. Distribution deals have been secured across the world, including the US and the UK.

"The investment for the distillery is about 55 million SEK [$8 million]," says marketing manager Lars Lindberger. "Construction started in November 2010, so it took us just over one year to build it. We have worked hard to make it environmentally friendly by reusing energy in all possible places. We use biofuel for heating. And it is built to use gravity—we lift water, malt, and yeast only once and it will fall downward during the process. To our knowledge it is the only distillery today that uses this technique.

"We call the new area Mackmyra Whisky Village—it's a couple of miles from Mackmyra Bruk and the other distillery. In the Whisky Village, we have also built a warehouse for our customers' 30-liter [8-gallon] casks. Today there are 2,500 barrels stored in that warehouse."

MACKMYRA "BRUKSWHISKY"

The Whisky Village

Mackmyra Whisky Village is just outside Gävle, about 90 minutes from Arlanda Airport. It will allow the company to quadruple output to a staggering 317,000 gallons (1.2 million liters). "The year 2011 was great, with a lot happening," says Lindberger. "The new distillery and the Whisky Village has been the biggest thing, but also the financing for the coming years is in place. And we have started to reach out better beyond Sweden and Scandinavia. Since April 2010 our colleague Jonathan Luks has been based in New York, and you can now find our whiskey, "The 1st Edition," in 25 stores and 20 restaurants in Manhattan. We're going to work from there. We've also visited China and Taiwan four times and have been met with great interest.

"We're also working to get better coverage in markets such as France and Spain. We now have more than 50 employees, so we're getting bigger. And we're in a position to release interesting bottles. We have done limited edition bottlings under our "Special" series and very small quantities of releases such as the "Moment" series. In Sweden we are still the best-selling malt whiskey in the premium and super-premium segment." A big year, then, so what's next for Mackmyra? "Next is to fine-tune the new distillery and start producing as much as we can," says Lindberger. "It will take a while before we can sell it, of course. And during that time international expansion will be important. The response we have had so far tells us that our Swedish whiskey has a bright future."

WHISKEY'S VIKING INVENTOR?

In 2011, during the construction of the new distillery, the builders came across an old tomb just where the new road leads to the distillery. The man buried must have been a wealthy man; he was interred wearing an exclusive robe and with horses, dogs, and cats. In the grave the archaeologists also found a lot of barley. Could this be the grave of the legendary Viking Orm, who is credited in Norse circles with discovering whiskey distillation? And if so, was this the place where he mastered the art of making malt whiskey? Mackmyra's people would certainly like to think so, and that the new distillery is bringing the whiskey story back home.

MACKMYRA "THE 1ST EDITION"

TASTING NOTES

MACKMYRA "THE 1ST EDITION"

single malt, 46.1% ABV, matured in Swedish oak casks
The trademark saltiness and earthy Swedish savory smorgasbord have been toned down here, and the sweet peach, apricot, and orange fruity heart allowed to glow. Vanilla and candy suppress the peppery notes, making this an easy-drinking delight.

MACKMYRA "BRUKSWHISKY"

single malt, 41.2% ABV, matured in Swedish oak casks
Up until this release, delicate, subtle, and sophisticated weren't words that you would normally have associated with Mackmyra. This, though, is Mackmyra Lite, a delicate, subtle, and sophisticated release designed to bring in a generation of new admirers.

MACKMYRA "MOMENT" SERIES

various strengths and cask treatments
Like a rock band returning to its roots and playing the earliest hits for diehard supporters, the "Moment" series explores all sorts of weird and wonderful versions of Mackmyra, many of them a throwback to the most intense salted, peated, and juniper-soaked releases. There are a couple of sweet fruit surprises, but most are Mackmyra doing thrash metal—dark and heavy.

MACKMYRA "MOMENT MEDVIND"

ENGLAND

After more than a century without any whiskey-makers in England, there are now four at various stages of production and with varying degrees of commitment. Far and away the most advanced is St. George's distillery in Norfolk, which swung into operation in November 2006—but the oldest whiskey, beating St. George's by a year, has been produced by a partnership between a cider farm and a brewery in Cornwall.

THE ENGLISH WHISKY CO. "CHAPTER 7"

ST. GEORGE'S

OWNER The Nelstrop family
FOUNDED 2004 **CAPACITY** 55,500 gal (210,000 liters)
ADDRESS Harling Road, Roudham, Norfolk NR16 2QW
WEBSITE www.englishwhisky.co.uk

When English whiskey distiller David Fitt was asked whether he and his team could keep on producing great whiskeys, following another wave of critical acclaim for the launch of St. George's five-year-old and a new version of "Chapter 7" rum cask finish, this is what he had to say: "I don't think we are making it tough for ourselves going forward. Inevitably, we will one day make a whiskey people don't like—I'm sure of it. Not because we want to, just because you can't please all of the people all of the time, and whiskey is such a personal thing."

You suspect that if and when it happens, Fitt will be as good as his word and will let such a small setback simply wash over him. After all, the occasional wobble in what has been a meteoric rise for their distillery will hardly matter.

Sprint to success

From the outset, farmers James and Andrew Nelstrop set out to make fine whiskey, and they did so by refusing to cut corners. They were up and running quickly; it took them just 11 months to go from obtaining planning permission for a rural distillery in the depths of Norfolk in eastern England to distilling spirits.

By the end of 2006 they were making spirits on Forsyths stills using the skills of the eminent Scottish distiller Iain Henderson, whose previous distilleries included Laphroaig and The Glenlivet. Even the very first runs were good enough to put in casks. From there it has been one success after another—too much success at first, because all of the original stock went in half a day when it was bottled at three years old.

What sets St. George's apart from many other fledgling distilling businesses is that even from the earliest days, the distillery was taking a

This very English distillery, by the Thet River in rural Norfolk, draws on the Scottish whiskey-making tradition.

ENGLAND EXPECTS

St. George's is the first English distillery to bottle a whiskey for more than 100 years, but it wasn't the first to distill in the 21st century and currently there are no fewer than four English operators. In his definitive and celebrated book *The Distilleries of the United Kingdom*, published in the 19th century, Alfred Barnard wrote of several English distilleries, most of which were making whiskey to be sent north for adding to Scottish blends. The last one to be demolished was on the site where the London 2012 Olympic Stadium now stands. Plans are underway to produce whiskey in London once more, and pressure is growing on lawmakers to reform English distilling laws in order to facilitate more small operators.

Scottish blueprint and tweaking it at every opportunity. This has included even simple things such as cask storage: to avoid the health and safety issues of such a small distilling team moving casks in and out of warehouses for filling and emptying, the distillery created a system by which every cask can be accessed in place and filled and drained without moving it.

Distillery diversity

As for the whiskey itself, the distillery is going to offer a lot of diversity. Given Iain Henderson's history, you'd expect a range of peated casks, and there are—but there's more. Henderson and then his replacement, former Greene King brewer David Fitt, showed a willingness to experiment with cask type to recask whiskey, so they effectively created second-fill casks earlier than would happen naturally, and the results of this experimentation will become evident as time goes by.

According to Fitt, the widely celebrated "Chapter 7" rum cask finish is the tip of a taste iceberg. "We have a real mixture of casks in bond and I'm keeping a very close eye on some of these," says Fitt. "For example, instead of finishing whiskey in wine casks, we are actually carrying out the full maturation in these casks. The Moscatel and Sauternes casks are coming along very nicely!"

Certainly the distillery has left its options open for the future—and almost certainly it will continue to surprise and delight whiskey-drinkers in times to come.

HICKS & HEALEY

TASTING NOTES

THE ENGLISH WHISKY CO. "CHAPTER 6"
single malt, 46% ABV
Delightful lemon and bitter orange malt with fresh sweet barley, zesty fizzy vanilla and a dose of pepper to give it body and depth. Young, yes, but coming along apace. Very well made malt.

THE ENGLISH WHISKY CO. "CHAPTER 7"
single malt, 46% ABV, finished in rum casks
This is sweet rum and raisin, lime candy with a milk chocolate center, and canned fruits with evaporated milk all rolled into one. There is little trace of the youthfulness of the malt, but the whole experience is clean, sharp and refined.

THE ENGLISH WHISKY CO. "CHAPTER 11"
CASK STRENGTH
single malt, 59.7% ABV, cask strength
The first monster premier league release from St. George's, a growling, rich, full-flavored citrus, green fruit, and bitter cherry whiskey wrapped up in country bonfire and steam engine smoke. It's all totally in balance and the gooseberry and peat finale is an absolute treat.

THE ENGLISH WHISKY CO. "CHAPTER 11"
CASK STRENGTH

ADNAMS BREWERY

REGION Suffolk
WEBSITE www.adnams.co.uk

Beautifully positioned right in the center of the unspoiled Victorian seaside resort of Southwold, on the East Anglian coast, this innovative brewery has built a fine reputation for its ales and has branched out into spirits. Unusual vodkas and gins have appeared, which make a virtue of using all natural products from grain to glass. The company is also maturing malt spirits with a view to start bottling from the very end of 2013. There are three core and fascinating whiskeys maturing here: a standard single malt maturing in virgin oak; an American-style whiskey made with 60 percent wheat, 35 percent barley, and 5 percent oats; and a 100 percent rye whiskey.

HICKS & HEALEY

REGION Cornwall
WEBSITES www.staustellbrewery.co.uk;
www.thecornishcyderfarm.co.uk

Healey's distills cider into apple brandy on its family-run farm in Cornwall. At the turn of the millennium, the company went into partnership with local brewer St. Austell to produce a small amount of whiskey. The first bottling of the malt was released as a seven-year-old in 2011, making it England's oldest-ever whiskey. How widely the whiskey will be made available in the future remains to be seen, but certainly a small amount of even older stock is being held back for the future.
Hicks & Healey (single malt, 68% ABV, cask strength) *A delight—apple crumble and vanilla ice cream with some cinnamon in the mix.*

THE LAKES DISTILLERY

REGION Cumbria
WEBSITE www.lakesdistillery.com

England's newest distillery was finally given the green light in late 2011 and started producing its first spirit in the fall of 2012. Earliest bottlings, therefore, won't be available until 2015 at the earliest. There have been plans for a distillery in the Lake District for some years now and previous projects have stalled. But after overcoming understandably tough planning restrictions—the Lake District is in a conservation area—the future looks bright. The area attracts large numbers of tourists and has much in common with Scotland.

WALES

Whiskey making in Wales has faced its trials. Making alcohol was historically frowned upon due to the strength of the Temperance movement, and eventually legal whiskey-making was abandoned altogether. Many distillers crossed the Atlantic and their skills helped shape their adopted country's whiskey industry. Recent attempts to revive the Welsh whiskey industry have been dubious at best—until The Welsh Whisky Company came along, that is.

PENDERYN "PORT WOOD"

INDEPENDENT BUT UNITED

The combination of being an independent Welsh distillery and part of a growing movement in world whiskey hasn't hurt Penderyn, says distiller Gillian Macdonald. "Being the only distillery in Wales is really amazing. The Welsh people, since the launch on St. David's Day 2004, have embraced everything about Penderyn and supported the company's growth. It is really becoming an icon that Wales can be very proud of and is now exported to over 25 countries. But at the same time it's great to see more distilleries opening across the world as it adds to the ever-growing diversity in the whiskey world. The more, the merrier! I think people are interested in finding out as much information as possible and realize that you don't have to be Scottish to make a great-quality whiskey. The consumer is interested to find out about the different ways in which you can make whiskey, and this takes them all around the world."

PENDERYN

OWNER The Welsh Whisky Company	
FOUNDED 2000 **CAPACITY** 185,000 gal (700,000 liters)	
ADDRESS Penderyn, Powys CF44 9JW	
WEBSITE www.welsh-whisky.co.uk	

If you decide to distill malt whiskey, you have two fundamental choices: you can seek to emulate the tried and trusted system they use with such great effect in Scotland—or you can rip up all the books and invent a brand-new way to do it.

The latter is what they did at Penderyn. Calling on the skills of whiskey's "Mr. Fix-It," Dr. Jim Swan, and employing Dr. David Faraday—a direct relation of the scientist Michael Faraday of electricity fame—to invent a brand-new distilling system, Penderyn's management went off into uncharted territory. Former Master Distiller Gillian Macdonald—not the only female distiller, but a rarity when she was appointed—explains where the distillery stands out from the rest. "There are several points of difference," she says. "First, the start of the process—the brewing—is not done

The distillery benefits from its location in a national park close to the picturesque Brecon Beacons.

in-house but is carried out by an independent brewer to our specification. In Scottish law there is a requirement to have this on site at the distillery. Brains Brewery in Cardiff sources the malt from the UK only and uses its own strain of brewer's yeast in the fermentation process, producing a full-flavored, fruity, malted barley, which is then transported to the distillery. Then there's our Faraday Still. Penderyn has a single-pot system that is unique. It produces much higher-strength spirits than the traditional two-pot set-up. Our product cut is 92–86 percent ABV, compared to a typical Scottish product cut of 75–65 percent, and as a result produces a different style of spirit—lighter in style than the typical Scotch—retaining the fruity character of the malted barley wash."

Maturation matters

There are differences in the way the whiskey is matured at the distillery, too. American Bourbon casks are used for most of the maturation, but for the last six months the whiskey is placed in Madeira casks. Such has been the demand that after four years of maturation—a short time compared to Scotch but enough for this part of the world and not unlike many distilleries across the world—all the dumped whiskey is bottled. As a result, the flavor profile varies slightly from batch to batch and so a month and year are put on each bottle.

The distillery makes three styles of whiskey: the standard one outlined above, a sherry wood, and a peated whiskey. But again, not peated in the normal Scottish sense. "Our Penderyn "Peated" edition is in essence an unpeated peated," says Macdonald, cryptically. "We don't peat any of our malt, and the peat flavor is imparted to the whiskey via the use of ex-Scotch casks that previously contained a peated whiskey. The spirit is either fully matured in these casks or transferred into them for some time for the peat flavor to be extracted by the spirit."

The visitors' center

As Penderyn is still a relatively young distillery, its aromatic and fruity whiskeys are just starting to come into their own. The distillery, which is close to a national park in the Brecon Beacons, has a visitors' center and benefits from the big influx of tourists. "It's a wonderful setting to be in and the area attracts a large number of tourists each year. When it's too wet to climb the Beacons, we are the ideal alternative, and our visitors' center is attracting 25,000 people a year. We run a range of tours and in-depth masterclasses to cater to the range of visitors we attract," says Macdonald.

TASTING NOTES

PENDERYN "MADEIRA"
single malt, 46% ABV, finished in Madeira casks
A ballet dancer of a whiskey, with a curious liqueur-like quality, some floral, almost perfumed notes, and some complex, fruity notes that make for a unique and intriguing whiskey. Might appeal to non–whiskey fans.

PENDERYN "PEATED"
single malt, 46% ABV
This walks a tightrope between a prodding, prickly peat bouncing off vanilla, apricot, and orange fruit on the one hand, and a more comfortable, wispy, smoke and fruit partnership on the other. It falls between two stools in some ways, the peat scuzzing up the clean fruit but not assertive enough to excite smoke heads. Intriguing nevertheless.

PENDERYN "PORT WOOD"
single malt, 60.6% ABV, finished in port wood casks
Is port wood overtaking sherry as the source of quality whiskey? Certainly we're seeing some great world whiskey coming from port, and here's one of them. Rich, full, winey, tasteful, complex, and unusual, this is Penderyn at its best. Has been bottled at cask strength—and the Scotch Malt Whisky Society had a cask—and it's even better.

PENDERYN "PEATED"

PENDERYN "MADEIRA"

SPAIN

While Spain has long been a whiskey drinking country, until 2011 it had only one distillery of its own—but it's an amazing one. Destilerías y Crianza is owned by Beam Global and is a one-stop whiskey shop.

DYC

OWNER Beam Global	
FOUNDED 1958 **CAPACITY** Not given	
ADDRESS Palazuelos de Eresma, Segovia, Castile and León	
WEBSITE www.dyc.es	

Travel about an hour north of Madrid and you find yourself in the historic town of Segovia, a pretty old town dominated by a stunning Roman aqueduct. You don't associate Spain with making whiskey, but in winter it's bitterly cold here, with snow caps on the mountains, and whiskey doesn't seem so far away. Indeed, it's not.

For more than 50 years, Destilerías y Crianza del Whisky—DYC—has made whiskey close by. For many of those years the distillery was something of a secret, but since it passed its 50th anniversary it has become part of the Segovian tourist trail—and boy, does it deserve to be.

DYC is a big distillery and part of the Beam Global empire. Visit—it has excellent tours and tastings—and you'll find it hard not to be impressed by the mix of Spanish architecture and whiskey distillery. They make a range of spirits here, including the respected premium gin Larios; there are pot stills for malt production and column stills for grain whiskey production; and they blend, bottle, and make up gift packs on site. It's some operation.

The evolution of DYC

DYC founder Don Nicomedes García had been involved in the spirits business since 1919 when he took over the running of his father's small distillery at the tender age of 18. Yet it wasn't until 1958, following several trips to Scotland to learn the secrets of Scotch whiskey-making, that he established the DYC plant, which began distilling the following year and bottling in 1963.

DYC is an evolving distillery. For many years it was content to serve Spanish blended whiskey to one of the world's biggest on-premise whiskey-drinking markets. It also produced what it called a pure malt, which was made up with malt from the distillery mixed with supplies of "malt allsorts" from Beam, including Ardmore and Laphroaig. But the story starts to get interesting with the launch of single malts—first an eight-year-old, then a 50th-anniversary bottling, and then a 10-year-old, each one better than the last.

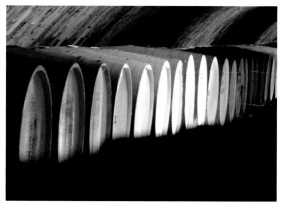

Maturation takes place *in American oak barrels, and the spirits are primarily produced for the domestic market.*

Segovia is already renowned for its fine dining and for the quality of the wines produced in the region. Now it is also seeking to place whiskey and the DYC distillery at the heart of its gastronomic offering, a move that augurs well for the future.

"We are encouraging people to ask for 'a Segovian' when they order their whiskey," says the local tourist board. "We have something to be proud of but we have never showed it off properly. That's changing now."

TASTING NOTES

DYC "PURE MALT"
blend, 40% ABV, mix of single malts from DYC and various Scottish distilleries
Tastes like a perfectly inoffensive blended whiskey. On the plus side, it's smooth, fruity, and easy-drinking; on the negative, it's too shy, doesn't want to offend, and in trying to be all things to all people, won't excite or over-delight anyone.

DYC 8-YEAR-OLD
aged blend, 40% ABV, mix of various grains
That's better—a step in the right direction. A Duran Duran of a whiskey; you can't help but admire how well it's put together, it hits the right sweet spots and is fruity in a good way, but it never really rocks out. Accept it as a light, fluffy, fun whiskey and it won't let you down.

DYC 10-YEAR-OLD "COLECCIÓN BARRICAS"
single malt, 40% ABV, matured in ex-Bourbon casks
A welcome addition of pepper spice and tannin wrapped around the light vanilla, orange, and yellow fruit heart of this malt makes this the best DYC single malt so far, and hints of great things to come. Still light, candy coated, and easy-drinking but with more body and a pleasant finish.

DYC 10-YEAR-OLD "COLECCIÓN BARRICAS"

FRANCE

France is so well known for its wines, Champagne, and Cognac, it is often overlooked that the country offers greater diversity of alcohol production, and that in the north the tradition is of apple and grain, not grape. While Normandy makes fabulous cider and Calvados, Brittany has a Celtic heart where beer and whiskey fit in easily. There is no recognizable Breton style but the region's distilleries are making increasingly fine whiskey.

DISTILLERIE DES MENHIRS

OWNER Guy Le Lay

FOUNDED 1986 **CAPACITY** 6,600 gal (25,000 liters)

ADDRESS 7 Hent Saint Philibert, Pont Menhir, 29700 Plomelin, Brittany **WEBSITE** www.distillerie.fr

Brittany is noted for its apples and the drinks made from them—Pommeau, cider, *gwenaval* (brandy), and *lambig* (cider brandy)—and it was these that Guy Le Lay focused on before deciding to turn his hand to whiskey. Before putting his plan into practice, he thought about it very carefully indeed, his main aim being to make sure that he applied the same high standards as the Scotch producers to the business of whiskey distillation. Rather than use his existing apple distillery, therefore, he invested in a separate operation.

Distillerie des Menhirs—the name referring to the standing stones that are one of the local attractions in this rugged and remote part of the world—was built in 1998. To produce spirits with a unique flavor, Le Lay has used not malted barley but local buckwheat, known as *blé noir* in French and *eddu* in Breton. It's a moot point as to whether buckwheat is actually a grain or not, and therefore whether the Eddu range actually constitutes whiskey, but there can be no doubt that the distillery is making unusual and impressive spirits.

TASTING NOTES

EDDU "SILVER"
single malt, 40% ABV
Full-bodied and rich in flavor, this is a single malt whiskey with floral and fruity notes, flavors of cloves, cinnamon, and nutmeg, and a caramel note toward the end.

EDDU "GOLD"
single malt, 43% ABV
A big, proud whiskey, with everything turned up. Fresh spring flavors, velvety and oily peach and apricot, and dancing spice and oak. Some vanilla, too.

EDDU "GREY ROCK"
blend, 40% ABV, mix of 30% Eddu whiskey and 70% grain
The weakest of the three bottlings but pleasant, drinkable, and inoffensive, with orange, peach, and some sharper apple notes.

DISTILLERIE WARENGHEM

OWNER Warenghem

FOUNDED 1900 **CAPACITY** Not given

ADDRESS Route de Guingamp, 22300 Lannion, Brittany

WEBSITE www.whisky-breton.com

In common with many other distilleries in Europe, Distillerie Warenghem was set up to make fruit liqueurs and to distill the abundant local apple crop. However, like Distillerie des Menhirs, it has adapted the Breton region's tradition of making cider brandy and brandy and embarked on the production of whiskey.

The distillery has a history stretching back well over 100 years but focused its attention on whiskey only at the turn of the millennium. Its main whiskey is called Armorik, and in addition to a standard version the distillery has experimented with double maturation using different casks and with sherry finishes. There is also a blended whiskey called "Whisky Breton," which is pleasant, rounded, and easy-drinking.

Although Brittany now boasts a number of whiskey distilleries, it has yet to develop any communal style, and of the three distilleries in this area (see next page for Glann ar Mor), Distillerie Warenghem is the one with a taste profile closest to the whiskeys of Scotland.

TASTING NOTES

ARMORIK "CLASSIC"
single malt, 46% ABV, non-chill-filtered, matured in a variety of oak casks
Bottled young—perhaps at only five years old—and using American and Breton oak casks, this is a whiskey on the move, its sappy notes retreating and being replaced with zippy, fizzy barley and apple fruit and a delightful wave of tangy spice and vanilla, salt, and pepper notes.

ARMORIK "SHERRY FINISH"
single malt, 42% ABV, aged in Bourbon casks and finished in ex-sherry casks
The green fruit, salt and pepper, and vanilla remain but the sherry adds a somewhat clumsy red berry and orange fruit that totters on the edge but just about gets away with it. The subtler original is preferred.

ARMORIK "ÉDITION ORIGINALE"

EDDU "SILVER"

GLANN AR MOR

OWNER Jean Donnay

FOUNDED 2004 **CAPACITY** Not given

ADDRESS 2, allée des Embruns, 22610 Larmor-Pleubian

WEBSITE www.glannarmor.com

The winemakers of France have done an outstanding job—so much so that when we talk of food and drink in France, we inevitably think of wine, wine, and wine; perhaps Cognac, possibly Calvados. It's far less likely that beer, cider, and whiskey will crop up. Yet all three of them have a place in the north of the country, and in Brittany, whiskey is very much part of the culture. The climate is ideal for grain production, and therefore for beer- and whiskey-making, and Brittany boasts three major distilleries—Distillerie Warenghem, Distillerie des Menhirs, and Glann ar Mor. The last of those is owned by the dedicated whiskey-maker Jean Donnay, who has produced two very different malts—a sweet and fruity delight under the name "Glann ar Mor," and a growling, feisty, peaty one called "Kornog." The distillery itself occupies a picturesque, rugged site close to the sea.

Expansion and experiment

Glann ar Mor is a work in progress, but each year the standard of the malt gets better, and in 2012 expansion work on the original distillery built in 2008 was completed. But, says Donnay, there's a long way to go, and progress is slower than he might have liked. "We still have to bottle at just over three years old, which fortunately is not a problem with the unusually favorable maturation conditions we enjoy," he says. "But I'm waiting impatiently for the time when our maturing stock will allow us to bottle at an older age. Every year we produce a little more than the year before, but we're still a long way from working at the distillery's full capacity.

"At the moment my priority is consistency, which certainly isn't the easiest thing with a new distillery, but I am quite happy with the consistency we have now reached with our bottlings. Delivering more exotic expressions is very easy, but that is not a priority and it will come later when we will have enough stock to afford it. Consistency means you have to progress with only small adjustments at a time. Doing so protects you from getting it wrong, but on the other hand the price you pay is that your learning curve is steeper than you might like. I keep asking myself a lot of questions such as, 'What would happen if I were doing this like this instead of like that?'

"I am finally trying a few of those things. Nothing really new or unusual in the traditional process of whiskey-making, as there are simply so many small things which can make a significant difference. And naturally, only time will really tell how relevant or not it is."

Influence from Scotland

While the distillers in the region communicate with each other, Donnay does not believe a distinctive Breton style is developing. "With only three Breton distilleries offering whiskeys, grouped in a small territory, we somehow manage to have a very wide variety of whiskey styles," he says.

"I don't make it a secret that my reference is Scotland. That does not mean I am trying to emulate whiskeys from Scotland. There are quite a few things I do in my distillery in the same way as they do it in Scotland, but there are also quite a few things I do very much my own way. Again, small changes can bring significant variations."

The Celtic personality

Whatever the future holds, Donnay believes that what he is producing is part of Breton, rather than French, whiskey. "To me, Glann ar Mor is, before anything else, a Breton and Celtic distillery, and the fact that it is located in France comes second to that. Only time will tell, but I think Brittany has what it takes to eventually become a whiskey force. Whiskey is a Celtic drink, part of a distinctive culture with distinctive traditions, as well as being related to geographical environment and climate.

"Brittany is not a land of wine, but a land of grains. When you have grains and no wine, you produce beer, and when you produce beer, you distill it and you make whiskey. Brittany has a long tradition of beer-making, and it was producing whiskey back to the middle of the 19th century at least, although it is difficult to say to what extent.

"As a drink, whiskey has to do with the personality of the people and of the land, and in this area Brittany has a lot to share with its Celtic cousins from Scotland and Ireland."

TASTING NOTES

GLANN AR MOR
single malt, 46% ABV
Very young, but this is a sweet and light delight, summer in a glass, with soft canned pears, fluffy apples, sweet grapes, and berry fruits. It's a simple and straightforward malt, but is pretty much blemish-free and is bursting with fresh, fruity promise.

KORNOG "TAOUARC'H KENTAÑ"
single malt, 46% ABV
If you doubt that France can produce world-class whiskey, you need to taste this. It's an oily, peaty, Islay-like delight, with bitter lemon and dark chocolate in the mix and the finest balance of flavors imaginable. There's not a weakness here, and the long peaty tail is outstanding.

CELTIC CONNECTIONS

When Jean Donnay declares Glann ar Mor a "Celtic distillery," he is drawing on a centuries-old affinity between Bretons and the Celtic peoples of Britain—the Scots, Welsh, and Cornish—who have long felt themselves nations apart from their English and French "partners." Celts fleeing the Anglo-Saxon invasion of Britain set off from the Cornish peninsula and settled in Brittany (hence the name), initiating a long shared history of language, culture, and trade. In later centuries, whiskey may well have figured among the goods shipped across the Channel, so it's fitting that Brittany once more boasts whiskey distilleries, while in Cornwall, Hicks & Healey are also producing a single malt.

GLANN AR MOR

KORNOG "TAOUARC'H EILVET 09"

BELGIUM

Belgium is well known for its beer and, to some degree, for its genever. But the difference between genever and malt whiskey is a fine one, and beer is the basis for whiskey. Belgium boasts three distilleries, of which the one enjoying widest distribution is The Belgian Owl.

THE BELGIAN OWL

OWNER Etienne Bouillon
FOUNDED 2004 **CAPACITY** Not given
ADDRESS Rue Sainte-Anne 94, 4460 Grâce-Hollogne
WEBSITE www.belgianwhisky.com

Few rapid-fire distillery visits immerse you so fully in the local culture as a trip to The Belgian Owl. Arriving by train, you alight in the center of Liège, a pretty, historic city, positioned at a key meeting point in the heart of Europe, which has made it both a cultural melting pot and a crossroads for an array of cultures. The region has been fought over repeatedly during the centuries, and the city has witnessed countless battles and hosted any number of peace ententes and victory celebrations, which it has celebrated with a hedonistic joy. As a result, Liège is a city that knows how to party, and food and drink are woven into the fabric of the local community. That a whiskey-maker should have hung out his shingle here should come as no surprise.

The distillery itself further reflects the community that created it. It operates across three sites—one rural, one suburban, and one in an industrial city. It's a unique operation that has developed by default and isn't exactly as whiskey-maker Etienne Bouillon would have it. "It has long been my intention to have the whiskey-making all done in one place, and I hope that will happen soon, but it has taken longer than I would have liked," he says.

A small-scale operation

Bouillon is very serious about his whiskey. He learned his skills partially from the legendary and highly respected Jim McEwan, the whiskey-maker at Bruichladdich on Islay in Scotland. McEwan still pops over occasionally, and provides comments on each bottling.

You can see why the two get along. Bouillon is an adherent of the concept of terroir, and his barley is grown on the nearby farm of one of his investors. Given the chance, he can explain the constitution of the soil here, and why it's ideal for growing barley—and make a convincing argument for why this particular barley has a bearing on the finished whiskey. Standing on the edge of the farm, looking across the fields of barley, reinforces the small scale of the whole operation.

WHAT'S IN A NAME?

The Belgian Owl's ultra-stylish packaging, and its distinctive logo showing an owl perched on the bare branch of a tree, suggest that Etienne Bouillon knows a thing or two about marketing. The name remains something of a curiosity, deriving from an old folk tale about an owl enchanter who turned a dirty little stream into the purest water and subsequently taught the local populace how to create a pure single malt. But why is the name English? It all comes down to the divisions within Belgium. "If I used a French name it would offend the Flemish, if I used a Flemish name it would offend the Walloons. So I went for a name that would equally offend everyone," says Bouillon, smiling.

THE BELGIAN OWL "BELGIAN SINGLE MALT"

The charming, historic city *of Liège, on the Meuse River, has always been a hotbed of culture.*

The malt is sent away for malting and then fermented at the farm before being transported to a suburban building where the distillery is housed. Actually, "distillery" is a little too grandiose. The building is more of a glorified garage and is decorated with bottle samples, packaging, posters, and newspaper articles about The Belgian Owl. The still itself is a historical curiosity, an oversized copper kettle on a wooden cart with wheels. "It's French," Bouillon explains. "The owners of the vineyards would have rented it and its owner would have moved it around the countryside to distill grape wine for brandy."

Everything about the operation is small-batch and handcrafted, and Bouillon is immensely proud of it. "It's a small operation, but I can put my time into ensuring that the quality of the spirits is as good as it could be. I work very hard at it," he says.

A strong, sweet whiskey

Once distilled, the whiskey is transferred to a cask, and when the cask is full—which doesn't happen in one fill—it is transferred to the most incongruous of maturation warehouses. Close to a busy road and on the edge of one of those soulless and faceless industrial parks you find in every city is a unit normally used for storing factory overstock. It's a warm, brightly lit site and in four years, the casks stored here will go up in strength during maturation—well up. It's unusual to have cask-strength whiskeys pushing well above 70 percent ABV but they manage it at The Belgian Owl.

Bouillon matures the whiskey in Bourbon casks, and so far he has remained firmly with a light, vanilla-y dessert whiskey, which is rich in sweet apple and pear notes.

The small nature of the distillery and the increasing popularity of the whiskey has hindered further expansion, but the malt has started to appear in stores as far away as Canada. For Bouillon, the final piece of the jigsaw puzzle will be when the whole operation can be transferred to the farm and production can be stepped up. "We know exactly what we need to do and the day is coming when we will do it, but all the pieces have to fall into place," he says. Without doubt, The Belgian Owl is a whiskey worth waiting for.

TASTING NOTES

THE BELGIAN OWL "BELGIAN SINGLE MALT"
single malt, 46% ABV, non-chill-filtered
At four years old, this whiskey is creamy, banana-flavored, and packed with dessert fruits, including sweet apples and pears in syrup. What spice there is, trims off any slight flabbiness there may be from the relative youthfulness of the malt. Honey, toffee, and dough ball notes add to the overall exquisite delights.

THE BELGIAN OWL "BELGIAN SINGLE MALT" CASK STRENGTH
single malt, 74.1% ABV, cask strength, non-chill-filtered
Approach this carefully—there's a wall of alcohol between you and the flavors contained therein. When it does tip over, it does so with a quite literally breathtaking intensity. It needs water, but take care here, too, because it sips better well above a standard strength. Marzipan, sweet citrus, bananas, and canned pears are all in attendance.

THE NETHERLANDS

With a long history of beer-making, one might expect the Netherlands to have a history of whiskey, too. But the grain spirits made here, often matured in oak barrels, have tended to be used for genever, the source of gin. The country has an enthusiastic whiskey drinking community, however, and hosts several whiskey shows, and the malts made by Zuidam are worthy of these Dutch diehards.

ZUIDAM

OWNER The Zuidam family	
FOUNDED 1975 **CAPACITY** 13,000 gal (50,000 liters)	
ADDRESS Smederijstraat 5, 5111 PT Baarle Nassau	
WEBSITE www.zuidam.eu	

One of the recurring themes when talking of emerging world distilleries is the propensity to bottle whiskey when it is too young in a bid to generate cash flow. At Zuidam, this isn't an issue. The distillery has no fewer than 600 product lines and has been producing spirits for more than 35 years. When it came to making whiskey, the mantra was simple: good things come to those who wait.

Order out of chaos
The Zuidam distillery isn't much to look at; it appears like any other industrial warehouse unit. But enter the building and you find yourself in an Aladdin's cave of pot and column stills, and large glass extracting vessels containing everything from cinnamon and cocoa to roses and vanilla pods for the distillery's naturally flavored liqueurs. There are boxes of fruit, and teams of workers cutting oranges and lemons, piling up boxes of black currants, or squeezing casks in between distilling equipment.

"It is an organizational nightmare," admits Managing Director Patrick Zuidam, "because there are so many different product lines here and each has to fit into the schedule."

Zuidam is very much a family firm. Set up by Patrick's father, Fred, and with mother, Hélène, still involved with what is outstanding design and packaging, Patrick runs the business and genial brother Gilbert heads up sales. Spend any time with Patrick and it becomes obvious that he is, in the nicest possible way, a distilling geek. His distillery allows him to experiment with drinks such as sherry-aged and five-grain genever.

"I use corn, malted barley, wheat, rye, and spelt," he says. "Spelt is an ancient form of wheat and I'd like to say it adds something special, but the truth is it's pretty useless. I use it because I wanted five grains." Such disarming directness coupled with confidence and humor make Patrick an engaging and formidable host. He is equally frank about the way his Millstone malt whiskey range is made with malted barley produced at local windmills.

"It might seem like a gimmick, yet the truth is that when I took over here I wanted to introduce a new genever but there was absolutely no money—so I asked a local miller if he would do it cheaply and he said he would do it free in return for a bottle of genever. We now use seven local windmills and it's a big job because you can't drive a truck to the windmill as it's up a hill. Every bag of barley must be carried up and back again.

"The millers say that making the grist this way without heat makes for an unscorched and better product. To be honest, though, I don't believe it." Patrick might be a bit cynical about the milling process, but the fact that the distillery pays such attention to detail, reflected elsewhere in the distillery process, is indicative of the high standard it sets itself. It has taken to whiskey making with the same determination to be the very best. "In Holland, there are not many people doing what we do," says Patrick. "We take our whiskey very seriously."

Zuidam makes peated and unpeated malt whiskey matured in virgin American oak casks as well as small 66-gallon (250-liter) sherry casks. The distillery also makes an impressive rye whiskey.

TASTING NOTES

MILLSTONE SINGLE MALT
single malt, 45% ABV
Young by Scottish standards, the maturation conditions help this punch above its weight. Smooth, richly fruity, and with peach and apricot in the mix, this is a tasty malt with no jagged edges and a pleasant vanilla finish.

MILLSTONE "PEATED"
single malt, 40% ABV
The peat isn't overly dominant, complementing the fruit, toffee, and vanilla of the standard bottling. Nor does it linger too long in the finish.

DUTCH RYE
single malt rye whiskey, 40% ABV
This has improved significantly in recent years and now the rye is an assertive senior partner in a whiskey that boasts aniseed, licorice, cherry, and dark chocolate as well as some citrus fruit in the mix.

DUTCH RYE

THE CHALLENGE OF RYE

Rye is notoriously difficult to malt, and doesn't convert sugars to alcohols without a fight, either. Most rye whiskey is made with a proportion of malted barley to help the conversion process. You can make 100 percent malted rye whiskey, but be prepared for a struggle. Patrick Zuidam explains, "I really like the taste of the rye whiskey, but it is a hard grain to distill. The mash gets thick like wallpaper paste and has the same oily texture. If it ferments too quickly, big bubbles of carbon dioxide explode, sending thick substance all over the place that you have to wade through. It takes some cleaning up."

MILLSTONE SINGLE MALT

MILLSTONE "PEATED"

GERMANY

The production of malt whiskey in Germany began at Robert Fleischmann's Blaue Maus distillery in 1983. In the 21st century the number of whiskey-makers has increased rapidly. By 2012 more than 50 distillers had produced a whiskey at least three years old or were about to release their first batch of liquid gold. The fashion for whiskey is certainly growing in Germany.

"BLAUE MAUS" SINGLE CASK MALT WHISKY

"GRÜNER HUND" SINGLE CASK MALT WHISKY

BLAUE MAUS

OWNER Robert Fleischmann
FOUNDED 1978 **CAPACITY** Not given
ADDRESS Bamberger Strasse 2, 91330 Eggolsheim, Frankonia, Bavaria
WEBSITE www.fleischmann-whisky.de

When you talk to Robert Fleischmann about whiskey, his eyes light up as he embarks on stories about distilling, the German navy, and the Scotch Whisky Association—the stories of a man driven by a challenge and by the idea of making whiskey in Frankonia, a region of northern Bavaria.

His small distillery was established in 1978, starting with fruit brandies, like most German distilleries. Fascinated by the story of Racke Rauchzart, a German whiskey blend founded in 1959, Fleischmann decided to make whiskey himself. But it took some help to get his fledgling project underway, and from a source you would not expect: he was encouraged and inspired by his local customs and excise officer, who later became a close friend of the family.

The production of his pure malt started on February 15, 1983. His first whiskey was called "Piratenwhisky" ("Pirate Whiskey") and, as he says today, "it had room for improvement." So he kept developing his capabilities and stock, and today he produces several different malt whiskeys, most of them single cask. Fleischmann purchases his malted barley from local maltsters and the oak casks for maturation are also obtained locally.

The "Glen Mouse" controversy

When Fleischmann started his whiskey-making journey, he never expected to attract as much attention as he received in 1998, when the Scotch Whisky Association forced him to change the name of one of his whiskies: "Glen Mouse" would be too close to some well-established Scotch whiskies and the term "Glen" was anyway reserved for Scottish whiskey only. He was also forced to change his labels several times as the ship on "Glen Blue," another early whiskey, was found to be too close to that on the famous Cutty Sark whiskey blend. Fleischmann was beset by many troubles, but as a true resilient

Frankonian dedicated to his passion, he kept on distilling, and survived to tell the tale.

He had served in the navy for many years and never lost his attachment to the sea, so names such as "Spinnaker," "Grüner Hund," and "Old Fahr," which are related to sailing and the navy, replaced the ones under dispute. Today he still produces whiskey in his small distillery, now supported by his daughter and other members of his family. He doesn't show a public face very often, but the whiskeys are surely a true German original and an iconic symbol of the beginning of whiskey making in Germany.

TASTING NOTES

"BLAUE MAUS" SINGLE CASK MALT WHISKY
single malt, 40% ABV, single cask, matured in German oak casks
Light amber color and nose primarily of nougat crème with some malty notes to finish. On the palate the whiskey is very creamy, almost buttery, and suddenly reveals a nutty flavor. This lingers on in the long creaminess of the finish.

"SPINNAKER" SINGLE CASK MALT WHISKY
single malt, 40% ABV, single cask, matured in German oak casks
Light amber in color, almost like dark straw. On the nose some citrus notes and lots of dryness are dominant. The palate shows a very sweet maltiness, again with some citrus notes, and is slightly bitter. This continues in the finish, which is dry and surprisingly very short.

"GRÜNER HUND" SINGLE CASK MALT WHISKY
single malt, 40% ABV, single cask, matured in German oak casks
Much darker amber in color and with more woodiness on the palate, with a long-lasting dryness, suddenly showing notes of pepper and bitter chocolate. The finish turns to black pepper and malt. It needs water to take away some of the dryness and woody notes and give more room for the spiciness.

"OLD FAHR" SINGLE CASK MALT WHISKY
single malt, 40% ABV, single cask
Dark amber color and a nose of bitter chocolate with heavy alcohol. The palate is astonishingly mild, opening up to nuttiness and some medium bitterness, which continues to the finish. Chocolate notes complete the very pleasant medium-long finish.

BOSCH "GELBER FELS" SINGLE GRAIN WHISKY

BOSCH "JR" SCHWÄBISCHER WHISKY

BOSCH

OWNER Andreas Bosch

FOUNDED 1948 **CAPACITY** Not given

ADDRESS Kirchheimer Strasse 43, 73252
Lenningen-Unterlenningen, Schwaben

WEBSITE www.bosch-edelbrand.de

The distillery owned by Andreas Bosch was founded by his grandfather, Johannes Renz, after whom its principal offering, "JR," is named. Over the last few years many distilleries in the region of Swabia that were originally dedicated to fruit brandy have turned to making whiskey instead, and for some it has become an important product. Once a year the distillers gather together and showcase their products at a "Schwäbischer Whisky Tag" (Whiskey Day) where everyone can enjoy the variety of whiskies available.

Andreas Bosch learned how to distill from his father and grandfather while he was a little boy, watching them at work. Hearing them deciding about head and tails and making assessments of taste was so fascinating to him that when he grew up, he became a distiller himself. Today he's in charge of the family business and controls the distillation with the same passion as his forebears.

The Bosch portfolio

Locally grown spelt is used as the main ingredient, but a pure wheat whiskey is also part of his portfolio. To increase the flavor profile, Bosch prefers to add different malts to the mash—spelt, barley, and rye—but doesn't give details of the proportions. For each double distillation he uses 264 gallons (1,000 liters) to start with. How much alcohol for maturation he receives also remains a secret between him and his customs officer.

There are three expressions offered at present, all matured in Limousin oak casks from France, as Bosch believes the quality and porosity of these casks adds the final touch of sweetness and balance to his whiskeys.

TASTING NOTES

BOSCH "JR" SCHWÄBISCHER WHISKY
spelt whiskey, 40% ABV, matured in Limousin oak
Apricot on the nose, followed by prunes, a hint of spice, and some light smokiness. On the palate, caramel, honey, and a hint of woodiness for astringency. The medium finish starts sweet, ending with intense woodiness.

BOSCH "GELBER FELS" SINGLE GRAIN WHISKY
single wheat malt, 40% ABV, matured in Limousin oak
Smokiness on the nose, followed by a rich fruitiness of apples and pears plus some vanilla. On the palate sweetness is dominant and caramel comes toward the end. The finish is again long and surprisingly mild.

SLYRS

OWNER SLYRS Destillerie GmbH & Company KG
FOUNDED 1999 **CAPACITY** Not given
ADDRESS Bayrischzeller Strasse 13,
83727 Schliersee/Ortsteil Neuhaus
WEBSITE www.slyrs.de

It was in 1998 that the idea of making the first malt whiskey in southern Bavaria dawned on Florian Stetter, who until that point had been engaged in brewing beer and distilling fruit brandies. With a skilled brewer's understanding of the relationship between hop and malt mashes, and the benefit of pure spring water from the Bavarian mountains, Stetter was well placed to fulfill his dream. After a visit to Scotland to learn the tricks of the Scotch malt whiskey trade, he started producing his first whiskey in 1999, using the stills formerly employed for fruit brandy and obtaining casks from local suppliers. Maturation took place in the clean fresh air in the town of Schliersee, known for its fine climate and panoramic views of the Alps.

The first distillate was released as a three-year-old whiskey in 2002 and received attention in Germany as a real curiosity. Surprising everyone, the whiskey took off and demand for it grew immediately; the new vintage expressions were released in early May each year, and had usually sold out by the end of the month. The distillery rapidly became famous and expansion was an obvious decision, but as it could not be done in the original buildings, a new distillery was constructed a short distance down the road and opened in 2007. Modern pot still distillation equipment was put in place for the double distillation and capacity was increased dramatically—a huge initial investment and a long-term high-risk one, given the increasing number of new whiskey distillers arriving on the German market since Stetter first turned his whiskey-making ambition to reality.

Expansion under way

When in 2007 Head Distiller Hans Kemenater started the first double distillation and the first drops of new-make spirit ran off the still, it was a tense moment for those who came to see the inauguration of the new distillery. But all went well; the new make was light, with a hint of smoke derived from the smoked barley supplied by a famous maltster in Bamberg, and the fruitiness that was already present in the fresh distillate in the old distilling plant remained.

Today, all Slyrs whiskey is produced in the new distillery, where mashing and fermenting is done in stainless steel vats opposite the two new copper pot stills. A very slow double distillation helps to retain the flavor profile from the Bavarian wood-smoked barley malt, while maturation takes place in a newly built warehouse right behind the distillery complex. Fresh white oak casks from the Ozark Mountains in the US, toasted as well as charred, are used for three years only to produce the current vintage expressions, which are released every year. After their first use the casks are refilled and are now in stock waiting to mature for a longer period; the annual angel's share is currently 4 percent on average at present. There are plans to release a 12-year-old expression in 2014.

RARITAS DIABOLI (2010 EDITION)

RARITAS DIABOLI (2008 EDITION)

One of the modern copper pot stills *installed at the new distillery, which first fired in 2007.*

TASTING NOTES

SLYRS 3-YEAR-OLD (2011 EDITION)
single malt, 43% ABV, matured in new American white oak barrels
Vanilla is the most dominant impression on the nose, followed by honey and citrus. On the palate the vanilla lingers on, followed by caramel, a light sweetness, and finally a spicy finish. The overall finish is medium long with lots of dry caramel.

RARITAS DIABOLI (2010 EDITION)
blend, 55% ABV, cask strength, non-chill-filtered
Raisins, dried fruits, a hint of smoke, licorice, and tobacco followed by dark chocolate are the main aromas in this dark mahogany-colored whiskey.

RARITAS DIABOLI

Slyrs also bottles Raritas Diaboli, a unique blended whiskey that includes some Slyrs whiskey in the mix, created by Jürgen Deibel and Hans Kemenater. Each year cask strength varies and the blend is characterized by special touches: the 2008 vintage could be described as sweet as an angel but devilish in the finish as soon as you add some drops of water, while 2009 is more heavily peated. There will not be a vintage every year, as Deibel wants to blend a whiskey only when he finds the right casks and when his style of blending and the quality of the available whiskeys are a match.

SLYRS 3-YEAR-OLD (2007 EDITION)

SLYRS 3-YEAR-OLD (2008 EDITION)

AUSTRIA

Inspired by the popularity of Scotch and their experience in producing high-quality fruit brandies, Austrian distillers have entered into whiskey production with gusto. In 1998, Johann Haider and Hans Reisetbauer were the first to make their mark, and today not only distillers but also brewers in increasing numbers have started to distill "whiskey made in Austria."

REISETBAUER

OWNER Hans and Julia Reisetbauer	
FOUNDED 1995 **CAPACITY** 2,600 gal (10,000 liters)	
ADDRESS Zum Kirchdorfergut 1, A-4062 Kirchberg-Thening	
WEBSITE www.reisetbauer.at	

He is a real character, Hans Reisetbauer, fanatically driven by the quest for quality and for creating new and exciting products. Yet when he began distilling fruit brandies in 1994, he did not foresee that in 1998 he would become Austria's first-ever whiskey producer.

The distillery owned by Reisetbauer and his wife, Julia, is located in Axberg, between Linz and Vienna. Reisetbauer's dedication to the quality of his whiskey starts with his own barley, grown in the region. The unsmoked barley is malted by a nearby maltster and later, after milling, is mashed at a constant 149°F (65°C) to carefully control the transfer from starch to sugar. Fermentation lasts for 70 hours to allow for full flavor development and the double distillation is carried out in copper pot stills that have been modified several times by Reisetbauer to achieve the full, rich aromas he wants his whiskey to have.

The distillate is given its final rounding by maturation in ex-wine casks formerly used for storing Chardonnay and Trockenbeerenauslese, a wine made from selected grapes left to dry on the vine at the end of the season, giving the whiskey a truly individual flavor. The distillate goes in at 71 percent ABV, which allows for a fast extraction of cask flavors.

TASTING NOTES

REISETBAUER 7-YEAR-OLD
single malt, 43% ABV, matured in ex-wine casks
Some winey notes and maltiness on the nose but no big expression of sweetness or wine. This changes on the palate, when suddenly honey, wine, and dark chocolatey flavors blend harmoniously. Together with dark fruits and nuts, it makes its way to a long finish of fruitcake.

REISETBAUER 12-YEAR-OLD
single malt, 48% ABV, matured in ex-wine casks
Velvety and soft on the nose. Almost oily on the palate, with maltiness, hazelnuts, and roasted aromas. Some chocolate notes and lingering spice in the very long finish.

REISETBAUER 7-YEAR-OLD

REISETBAUER 12-YEAR-OLD

ROGGENHOF

OWNER Johann and Monika Haider
FOUNDED 1995 **CAPACITY** 7,900 gal (30,000 liters)
ADDRESS Roggenreith 3, 3664 Roggenreith
WEBSITE www.roggenhof.at

Johann Haider and his wife Monika established their distillery in Roggenreith, a little village in the Austrian region of Waldviertel, back in 1995. Today it's one of the most picturesque distilleries in Austria, with both a museum and "Fire and Water Garden" for visitors to enjoy.

Almost 80 tons of grain go into producing the whiskey each year. Rye is mostly used for the five whiskeys in the range, apart from one single malt based on barley malt exclusively, because it is the main grain crop of this region of Austria; in fact, the name "Roggenhof" means "rye farm." The distillery hosts two high-capacity copper spirit stills from Germany and warehousing takes place on site, where the newly distilled spirit matures in whiskey cellars in which a water well ensures the necessary humidity to reduce evaporation.

Maturation matters

At Haider's distillery, maturation barrels are used a maximum of three times. The first-fill barrels are matured for only three years as the oak already gives a lot of character to the whiskey, while a second fill can last much longer and usually reaches its peak after six years of maturation. Before using the barrels for a third time, Haider prefers to take them apart so that each stave can be charred and planed, after which these barrels can then be used to store whiskey for 12–18 years. All his whiskeys, under the name Waldviertler, are also offered at cask strength.

TASTING NOTES

WALDVIERTLER J.H. "ORIGINAL RYE-WHISKY"
rye whiskey, 41% ABV, matured in Austrian oak casks
Made from 60% rye and 40% malted barley, with a taste harmoniously balanced by the two grain varieties. Maturation in Manhartsberger summer oak infuses the whiskey with a gentle vanilla flavor.

WALDVIERTLER J.H. "SPECIAL RYE MALT—NOUGAT"
pure rye malt, 41% ABV, matured in Austrian oak casks
The malt is roasted to a darker shade that gives the whiskey an intense malty taste with a touch of chocolate and nougat. A minimum of three years of maturation takes place in Manhartsberger summer oak barrels.

WALDVIERTLER J.H. "SINGLE MALT"
single malt, 41% ABV, matured in Austrian oak casks
The palate first recognizes a light, crisp, malty, caramel flavor that dominates the whiskey to the finish. Maturation takes place in Manhartsberger summer oak for at least three years.

WALDVIERTLER J.H. "SPECIAL SINGLE MALT—KARAMELL"
single malt, 41% ABV, matured in Austrian oak casks
Made from 100% barley roasted and malted to a dark shade, giving a taste that's smoky and dry, with an intense flavor of caramel. Manhartsberger summer oak maturation for three years provides balance.

WALDVIERTLER J.H. "SPECIAL RYE MALT—PEATED"
pure rye malt, 46% ABV, matured in ex-wine casks
This limited-edition pure rye whiskey is produced from 100% dark, peat-roasted rye malt, and maturation is carried out in used wine casks from the Langelois region of Austria. The palate offers a long-lasting chocolate-nougat combination, which adds fruity notes and some bacon to it. Apple notes in the finish.

Steam punk–esque copper stills *from Germany fire this striking Austrian distillery.*

WALDVIERTLER J.H. "ORIGINAL RYE-WHISKY"

WALDVIERTLER J.H. "SINGLE MALT"

SWITZERLAND

Until 1999, Swiss distilleries were exclusively focused on the production of fruit brandies and whiskey was not on the map. However, when regulations changed to allow the distilling of grain, whiskey-making began in earnest. Today the country boasts around 20 distillers, some of them dedicated exclusively to the production of Swiss whiskey.

WHISKY CASTLE "DOUBLEWOOD"

WHISKY CASTLE "CHÂTEAU"

KÄSER'S WHISKY CASTLE

OWNER Ruedi Käser

FOUNDED 2000 **CAPACITY** 5,300 gal (20,000 liters)

ADDRESS Schlossstrasse 17, 5077 Elfingen

WEBSITE www.whisky-castle.com

It doesn't really look like a castle—more like an American farmhouse or maybe a church. In fact, it's a distillery built by Ruedi Käser, one of Switzerland's most successful distillers, for the purpose of making whiskey.

Käser's personal dedication to hands-on distilling began in 1995, when he, not yet a distiller, asked a producer to distill some fruit brandy for him. Confident of its quality, he entered the distillate into a competition, only to have it

Famous for its alpine landscapes, *Switzerland has only recently developed a reputation for whiskey-making.*

rejected as "undrinkable." Shocked by the experience, Käser decided to learn the art of distilling for himself, so that he could be confident of the quality of the spirits he intended to sell. Just a few years after this early setback, Käser was receiving awards for the quality of his spirits and, after many years of experience with fruit brandies and other exotic distillates, with the change in the law he decided to diversify into whiskey. Today his small establishment produces no fewer than 18 different varieties.

To make his whiskey as authentic as possible he installed a pot still, similar to those used by Scottish whiskey producers, for the second distillation. Different varieties of grains are used to produce the whiskeys, but Käser still believes in malted barley as a very important ingredient. The casks have different origins and all contribute to the final character of the product, which Käser intends to be a truly individual "Swiss-style" whiskey.

Not as picturesque as a real castle, *Käser's modern distillery still blends harmoniously with its surroundings.*

TASTING NOTES

WHISKY CASTLE "DOUBLEWOOD"
single malt, 43% ABV
Smoked malted barley is the grain used for producing this whiskey. The nose is distinctively nutty, some fruitiness is detectable, and malt with some smokiness is dominant. On the palate the whiskey again has the notes of many different nuts plus some roasted chestnut flavor. In the finish there is some woodiness, but surprisingly mild and pleasant.

WHISKY CASTLE "SMOKE BARLEY"
single malt, 43% ABV, matured in new French oak casks
Together with the smoked barley malt, smokiness is a first impression on the nose, followed by some almonds and hazelnuts and dominant malt character. The nose finishes with hints of fresh bacon. On the palate, malt predominates, defined with the sweetness of malted barley that continues into the medium-long finish.

WHISKY CASTLE "EDITION KÄSER"
single malt, 68% ABV, cask strength
Starts with some chocolatey and nougat notes on the nose, needing some water to release the full flavor portfolio of lush green fruity aromas and a hint of nuts. On the palate, some wood-smokiness and sappy, fruity, and malty aromas blend with coconut and vanilla. The finish is very long and dominated by malt and vanilla.

WHISKY CASTLE "CHÂTEAU"
single malt, 50% ABV, matured in ex-Sauternes wine casks
Sauternes wine casks from Château d'Yquem give this whiskey its nose and character. Fruitiness of apricot and quince plus some sweet grapes push to the foreground and cover the maltiness that only has a chance to show in the mild and lengthy finish. On the palate, apricot marmalade and a long-lasting sweetness of grapes and malt. Overall, a very unusual whiskey.

LANGATUN "OLD DEER"

LANGATUN "OLD BEAR"

LANGATUN

OWNER Hans Baumberger
FOUNDED 1857 **CAPACITY** Not given
ADDRESS St. Urbanstrasse 34, 4900 Langenthal
WEBSITE www.langatun.ch

The long history of Langatun began in 1857, when Jakob Baumberger returned home to Switzerland from his studies in Munich as a newly graduated master of brewing and founded a distillery at his father's farm. Three years later he took over a brewery in the nearby village of Langenthal and developed both the distillery and the brewery into successful enterprises, subsequently purchasing the rights to a clear spring in the hills above the village and installing pipes to guide the water directly to his distillery.

Thanks to the farsightedness of his great-grandfather, third-generation Master Brewer and Distiller Hans Baumberger can today rely on the fine spring water which, together with his malted barley, is said to lie behind the quality of his whiskey. The barley is either lightly smoked (as in "Old Bear") or a mixture of non-smoked and lightly smoked barley malt ("Old Deer"). The peat for smoking the barley is obtained locally, while the yeast for fermentation is stout yeast from England.

Triple distilled, wine cask matured
Perhaps the most important element in Langatun's whiskeys is the triple distillation in copper pot stills. Unusually for European whiskey-makers, who prefer to distill twice, this distillation allows for a smooth, silky, and malty taste profile in the make.

Finally, maturation adds complexity and finesse to the whiskey. "Old Deer" is matured in sherry and Chardonnay casks, while Châteauneuf-du-Pape casks are used for "Old Bear." The latter give the whiskey a deep reddish-amber color and are also clearly detectable in the nose and palate.

TASTING NOTES

LANGATUN "OLD BEAR"
single malt, 40% ABV, matured in ex-Châteauneuf-du-Pape wine casks
Wine elements present in the oak barrels can easily be detected: an intense auburn color, nice flavors of wood and peat, and the typical malty aroma with a slight touch of the taste of wine.

LANGATUN "OLD DEER"
single malt, 40% ABV, matured in ex-sherry and ex-Chardonnay wine casks
A very complex and elegant whiskey. At first, a smooth, tender and malty character, followed by a mixture of honey, wood, spiciness, and finally roasted aromas. Bitter chocolate and tobacco can be found on the palate and continue to linger in the finish, along with further winey notes and complexity.

LOCHER

OWNER Brauerei Locher AG

FOUNDED 1999 **CAPACITY** 13,200 gal (50,000 liters)

ADDRESS Industriestrasse 12, CH-9050 Appenzell

WEBSITE www.saentismalt.ch

BEAR LOGO OF SÄNTIS MALT

Beer is the main product of Locher Brewery, the last remaining one of its kind at the foot of the Alpstein Mountains in northeastern Switzerland. When the brewery was established in Appenzell by the Locher family in 1886, they could not have foreseen that five generations later their beer casks would be used not only for making beer but for single malt whiskey too.

The man behind the idea of making whiskey is Karl Locher. When he turned 40 some years ago, he conceived the idea of drinking his own malt when he reached 60. Distillation had already been carried out in the brewery prior to World War II, so it was just a matter of revitalizing the stills and returning to making spirits. The first distillation of local barley malt took place in 1999, after the legalization of grain distilling in Switzerland.

The development of Säntis whiskeys
Several editions of Säntis Malt, named after the highest mountain in the region, have been released since whiskey production began in 1999. The whiskeys are bottled at different alcoholic strengths and while most of them mature in regular beer barrels of 53 gallons (200 liters) or more, "Edition Sigel" matures in very small barrels of only 13–20 gallons (50–75 liters).

As with most Swiss whiskeys today, the malts from Säntis are notable for their fruitiness and the character of the spicy barley malt. In the case of all the Säntis malts, the beer casks are responsible for a major part of the aroma profile. Maybe in a few years we will see more roasted aromas and nutty flavors coming from longer-aged whiskey produced by Säntis and other Swiss distillers.

TASTING NOTES

SÄNTIS MALT "EDITION DREIFALTIGKEIT" (CASK STRENGTH PEATED)
single malt, 52% ABV, cask strength, matured in oak ex-beer casks
Earthy, woody, and spicy-smoky on the nose. On the palate, caramel is dominant, but the fruitiness present in most of the whiskeys is well balanced with the peatiness. Both, together with spiciness, are present in the finish.

SÄNTIS MALT "EDITION SÄNTIS"
single malt, 40% ABV, matured in oak ex-beer casks
Careful selection of small beer barrels gives this whiskey a surprisingly fresh aroma of green figs and a very low fruitiness. The spiciness remains a very long and dominant aroma into the finish.

SÄNTIS MALT "CASK 1130"

SÄNTIS MALT "EDITION DREIFALTIGKEIT"

LIECHTENSTEIN

With only a small number of inhabitants and bounded by its much larger neighbors Austria and Switzerland, Liechtenstein is best known today for its banks and the secrecy they offer those rich enough to have an account. Secrecy, however, is not the case for the single brand of whiskey made in the principality. With water sources from the mountains and a family tradition of distilling, it was only a matter of time before whiskey making would start.

TELSER

OWNER Brennrei Telser Ltd. FOUNDED 2006 (whiskey)

CAPACITY approx. 60 gal (230 liters)

ADDRESS Dorfstrasse 67, 9495 Triesen

WEBSITE www.telsington.com

Like many other whiskey producers today, Marcel Telser was inspired by his trips to the heartlands of Scotland to make his own whiskey. After several years of experimentation and trials in his distillery—which was first recorded in documents for distilling in 1880—he finally brought his first-ever Liechtenstein whiskey onto the market in July 2009, naming it Telsington.

Crystal-clear mountain spring water from the local Triesner Bergquelle source is a major factor in the success of Telsington. The grain used is barley but, unlike in the production of Scotch single malt, the wort is allowed to rest for a period of ten days to achieve a full, round fermentation profile. Distillation is supervised by Marcel's father

and is carried out in copper pot stills, which are heated over a wood fire in traditional fashion. The whiskey is then matured in 500-year-old cellars with a natural soil floor, which allows for an exchange of soil and the locally sourced ex-Pinot Noir casks, giving the whiskey a mild character.

TASTING NOTE

TELSINGTON
(DISTILLED 2006, BOTTLED 2009)
single malt, 42% ABV, matured in ex-Pinot Noir wine casks, non-chill-filtered
There is some maltiness on the nose, but the red wine aroma is clearly detectable in the back. A hint of peatiness and tobacco smoke completes the first impression. On the palate the wine aroma is again present, later supported by some roasted notes. The finish is driven by the sweetness of the malt, but surprisingly spicy with notes of bitter chocolate.

Telser has brewed beer *in its traditional wooden buildings since 1880, but only began distilling in 2006.*

TELSER "TELSINGTON"

TELSER "TELSINGTON III"

BIRKENHOF

WEBSITE www.birkenhof-brennerei.de

Neutral grain spirit was the core product of this 19th-century distillery in the remote region of Westerwald, western Germany, where whiskey was recently added to the portfolio. The first whiskey released, Fading Hill, is only the start, as more casks of spirit based on different grains and with many finishes are awaiting maturation and blending in the new warehouses on site. **Fading Hill 3-year-old "2012"** (single malt, 65% ABV, cask strength, matured in ex-Bourbon casks) *Fruity and malty nose, supplemented by honey and vanilla. Pronounced alcohol on the palate, with fruits, honey, and some almonds. Malty, slightly bitter finish. Reminiscent of a much longer-matured Gaelic spirit.*

COILLMÓR

WEBSITE www.coillmor.com

Situated in the middle of the Bavarian Forest, this distillery produces its whiskey from Bavarian malted summer barley and the clear water of the region. In 2006 the first whiskey was distilled, released in 2009 as a three-year-old. The name Coillmór is Gaelic, meaning "huge forest"—referring to its location and the Scottish method of double distilling that is used. Aging is mostly in American oak, but sherry, port, or other casks are also used. **Coillmór 3-year-old** (single malt, 46% ABV, single cask, matured in American oak) *On the nose a lot of fruitiness, mainly pears, and some cookie flavors. The palate is again fruity, with apples and pears, but slightly citrus on top. The medium-long finish is fruity and intense.*

ETTER

WEBSITE www.etter-distillerie.ch

Famed for their fruit brandy, Hans Etter and his family turned to the distillation of whiskey in 2007, using only locally grown and malted barley. The whiskey gains complexity and smoothness from spring water from a nearby cave, while maturation takes place in oak barriques from a winery in the region. **Johnett Whisky** (single malt, 42% ABV, matured in ex-wine Barriques) *A pleasant maltiness is the dominant aroma. Candied fruits, light spiciness, and some nutty notes make for a very smooth and balanced flavor profile, which lingers on in the medium finish.*

GOUDEN CAROLUS

JOHNETT WHISKY

FINCH

WEBSITE www.finch-whisky.de

Triple distillation and the use of spelt and wheat from the distillery's own fields are the main characteristics of these whiskeys from the southwestern region of Swabia in Germany. They are all three to five years old, the three-year-olds matured in barrique barrels, most of which held retsina; a four-year-old made from spelt was aged in port casks. **Finch 4-year-old "Schwäbischer Highland Whisky"** (grain whiskey, 40% ABV) *Made from 70 percent spelt and 30 percent wheat, the grain is dominant on the nose, followed by vanilla and some woodiness. On the palate, fresh bread and some spices; bitter notes of chocolate are in the foreground in the medium-length finish.*

HAMMERSCHMIEDE

WEBSITE www.hammerschmiede-spirituosen.de

Mild, pure spring water and unpeated malted barley make a large contribution to the smoothness of this distillery's whiskey. Small pot stills are used, along with casks of various origin, including fino, Manzanilla, Amontillado, Oloroso, cream sherry, Madeira, Marsala, and port. **Glen Els "Unique Distillery Edition"** (single malt, 45.9% ABV, matured in first-fill ex-fino, Manzanilla, Amontillado, Oloroso, and cream sherry casks in combination) *Dried fruits and some fresh fruitiness to follow; vanilla and caramel are also present. On the palate, very full-bodied and complex. The cream sherry casks seem to have the biggest influence as toffee and wood combine. The finish is again driven by the sherry character.*

HET ANKER

WEBSITE www.hetanker.be

Het Anker brewery is famed for producing great Belgian beer—they are the makers of the Gouden Carolus Tripel beer—and it also makes the juniper-based liquor called genever. The owners experimented with a triple-distilled whiskey in 2003, but since then a dedicated distillery with pot stills made by Forsyth's of Scotland has been built. In 2008 a three-year-old malt spirit under the same Gouden Carolus name was bottled in small quantities. Proper whiskey is due for release in late 2013. **Gouden Carolus** (single malt spirit, 40% ABV) *Nicely balanced for a young whiskey, with fruity and some woody notes.*

LIBER

WEBSITE www.destileriasliber.com

Originally set up as a cooperative in the Grenada region of Spain, Destilerías Liber is the realization of a dream for Fran Peregrina, who wanted to take advantage of the region's outstanding natural resources. The distillery makes a non-chill-filtered single malt under the name Embrujo, bottled at 40 percent and about five years old. Maturation is fast here—the evaporation rate of the spirit is three times that of Scotland—but nevertheless the whiskey tastes young and, while showing glimpses of outstanding quality, it's still a work in progress.

Embrujo de Granada (single malt, 40% ABV) *Thin, easy-drinking fruity whiskey with orange notes, not unlike a fruity Speysider, but still a little on the sappy, grainy side.*

SPIRIT OF HVEN

WEBSITE www.backafallsbyn.se

A microdistillery located on an island in the strait between Denmark and Sweden, Spirit of Hven bottled its first whiskey in very limited quantities in 2011. The plan is to produce two very different whiskeys, one a fruity, vanilla-y, and fresh whiskey, the other described as smoky with seaweed notes.

Hven "Urania" (single malt, 45% ABV, matured in American, French, and Spanish oak) *The nose is stringent, with fresh wood, herbs, and peppery notes, and a hint of vanilla released by a dash of water. Pepper continues on the oily palate, along with licorice and touches of tobacco. The finish is long, with grassy notes ending in citrus and apples.*

US HEIT

WEBSITE www.usheitdistillery.nl

Aart van der Linde, owner of the brewery Us Heit, is also an avid whiskey fan and has been bottling Frysk Hynder (Friesian Horse) as a young whiskey and in the tiniest of quantities since 2005. Aart enjoys experimenting with his whiskeys, so there are several different expressions of it and different casks have been used in maturation at different times. The later casks formerly contained port.

Frysk Hynder 3-year-old "Sherry Matured" (single malt, 43% ABV, matured in ex-sherry casks) *Sweetish and remarkably soft for a young whiskey. Tasty, with a beautiful full body and distinctive sherry notes.*

FRYSK HYNDER

EMBRUJO DE GRANADA

WAMBRECHIES

WEBSITE www.wambrechies.com

Genever has been the *raison d'être* of Wambrechies for nearly 200 years, and whiskey is a more recent addition. The process here is quite unusual—it's double distilled but in a column rather than a pot still. The resulting spirit tends to be bottled at three years old and is a little thin and reedy, but the older version is worth seeking out.

Wambrechies 8-year-old (single malt, 40% ABV) *Delicate nose, with aniseed, vanilla, and cereal notes. Smooth palate, with a fine malty profile. Spicy finish of ginger and chocolate.*

WEIDENAUER

WEBSITE www.weidenauer.at

When Oswald Weidenauer produced whiskey from oats and spelt in 1997, he distinguished his products from other Austrian distillers. Oats are a very uncommon grain for distillation, and tricky, too, as there is limited availability of harvests. Malting is done by a local maltster, but milling, mashing with enzymes (like American whiskey), and double distillation takes place in Weidenauer's own distillery. Maturation is in fresh medium-toasted 30-gallon (115-liter) barrels, which quickly deliver a light color and aroma to the final product.

Waldviertler Whisky (single malt oat whiskey, 42% ABV) *Starts surprisingly fresh and fruity on the nose, quickly followed by vanilla. The oat malt is very sweet on the palate and this sweetness lingers into the finish. Very well rounded overall.*

ZIEGLER

WEBSITE www.brennerei-ziegler.de

The house of Ziegler has been distilling fine spirits, mostly fruit brandies, for almost 150 years. Now, after several years of maturation, a whiskey is added to their portfolio. Organic, local barley is malted at a nearby brewery, which also produces the mash for Ziegler's home distillery. Double distillation in small stills results in a clear spirit that is matured in lightly toasted French oak or chestnut barrels. The final character of the whiskey comes from the location, which has a microclimate almost like the Mediterranean.

Aureum "1865" (single malt, 43% ABV, finished in ex-Bourbon barrels) *Hints of blossoms and hay meadows provide the first impression on the nose. Slightly floral on the palate, too, with additional cookie flavors. The vanilla-style finish comes from final maturation in Bourbon barrels.*

NEW WORLD

AUSTRALIA

The vast country of Australia is known for its harsh and extremely hot climate, conditions totally unsuited for whisky production – or so it may seem. Forty years ago nobody considered it to be suited to decent wine production either, and look what happened. And in fact Tasmania, to the south of the mainland, is just about perfect for making grain spirit, with an abundance of water, a mild climate, lots of peat, and ideal conditions for farming grain. More recently, Victoria has proved to be a garden for Australia, and whisky is starting to flourish here, too. There are also distilleries close to Perth and Adelaide; overcome the temperature issues here and the benign climate accelerates maturation

Regional Styles
Despite the overall diversity there is a core style emerging – single malt whisky matured in small quarter casks previously used for port production.

Author's Choice
The pioneers are Lark, Sullivan's Cove, and Bakery Hill, and they're all now making excellent whisky. Then there are the likes of Nant, Limeburners, and Old Hobart producing, but as yet works in progress. After them, the new kids on the block who are up and running but not yet ready to bottle. Today, then, seek bottles from the first pioneers.

Regional Events
Australia's biggest problem is that not much Scotch whisky makes it as far as Sydney and Melbourne, and that which does is very expensive. There was an attempt to stage a Whisky Live Sydney but it had mixed success. The country does, though, have a lively organization for whisky aficionados, the Malt Whisky Society of Australia (www. mwsoa.org.au) and this has also held its own whisky festivals.

Australian whisky may be in its infancy but as is the Aussie way, there's a growing confidence Down Under that the country will become a world force in this field. Some of the distilleries featured in this section have yet to bottle spirit, and almost certainly new projects will have sprung up by the time of publication. Much of the whisky so far has been sucked up by South East Asia and, as with many other Australian products, it's this region that would seem to offer the country its future. There has been a big change in Australia in ten years, and Europe is no longer a priority – why try to compete against Scotland and Ireland in Europe when there are new territories to the West and East to explore?

Australia has a long history of distilling that stretches back to colonial times, and there are still many examples of snake-oil dealers selling grog. However, there are also some sharp businessmen

Located on Tasmania's northern coast, *Hellyers Road distillery produces a whisky unlike any other on the island.*

in this region and they have hitched their future to competing at the quality end of the market. Much inspiration comes from Scotland but, perhaps unsurprisingly given the large Irish contingent, other grain whisky styles are also emerging.

The hot, dry Australian bush *is hostile to producing whisky, but along the temperate coast distilling flourishes.*

GETTING AROUND

In view of the size of Australia it's very difficult to find a suitable base for exploration of its whisky. The obvious exception is Hobart, on the island of Tasmania, which can be reached by flights from Sydney and Melbourne and gives access to the island's distilleries. Call ahead and the Tasmanian whisky industry will welcome you, but you'll need to hire a car. Melbourne is also a good base for exploring the emerging distilleries of Victoria as well as the region's other food and drink attractions.

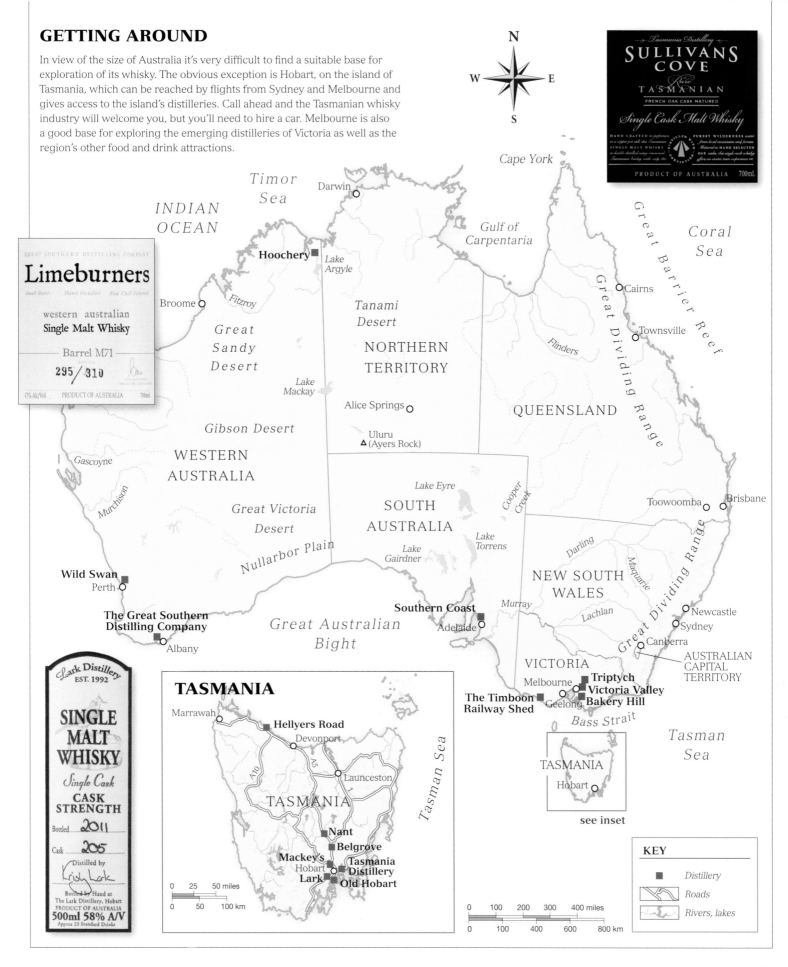

SULLIVANS COVE
Rare
TASMANIAN
FRENCH OAK CASK MATURED
Single Cask Malt Whisky
PRODUCT OF AUSTRALIA 700mL

GREAT SOUTHERN DISTILLING COMPANY
Limeburners
Small Batch   Hand Distilled   Non Chill Filtered
western australian
Single Malt Whisky
Barrel M71
295/310
43% Alc/Vol   PRODUCT OF AUSTRALIA   700mL

Lark Distillery
EST. 1992
SINGLE MALT WHISKY
Single Cask
CASK STRENGTH
Bottled 2011
Cask 205
Distilled by
Kristy Lark
Bottled by Hand at
The Lark Distillery, Hobart
PRODUCT OF AUSTRALIA
500ml 58% A/V
Approx 23 Standard Drinks

Map labels

N W E S

Timor Sea
INDIAN OCEAN
Cape York
Darwin
Hoochery
Lake Argyle
Gulf of Carpentaria
Coral Sea
Great Barrier Reef
Broome
Fitzroy
Great Sandy Desert
Tanami Desert
NORTHERN TERRITORY
Flinders
Cairns
Townsville
Great Dividing Range
Lake Mackay
Gibson Desert
WESTERN AUSTRALIA
Alice Springs
Uluru (Ayers Rock)
QUEENSLAND
Gascoyne
Murchison
Great Victoria Desert
Lake Eyre
SOUTH AUSTRALIA
Cooper Creek
Toowoomba
Brisbane
Wild Swan
Perth
Nullarbor Plain
Lake Gairdner
Lake Torrens
Darling
NEW SOUTH WALES
Macquarie
The Great Southern Distilling Company
Albany
Great Australian Bight
Southern Coast
Adelaide
Murray
Lachlan
Great Dividing Range
Newcastle
Sydney
Canberra
AUSTRALIAN CAPITAL TERRITORY
VICTORIA
Melbourne
Triptych
Victoria Valley
The Timboon Railway Shed
Geelong
Bakery Hill
Bass Strait
Tasman Sea
TASMANIA
Hobart
see inset

TASMANIA

Marrawah
Hellyers Road
Devonport
A10
A5
Launceston
TASMANIA
Nant
Belgrove
Mackey's
Hobart
Lark
Tasmania Distillery
Old Hobart
Tasman Sea

0   25   50 miles
0   50   100 km

0   100   200   300   400 miles
0   100   400   600   800 km

KEY

■ Distillery
Roads
Rivers, lakes

263

BAKERY HILL

OWNER David Baker **FOUNDED** 1998

CAPACITY 26,400 gal (100,000 liters)

ADDRESS 1/20 Gatwick Road, North Bayswater, Victoria 3153

WEBSITE www.bakeryhilldistillery.com.au

BAKERY HILL *"CLASSIC MALT"*

Australia is undergoing a whiskey revolution and, as with its wine, is deadly serious but approaching production in a refreshing new way. On Tasmania the distillers have created a whiskey community and raised their profile through power in numbers. Take pity, then, on David Baker, who has battled alone against the odds to make some of the Southern Hemisphere's finest malt.

Baker, who was a biochemist before turning to the distillation of malt spirits, set up his distillery to make both peated and non-peated whiskey in a manner not dissimilar to Scotch single malt. Now the distillery is just starting to reap the full rewards after several years of struggle.

"Establishing a single malt distillery in a country that isn't a traditional producer of malts has been hard because of the lack of engineering know-how," he says. "Whether it was brewing our mash or distilling, the lack of technical expertise meant that we had to do all the research, development, and design ourselves."

Struggle and success

Trial and error paid off and quite quickly the distillery began making quality malt. Unexpected curveballs have created difficulties for Baker, and the lack of a ready-made community to fall back on has made for a solitary existence. Baker is a fighter and a survivor, and he has now started to export stock, having built up sufficient quantities.

"At Bakery Hill, 2011 was a consolidation year," says Baker. "Continuing to distill our malts and lay them down has been our major focus, together with growth into various new export markets."

Bakery Hill makes five different expressions of whiskey. "Where we are different is that we use a very long fermentation process," says Baker, "which we believe further enhances the flavor and character. The wash is then double distilled to typically 72 percent ABV and then reduced to 65 percent for casking in either 200-liter or 100-liter American oak barrels. Because of the different climatic conditions in Melbourne compared to Scotland, we can achieve a quicker maturation and bottle our single cask expressions at eight years old."

Into the future

Established in 1998, Baker's distillery has ridden the wave of New World whiskey growth and seen huge changes, but he's excited about the future. "The most satisfying high point recently has been

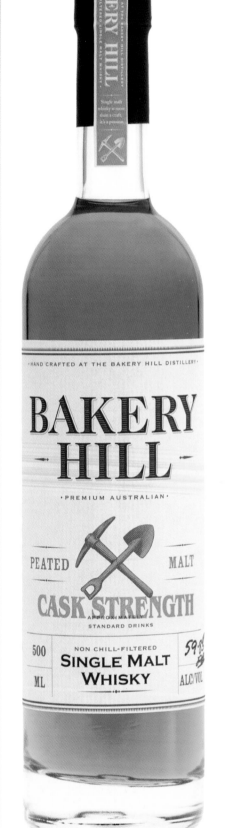

BAKERY HILL *"PEATED MALT"* CASK STRENGTH

Bakery Hill evokes *the Gold Rush era, when prospectors braved the hot plains of Victoria in search of a fortune.*

the way the public both locally and overseas has embraced our malts. Eleven years ago, the malt whiskey consumer considered malts coming from nontraditional countries as a curiosity, but once it was seen that our malts were as good, if not in some cases better, the situation changed in our favor.

"From now on we'll be expanding, with the distillery operating round the clock 365 days a year, putting together the volumes of spirits that will enable us to grow to the next stage. As we are part of the Pacific Basin where new markets are opening up all the time, Bakery Hill is focusing its marketing on these nontraditional areas."

TASTING NOTES

BAKERY HILL "CLASSIC MALT"
single malt, 46% ABV, non-chill-filtered
Surprisingly delicate nose, with fresh meadow, sweet barley, gin blossom, honey, and citrus. The palate has more green fruit but traces of orange, vanilla, and enough wood and pepper to hold the malt in check.

BAKERY HILL "PEATED MALT" CASK STRENGTH
single malt, 59.5% ABV, cask strength, non-chill-filtered
Intense peat, fresh salad, grape, and melon on the nose, and on the palate a big burst of peat, graham cracker, some vanilla, apple, blood orange, and sweet pepper. Water releases a complex array of flavors, with pepper and peat dominating the finish.

BAKERY HILL "DOUBLE WOOD"
single malt, 46% ABV, non-chill-filtered
Fragrant nose with fruit cocktail in syrup. The taste is soft, rounded, and with exotic fruits to the fore. Very easy drinking, sweet and balanced with vanilla, peach, and summer berries. The most complete Bakery Hill whiskey.

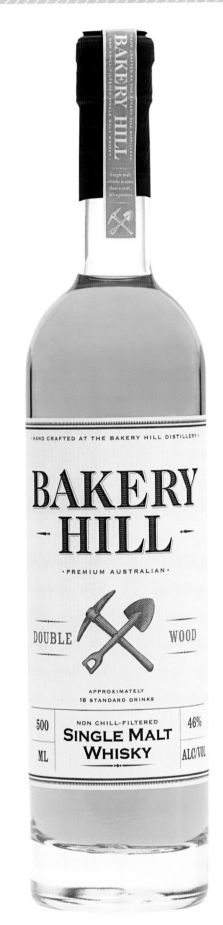

BAKERY HILL "DOUBLE WOOD"

THE COST OF GOLD

The place this distillery is named after became infamous for a gold miners' uprising in the mid-19th century and the bloody aftermath that saw at least 25 people killed by the authorities. The area had become a magnet for miners, who were forced to buy expensive licenses for relatively small plots of land regardless of whether they actually found gold, and in the general atmosphere of lawlessness, disputes, and drunkenness, it was not uncommon for police to use savage violence. Finally, a group of miners rebelled under a blue Southern Cross flag, but after days of standoffs, order was restored by government troops through violence and bloodshed.

LARK

OWNER Bill Lark
FOUNDED 1992 **CAPACITY** 31,700 gal (120,000 liters)
ADDRESS 14 Davey Street, Hobart, Tasmania
WEBSITE www.larkdistillery.com.au

The modern Australian whiskey industry begins and ends with Bill Lark. Much has been written about his role as the godfather of whiskey-making in Tasmania.

Tasmanian whiskey reborn

Out fly-fishing with friends one day, Lark mused over a dram of Cardhu whether it would be possible to make a good Scotch-style malt whiskey in Tasmania, which, after all, was in many ways bountiful in all that was needed to make great whiskey: world-class barley, pure water, peat bogs, and, perhaps most importantly, a climate with the right balance of temperature and humidity for maturation. He resolved to give it a try but, seeking a license at the customs and excise office, discovered the island was subject to a 150-year-old prohibition law. He lobbied hard, won a repeal, and sparked Australia's ongoing whiskey renaissance.

"When we started," says Lark, "the idea was simply to see if we could make good malt whiskey in Tasmania, not necessarily with the idea to establish an industry. The fact is that the whiskey soon proved to be of such good character that the business quickly grew up around us."

For the customs and excise staff he has nothing but praise. "They were very supportive right from the start, and I think that it just made a pleasant change looking at whiskey-making laws rather than the normal daily work. They couldn't have been more helpful," Lark says.

The law banning the production of spirits on Tasmania dated back to the days when the island was a prisoner colony and the inhabitants became adept at making strong alcoholic potions, seriously affecting the food supply and leading to a raucous, lawless, and drunken island. These days Tasmania is an altogether more sedate and ordered place, but there's a delightful old-fashioned Aussie rebelliousness about the people here, and a certain bohemian charm.

An influential distillery

Lark Distillery is a short distance outside of the city of Hobart, surrounded by farmland and nestled in the heart of the island's wine-making regions. In early 2012 the arrival of its own herd of Highland cattle was being planned, and the Scottish parallels extend to the rugged grasses, hilly skyline, and rough-and-tumble natural beauty. The distillery itself, housed in farm outbuildings, is small and has stills built by an Australian company especially for Lark—though two or three distilleries on the island have very similar equipment, reflecting the influence Bill Lark has on the thriving whiskey industry there.

Since founding their distillery in 1992, the Larks have been making whiskey in a very hands-on

While the distillery *lies on the outskirts of Hobart, Lark has an office and shop on the city's busy harborfront.*

LARK SINGLE MALT WHISKY "CASK STRENGTH"

manner. Everything is manual at Lark Distillery—the spirit running off the still tasted by the small distilling team and cuts made not by formula but as circumstances dictate. It's a sign of the growing confidence here that, should you so wish, you can distill your own version of Lark, choosing when to make the cut yourself.

A similar small-scale, hands-on approach is reflected in the distillery's use of peat, which is dug out by hand from its very own bog in the Central Highlands of Tasmania—a peat Lark claims is subtly different from Scottish peat thanks to the influence of Tasmanian native flora. Yet for all his respect for Scottish traditions, Lark is never afraid to innovate and has developed a unique "post malt smoking" method for imparting peat flavors to his whiskey—and it's certainly caught the attention of the Scotch whiskey makers he so respects.

The smaller-is-better theme continues in Lark's very considered choice of quarter casks for maturation, which not only speed up the natural aging but also deliver a "richness of character" that helps give Lark whiskeys their "big finish." Small means harnessed for big ends. And if you want a reminder of how much this tiny distillery at the bottom of the world punches above its weight, it's there in the small collection of maturing casks and the sweetest maltings room—more a beehive than a room—with handheld removable tracks on which the local barley is placed for peating.

Reaching out to the world

If the distillery is doing a passable impression of a Scottish microdistillery, the "cellar door" site in the center of Hobart offers a different view. Upstairs are the administration offices, and here there's an altogether more businesslike feel to proceedings. Downstairs there's a bar, shop, and sitting area—all very cosmopolitan. Bill confirms that Australia has come of age. "We're doing excellent business and that's taking most of my time now," he says. "We're opening new markets and there are big opportunities opening up in South East Asia. These are exciting times for Australia." Indeed they are—and Bill's legacy is enshrined in an unfolding story.

TASTING NOTES

LARK SINGLE MALT WHISKY "SINGLE CASK"
single malt, 43% ABV, single cask, matured in ex-port oak quarter casks
This is big, bold, loud, and brash, but far cleverer and more nuanced than on first taste. No other whiskey on earth tastes like this. This is all about stewed overripe apples dipped in anisette or Benedictine, giving herbal and medicinal notes, then left to cook like a Madeira might, so that oak is infused in the mix. Utterly delightful.

WHISKEY WOMAN

Always a pace setter in Australia, Lark Distillery broke new ground when Bill appointed his daughter, Kristy, as Master Distiller a few years back. The very male world of Aussie whiskey greeted the appointment with bemusement, but it made total sense; Kristy grew up surrounded by distilling and her father's enthusiasm for it, and her appointment freed Bill to play an ambassadorial role and open new markets for the malt. Kristy has now stepped down to start her own family, but is proud of her place in the growing success story of Australian whiskey.

LARK SINGLE MALT WHISKY "SINGLE CASK"

TASMANIA DISTILLERY

OWNER Patrick Maguire	
FOUNDED 1994 **CAPACITY** 6,340 gal (24,000 liters)	
ADDRESS 1/14 Lambs Place, Cambridge, Tasmania	
WEBSITE www.tasmaniadistillery.com	

While Bill Lark of Lark distillery has correctly been credited for the rebirth of whiskey-making in Tasmania, it's easy to overlook the crucial role that Patrick Maguire has played in the Australian whiskey story. While he has been happy to take a back seat and quietly get on with the business of making and exporting whiskey, he is in fact key to the overall whiskey story, a point acknowledged by the other distillers on the island, particularly Lark.

Maguire worked with Lark at the latter's distillery when it first opened, but it wasn't long before he branched out on his own, eventually steering the Sullivans Cove brand to become not just the best-known Australian whiskey outside its homeland, but pretty much the only one to sell in any quantity overseas.

Against the hooch merchants

Australia's history as a penal colony is well documented—Sullivans Cove has referred directly to it in its advertising and marketing campaigns—and with so many former British and Irish citizens, it should come as no surprise that whiskey flourished here. But much of the illicitly produced

Sullivans Cove whiskey is named after the early British settlement at what would become Hobart in Tasmania.

SULLIVANS COVE "FRENCH OAK CASK"

spirit was little more than foul-tasting grog, and there was little attempt to make whiskey worthy of the name. Indeed, when Australian whiskey-makers such as Bill Lark and Patrick Maguire started making single malt properly, they went out of their way to distance themselves from the hooch merchants, shunning an Australian government initiative to scrap minimum maturation periods and insisting on adopting production regulations in line with those of Scotland.

Heritage potential

When Maguire struck out on his own, rather than start from scratch, he recognized the marketing potential in an existing whiskey brand which, to put it bluntly, was pretty dire and could have not only sunk without a trace but also pulled the entire Australian single malt industry down with it. What Maguire saw was a name and a label that told a story about the country the whiskey was produced in. Evoking Tasmania's early colonial heritage as well as its beautiful coastline, Sullivans Cove is named after the place where, in 1804, Captain David Collins founded the British settlement that would later become Hobart.

If you've tasted early bottlings of Sullivans Cove, you may have been underwhelmed. Early offerings were ordinary in the extreme, and although they represented a genuine attempt to produce a proper single malt, they were poor imitations of the whiskey that was being made in Scotland. For credibility's sake, the faltering flagship that was Sullivans Cove had to be salvaged, and Maguire was the man responsible

for doing it. Sullivans Cove falls into three distinct periods—the early grim one, a middle "not bad but why would you bother?" one, and the most recent "hello, what have we here?" one. In 2011 the distillery bottled an 11-year-old, the oldest official distillery bottling (though an independent bottler in the country has put out an older whiskey still, probably originally made by this distillery), and Maguire has been signing distribution contracts across the world ever since. Sullivans Cove is an ugly duckling no more.

The butterfly takes wing?

Yet there remains a delicious irony about the distillery. Whatever you imagine the home of Sullivans Cove whiskey might look like, almost certainly the reality will come as something of a shock. White-tipped waves crashing onto rocky beaches, perhaps? Barren and bleak cliff views across delightful sandy Australian beaches? A fishing port, maybe?

Unfortunately not. Australian whiskey is still a work in progress, a butterfly struggling to break free of its chrysalis, and no distillery represents this better than Sullivans Cove. With Maguire focused on selling whiskey, there has been little time for niceties; this isn't so much a distillery as a collection of distilling equipment heaped together in a large storage unit in an industrial park on the outskirts of Hobart, and you have to look hard to see the distilling equipment in among the mess. There are plans to move to a new site eventually, when time allows.

TASTING NOTES

SULLIVANS COVE "DOUBLE CASK"
single malt, 40% ABV
Matured in both Bourbon and port casks, this has a sweet, fruity nose with plenty of vanilla but clean and refreshing barley, too. On the palate red berries, soft toffee, mince pie, and sweet spices combine. The finish is medium-long and pleasant.

SULLIVANS COVE "AMERICAN OAK BOURBON CASK MATURED"
single malt, 60% ABV
The nose doesn't open up readily and needs water from the outset, but once it's added you get a zippy, zesty, buoyant nose. The flavors kick around all over the place but the Bourbon vanilla notes and honey just about hold everything in place. There are some spring fruits toward the end and delicate spice.

SULLIVANS COVE "FRENCH OAK PORT CASK MATURED"
single malt, 60% ABV
The biggest beast in the portfolio, this has rich berries and some citrus fruits on the nose and if you add water to bring the strength down to 44–46% it is a joy, with a fruit bowl of flavors, clean barley, and a very drinkable, weighty, big-hearted malt.

ALL THE FUN OF THE FAIR

Australian whiskey has come a long way in a short time, and the nation's distillers have embraced their own standards code and taken it seriously. But that wasn't always the case, and in the early days there were those who would try anything to win over a doubting public. "The previous owner of Sullivans Cove used to bring tours to what he called 'the distillery', but there wasn't really anything to see," says Bill Lark. "So he fixed it up with music and lights, and when he pushed the switch it would look and sound like a fairground attraction."

SULLIVANS COVE "AMERICAN OAK BOURBON CASK MATURED"

THE GREAT SOUTHERN DISTILLING COMPANY

OWNER Cameron Syme

FOUNDED 2004 **CAPACITY** 52,800 gal (200,000 liters)

ADDRESS 252 Frenchman Bay Road, Robinson, Albany WA 6330 **WEBSITE** www.distillery.com.au

It's a grandiose enough name, The Great Southern Distilling Company, but it suits the landscape it stands in as well as the ambition of one of Australia's true whiskey pioneers, founder Cameron Syme. In the distillery's most recent whiskey, called Limeburners, you can taste the treeless plains and wide open roads of mainland Australia in every sip.

Taking on the challenge

Limeburners is a whiskey whose time is right now—a whiskey coming into focus and confidently exploring whiskey paths untraveled by anyone else. It wasn't always this way: the distillery made the mistake of bottling its first whiskeys too young, and they were sappy and difficult.

But apart from the economic issues there were other mitigating circumstances, not least coming to terms with the climate. In many ways Tasmania and even Victoria have it easy—there is strength in numbers in those regions and they have a long history of food and drink production, which at least gives them some form of blueprint. Not here, though. With the inland heat on the one hand, and the gusty, salted coastal air coming from the other,

Syme is doing what Australian pioneers have always done—taken on the challenge of the elements and conquered them through indefatigable spirit. In practice, the cool maritime air wins the environmental battle and maturation is relatively slow here. More than that, a plentiful supply of pristine clean water, peat, and barley make Albany ideal for whiskey.

Limeburners is bottled in single cask batches, and each expression is therefore different. The whiskey is named after an area where lime was burned during convict times, and the distillery is a modern state-of-the-art one with a highly trained Bavarian-born distiller, specializing in small-batch boutique spirits of which whiskey is just one.

Cameron Syme's importance to Australian whiskey is well known and he plays a senior role within the Australian whiskey community. It's a sure bet that The Great Southern Distilling Company will continue to develop into a major force on the whiskey scene.

TASTING NOTES

LIMEBURNERS "BARREL STRENGTH"
single malt, 61% ABV, non-chill-filtered

A big, big whiskey with an almost liqueur-like quality to it. The casks used here are Australian brandy and Bourbon, and the result is a gentle, honeyed, and slightly aniseedy whiskey with lots of fresh grape and barley.

In Western Australia *whiskey-makers must contend with arid heat emanating from the treeless inland plains.*

LIMEBURNERS WHISKY LIQUEUR
The Limeburners single malt is infused with spices and sweetened with karri blossom honey to produce this unusual whiskey liqueur.

LIMEBURNERS "BARREL STRENGTH"

HELLYERS ROAD

OWNER Whisky Tasmania Pty. Ltd.
FOUNDED 1997 **CAPACITY** 52,800 gal (200,000 liters)
ADDRESS 153 Old Surrey Road, Burnie, Tasmania 7320
WEBSITE www.hellyersroaddistillery.com.au

Tasmania's biggest distillery, Hellyers Road is also its most esoteric. It makes a style of whiskey unlike anything else on the island—a plus, because Tasmania is proving itself capable of a wide range of different whiskey styles. Hellyers Road has more in common with a Scottish Lowland whiskey, and is the least assertive on the island.

The history of Hellyers

The distillery is a wholly owned subsidiary of Betta Milk, Tasmania's large milk-producing cooperative set up by local farmers in the 1950s, and is named after Tasmanian pioneer Henry Hellyer. He was the first to explore the interior of the island back in the 1820s, and his determination and spirit are the inspiration for the whiskey-making side of the business, which was established as an attempt to diversify and avoid being swallowed up by an aggressive mainland dairy operation.

As is often the case with fledgling distilleries, the first bottlings were nothing to write home about, but Hellyers Road has diversified since then and offers a number of different styles, most of which are sold on the island or to selected outlets on the Australian mainland. The distillery offers two main expressions, the "Original" and "Peated," and two variations: "Slightly Peated" takes the former and adds a pinch of the latter, while "Pinot Noir Finish" is produced by finishing "Original" malt in pinot noir casks.

This is a sizable distillery located away from the others in the northwest of the island, but if you travel there, you will find a modern establishment with a visitors' center, a shop, and even a restaurant.

TASTING NOTES

HELLYERS ROAD SINGLE MALT WHISKY "ORIGINAL"
single malt, 46.2% ABV, matured in American white oak casks, non-chill-filtered
With enough alcohol bite to show teeth, this is nonetheless a cereally, sappy, grassy, and grapey whisky. Lots of malt with a clean, drinkable aspect.

HELLYERS ROAD SINGLE MALT WHISKY "PEATED"
single malt, 46.2% ABV, matured in American white oak casks, non-chill-filtered
Subtle, complex, and well-made whiskey with peat not dominating but adding a much-needed depth. There's citrus, vanilla, and a distinctly floral aspect to this—all very pleasant.

HELLYERS ROAD SINGLE MALT WHISKY "ORIGINAL"

HELLYERS ROAD SINGLE MALT WHISKY "PEATED"

NANT

OWNER The Batt Family
FOUNDED 2005 **CAPACITY** 7,900 gal (30,000 liters)
ADDRESS The Nant Estate, Nant Lane, Bothwell,
Tasmania 7030 **WEBSITE** www.nantdistillery.com.au

Of all Tasmania's distilleries, Nant is the most suitable when it comes to meeting the demand of the modern whiskey fan, edging out Lark Distillery because that distillery is split over two sites, one in the center of Hobart, the other some drive away in the countryside.

You don't need much in the way of premises to distill malt spirit, so some distilleries are decidedly underwhelming. Not Nant. It occupies an all-but-perfect site, it has been thought out properly, and it is the product of some serious investment. No wonder the owners are proud of it.

The distillery takes some finding; it's a fair distance from Hobart, out into the rural areas, and you have to approach it down a small track. A restored and working water wheel is close by, a pretty brook flows through the center of the site, and the buildings that house the distillery are new and pristine.

Everything inside is how one would hope a small hands-on distillery would be. The stills, made in Australia, are similar to Lark's. Both pine

Dating from 1823, the water-driven *flour mill at Nant is now used to grind the malted barley for whiskey-making.*

and stainless steel washbacks are on site, and Nant is making separate whiskeys with each to find out once and for all whether there is a difference. The whiskey, still young, is as delicate as anything you'll find in Australia, and with conference and meeting areas, a chic bar area with a terrace, and a sedate, rural environment to relax in, you can't help but fall in love with the whole experience. There are plans to build a distillery similar to this at the Kings Barns golf course estate in Fife—a real treat for the Scots if they do.

TASTING NOTES

NANT "SHERRY CASK" (BOTTLED 2011)
single malt, 43% ABV, matured in ex-sherry casks
The sappiness of a too-young whiskey is still there—this is bottled not much past three years old—but there are delicate red berry notes, an almost effeminate sweetness, and an emerging complexity that suggests that despite the cask, this is going to be a sophisticated, velvety, sweet treat.

NANT "PORT CASK" (BOTTLED 2011)
single malt, 43% ABV, matured in ex-port casks
Given its age, this is an immense whiskey. Port, more than most casks, will send maturing spirit along all sorts of undesirable roads before settling down, but here rich red currant, blackberry, raspberry, and blueberry are already vying for attention.
Give this another four years, and wow!

NANT "PORT CASK"
(BOTTLED 2011)

OLD HOBART

OWNER Casey Overeem	
FOUNDED 2007	**CAPACITY** Not given
ADDRESS Hobart, Tasmania	
WEBSITE www.oldhobartdistillery.com	

This is a distillery that at the time of writing was in the process of moving premises and didn't quite live up to its name. Old Hobart wasn't in Old Hobart at all, but some distance along the coast in the outbuildings and garage of a modern suburban house built on a hillside overlooking Tasmania's stunning coastline.

Moonshine inspiration

However, there's absolutely nothing artificial or contrived about the distillery's owner, Casey Overeem, a wealthy and very astute local businessman with a passion for whiskey. His interest in whiskey was first ignited in the early 1980s on a trip to Norway to visit relatives. In a country where people struggle to keep warm and alcohol is taxed to the hilt, the making of homemade moonshine, or *hjemmebrent* ("home-burned"), is common and, while there, Overeem witnessed small-scale distilling for the first time.

"Many people had microdistilleries in their cellars and I really admired them, so I started experimenting when I got home," he says.

It took another two decades of research and experimentation, and a successful campaign by long-time friend Bill Lark, of Lark Distillery, to amend Tasmania's century-old law banning small-scale distillation, before Old Hobart Distillery finally secured a distiller's license in 2005. Overeem then supplemented his home-taught skills with a fact-finding trip to Scotland, to him the spiritual home of whiskey-making, where he managed to visit some 15 distilleries and happily reports their willingness to share knowledge and pass on advice.

Nothing accidental

As with Nant, there are two malts offered here, and at the time of visiting they were just three years old—indeed, tasting samples were drawn from the cask and only one was bottled as this book went to press. Since the distillery was changing its location, it's hard to pass judgment on the environment, but Casey has invested in the same stills as Nant and Lark—Australian-made and smaller than anything in Scotland, but still properly constructed and not designed as a folly.

Time and effort have gone into cask selection, too, and Casey Overeem's whiskey follows an emerging Tasmanian style of port-finished whiskey matured in small casks. There is a quiet confidence about the Tasmanian producers and they feel no need to rush what they are doing to jump on any current bandwagon. The chic bottles that the whiskey will be sold in and the attractive packaging also suggest that there is nothing accidental about the burgeoning Tasmanian whiskey scene.

OVEREEM "SHERRY CASK MATURED"

TASTING NOTES

OVEREEM "CASK STRENGTH PORT CASK MATURED"
single malt, 64% ABV, cask strength, aged in ex-port French oak quarter casks
The nose is decidedly fruity but the spirit itself is a work in progress—still very young, unrefined, and coarse, and the flavors are all over the place. But this is like seeing a talented baseball player joining the major leagues too young: some of the delivery is wayward but the power, energy, and enthusiasm are there in abundance, and the odd palate bouncer provides a tasty morsel of what is to come.

OVEREEM "CASK STRENGTH PORT CASK MATURED"

OVEREEM "CASK STRENGTH SHERRY CASK MATURED"

BELGROVE

WEBSITE www.belgrovedistillery.com.au

Peter Bignell isn't your average distiller. He's a farmer; a skilled sand and ice sculptor; he has restored a water mill; and most recently, he built an ecological distillery in which he then distilled rye grown on his farm—and as anyone who's ever distilled rye knows, that's no easy task. The tiny distillery is run on a part-time basis and is still a long way from bottling a proper whiskey, but a white rye spirit has been bottled which has a unique taste. Early days yet, but maturation in port casks means Bignell's is almost certainly a unique rye whiskey, and certainly another big plus for Tasmania's ever-expanding whiskey industry.
Belgrove "White Rye" (new spirit, 40% ABV)
Clean and fresh with a distinct spearmint menthol taste, and with a licorice, hickory, and pepper twist.

HOOCHERY

WEBSITE www.hoochery.com.au

It's often assumed that if someone is making whiskey in a place such as Australia, they must be taking Scotch as their blueprint. This isn't always the case—there are other whiskey styles, and newly invented grist recipes are taking whiskey into new areas. Hoochery is best known for its rums and innovative range of spirits, made mainly with Australian ingredients. Its Raymond B. Whiskey is made from 100 percent corn mash, which in the US would be called Bourbon. The spirit is then poured through mahogany to give it a smoother taste and finish. No samples were yet available.

The spirits maturing in oak barrels *at the Hoochery warehouse will be bottled as Raymond B. Whiskey.*

MACKEY'S

WEBSITE www.mackeysdistillery.com.au

Such is the speed of change in Australian whiskey it's not always easy to pin down the product. Mackey's is the brainchild of Damian Mackey and in 2009 local Tasmanian whiskey groups were reporting that they had tasted samples. By 2012, though, no whiskey had been released and the word was that as recently as October 2011 new stills were being put in. There definitely will be a Mackey's whiskey in Tasmania at some point, though, and the word is that Damian will look to his Irish roots and market a triple-distilled whiskey.

SOUTHERN COAST

WEBSITE www.southerncoastdistillers.com.au

Australian whiskey is rapidly starting to develop some national characteristics, even though the distilleries can be located massive distances apart. With ex-sherry casks in short supply, much of the whiskey from Australia is being matured in former port casks, often refilled into small 26-gallon (100-liter) barrels, further accelerating maturation. Southern Coast Distillers is making very small batches of whiskey that is already turning heads. Owner Ian Schmidt is a former flagpole maker who started distilling whiskey as a hobby—and with typical Aussie swagger he says the Scots have been hoodwinking the world for centuries because making good whiskey is easy.
Southern Coast "Batch 5" (matured in American oak ex-port casks, ABV varies) *Apricots, toffee, pears, and traces of wood on the nose, and a rich, sweet palate with honey, roasted nuts, coconut, marzipan, and orange fruit.*

BELGROVE "WHITE RYE"

RAYMOND B. WHISKEY

A renovated train shed *dating from around 1910 provides Timboon with its distillery building.*

THE TIMBOON RAILWAY SHED

WEBSITE www.timboondistillery.com.au

This distillery has a history stretching back to the days when pioneers were founding the state of Victoria and building railroads through it. The whiskey link is even older, for tough moonshiners, including the notorious whiskey maker Tom Delaney, made mountain dew here for years before it was stamped out a century ago. The Timboon Railway Shed is a tourist center selling local produce as well as brewing and distilling a range of products, including a single malt whiskey that looks to Scotland for inspiration. The whiskey is matured in 13-gallon (50-liter) and 24-gallon (90-liter) casks made with wood from ex-port casks.

Timboon (single malt, 45–50% ABV, matured in wood from ex-port casks) *Sweet, fruity malt with milk chocolate, honeycomb, raisins, some citrus, and red berries.*

TRIPTYCH

WEBSITE www.triptychdistillery.com.au

A distillery that's something of an enigma, Triptych is so new that at the time of writing, very little information was available about it. It's described as small batch, and Triptych is defined on its website as "a work in three parts" and, most tellingly, "three mates, one vision." There are references to small batch production of single malt but also American-, Canadian-, and Irish-style whiskey. Pretty ambitious, then, and one to watch.

VICTORIA VALLEY

WEBSITE www.victoriavalley.com.au

While it hasn't bottled any whiskey yet, Victoria Valley embodies the growing confidence and burgeoning size of the Australian whiskey industry. The whiskey's not that far away and undoubtedly there is a genuine excitement about it, since the distillery was created and built by a business group linked to Tasmanian whiskey veteran Bill Lark. Now, under the direction of Managing Director and Head Distiller David Vitale, all the focus is on producing a great malt. When that comes on line, Victoria Valley will be Australia's biggest malt whiskey producer, and it's likely to market a range of whiskeys because it's maturing spirits in a range of different cask types and sizes. The distillery is selling barrels to those interested, and is set to export extensively to Southeast Asia.

WILD SWAN

WEBSITE www.wildswandistillery.com.au

The Swan Valley has been known for quality fruit, wine, and beer for many years now, and as far as the team behind Wild Swan Distillery was concerned, there was no reason why spirits shouldn't be part of the regional story. Wild Swan is run by the Angove family, and John Angove brings experience from working in a Canadian distillery and being an avid home brewer, too. At the time of writing, no whiskey had been released, but vodka and gin are in production and in 2008 the distillery picked up its first international awards in the San Francisco World Spirits Competition, with further successes in 2011.

TIMBOON

NEW ZEALAND

Given that a large proportion of its population is of Scottish descent and that there are similarities between its South Island and the Scottish Highlands, New Zealand would seem to be ideal territory for quality single malt whiskey. However, the economic reality of producing spirits for such a tiny population, and one with more home stills than anywhere else, means that this is not the case. Two or three distillery projects are said to be in the pipeline, but for the time being, the country relies on dwindling quantities of old stock.

NEW ZEALAND WHISKY COMPANY

OWNER	New Zealand Whisky Company
ADDRESS	14–16 Harbour Street, Oamaru
FOUNDED 2009	**CAPACITY** None
WEBSITE	www.thenzwhisky.com

The address is certainly a local one: the company is based in a 125-year-old harborside site in a small New Zealand town. Scratch beneath the surface, however, and you will find this is an Australian operation. Yet Greg Ramsay, who was previously involved in funding and setting up Nant Distillery in Tasmania, is taking New Zealand whiskey very seriously. Having purchased the last of the stock from the closed Willowbank Distillery in Dunedin, the company marked its commitment with two of the best bottles of New Zealand whiskey ever released, bookending the successful 2011 Rugby World Cup. "Touch. Pause. Engage." was a 24-year-old whiskey distilled in the year the All Blacks last won the World Cup in 1987, and "Vindication," a 16-year-old distilled in 1995, the last time the All Blacks reached a final. Further bottlings are planned and there are mutterings about a new distillery...

TASTING NOTES

NEW ZEALAND'S 1987 24-YEAR-OLD "TOUCH. PAUSE. ENGAGE."
single malt, 49–60% ABV, cask strength, matured in oak barrels
This has an incredibly soft banana and vanilla ice cream heart, with apple turnover and freshly baked sweet bread, too. Only a hint of oak but enough pepper to hold the malt in check. Doesn't taste 24 years old but it's a creamy, honeyed delight.

NEW ZEALAND'S 2011 16-YEAR-OLD "VINDICATION"
single malt, 52.3% ABV, cask strength, matured in oak barrels
A heart of zingy lemon sherbet, sweet cinnamon, and apple Danish, plus a sprinkling of salt and pepper, and some sharp barley. Little sign of the 16 years in oak, but the cask strength means plenty of bite, and it seems this is the age when Willowbank malt hits turbo gear.

SOUTH ISLAND 21-YEAR-OLD

NEW ZEALAND'S 1987 "TOUCH. PAUSE. ENGAGE."

THOMSON

OWNERS	Matt and Rachael Thomson
ADDRESS	Not given
FOUNDED Not given	**CAPACITY** None
WEBSITE	www.thomsonwhisky.com

When it comes to whiskey, New Zealand's neighbors across the Tasman Sea are much more visible and noisy. Indeed, it's taken an Australian company to form the New Zealand Whisky Company and to pick up the New Zealand whiskey message by bottling old stocks from the now defunct Willowbank Distillery. Willowbank was responsible for the biggest New Zealand whiskey names—Lammerlaw, Milford, Wilson's—and apart from some very small producers such as Kaiapoi and Hokanui, there's no current whiskey maker in the country.

Thomson is included here, though, because the company is releasing old bottles of Willowbank stock and building a reputation for whiskey. So could it be that a New Zealand whiskey industry is slowly reemerging?

"I don't really think it's that slow," says company co-owner Rachael Thomson. "It's more that there hasn't been the choice available, so most people assume there is no such thing as New Zealand whiskey. They simply haven't come into contact with it. Loads of people in New Zealand love whiskey—it's in our Scottish and Irish heritage, so it's an established category here—and people always have their favorite brand, which often by default happens to be a Scotch or an Irish whiskey.

The South Island's stunning scenery is reminiscent of the Scottish Highlands—and the whiskey is similar, too.

It's simply an education and awareness thing. People are delighted when they see that Thomson is New Zealand whiskey, as they feel whiskey is in their roots somehow and it makes complete sense to them that we should have our own product and brand. The interest in New Zealand whiskey is definitely growing, and quite quickly, the more awareness that is built, and the more opportunities presented for people to try it.

"2011 was the year we gained loyal customers— the repeat buyers who trust the brand name to deliver excellent bottlings. So it was a cornerstone year for Thomson. We're working on some new single cask bottlings and growing our base here in New Zealand. We'll continue to establish ourselves and keep the whiskey flowing."

TASTING NOTES

THOMSON 8-YEAR-OLD
blend, 40% ABV, matured in ex-Bourbon barrels, non-chill-filtered
This is described as a blend, though there are no details about how much grain is in the mix or where it comes from. But this is a light, easy-to-drink, and tasty whiskey with floral, zingy, and citrus notes and a hint of pepper.

THOMSON 10-YEAR-OLD
single malt, 40% ABV, matured in ex-Bourbon barrels
A lightweight malt whiskey and very Lowland in style, with a thin, sappy, buttery, and reedy taste and some pepper spice later on.

THOMSON 18-YEAR-OLD
single malt, 46% ABV, single cask (197 bottles), matured in ex-Bourbon barrels, non-chill-filtered
The best bottling from Thomson so far. It seems 16–20 years is perfect for this distillery. Oak, spice, vanilla, lemon and lime, and some soft toffee are all in the mix.

THOMSON 18-YEAR-OLD

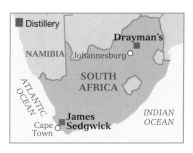

SOUTH AFRICA

South Africa is playing catch-up when it comes to whiskey. Well known for its wine and beer, a new emerging black middle class has generated demand for premium Scotch whiskey, and South African whiskey-makers have imitated Scotch production methods to meet local demand. Now, though, there are signs that domestic whiskey is evolving into something distinctly South African.

DRAYMAN'S

OWNER Moritz Kallmeyer	
FOUNDED 2006 **CAPACITY** 357 gal (1,350 liters)	
ADDRESS 222 Dykor Road, Silverton, Pretoria 0127	
WEBSITE www.draymans.com	

Given the size of South Africa and the amount of beer the country drinks, it's surprising that there aren't more whiskey-makers; until Moritz Kallmeyer decided to try to emulate the great single malt whiskeys of Scotland, the James Sedgwick Distillery was the only producer. It's still early days for Drayman's, but the signs are extremely good.

When Kallmeyer gave up his career and focused on making craft beers in the mid-1990s, he was ahead of his time, for while craft brewing is well established now, it wasn't back then. Kallmeyer was driven by two ambitions—to have fun doing something he loved and to bring the special tastes of quality German beers to a South African population.

Today he makes wheat beers, smoked beers, lagers, and even mead. Oh, and mampoer—a fiery indigenous spirit distilled from various fruits, which is made only in South Africa. Kallmeyer's version of it comes in a bottle wrapped in barbed wire and with an alcohol strength of 50 percent ABV.

The science of whiskey

Kallmeyer's brewery and distillery can be found in the Highveld near Pretoria, and Drayman's is the first whiskey ever to be made there. Its owner has a science background and it shows. His detailed website gives precise and extensive details about the brewing and distilling process he's developed over the years—and if it seems a bit dry, what he's making most certainly isn't. Kallmeyer is an enthusiast but he's also good at what he does, and his intention is to make fruity and rich whiskeys in the style of those found in the Scottish Highlands. It's an ambitious aim, but he makes no claim that he will make anything as good as Scotch single malt.

"I know that in consumer perception I can never in a hundred years hope to match the legendary counterparts from Speyside or Islay," he says. "However, I am both humbled by and enthusiastic about the challenge of striving to achieve Scotch perfection in South Africa."

He's made a great start. A four-year-old richly sherried whiskey tastes significantly older than it is, and Kallmeyer puts this down to the unique conditions on the Highveld, which may well intensify the distillation process.

The solera system

Where most fledgling distilleries turn to vodka and gin production, Drayman's has introduced a solera system for making whiskey. Eight 60-gallon (225-liter) casks made of French oak are used. The first four were filled in 2006 and the rest filled with Scottish and South African whiskeys at six-month intervals.

Eventually, in 2009, the first portion of the first cask was drawn off and bottled, then the cask refilled from the second-oldest cask. That in turn was refilled from the third, and so on. No cask is ever totally emptied and the process is ongoing, with whiskey from the oldest cask always drawn off for bottling. That's how it works at the distillery, but Kallmeyer encourages customers to take home specially made 1.2-gallon (4.5-liter) casks and set up a solera system at home, either with a series of small casks or by simply topping off one cask with something different when some of the whiskey has been drunk, effectively changing the contents each time.

"This is probably the largest capital investment for us, and a valuable asset that will be passed down to our descendants," he says. "Managing a solera is very labor-intensive by nature, requiring care and skill in transferring whiskey from cask to cask, but the effort is rewarded in the end with silky smoothness and enjoyment in every sip." Production at the distillery is tiny—just one 60-gallon (225-liter) cask is filled every two months.

TASTING NOTES

DRAYMAN'S "HIGHVELD"
single malt, 43% ABV, matured in rejuvenated
4th or 5th refill American oak ex-wine barrels
A work in progress, with the berry fruit, orange, and grape flavors veiling the youthful barley, but it seems to be latched together rather than fully bonded. There are vanilla and citrus notes in there, too. Lots to like, with some late-developing spice.

DRAYMAN'S "HIGHVELD"

JAMES SEDGWICK

OWNER Distell	
FOUNDED 1991	**CAPACITY** 713,000 gal (2.7m liters)
ADDRESS Distillery Road, Wellington 7655	
WEBSITE www.threeshipswhisky.co.za	

Its history may stretch back to the 19th century but its whiskey production program started in earnest only in 1991, so there's nothing backward-thinking about James Sedgwick.

In 2009 the distillery was upgraded and expanded, with new equipment and increased capacity. The improvements included two new pot stills made by Forsyth's of Scotland and designed in the style of those at Bowmore on Islay.

Future ambitions
The distiller is Andy Watts, a former cricket player who came over from the UK to coach cricket and settled in South Africa. He says that the whiskey from the distillery is evolving and starting to pick up international accolades as a result.

"Since 1994, the introduction of whiskeys from other parts of the world and an emerging market of new whiskey drinkers have allowed us to create new styles with our own unique characteristic," he says. "We respect the tradition of the established whiskey-producing nations but we are not held back by them."

The distillery plans further innovation and experimentation in the future, and it's a reasonable expectation that the South African whiskey story is still in its infancy.

As part of the distillery's upgrade, an old maturation warehouse was renovated and converted into a tasting center for the company's salespeople to use with the trade. The next step will be to open the distillery to the public.

TASTING NOTES

THREE SHIPS 5-YEAR-OLD
blend, 43% ABV
Rich in character, with a zesty, zippy youthfulness, fizzy fruit, and some earthy, peaty notes that bring to mind a young Highland-style Scotch single malt. Balanced, well made, and with a long, smooth finish.

THREE SHIPS 10-YEAR-OLD
single malt, 43% ABV
Surprisingly subtle and sophisticated, with some salt and pepper notes, hints of peat, and more subdued fruit than the five-year-old. Another nod to the Highlands.

BAIN'S "CAPE MOUNTAIN WHISKY"
grain whiskey, 43% ABV, matured in ex-Bourbon barrels
A totally different beast altogether; a sweet, Bourbon-matured grain whiskey and a delight. On the nose there are summer flowers, sweet vanilla, and soft toffee; on the palate there are great dollops of honey and vanilla, some citrus fruits, and honey, with some late sweet spice.

BAIN'S "CAPE MOUNTAIN WHISKY"

THREE SHIPS 5-YEAR-OLD

THREE SHIPS 10-YEAR-OLD

INDIA

There's whiskey and there's "whiskey"—and India makes more "whiskey" than any other country in the world. The trouble is, much of it falls outside generally accepted definitions of what whiskey is. There are countless brands made with molasses. Most of the international producers sell blends of varying quality within the country, many made up of both Indian and Scottish ingredients. So Amrut is an aberration—while most Indian whiskeys sell only in the domestic market, Amrut single malts are almost exclusively exported, though they can be found in a few Bangalore hotel bars.

AMRUT

OWNER Amrut Distillers	
FOUNDED 1948 **CAPACITY** 53,000 gal (200,000 liters)	
ADDRESS 36 Sampangi Tank Road, Bangalore, Karnataka	
WEBSITE www.amrutdistilleries.com	

Bangalore is a traffic jam on a construction site in the sun, a contrary mix of tree-lined streets, pretty gardens, and stunning Hindu temples on the one hand and dust, dirt, and car exhaust on the other. The city is changing but, as in so much of India, poverty and wealth sit side by side. Money is pouring in here and new technology is big business. But progress means change and Amrut Distillery has abandoned its original offices, which are sullenly awaiting demolition, and now occupies a site a little under an hour from downtown, out in the suburbs of this sprawling city.

Molasses and malts
The distillery itself was established in 1948 to provide cheap alcohol for the military and has grown into a producer of molasses-based blended "whiskey" for the Indian market. Amrut is probably best known for its Indian brandy, however, made with grapes too rich in tannin to be sold as wine but the base for a full and tasty brandy.

The distillery's owners make no apology for using molasses for their spirits, a practice frowned upon by aficionados. "Taste the whiskey and it tastes fine," they say. "But think where we are. We have big problems in India. We need grain to feed people and, correctly, making whiskey is not a priority. We use what we can."

The malt whiskey resulted from an experiment for a thesis at Newcastle University by Riki Rao Jagdale, grandson of the distillery's founder, to see if it would be possible to take malts to Newcastle and sell Indian whiskey in Britain. He not only concluded that you could, but he also met Ashok Chokalingam, who is still the distillery's general manager based in the UK and is responsible for much of Amrut's worldwide

At the heart of India's IT boom, *the state of Karnataka is also a place of beautiful temples—and malt whiskey.*

AMRUT "FUSION"

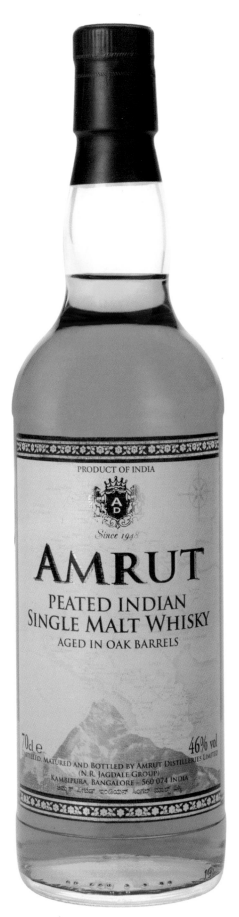

AMRUT "PEATED"

expansion. The main reason, though, is the whiskey, which is sublime and, judging from cask samples maturing in the warehouse, going from strength to strength.

"There were moments when we wondered if it could work and we made mistakes and had some lows along the way," says Riki's father, Neelakanta Jagdale. "But the whole process is taken very seriously here and we're experimenting with lots of casks, trying different things."

Departure from traditions

The distillery itself, on a tree-lined street where monkeys can be a problem in the still room, is a strange mix of a traditional whiskey distillery and a decidedly Indian operation. The still room is packed with a hodgepodge collection of stills, at the heart of which are the Indian-made pot stills that produce Amrut whiskey. The distillery is very labor-intensive, and in the bottling hall teams of full-time and part-time women workers hand-bottle every whiskey.

Peated barley is brought in from Scotland but Indian barley is key to the process, and Indian ingenuity has created a range of malts that challenge the typical way of doing things. At Amrut they will put spirit in a sherry cask, for instance, move it to Bourbon, and then transfer it back to sherry. They have made whiskey using malt matured in Scotland as well as India, and one release was matured on an island off the coast of Germany.

TASTING NOTES

AMRUT "PEATED CASK STRENGTH"
single malt, 62.8% ABV, cask strength, non-chill-filtered
The nose is shy and unspectacular at first but with water it explodes into a kippered fish stand, then some gritty, oily, smoke notes. There's sweet fruit on the palate, with the smoke quick-stepping around the core flavors. It's enticing and different, and the finish is long and peppery.

AMRUT "FUSION"
single malt, 50% ABV, made with mix of Indian and peated Scottish barley, matured in new American oak barrels
World-class whiskey by anyone's standards, this mixes peated malt from Scotland with unpeated malt from India at the grist stage—that is, before beer fermentation takes place. The result is a kickboxer of a whiskey, dark chocolate trying to battle with the peat heart, and fruit, pepper, and oak punching out at each other.

AMRUT "PORTONOVA"
single malt, 62.1% ABV, matured in a mix of new American oak and ex-Bourbon barrels, transferred to ex-port barrels, then returned to ex-Bourbon casks
Another world-class whiskey—a fireworks display that's close to being over the top but gets away with it and as a result is unforgettable. It's made by using virgin oak, then putting the spirit into port pipes, and finally returning it to oak again. Expect orange, dark chocolate, spices, blueberry, black currant, and pepper.

ENVIRONMENTAL CONCERNS

They take their environmental responsibilities very seriously at the Amrut Distillery, where almost nothing is wasted. The distillery recycles as much as it can and, in a country where water is a precious resource, has invested in water conservation equipment. It also has a small cooperage to char and rechar barrels and has invented its own unique system for firing the insides of the barrels. One cooper holds what is in effect a glorified blow torch on the end of a long pipe, and as he fires it up, another cooper rotates the barrel around the flame. It's an ingenious, and quintessentially Indian, practical solution to a traditional problem.

AMRUT "PORTONOVA"

McDOWELL'S

OWNER United Spirits	
FOUNDED 1971	CAPACITY Not given
ADDRESS Bethorda, Ponda, Goa 403401	
WEBSITE www.unitedspirits.in	

Most Indian "whiskeys" are created from continuous still spirits made with molasses, rice, or barley, mixed with whiskey extract and sometimes Scottish malt or grain. There has long been an attempt to close the gap between Indian and European definitions of whiskey, and when United Spirits' owner Vijay Mallya bought Whyte & Mackay, the link came one step closer.

Birth of Indian malt
United Spirits stands apart from many of the other domestic Indian companies in that as it does produce a genuine single malt whiskey, made at its distillery in Ponda, Goa, known as the Ponda Distillery or the McDowell's Distillery. Scotsman Angus McDowell founded McDowell & Company in Madras in 1826 as a trading company specializing in liquor and cigars. McDowell's was acquired by Vittal Mallya, father of Vijay and owner of United Breweries, in 1951. The McDowell's "No.1" blend of Scotch and "Selected Indian Malts" was launched in 1968 and, on the back of its success—it's now the world's fourth largest-selling whiskey—the company commissioned the malt whiskey distillery in Ponda three years later.

Produced using the same distilling regimen as Scotch malt, McDowell's "Single Malt" is bottled young, at only three or four years old, but Goa's hot climate and variance in temperature accelerate maturation. There's no attempt to sell the single malt outside India, and the market is so vast it's very hard to get an accurate picture of how much is produced, but if you find it, it's likely to be in the country's better hotels.

Diet whiskey?
For a country with such a basic whiskey industry, and one that is traditional in so many ways, the noncompliance on grain has led to surprising innovations. McDowell's makes a spirit drink mixing "whiskey" with gardenia, a shrub reputed to have the ability to fight fat. The drink, therefore, is marketed as the world's first "diet whiskey."

McDOWELL'S "NO.1"

McDOWELL'S "NO.1 PLATINUM"

TASTING NOTE

McDOWELL'S "SINGLE MALT"
single malt, 42.8% ABV, matured in oak casks
Young and sappy, with cereal and ginger notes, some citrus and a sweet honey taste. Not very complex but pleasant, easy to drink, and inoffensive.

McDOWELL'S "SINGLE MALT"

PAKISTAN

The idea of Pakistani whiskey has long been a source of bemusement, and it is indeed incongruous. But Pakistan does have a non-Muslim community and the making of alcohol is tolerated, so Murree Brewery's owners are able to provide whiskey and other alcoholic drinks for a domestic Christian and Hindu community in controlled outlets and on proof of non-Muslim status.

MURREE

OWNER Isfanyarul Khan Bhanaras
FOUNDED 1899 **CAPACITY** 137,000 gal (520,000 liters)
ADDRESS National Park Road, Rawalpindi
WEBSITE www.murreebrewery.com

Located in the far north of Pakistan, close to Islamabad in the Western Himalayas, Murree Brewery is the only distillery in a Muslim-dominated country and its presence there is historical, predating by nearly 50 years the formation of Pakistan upon the partition of British India in 1947. Murree was first established in the mid-1800s, with the distillery being added just before the start of the 20th century. It was first built to meet the demand for beer and then spirits among British soldiers serving in the region and, although there were moves to shut it down once Pakistan came into being, special dispensation was granted so that the non-Muslim owners could stay in business.

As well as being the only alcohol-producing establishment in a Muslim country, with more than 150 years behind it, Murree is also one of the oldest businesses in Asia. There are good reasons why it is tolerated; on the occasions when production has been stopped, illegal whiskey has appeared and there have been deaths from the consumption of poisoned alcohol.

Nevertheless, Murree has had something of a checkered history much in keeping with Pakistan's tightrope act between Muslim fundamentalists and liberal secularists. The plant has been shut down at various times and there are strict rules imposed on it by local and central government. Murree cannot export, for instance, and cut back production to a fraction of capacity in a dispute over tax. With no export market, most Murree whiskey is sold through Pakistan's hotels and can be bought by anybody with documentation showing they are not Muslims.

Whiskey making at Murree

It's hard to get an accurate estimate of what the distillery produces. It has four wash stills outdoors and with two spirit stills indoors could make large quantities of whiskey, but the plant is thought to be operating well below its capacity and also has an industrial alcohol function.

The spirit is made with barley from Scotland and matured in cooled cellars. The whiskey-makers try very hard to copy single malt from Scotland—too hard, really—and whiskey is matured to a range of ages up to 21 years old. Whatever's going on at the distillery, though, the anemic color of the 12-year-old suggests either tired oak or conditions that aren't conducive to maturation.

TASTING NOTE

MURREE 12-YEAR-OLD "MILLENNIUM RESERVE"
single malt, 43% ABV
Light, oily, and floral on the nose. Strangely disjointed palate, with weak fruits, some barley, and green vegetable notes, and a late taste of pepper. Light and mellow.

MURREE "VINTAGE GOLD"

MURREE 8-YEAR-OLD "MALT WHISKY CLASSIC"

TAIPEI

■ **Kavalan**

Taiwan Strait

TAIWAN

Kaohsiung

Taichung

Philippine Sea

South China Sea

TAIWAN

Given the huge economic growth across Asia and the growing demand for quality whiskey, both blended and single malt, it was perhaps inevitable that an entrepreneurial nation such as Taiwan, with an obvious and direct route to the growing Chinese market, would start producing whiskey. The country's climate isn't best suited to whiskey-making, however, with high temperatures causing the angel's share to evaporate at a far faster rate than in countries with more temperate climates. Yet Taiwanese ingenuity has overcome these barriers and turned the effects of "tropical aging" to its advantage.

KAVALAN

OWNER King Car Group	
FOUNDED 2005 **CAPACITY** 343,000 gal (1.3m liters)	
ADDRESS No. 326, Sec. 2, Yuanshan Road, Yuanshan, Yi-lan	
WEBSITE www.kavalanwhisky.com	

You would have to go a long way to find a more remarkable whiskey story than that of Kavalan in Taiwan. It's a distillery that came from nowhere in the new millennium to become a major player on the world whiskey stage.

The country's ability to respond to market demands and to emulate the greatest producers that supply those markets is well established, as is Southeast Asia's love of whiskey. So while the major Scottish producers were competing with each other to find a toehold in the region and battling to establish routes to market, King Car, a sizable Taiwanese business, wasted no time in building a distillery and getting it up and running.

Off and running

Where Japan has emulated Scotch whiskey by studying the country's distilleries and recreating them with impressive precision over several generations, the approach in Taiwan has been altogether different. Kavalan's plan was to spend whatever it took to get high-quality malt whiskey to market in the shortest possible time. True to their word, it took only nine months to build the distillery and start producing the spirit, and after just two years that spirit was being exported.

Burns Night gatecrasher

In the UK the story started with the submission of two Kavalan samples marked "China" to the World Whisky Awards, sent out by *Whisky Magazine*. One was sweet, creamy, honeyed, and bright yellow; the other was plummy, fruity, sherried, and very dark. They were both outstanding and sailed through the early rounds, and although neither won an award that year— Amrut was just hitting its stride as a great whiskey—the judges were highly impressed.

Just a few weeks later a Scottish newspaper thought it would be funny to trick local whiskey journalists by holding a Burns Night Supper— when patriotic Scots everywhere celebrate their national poet, national dish (haggis), and national tipple—accompanied by a blind tasting of young whiskeys that included some unusual international expressions. These non-Scotch interlopers included a whiskey made by the Auld Enemy, the English. Yet it wasn't the English whiskey that caused the greatest shock—it was a malt from Kavalan that really shone out. What makes the story even more remarkable is that the spirit— rich, full-bodied, and bursting with flavor—was only two years old and, in Europe at least, couldn't even be called whiskey.

So how could a country with no whiskey-making tradition, no trained distillers, and no specialty distilling equipment turn the world of whiskey on its head, and in three short years position itself as one of the most developed and accomplished producers of whiskey outside the five traditional whiskey-making territories?

Challenges overcome

Owned by King Car, a substantial company that has been making food and drinks for more than 50 years and employs about 2,000 people, Kavalan is named after the first tribe to inhabit the region of Taiwan where the distillery stands. According to the owners, the name symbolizes sincerity, honesty, and cultivation.

When King Car decided to make whiskey, it turned to the world's best, bringing in stills from Forsyth's in Scotland and employing Dr. Jim Swan, whiskey's "Mr. Fix-It," to carry out a feasibility study. There were considerable obstacles to overcome, not least the temperature and humidity; Taiwan has a high humidity similar to the Speyside region in Scotland, but the annual average temperature is 25°F (14°C) higher. This explains the rapid maturation and the high loss of liquid even in a relatively short period of time. But whiskey making requires great amounts of

KAVALAN "CONCERTMASTER PORT CASK FINISH"

cool water to recondense the spirits, so a cooling system had to be installed.

Taiwan has demonstrated time and again that it can work fast and learn fast, and that's exactly what happened when it came to making whiskey. The Kavalan distillery was built in 2005 and 2006 and was bottling "whiskey" in 2008. Since then there has been a regular stream of bold and rich expressions matured in both Bourbon and sherry casks. It's hard to believe how young they are, the only clues being the lack of astringency that long maturation in oak brings and the fact that the finish is relatively short. It's clearly far too early to gauge what will happen with these whiskeys when they have aged for more than 10 years, but some believe that they will peak sooner rather than later.

Unlocking the home market

The hardest challenge for King Car might be getting the whiskey taken seriously at home, a market that ought to be proving highly lucrative, given that it is currently the sixth-largest market for Scotch whiskey in the world. Yet the Kavalan and King Car labels carry a significant price tag by Taiwanese standards, particularly given that age statements are considered so important in Asia. But Kavalan has had no problem being accepted elsewhere, and can now be found in export markets across the world.

Annual visitor numbers to the distillery now top one million and this should stand as a good omen for the home market, and gives a sense of the sheer passion in Taiwan for all things whiskey.

TASTING NOTES

KING CAR WHISKY "CONDUCTOR"
single malt, 46% ABV, non-chill-filtered
A whiskey that starts off sweet and fruity, with peach and apricot, and then a wave of pepper cuts across it and it takes on a more earthy, savory tone and ends as a balanced Scotch Highland–style whiskey.

KAVALAN "SOLIST FINO"
single malt, 57.5% ABV, cask strength, matured in ex-fino sherry butts, non-chill-filtered
As the name suggests, this is from a fino sherry cask and is a big, bold, sherried whiskey that tastes as if it should have aged for 18 years but probably spent a fifth of that time in a cask. The clues are the fact that it's sweet and there's no astringency or finish of any note. Rich, plummy, sweet, and very palatable.

KAVALAN "CONCERTMASTER PORT CASK FINISH"
single malt, 40% ABV, matured in American oak casks and finished in ex-port wine barriques
Big, rich, and fruity nose and an intriguing but developed taste, with plum, grape, red berries, and a hint of sulfur, which is entirely appropriate here and gives this very young whiskey some much-needed gravitas.

KING CAR WHISKY "CONDUCTOR"

KAVALAN "SOLIST FINO"

GLOSSARY

ABV (alcohol by volume) This is the proportion of alcohol in a drink, expressed as a percentage. Whiskey is most commonly at 40 percent or 43 percent ABV.

Analyzer still *see* continuous distillation

Angel's share The expression given for the amount of liquid that evaporates from the cask during the period of *maturation*.

Batch distillation Distillation carried out in batches, as opposed to *continuous distillation*. Each batch may be marginally different, which gives the method an artisanal quality.

Barrel *see* cask

Blended malt A mix of single malt whiskeys from more than one distillery.

Blended whiskey A mix of malt whiskeys and grain whiskeys.

Cask The oak container in which whiskey is matured. There are many different styles and sizes, and a principal distinction between the type of wood used: American or European oak. In the US, whiskey is most commonly matured in barrels (48–53 gal/180–200 liters). American barrels are reused elsewhere; in Scotland they are often broken down and reassembled as hogsheads (66 gal/250 liters). Butts and puncheons (132 gal/500 liters) are the largest casks for maturing whiskey, having first been seasoned with, or used to age, sherry.

Cask finishing The practice of using a different cask (such as port, Madeira, French wine, or rum casks) for the final period of the whiskey's maturation.

Cask strength Whiskey that is bottled straight from the cask rather than first being diluted. It is typically around 57–63 percent ABV.

Column still Also known as a Coffey, patent, or continuous still, this is the type of still used for *continuous distillation*.

Condenser The vaporized spirit driven off the stills is turned into liquid in a condenser. The traditional type of condenser is a "worm tub"—a tapering coil of copper pipe set in a vat of cold water outside the still house. Worm tubs have largely been superseded by shell-and-tube condensers, usually situated inside the still house.

Continuous distillation The creation of spirits as an ongoing process, as opposed to *batch distillation*. Continuous distillation uses a *column still* (also known as a patent or Coffey still) rather than a *pot still*. It has two connected columns: the rectifier and the analyzer. The cool wash travels down the rectifier in a sealed coil, where it becomes heated. It then passes to the head of the analyzer, down which it trickles over a series of perforated copper plates. Steam enters the foot of the analyzer and bubbles through the wash, driving off alcoholic vapor, which rises up the analyzer then passes to the foot of the rectifier. Here it again ascends, to be condensed by the cool wash (which is thus heated) as it rises in a zigzag manner through another series of perforated copper plates. As the vapor rises it becomes purer and of higher strength, until it is drawn off at the "striking plate" at 94 percent ABV.

Cut points In the process of *pot still* distillation, the operator divides the run into three "cuts" to separate the usable spirit from rejected spirit, which must be redistilled. The first cut contains the *foreshots*; the middle cut is the section of usable spirit; the end cut contains the *feints* or aftershots.

Draff The Scottish name for the remains of the grain after mashing. It is a nutritious cattle fodder, used either wet or dried and pelletized.

Drum maltings Large cylinders in which grain is germinated during the industrial *malting* of barley. The drums are ventilated with temperature-controlled air and rotate so the grains do not stick together.

Dumping Emptying the contents of a cask into a vat, either prior to bottling or before putting into a different kind of cask.

Eau de vie Literally "water of life," and usually used in reference to grape-based spirits. Compare with *uisge beatha*.

Expression The term given to a particular whiskey in relation to the overall output of a distillery or spirits company. It may refer to the age, as in 12-year-old expression, or to a particular characteristic, such as a cask strength expression.

Feints The final fraction of the spirit produced during a distillation run in *batch distillation*. Feints (also called tails or aftershots) are aromatically unpleasant, and are sent to a feints and foreshots receiver to be mixed with *low wines* and redistilled with the next run.

Fermenter Another name for *mash tun*.

First fill The first time a cask has been used to hold whiskey other than Bourbon, it is referred to as first-fill cask. A first-fill sherry cask will have held only sherry prior to its use for maturing whiskey; a first-fill Bourbon cask will have been used once only to hold Bourbon prior to its use in maturing whiskey.

Foreshots The first fraction of the distillation run in *pot still* distillation. Foreshots (also known as heads) are not pure enough to be used and are returned to a feints and foreshots receiver to be redistilled in the next run.

Grist Ground, malted grain. Water is added to grist to form the *mash*.

Heads *see* foreshots

High wines (US) A mix of spirit that has had its first distillation and the *foreshots* and *feints* from the second distillation. With a strength of around 28 percent ABV, high wines undergo a second distillation to create *new make*.

Independent bottler/bottling A company that releases bottles of whiskey independently of the official distillery bottlings. They buy small quantities of *casks* and bottle the whiskey as and when they choose.

Kilning In the process of *malting*, kilning involves gently heating the "green malt" to halt its germination and thereby retain its starch content for turning into sugars (in the mashing stage). Ultimately these sugars will be turned into alcohol. Peat may be added to the kiln to produce a smoky-flavored malt.

Lomond still This *pot still* was designed so that a distillery could vary the character of spirits being produced. The level of *reflux* could be altered by way of an additional condenser on the still, so that a heavy or light style of spirit could be made, as required.

Low wines The spirit produced by the first distillation. It has a strength of about 21 percent ABV. Compare with *high wines*.

Lyne arm (or "lye pipe") The pipe running from the top of the still to the condenser. Its angle, height, and thickness all have a bearing on the characteristics of the spirit.

Malting The process of deliberately starting and stopping germination in grain to maximize its starch content. As the grain begins to germinate (through the influence of heat and moisture), it becomes "green malt" (grain that has just begun to sprout). The green malt undergoes *kilning* to produce malt.

Marrying The mixing of whiskeys prior to bottling. It most often applies to *blended whiskey*, where whiskeys of different types and from several distilleries are combined for a period in vats or *casks* to blend more fully before the whiskey is bottled.

Mash The mix of *grist* and water.

Mash bill The mix of grains used in the making of a particular whiskey. In the US, there are specific, legal requirements about the percentage of certain grains for making Bourbon, Tennessee whiskey, and rye whiskey, for example.

Mash tun The vessel in which the grist is mixed with hot water to convert starch in the grain into sugars, ready for fermentation. The fermentable liquid that results is known as *wort*; the solid residue (husks and spent grain) is *draff*.

Maturation For *new make* to become whiskey, it must go through a period of maturation in oak *casks*. The length of time varies: in Scotland and Ireland, the minimum period is three years; in the US, the minimum maturation is two years.

Middle cut *see* cut points

New make The clear, usable spirit that comes from the *spirit still*. It has a strength of about 70 percent ABV and is diluted to around 63–64 percent before being put into *casks* for *maturation*. In the US, new make is called "white dog."

Peating Adding peat to the kiln ovens when *malting* barley to impart a smoky, phenolic aroma and taste to the whiskey. Barley that has undergone this process is known as peated malt.

Phenols A group of aromatic chemical compounds. In whiskey making, the term is used in regard to the chemicals that impart smoky and medicinal flavors to malt and the whiskey made from it, which may be described as phenolic. Phenols are measured in parts per million (ppm). Highly phenolic whiskeys, such as Laphroaig and Ardbeg, will use malt peated to a level of between 35 and 50ppm.

Poteen *see* uisce poitín

Pot still The large onion-shaped vessels, nearly always made of copper, used for *batch distillation*. Pot stills vary in size and shape, and these variations affect the style of spirit produced.

ppm *see* phenols

Proof The old term for the alcoholic proportion of a spirit, now superseded by ABV. The American proof figure, which is different from imperial proof, is twice the ABV percentage.

Rectifier *see* continuous distillation

Reflux The process by which heavier alcoholic vapors fall back into the still rather than passing along the *lyne arm* to the *condenser*. By falling back, these vapours are redistilled, becoming purer and lighter. The size, height, and shape of the still, and how it is operated, contribute to the degree of reflux, and therefore to the lightness and character of the spirit. Long-necked stills have a greater degree of reflux and produce a more delicate style of spirit than squatter stills, which tend to make heavier, "oilier" whiskies.

Run In *batch distillation*—as carried out using *pot stills*—the extent of distillation is referred to as a run. The spirit produced during the run is variable in quality, and is divided by *cut points*.

Saladin box Used in the industrial *malting* of barley, this is a large rectangular trough in which the grains are germinated. Air is blown through the barley in the trough and the grain is turned by mechanical screws to prevent the grains from sticking together.

Silent distillery A distillery in which whiskey production has stopped—possibly only temporarily.

Single cask A bottling that comes from just one *cask* (often bottled at *cask strength*).

Single malt A malt whiskey that is the product of just one distillery.

Spirit safe A glass-fronted cabinet through which the distilled spirit passes and which is used to monitor the purity of the spirit. The stillman operates the spirit safe during a *run* to assess its quality and make *cut points*.

Spirit still In *batch distillation*, the spirit still is used for the second distillation, in which the spirit from the *wash still* is distilled again to produce *new make*.

Still The vessel in which distillation takes place. There are two basic types of still: a *pot still* for *batch distillation* and a *column still* for *continuous distillation*.

Triple distillation Most *batch distillation* involves two distillations: in a *wash still* and in a *spirit still*. Triple distillation—the traditional method in Ireland—involves a third distillation, which is said to produce a smoother and purer spirit.

Uisge beatha/uisce beatha The Scottish Gaelic and Irish Gaelic terms, respectively, from which the word "whiskey" derives. The term means "water of life," and is synonymous with *eau de vie* and *aqua vita*.

Uisce poitín Historically, the Irish Gaelic term for unlicensed whiskey, usually known as poteen.

Vatting The mixing of whiskey from several *casks*. This is usually done to achieve a consistency of flavor over time (*see also* marrying).

Viscimetric whorls The eddies and vortices observable when water is added to whiskey. The capacity of an individual whiskey to sustain viscimation is termed its viscimetric potential.

Wash The resultant liquid when yeast is added to the *wort*, fermenting into a kind of ale. Wash has an alcoholic strength of about 7 percent ABV. It passes into a *wash still* for the first distillation.

Wash still In *batch distillation*, the wash still is used for the first distillation, in which the *wash* is distilled.

Washbacks The fermenting vessels in which yeast is added to the *wort* to make *wash*. Called "fermenters" in the US.

Wood finish *see* cask finish

Worm/worm tubs *see* condensers

Wort The sweet liquid produced as a result of mixing hot water with *grist* in a *mash tun*.

INDEX

Page numbers in **bold** indicate main entries. Page numbers in *italics* indicate tasting notes. The definite article ("The") at the beginning of a name is ignored in the index order. Names including numbers appear as if the figures were spelled out.

XYZ

WHISKEYS BY STYLE

PICTURE CREDITS

Key: a-above; b-below/bottom; c-center; f-far; l-left; r-right; t-top

DK Images
Original photography by Peter Anderson © Dorling Kindersley: 15fl, cl, fr; 23cl; 38b; 42; 45l; 60b; 61l; 62tl; 64; 66l, tr; 68r; 69l; 70l; 72t; 74; 75b; 80–81; 83; 84l, br; 89; 90bl, r; 91r; 95; 103; 106bl; 107; 110r; 113l; 114br; 115t; 116; 120r; 123; 129l; 130; 131c; 140; 141br; 144–145; 152tl, r; 156; 176t; 177r; 180; 181c; 189; 192; 195tl; 207l; 220; 222r; 229l; 236tl; 237b; 241; 243; 247; 251; 259b; 266l; 267; 268t; 269; 280l; 281l

10fl, Alex Havret © Dorling Kindersley; 16bl, Tim Daly © Dorling Kindersley; 17cr, Ian O'Leary © Dorling Kindersley; 21tl, © Dorling Kindersley; 21cr, Peter Anderson © Danish National Museum; 24tl, Alex Havret © Dorling Kindersley; 28tl, Ian O'Leary © Dorling Kindersley; 32br, Alex Havret © Dorling Kindersley; 82bc, Linda Whitwam © Dorling Kindersley; 85tl, Paul Harris © Dorling Kindersley; 91bl, Alex Havret © Dorling Kindersley; 101tl, Joe Cornish © Dorling Kindersley; 102br, Paul Harris © Dorling Kindersley; 106br, Linda Whitwam © Dorling Kindersley; 112tr, Alex Havret © Dorling Kindersley; 114bl, Joe Cornish © Dorling Kindersley; 141tl, Paul Harris © Dorling Kindersley; 142br, Paul Harris © Dorling Kindersley; 153tl, Alex Havret © Dorling Kindersley; 160ar, Tim Daly © Dorling Kindersley; 164br, Bob Langrish © Dorling Kindersley; 203tr, Enrique Uranga © Rough Guides; 204br, Nigel Hicks © Dorling Kindersley; 206br, Peter Wilson © Dorling Kindersley; 209tl, Francesca Yorke © Dorling Kindersley; 228tr, © Dorling Kindersley; 234cr, Peter Hanneberg © Dorling Kindersley; 238cr, Paul Whitfield © Rough Guides; 245tl, Paul Tait © Dorling Kindersley; 254br, Katarzyna and Wojciech Medrzakowie © Dorling Kindersley; 262br, Terence Carter © Dorling Kindersley; 265tl, Katherine Seppings © Dorling Kindersley; 266br, Andrew Harris © Dorling Kindersley; 268bc, Andrew Harris © Dorling Kindersley; 270bl, Katherine Seppings © Dorling Kindersley; 277bl, Peter Bush © Dorling Kindersley; 280br, Dave Abram © Rough Guides

The publisher would like to thank the following for permission to reproduce their images:

Alamy Images: 6bl, V&A Images; 21tr, 19th era; 23bl, Patrick Guenette; **Asahi Group Holding:** 23t; **The Bridgeman Art Library:** 22tl, Apsley House, The Wellington Museum, London, UK/© English Heritage Photo Library; 22r, Private Collection; 21br, Private Collection/The Stapleton Collection; **Corbis:** 20bl, Gianni Dagli Orti; **Davin de Kergommeaux:** 207tr, br; 210l; 211br; 212–213; 214t; 215b **Mary Evans Picture Library:** 20r; **Science Photo Library:** 20cl, George Bernard; **TopFoto.co.uk:** 22cl, The Granger Collection, New York

Amrut Distillers; Andreas Bosch; Angus Dundee Distillers PLC; Barry Bernstein and Barry Stein; The Batt family; Beam Global and Beam Inc.; Ben Nevis Distillery (Fort William) Ltd; The BenRiach Distillery Company Ltd; Berry Brothers & Rudd; Bill Lark; Brauerei Locher AG; Brennerei Telser Ltd; Brouwerij Het Anker; Brown Forman; The Bruichladdich Distillery Company Ltd; Burn Stewart Distillers Ltd (CL World Brands); Cameron Syme; Campbell Distillers Ltd; Casey Overeem; Chivas Brothers Ltd (Pernod Ricard); Cisco Brewers; Coordinated Development Services Ltd; The Cuthbert family; David Baker; Destilerias Liber; Diageo PLC; Distell; Dry Fly Distilling Company; The Edrington Group; Etienne Bouillon; Glenglassaugh Distillery Company Ltd; The Glenmorangie Company Ltd; Glenora Distillers; Gordon & MacPhail; The Griffin Group; Gruppo Campari; Guy Le Lay; Hans and Julia Reisetbauer; Hans Baumberger; Hans Etter; Highwood Distillers Ltd; Ian Macleod Distillers Ltd; Ichiro Akuto; Inver House Distillers Ltd (Thai Beverages PLC); Irish Distillers; Isfanyarul Khan Bhanaras; Isle of Arran Distillers Ltd; J. & A. Mitchell & Company Ltd; J. & G. Grant; Jean Donnay; Johann and Monika Haider; John Clotworthy; John Dewar & Sons Ltd; Julian Van Winkle; Kentucky Bourbon Distillers Ltd; Kilchoman Distillery Company Ltd; King Car Group; Kirin Brewery Company; Kittling Ridge Estate Wines & Spirits; La Martiniquaise; Lawrenceburg Distillers, Indiana; Loch Lomond Distillery Company Ltd; Mackmyra; Mark Tayburn; Matt and Rachael Thomson; Moritz Kallmeyer; Morrison Bowmore Distillers Ltd; Nadim Sadek; The Nelstrop family; New Zealand Whisky Company; Nikka; Patrick & Kimm Evans; Patrick Maguire; Peter Bignell; Piedmont Distillers; Rick Wasmund; Robert Fleischmann; Rogue; Ruedi Käser; Sazerac; Scott and Todd Leopold; The Shapira family; Signatory Vintage Scotch Whisky Company Ltd; SLYRS Destillerie GmbH & Company KG; Speyside Distillers Company Ltd; Spike Dessert; Stephen McCarthy; St. George Spirits; Stranahan's Colorado Whiskey Company; Suntory Ltd; Timboon Railway Shed Distillery; Tomatin Distillery Company Ltd; Tullibardine Distillery Ltd; United Spirits; Us Heit Distillery; Warenghem; The Welsh Whisky Company; Whisky Tasmania Pty Ltd; Whyte & Mackay Ltd; William Grant & Sons Ltd; The Zuidam family

ABOUT THE AUTHORS

Gavin D. Smith is one of the world's leading whiskey writers and authorities on the subject. Editor, author, and journalist, he contributes feature material to a wide range of specialist and general interest publications. He is also the author of more than 20 books. Gavin provided tasting notes and editorial material for the 6th edition of Michael Jackson's *Malt Whisky Companion* (2010), and his latest book, *Discovering Scotland's Distilleries*, was published in spring 2010. Gavin has been made a Keeper of the Quaich, the Scotch whiskey industry's highest honor. He is in demand for consultancy work, hosting whiskey-related talks, and tutored tastings.

Dominic Roskrow has been a journalist for more than 20 years and has written about the drinks industry since 1991. He was editor of *Whisky Magazine* for four years before setting up his own business, and launched *Beers of the World Magazine in 2005.* He is editor of *Whiskeria* and his own online magazine *World Whisky Review*, is whiskey editor for *The Spirits Business*, covers world whiskey for *The Whisky Advocate*, and runs The W Club website. The Whiskey Opus is Dominic's sixth book on whiskey. He travels across the world regularly to visit distilleries and to speak on Irish and world whiskey. He is a proud Keeper of the Quaich and Kentucky Colonel, and occasionally finds time to watch his beloved Leicester City and New Zealand All Blacks. He lives in Norfolk, and he is married with three children.

Davin de Kergommeaux has been analyzing, writing, and talking about whiskey as an independent commentator for more than 12 years. He writes regularly for a variety of drinks and lifestyle magazines, and on the web for MaltManiacs.org and CanadianWhisky.org, among others. He was appointed Canadian contributing editor to *Whisky Magazine in 2011.* His first book, *Canadian Whisky: The Portable Expert*, was published in May 2012, and he has also contributed to *The World Atlas of Whisky* (2010) and *1001 Whiskies You Must Taste Before You Die (2012)*. Davin is often asked to judge at international whiskey competitions, including the World Whisky Awards, and since 2003 has served as a judge for the annual Malt Maniacs Awards. He is also the founder, head judge, and coordinator for the Canadian Whisky Awards.

Jürgen Deibel has been working in spirits for 30 years, hosting tastings, seminars, and training sessions all around the world on whiskey and other spirits. He has contributed to *Whiskey: The Definitive World Guide* (2005) and written books on vodka, tequila, and sherry. In 1995 he founded his first consultancy company for spirits. Since this time he has worked professionally for producers, importers, distributors, and trade. Today he is owner of Deibel Consultants and works and lives in Hanover, Germany and Lima, Peru.

ACKNOWLEDGMENTS

AUTHORS' ACKNOWLEDGMENTS

Gavin would like to thank the following people for their generous assistance in researching the book: Kirsteen Beeston, Morrison Bowmore Distillers Ltd; Jim Beveridge, Diageo plc; Sarah Burgess, Diageo plc; Andy Cant, Diageo plc; Graeme Coull, La Martiniquaise; Georgie Crawford, Diageo plc; Keith Cruickshank, Gordon & MacPhail; Graham Eunson, Tomatin Distillery Company Ltd; Kay Fleming, Diageo plc; Peter Gordon, William Grant & Sons Ltd; John Grant, J. & G. Grant Ltd; Ken Grier, The Edrington Group; Stuart Hendry, Ian Macleod Distillers Ltd; Brian Kinsman, William Grant & Sons Ltd; Mark Lochhead, Diageo plc; Jim Long, Chivas Brothers Ltd; Dr Bill Lumsden, The Glenmorangie Company Ltd; Des McCagherty, Signatory Vintage Scotch Whisky Company Ltd; Neil Macdonald, Chivas Brothers Ltd; Frank McHardy, Springbank Distillers Ltd; Ewan Mackintosh, Diageo plc; Ewen Mackintosh, Gordon & MacPhail; Ian Macmillan, Burn Stewart Distillers Ltd; 'Ginger' Willie MacNeill, Morrison Bowmore Distillers Ltd; Dennis Malcolm, Gruppo Campari; Stephen Marshall, John Dewar & Sons Ltd; Gavin McLachlan, Springbank Distillers Ltd; Ann Miller, Chivas Brothers Ltd; Euan Mitchell, Isle of Arran Distillers Ltd; Dr Nick Morgan, Diageo plc; Douglas Murray, Diageo plc; Richard Paterson, Whyte & Mackay Ltd; Mark Reynier, Bruichladdich Distillery Company; Pat Roberts, Cognis Public Relations; David Robertson, Whyte & Mackay Ltd; James Robertson, Tullibardine Distillery Ltd; Colin Ross, Ben Nevis Distillery Ltd; Caitriona Roy, Richmond Towers Communications; Jacqui Seargeant, John Dewar & Sons Ltd; Colin Scott, Chivas Brothers Ltd; David Stewart, William Grant & Sons Ltd; Andrew Symington, Signatory Vintage Scotch Whisky Company Ltd; Gerry Tosh, The Edrington Group; Mike Tough, Diageo plc; Billy Walker, BenRiach Distillery Company Ltd; Anthony Wills, Kilchoman Distillery Company Ltd; Alan Winchester, Chivas Brothers Ltd

Dominic would like to thank all the distillers and whiskey -makers in the far flung corners of the world who have regularly given up their time to answer my questions, and my family for putting up with my incredibly unsocial working hours and the strange out-of-hours phone calls from Australia and Asia.

Davin would like to thank the following people for who kindly helped in providing information: Michael Nychyk at Highwood; David Dobbin, at Canadian Mist; John Hall and Beth Warner at Forty Creek/Kittling Ridge; Dan Tullio and Tish Harcus at Canadian Club; Carolyn McFarlane and Trevor Walsh at Gibson's; David Doyle and Don Livermore at Corby's; Rob Tuer, Rick Murphy and Jeff Kozak at Alberta Distillers; Donnie Campbell and Bob Scott at Glenora; Patrick Evans and Mike Nicholson at Shelter Point; Barry Bernstein and Barry Stein at Still Waters; Lorien Chilton and Tyler Schramm at Pemberton; Richard Zeller, Jim Knapp, Adam McCarthy and Keith Casale at Masterson's. Thanks also go to his wife Janet de Kergommeaux and able nosing assistant Ronan Oneida de Kergommeaux.

Jürgen would like to thank Petra Feiss, Helmut Knöpfle, and Erhard Ruthner for help researching German and Austrian whiskey; all the distillers and producers in Germany, Austria, and Switzerland for their patience in answering questions; Yvonne Deibel and Ruth Castillejo for their abundance of patience and love.

PUBLISHER'S ACKNOWLEDGMENTS

Editor Diana Vowles
Designers Mandy Earey, Heather McCarry, Anne Fisher
Proofreader Holly Kyte
Indexer Susan Bosanko
Original Photography Peter Anderson
Front Cover Photograph William Reavell

Dorling Kindersley would also like to thank Charlotte Seymour, Ligi John, Divya PR, and Aastha Tiwari for editorial and design assistance; Andrea Göppner at DK Verlag; Melita Granger and Rosie Adams at DK Australia; Jo Walton and Romaine Werblow for picture research; Thomas Morse for color repro assistance; Michael Orson and everyone at Master of Malt for kindly supplying images and efficiently processing orders; Pat Roberts at Cognis Public Relations; Will Wheeler at Maloney & Fox; Aja Schmeltz at Tuthilltown; Greg Ramsay; Tom Holder at Experience Consulting; Olivia Plunkett at Marussia Beverages UK Ltd.